THE COMPLETE IDIOT'S GUIDE® TO

Acing the GRE

by Henry George Stratakis-Allen

ALPHA

A member of Penguin Group (USA) Inc.

ALPHA BOOKS

Published by the Penguin Group

Penguin Group (USA) Inc., 375 Hudson Street, New York, New York 10014, USA

Penguin Group (Canada), 90 Eglinton Avenue East, Suite 700, Toronto, Ontario M4P 2Y3, Canada (a division of Pearson Penguin Canada Inc.)

Penguin Books Ltd., 80 Strand, London WC2R 0RL, England

Penguin Ireland, 25 St. Stephen's Green, Dublin 2, Ireland (a division of Penguin Books Ltd.)

Penguin Group (Australia), 250 Camberwell Road, Camberwell, Victoria 3124, Australia (a division of Pearson Australia Group Pty. Ltd.)

Penguin Books India Pvt. Ltd., 11 Community Centre, Panchsheel Park, New Delhi—110 017, India

Penguin Group (NZ), 67 Apollo Drive, Rosedale, North Shore, Auckland 1311, New Zealand (a division of Pearson New Zealand Ltd.)

Penguin Books (South Africa) (Pty.) Ltd., 24 Sturdee Avenue, Rosebank, Johannesburg 2196, South Africa

Penguin Books Ltd., Registered Offices: 80 Strand, London WC2R 0RL, England

International Standard Book Number: 978-1-59257-515-2
Library of Congress Catalog Card Number: 2007926844

09   8   7   6   5   4   3

Interpretation of the printing code: The rightmost number of the first series of numbers is the year of the book's printing; the rightmost number of the second series of numbers is the number of the book's printing. For example, a printing code of 07-1 shows that the first printing occurred in 2007.

Printed in the United States of America

Note: This publication contains the opinions and ideas of its author. It is intended to provide helpful and informative material on the subject matter covered. It is sold with the understanding that the author and publisher are not engaged in rendering professional services in the book. If the reader requires personal assistance or advice, a competent professional should be consulted.

The author and publisher specifically disclaim any responsibility for any liability, loss, or risk, personal or otherwise, which is incurred as a consequence, directly or indirectly, of the use and application of any of the contents of this book.

Most Alpha books are available at special quantity discounts for bulk purchases for sales promotions, premiums, fund-raising, or educational use. Special books, or book excerpts, can also be created to fit specific needs.

For details, write: Special Markets, Alpha Books, 375 Hudson Street, New York, NY 10014.

Publisher: *Marie Butler-Knight*
Editorial Director: *Mike Sanders*
Managing Editor: *Billy Fields*
Executive Editor: *Randy Ladenheim-Gil*
Development Editor: *Michael Thomas*
Senior Production Editor: *Janette Lynn*

Copy Editor: *Michael Dietsch*
Cartoonist: *Shannon Wheeler*
Cover/Book Designer: *Becky Harmon*
Indexer: *Angie Bess*
Layout: *Becky Harmon*
Proofreader: *Aaron Black*

Contents at a Glance

Contents

Appendixes

Introduction

If you're thinking about graduate school, you must be thinking about the GRE. You probably have fond memories of the SAT. Okay, maybe not. Unfortunately, the GRE is the SAT's bigger brother. The GRE will feel awfully familiar in some ways and totally foreign in others. The vocabulary can be brutal and you probably haven't seen most of the math in years. Fret not, this book contains everything you need in order to master the GRE. Sure, raising your score will take a few hours, but it's easier than raising your undergraduate GPA.

What's in This Book

Part 1, "Taking Control," gives you all the background to the GRE, how it's created, and how you can take it apart. These chapters also give you all of the nuts-and-bolts details about registering, scoring, and fundamental test-taking strategies. After reading these chapters, you'll understand how standardized tests are made and how they can be controlled. These chapters also put the GRE in the context of graduate admissions.

In **Part 2, "Verbal: Smorgasbord of Standardized Testing,"** we'll dissect the verbal sections of the GRE. We'll start with sentence completions and move on to long and short reading passages, and explore the new logic passages. If you've feared the GRE verbal sections, then these chapters are for you! The final chapters are verbal practice sets to help you hone your verbal skills.

Part 3, "Math: All Bark, No Bite," covers all of the math you need to know for the GRE. If you miss eighth grade, then our arithmetic chapter will take you back. What took you a year to learn is crammed into one arithmetic-packed chapter. Then if you miss high school, we have algebra and geometry. These chapters are great if you want to improve once-great math skills or recover from mathophobia. We'll also explore charts, graphs, tables, and other random GRE math.

If you're wondering what to do about the two scored essays on the GRE, then **Part 4, "Analytical Writing: First Impressions Are Everything,"** will cover it all! First, I'll give you the details of what the two essays test and how they're scored. Next, we'll review essay structure. Finally, you can read through some sample GRE essays.

The real fun is in **Part 5, "GRE Vocabulary."** The vocabulary used on the GRE is insane. Take a few minutes to look through *The Complete Idiot's Guide (CIG)* list and you'll discover that working on your vocabulary is probably a good idea. Start soon! It takes a while to improve one's vocabulary. Part 5 also includes quizzes, roots, and prefixes.

Extras

Watch for these sidebars along the way:

FAIR WARNING

In these sidebars, you'll find warnings about common mistakes.

BET YOU DIDN'T KNOW

Here you'll find bits of intriguing information.

VEXING VOCABULARY

These sidebars define words and jargon.

INFO TO GO

These sidebars contain bits of information to take with you into the test!

Trademarks

All terms mentioned in this book that are known to be or are suspected of being trademarks or service marks have been appropriately capitalized. Alpha Books and Penguin Group (USA) Inc. cannot attest to the accuracy of this information. Use of a term in this book should not be regarded as affecting the validity of any trademark or service mark.

Taking Control

To really take control of the GRE, you need to know how it's created and how you can take it apart. These chapters also give you all of the nuts-and-bolts details about registering, scoring, and fundamental test-taking strategies. I'll also introduce the idea of Tom, the standard test-taker, and how you can use that knowledge to your advantage. After reading these chapters, you'll understand how standardized tests are made and how they can be controlled. These chapters also put the GRE in the context of graduate admissions.

Chapter 1

Taking the GRE Apart

In This Chapter

- Who makes the GRE and why?
- What's on the GRE?
- Learning about "order of difficulty"
- How *not* to approach the GRE
- Taking the guesswork out of guessing

I know: what does the GRE have to do with your ability to succeed in graduate school? Think of the GRE as a battle between good and evil. You probably think I'm exaggerating, so let me explain.

I've been on the inside of the standardized testing world for more than 10 years, and I'm about to spill all the secrets. Now you're going to know everything there is to know about the GRE.

In the Beginning

Slouching out of Princeton, New Jersey, several times each year, the GRE is the 700-pound gorilla of the standardized testing world. No one likes it, but no one can seem to kill it. It throws its weight around the admissions world and usually gets its way. Some day, some brave soul will free us from this beast, but until then, we endure.

The GRE is a derivative of the SAT, which has a murky past as an Army IQ test during World War I. The Army got sick of the test, and the shrink who invented it had to find another use for it. He eventually convinced Princeton University that they needed the test (probably because they regretted admitting F. Scott Fitzgerald). What followed was decades of pain and suffering for millions of innocent students.

INFO TO GO

In the nineteenth century, everyone from Queen Victoria to Walt Whitman loved phrenology, which was the "science" of reading the bumps on your head. Some head doctors thought that strong personality traits would cause different parts of your brain (called "brain organs") to expand, thereby making bumps on your noggin. So if you were going to be a great musician, the head doctor would find a bump on your head that corresponded with the "Organ of Tune." Head doctors thought they could read children's heads and predict if they were going to grow up to be musicians, mathematicians, poets, or thieves. Now we know that phrenology is totally bogus, but we've gone from reading bumps to scoring analogies.

Where Does the GRE Come From?

A recent FBI investigation reported that the GRE does, in fact, come straight from hell. (Just kidding.)

The company that makes the GRE is the Educational Testing Service (ETS). ETS is a mammoth standardized test-making company; it makes over 500 different tests, torturing people of all ages all over the world! All ETS does is make tests. Golf pros, barbers, firefighters, and you sit down to take ETS tests. The test-makers aren't brain scientists or Nobel Prize winners; they are just ordinary people who sit around all day and put together little bubble tests. Sounds fun, doesn't it?

No serious scholar would suggest that the GRE predicts how well you will do in college; there is no study that shows a statistically valid correlation between the GRE and college grades. No graduate

school really thinks that the GRE tells them how smart or how motivated you are.

Yet ETS makes millions each year from standardized tests, which is pretty good for a nonprofit company. Then it makes purchases that help it improve the GRE. For example, in 1992, ETS bought the Princeton Country Club for about $42 million. That's right, ETS bought a posh country club with your GRE registration fee (well, yours and a million others). While you are sitting on your derriere for three hours, the fine folks at ETS are enjoying their duck pond and horse trails.

Why Do Grad Schools Want It?

But why do graduate schools like this test? Well, imagine sitting in a college admissions office and receiving 500 applications in two months, and you and maybe one other person must decide who gets admitted and who gets rejected. Furthermore, those 500 applications include 450 different transcripts; 1,700 letters of recommendations; activities lists; essays; writing samples; and thousands of other pieces of paper. How do you do it?

Most graduate programs spend about 10–15 minutes on the typical application. Why don't they spend more time? Because they don't have the staff. If they charged you $500 to apply, then maybe they'd throw out the GRE and read your essay a few times, interview you, and talk to your professors.

Graduate schools also use the GRE to check for grade inflation. Some colleges have grade inflation, which means that most students will have As and Bs. Harvard is famous for grade inflation, and some joke that it's harder to get a C than an A at Harvard. Colleges engage in grade inflation to make their graduates more competitive when applying to graduate and professional schools. But this also means that grad schools can be skeptical of your grades. If you're getting straight As, then they will want to see reasonably high GRE scores. If your GRE scores are comfortably below average, that will indicate that your college inflates grades or your courses were easy. So GRE scores act as a check on undergraduate grade inflation.

? BET YOU DIDN'T KNOW

Grad schools inflate grades, too. It's actually rare to see low grades in grad schools, and most grad schools give As to all their students.

So ETS likes the GRE because it brings in a wad of cash, and the colleges like the GRE because it allows them to process applications a little more quickly and gives them a grade-inflation check. Did you notice how much of this actually has to do with education? But this shouldn't stop you from kicking this test in the butt.

Now do you see what I mean by good versus evil? There is no other way to describe this test other than evil. This test has nothing to do with all the hard work you did in college or any of the hard work you will do in grad schools.

No one in his right mind would ever suggest that the GRE measures anything other than how well you take the GRE. It doesn't measure how well you did in college or will do in grad school. It doesn't measure how smart you are or how much you know. If anyone suggests that the GRE tests anything worth knowing, you should tell him to seek medical attention.

That's the bad news. The good news is that this test is "standardized," which means that supposedly everyone's scores are completely comparable. Now we know that's silly, but that's the story and ETS is

sticking to it. The good news is that "standardized" means "same stupid test every year." The fundamental way that this test is made doesn't change. So if you can figure out how the test is made, then you can raise your score because ETS can't change the test. ETS is not going to tell you all its dirty little secrets; that's my job.

! INFO TO GO

Did you know that there is a strong correlation between which conference wins the Super Bowl (AFC or NFC) and the performance of the U.S. stock markets for that year? The correlation is so strong that the German national bank follows the Super Bowl just to see how the stock market will perform. But no one in his right mind would actually claim that the Super Bowl really predicts the stock market—it's just a superstitious statistical fluke. ETS claims the GRE can predict your first year grad school performance—but that's just another superstitious fluke.

What's on the GRE?

Generally, the GRE includes …

- ◆ Two essay sections that ask you to write essays; one is 30 minutes and one is 45 minutes.

- ◆ One 30-minute verbal section that includes all kinds of sentence completion and reading passage questions; usually 30 questions total.

- ◆ One 45-minute math section composed of multiple choice questions and quantitative comparison questions ("Which side is bigger?" questions); usually 28 questions total.

- ◆ One research or experimental section.

Keep in mind that ETS can and will vary the test. So the exact number of questions and the question types may be a little different from what's above.

Will there be analogies? Most likely, but it's conceivable that there will be only two or three analogies or even no analogies. Don't freak out. We're going to prep you so you will be ready for everything.

The experimental section is just that: you're the guinea pig and this section experiments on you. This would be like Ford putting some brakes on a car, selling you the car, then calling you the next day to ask whether the brakes worked. "Those were some new, untested brakes we put on that car. Did they stop the car?" Of course, Ford would never do this, but for some reason ETS gets away with it. Thanks, ETS.

What's the purpose of the experimental section? Mostly three things:

1. Tries out new questions. So you will see things on this section that you know aren't tested on the GRE (like calculus). Because the GRE is always changing, ETS will be testing new question types.

2. Gauges question difficulty. ETS knows exactly how hard a question is because it was first tried out on this section.

3. Develops great wrong answers. One of ETS's dark secrets is that it works just as hard making up wrong answers as it does making up correct answers. Most GRE multiple-choice problems have five answer choices: four wrong choices and one correct answer. Do you think ETS just makes up four random wrong answers? Nope. ETS works very hard to make up great wrong answer choices, so if you make a tiny mistake on the problem and get a wrong answer, chances are that your wrong answer will be an answer choice.

So what does this mean?

If you get to a section on the GRE and it totally freaks you out, it's probably the experimental section. Don't freak out. Just try your best to finish the section, but don't let ETS blow your concentration.

Just because your answer to a question is listed in the answer choices doesn't mean it's correct. If there are four wrong ways and one correct way to do a problem, I guarantee that ETS will list the four wrong answers next to the one right answer.

Order of difficulty is determined by testing the questions. We'll talk more about this later, but remember this: easy questions are easy because more than 75 percent of all students will get them correct; medium questions are medium because 40–75 percent will get them correct; and hard questions are hard because fewer than 40 percent will get them correct.

ETS sometimes informs you that you're about to do an experimental section. In most cases, a labeled experimental section is called a "Research" section. ETS will offer you something (money, for example) to take the research section. These sections are optional and do not affect your score.

The Big Picture

Once you understand the Big Picture, then all the little parts start coming into focus. The Big Picture starts with this crazy assertion: you can get a perfect score on the GRE without even doing one third of the math or verbal problems. Sounds crazy, doesn't it?

Sure, you'll read all the problems and fill in a bubble for every one, but you're not going to actually do every problem. On many math problems, you can get the correct answer without doing the problem! On verbal problems, you can often get the correct answer without knowing what the words mean or, in critical reading, without reading the passage! This sounds crazy only because you don't usually take tests like this. In school, your teacher isn't trying to trick you; the test actually tests your knowledge of the subject; the teacher cares not only about whether you got the correct answer, but also how you got the correct answer. None of this is true on the GRE.

In fact, the GRE is the evil opposite of your normal school tests. On the GRE, no one cares whether you know how to do the problem. No one cares if you show your work. The test isn't about anything you learn in school. Does anyone study sentence completions in school? No. Why not? Because they're stupid. Some people might say "What about geometry? That's on the GRE and you study it in school." Unfortunately, the geometry on the GRE still doesn't test your knowledge of geometry. If it did, then why would ETS put all the geometry formulas you need to know at the beginning of each math section? Because ETS isn't really testing geometry—they just need a bell curve.

The more you understand that the GRE is the evil opposite of normal college tests, the better your score will be.

Content, Anyone?

The actual content of the GRE is surprising. Many people think that since very few get perfect scores on the GRE, the math and verbal must be difficult. If you believe this, then I've got two tickets to Elvis's next concert that you might want to buy.

The GRE math section tests arithmetic (you know, $2 + 3 = 5$), basic algebra (the stuff you learned in seventh or eighth grade when letters, like x, y, and z, first appeared in math problems), and basic geometry. You learned all of the GRE math by November of your sophomore year in high school; the trick is remembering it! The GRE Verbal section is nothing more than a vocabulary and reading

test. And while GRE vocabulary is a little difficult, you'll be glad to know that ETS has decreased the amount of vocabulary on the GRE. So you should work hard to improve your vocabulary, but you can get a decent score without a great vocabulary.

Many students who are in advanced math courses are confused by the GRE. Not only is the content of the GRE simple, but each math (and verbal) concept is boiled down to the simplest rule possible and it's applied uniformly. For example, everyone knows that the square root of 25 is 5 or -5. Not so on the GRE. The square of any number (like 25) is usually the positive root only (in this case, 5). This is how you were first taught square roots in fifth or sixth grade, and this is the way they are on the GRE. Every rule is boiled down to its simplest version and it's never broken. By now, you have probably moved on to more complex versions of simple math and verbal rules, but not ETS. It's still stuck in fifth grade, making everyone apply the same simple rule over and over (and swatting your knuckles with a ruler if you don't stick to the rule).

X FAIR WARNING

The GRE is like a Fascist fourth-grade teacher: every math and verbal rule is applied in its most elementary form, and the rule is applied ruthlessly. If you know it, you get all the points. If you don't know it, you get none of the points.

How the GRE Is Scored

The sections on the GRE are scored on a 200–800 scale. You get a 200 on each section for showing up to the test and an 800 for getting 99 percent of the questions correct (you can still miss a few). No one really knows why ETS chooses this scale, but we think it's because ETS wants everyone to think the GRE test is special.

Right after you finish taking the test, you will be asked whether you want to know your score or cancel it. If you want to know, you will immediately be told your verbal and math scores. If you choose to cancel it, the score will never be known. It takes a few weeks for ETS to grade your essay, so you can find out only your math and verbal scores immediately.

About five weeks after you take the GRE you will receive a report from ETS with a math, verbal, and essay score. You will get a score between 200 and 800 for the math and verbal sections. The best score on either section is 800. The average score is about a 500. The essay scores are reported on a 0–6 scale, with 6 being the best score.

How the GRE Is Made

Now for the good stuff. The basic way ETS writes all GRE problems can be summed up in four steps:

1. Write simple, straightforward math and verbal problems.

2. Mess them up.

3. Add distracting and confusing answer choices.

4. Repeat Step 2.

To show you how ETS does this, take a crack at the following problem:

> The volume of Jimi Hendrix's amplifier goes up to $3x = 9$, Paul McCartney's amplifier goes up to $2z = 4$, and Kurt Cobain's amplifier goes up to $3y = 6$. What is twice the value of $2(x + y)$?
>
>   a. 5
>   b. 7
>   c. 10
>   d. 15
>   e. 20

If your math teacher wrote this question, it would look like this:

> If $3x = 9$ and $3y = 6$, what is $4(x + y)$?

Same problem, just without ETS's dirty tricks. This is how ETS originally wrote the problem (remember step 1: write simple, straightforward math and verbal problems). You can now see that the actual math in this problem is from the seventh grade (at best). In fact, this problem is easy when your math teacher writes it. Now we can easily see that $x = 3$ and $y = 2$, so $4(x + y) = 20$. So the answer is 20.

ETS's GRE problems are the evil opposite of your normal college test problems, and you miss them because you approach them like normal college problems. Here are the differences:

College Prof	ETS The Test-Maker
Uses numbers in math problems	Uses words in math problems
Offers only relevant information	Puts in lots of crap to trick you
Is actually trying to see whether you know math	Is trying to get you to pick the wrong answer
Checks your work to see how you did the problem	Doesn't check your work and doesn't care—all that counts is which oval you bubble in
Full credit for correct answer; partial credit for good work	No partial credit, and lists wrong answers choices that look correct just to fool you
Is not evil	Is very evil

It's All About Reading

So what are ETS's math problems really about? Critical reading! That's right: better readers get higher math scores. You'll notice in the problem above that the math was simple, but it took a careful reader to extract the math from that bogus amplifier problem. So it doesn't matter if you're good or bad at math: the math is easy, the reading is what makes it difficult.

FAIR WARNING

The test you take to get admitted to medical school is called the MCAT (8 hours of physics, biology, and verbal). Who do you think consistently scores the highest on the MCAT? Physics majors? Nope. Chemistry majors? Nope. Biology majors? Nope. (Give up yet?) Humanities majors! Crazy, isn't it? All standardized tests are about critical reading skills, and humanities majors (English, history) usually have better critical reading skills than biology majors. It's all about reading.

If you have more than three months to prep for the GRE, the best thing to start doing now is to read. Start reading long, boring essays. If you do that for 3+ months, your verbal *and* math scores will improve. What counts as good GRE prep reading? Any publication that uses big words: *Economist, National Review, Wall Street Journal, Scientific American*. Most major newspapers and big-circulation magazines (like *Time* or *Newsweek*) aren't well-written enough (the essays are short and dumbed down). So start reading today! Read everything you can get your hands on (and not just the *Sports Illustrated* swimsuit edition and *Cosmopolitan*).

Order of Difficulty

So the bad news is that ETS is hard at work screwing up perfectly good math and verbal problems just to confuse you. The good news is that it's given you a way to tell exactly how much it has screwed up each problem.

Everything on the GRE is in an Order of Difficulty. This means that in a section of 25 math problems, the first problems are easy, the middle problems are medium, and the last problems are difficult. So what does this mean?

Easy Problems

Easy problems are "easy" because, usually, more than 70 percent of all test-takers get them correct. Roughly the first third of any section of problems are easy. Easy problems are easy because ETS hasn't taken the time to screw them up.

Medium Problems

Medium problems are a little tricky. The average test-taker gets about 50 percent of these correct. ETS starts to introduce dirty tricks in medium problems, so be careful. Most test-takers start to get medium-level problems around questions 7–9.

Hard Problems

The last third of any section are "hard" problems. Why are they hard? Because most people miss them (usually fewer than 35 percent of test-takers get these problems correct). These problems are hard because ETS has introduced all its dirty tricks. Usually, the hard questions start around questions 16–20.

Meet Test-Taker Tom

To give you an idea of how you're going to approach the GRE, I'm going to tell you a story. Let's say Tom, a junior from Frost College in Cornpone, Indiana, is about to take the GRE. Tom is a typical test-taker. He wakes up that Saturday in May around 6 A.M. and drives to Frost College. Tom has no idea what ETS has cooked up back in New Jersey. Tom didn't really prepare for the GRE (and never even thought about it). Tom assumed that the GRE would be just like the tests in college, and he gets As in school. Why worry?

How Tom Takes the GRE

So Tom gets to section one, and it's a 45-minute math problem-solving section. On problem #1, Tom reads the problem, spends just a few seconds figuring out the answer, and picks the answer choice that seems right. (He got this one correct!)

Tom keeps working on section 1. He works quickly through the easy and medium problems to get to the hard ones. He figures that if he has more time on the hard problems, he will get more of them correct. So on problem #12, Tom spends just a few seconds; he reads the problem, works quickly on it, and picks the answer choice that seems right. (He missed this one!) On problem #14, he quickly reads the problem, figures out an answer, and picks the answer choice that seems right. (He got this one correct!)

On the first hard problem, he spends three whole minutes. He reads the question (twice), figures out an answer, and picks the one that seems right. (He missed this one!) On the next hard problem, he reads the question (three times), figures out an answer, then picks the one that seems right. (He missed this one, too!)

Tom gets his GRE score right after the test: 500 on math and 500 on verbal. Right in the fiftieth percentile on both. Right in the middle. Not good. Not bad. Just average.

The majority of students take the GRE the same way Tom does—and the national average score is 500 in each section. Chances are that you do many of the same things that Tom does.

Don't Be a Tom

What did Tom do wrong and how can he raise his score? Here's a summary of how Tom took the GRE:

Problem Level	Time Tom Took	Answer He Chose	How He Did
Easy	Very little time	The one that looked right!	Got most right
Medium	Not much time	The one that looked right!	Got half right
Hard	Lots of time	The one that looked right!	Got most wrong

Here are the primary reasons that Tom's strategy failed:

♦ He missed easy and medium problems because he rushed through them to get to the hard problems, which he was going to miss anyway. If he had slowed down on the easy and medium problems, he would have gotten more right!

♦ On every problem, he chose the answer choice that looked right. Because ETS makes wrong answers "look" right on harder problems, he should have changed his strategy as the problems got harder!

If he keeps approaching the GRE this way, he will never get above the fiftieth percentile on either section.

Let's look more closely at the two mistakes. First, Tom speeds through the easy problems and works quickly through the medium problems just to get to the hard problems. He thinks that the reason he misses hard problems is that he doesn't have enough time. Tom's solution is to spend more time on the hard problems. But even with more time, Tom's score doesn't improve. Why? Because you don't need more time to get hard problems correct; you need a new strategy.

Which leads us to Tom's second big mistake: he approaches every problem the same way. He reads the question, does the problem, and chooses the answer that looks right. *Why does this fail?*

Remember order of difficulty? Why is a hard problem considered "hard"? Because everyone (like Tom) misses it! How do they miss it? Because they read the question, do the problem, and pick the answer choice that looks right. But on hard problems, the answer choice that "looks" right is wrong! That's how they got to be hard problems.

How does ETS trick Tom on verbal sections? ETS uses words like "enervate." What do you think "enervate" means? Most people will say—without hesitation—that it means "something like energy or with energy." ETS will give you an *analogy* such as "enervate : energy" and you will think "enervate means with lots of energy." All of this seems to make sense, but "enervate" actually means "to lose energy" or "to weaken." That's the opposite of what most people think it means and that's how Tom misses this problem. ETS loves to give you words that look like they mean one thing when they really mean the opposite. (Another Tom word: infinitesimal.)

VEXING VOCABULARY

A GRE **analogy** is a comparison of relationships. For example, "Apple : Fruit" and "Carrot : Vegetable." Apple is a kind of fruit and carrot is a kind of vegetable. These relationships are analogous because they are both "kind of" relationships. So when ETS gives you a pair of words, you try to determine the relationship, then find a pair in the answer choices with the same relationship. If you hate analogies, the good news is that they are becoming less frequent. The bad news is that analogy questions are being replaced with more reading passage questions.

A "hard" problem is one that everyone gets wrong. This happens because ETS creates the problem so that there is an "obvious" way to do the problem and an "obvious" answer choice to pick, but the "obvious" way to do the problem and the "obvious" answer choice are wrong. So if you pick the answer choice that "just seems right" on a hard problem, you'll miss it.

So here's how you should approach hard GRE questions: the amount of time you spend on each section and the way you choose answers should be the opposite of what Tom does and the opposite of what most test-takers do. This is the first step to improving your score.

Problem Level	Time You Should Take	What to Do with the Answer Choice That "Looks Right"	And You Should Get Them …
Easy	Enough! Don't make careless errors!	Choose it!	All correct!
Medium	Lots of time!	Be careful! (Sometimes the obvious answer is correct, sometimes not.)	Mostly correct!
Hard	Not much (or none, you may skip these).	Cross it out—it's wrong every time!	Some correct (or left blank).

ETS makes the GRE for people just like Tom: average test-takers who score in the fiftieth percentile every time on math and verbal regardless of what they do. Tom can try to improve his score, but it won't help because Tom doesn't understand the test. ETS expects everyone to approach the GRE like Tom.

Here's another example of how ETS designs the GRE for Tom. Fill in the blank for each one of these "questions" with the first word you think of:

Question	Your Answer
Peanut butter:	_____
Fork:	_____
Cat:	_____
Ice:	_____
1:	_____
A negative #:	_____

Now here are the most commonly given answers. Did you write any of these?

Question	Common Answers
Peanut butter:	sandwich, jelly
Fork:	knife, spoon
Cat:	dog, kitten
Ice:	cube, tea, cold
1:	2
A negative #:	-1, -3

If you put some of the "Common Answers," then you're acting like Tom. What a test-taker will put on any question is fairly predictable, and ETS has tested all of his questions to see what Tom will put for each question.

Is this bad? Not on an easy question. If you're on question #2, and the question is "peanut butter," then "jelly" is correct. Easy questions have obvious answers. But if you're on question #24 and the question is "peanut butter," then find "jelly" and cross it off—you know it's wrong! Obvious answers are wrong on hard questions.

This is important:

> On easy questions, obvious answers are correct.
> On hard questions, obvious answers are wrong.

So ETS makes up questions and then figures out which answer choice Tom would pick as an answer. If the question is hard, Tom's answer is wrong.

No question will appear like this on the actual GRE. It's designed to situate your brain.

Try this one:

Question	Answer Choices
Cat	a. Dog
	b. Sea kelp
	c. Bird
	d. Canary
	e. Tree

What did you put? Hopefully, you asked, "Is this an easy or a hard question?" What's the correct answer if this is an *easy* question? Probably Dog (because it reminds Tom of Cat).

What if this is a *hard* question? Then the correct answer is probably Sea kelp (because it doesn't look like it has anything to do with Cat).

If this were a *medium* question, the correct answer is probably Bird, Canary, or Tree—they aren't directly related to Cat but they have something in common.

Got it? The entire GRE works like this—you must master the concept of Order of Difficulty and use it throughout the entire GRE. This is the hardest part: most students understand this concept and use it while studying, but they forget it when taking the actual test. Learn it now and use it later!

What Would Tom Choose?

So ETS designs the GRE around the predictability of Tom, the average test-taker. Your job is to ask: which answer choice would Tom choose? If it's an easy question, Tom's answer choice is correct. If it's a hard question, get rid of Tom's answer choice—it's wrong every time. Got it? Now you know how ETS puts together the GRE.

Right, Wrong, and Best

When taking normal college tests, you usually work in the world of "right" and "wrong" answers. In the instructions for the GRE, ETS tells you to look for the "best" answer. Forget about thinking about answer choices in terms of right answers, wrong answers, or best answers. The only answer that counts is the one that ETS thinks is correct.

Sometimes you might look at the answer choices for a particular problem and think that ETS is a fool. Keep in mind that ETS is giving out the points on this test, and the only thing that counts is that you're picking the answer choice that ETS thinks is correct.

INFO TO GO

Remember: the goal on the GRE is to pick the answer choice that ETS thinks is right—nothing else matters.

When it comes to your GRE score, *no one* cares …

- Whether you know how to do the problem.
- Whether you showed your work on the problem.
- Whether you're sure your answer choice is correct.

What they *do* care about is …

- Whether you choose ETS's answer.

Got it?

How the GRE CAT operates

The GRE is a CAT. "CAT" stands for "Computer Adaptive Test." This is different from a "linear" test. Your normal college tests are all linear, which means there are a standard set of questions that everyone answers, and those questions are "lined up" before the test begins. The CAT is different because the test doesn't actually exist until you start taking it. When you start, ETS will give you a 50th percentile question (about 470 verbal and 620 math). Let's say you're starting with a math section. Your first question is a 620 level question. If you get it correct, your next question will be more difficult, around the 650 range. If you get that correct, your next question will be even more difficult, around the 700 range. If you miss a question, you'll be given an easier one. Eventually, the CAT settles on a range for you. For example, perhaps you get almost every math question correct in the 640 range and lower. But you miss almost every question that's higher than a 640. The CAT will give a score of 640. So the test adapts to your answers.

Do not try to figure out whether a question is easier or harder than the previous question. Your brain will explode. Sometimes it's obvious that a question is more difficult, but most of the time it isn't that obvious. Spending precious minutes trying to determine if you got the previous question correct is a waste of time. Also, keep in mind that each section must be balanced, which means you must be given a minimum number of question types: *antonyms*, analogies, sentence completions in verbal, and arithmetic, geometry, and algebra questions in math. So if you are an analogy fiend, besides being the envy of all your friends, you'll possibly get all the GRE analogies correct. But that doesn't mean ETS will stop asking you analogy questions. For you to have a valid score, you must be asked a certain number of every question type, even if you're getting them all correct. So the CAT format isn't perfect—sometimes, even if you get a question correct, ETS may need to ask you a question which seems easy to you.

VEXING VOCABULARY

Antonyms are straightforward: ETS gives you a word, and you choose a word that is its opposite. Easy? Well, the words they give you are often fairly obscure. So a question may be "apotheosis" followed by five answer choices, one of which is "abasement" (the opposite of apotheosis). Yes, it's essentially a grad-level vocab quiz. The good news: antonyms are becoming less frequent. The bad news: antonyms are often the first questions, so if you're taking a computer adaptive version of the GRE, you really need to get them correct.

CAT Strategy

So your score starts in the middle and moves up or down depending on whether you answer the question correctly. Here's the rub: the first few questions on any section will largely determine your score for that section. So if you start the Verbal section by getting the first 12 questions correct, you'll probably receive a score above 700, even if you miss many of the remaining questions. Similarly, if you miss the first 7 questions in math, your math score will probably be below 500 even if you get 65 percent of the remaining questions correct. So the first 7–12 questions for any single section will have a disproportionately significant impact on your final score. Essentially, those initial questions set the range in which ETS thinks your final score will be, and that range is very difficult to break out of—in fact, only a consecutive string of 4+ correct or wrong answers will result in a score higher or lower than that initial range. Not to freak you out, but you must do well on those first questions.

It's also important that you answer every question. There's the obvious issue that the CAT is built on your answers, so you must answer the question for the test to continue. But your score is also determined based on how many correct answers you gave out of total questions answered, and ETS essentially penalizes you for taking a "shorter" test. So make your test as "long" as possible by answering all the questions.

So what's the strategy? Work slowly and carefully on the first 7–12 questions, then speed up to make sure you finish each section. This approach will maximize your potential score.

Dismantling the GRE

So now you know how the GRE is put together. Here's how we're going to take it apart.

The dissection starts with the answer choices. As you know, you need to look for ETS's answer choice. The nice thing is that ETS writes all the correct answers in the test! Every question has the correct answer written under it! Unfortunately, every question also has several wrong answer choices written under it, too. But because the test is multiple-choice, it means that sometimes you can get the right answer just by getting rid of the wrong answer choices. For example, you might be asked a question like this on a normal high-school test:

> In what modern country did Napoleon's Piedmont campaign take place?

And if you had no idea, you would skip the problem. But if ETS wrote your high school tests, this problem would look like this:

> Napoleon's Piedmont campaign took place in which modern country:

a. South Korea

b. United States

c. Brazil

d. Italy

e. Japan

Spend 20 seconds reviewing the answer choices and you realize the answer must be Italy. No other answer choice makes sense. You'd be surprised how many GRE questions are like this—many answer choices won't even make sense. So make sure you're always using the answer choices to your advantage.

Take a look at this question and keep Tom in mind.

Level: Medium

Jane buys a dress that is discounted by 20 percent. If Jane pays $100 for the dress, what was the original price?

a. $80

b. $100

c. $120

d. $122

e. $125

This problem is designed by ETS to get Tom to pick the wrong answer. It looks easy, but any problem that's a medium question can't be this easy—so ETS must be up to some tricks. Tom almost always misses this question even though the math is painfully easy (it's sixth-grade math!). The primary mistake that Tom makes is in not reading the problem closely enough. Remember: good verbal and math scores depend on good reading skills! Tom makes the mistake of simply adding 20 percent to $100 and getting $120. Here are the ways ETS writes GRE problems like this one to lead the Toms of the world to the wrong answer choice.

- ETS writes the problem in a way that encourages Tom to misread it. Often, if Tom gets the wrong answer, it's because Tom didn't read the question correctly.

- ETS will put obviously wrong answer choices in the problem so Tom will cross them off and think he's being smart. The joke is on Tom. ETS plants these wrong answer choices just to give Tom a false sense of security.

- ETS will disguise the correct answer choice with some wrong answer choices that look similar. In this problem, answer choices $122 and $125 are close together, and some will conclude that since $122 is wrong, so is $125. Be careful: don't get rid of one answer choice just because it's close to another. The correct answer is $125.

- Finally, ETS loves problems that are deceptively easy: this problem seems very easy when you first read it. Don't be fooled by problems that appear easy!

Here's one more example of a problem you might see on a college test:

During his North Africa campaigns, Field Marshall Rommel was called the "Desert _____" because he was wily and cunning.

Here's the same question as it would appear if ETS wrote it:

During his North Africa campaigns, Field Marshall Rommel was called the "Desert _____" because he was wily and cunning.

a. Oak Tree

b. Polar Bear

c. Badger

d. Fox

e. Snake

ETS adds distracting answer choices to otherwise simple questions. You know the answer is Fox, but those answer choices sure make you think twice.

To Guess or Not to Guess

Tom has heard of a guessing penalty that ETS charges for each guess. Maybe you have heard of it, too. Well, I'm here to tell you it's just a load of bull. You don't get any points deducted for guessing—not a single point! ETS doesn't know when you guess—so how can it deduct points?

On a paper version of the GRE, you do get $\frac{1}{4}$ point subtracted from your raw score for each wrong answer (whether you guessed or not—sometimes, you work very hard on a problem and still get a wrong answer). On the CAT version of the test, you get knocked down a level of difficulty for each wrong question. So missing a question will make the computer think you've reached your limit.

But none of this should discourage you from guessing. Why? First, because if you're taking the GRE CAT then you must answer every question. You don't have a choice.

But even if you did have the choice, you should guess. Because sometimes when you guess, you will guess correctly! But there are two types of guesses:

good guesses and wild guesses. If you can eliminate one or more answer choices as wrong, then you increase your chances of guessing correctly. That makes it a good guess. So if you can get rid of at least one wrong answer choice, you should guess.

A wild guess is when you have no idea about any of the choices. But even if you guess wildly, you may still (occasionally) get a few answers correct. If you guessed wildly on the entire GRE—never knowing what the correct answer is—your score won't go up or down. So guessing wildly doesn't hurt your score—but it could be a waste of time.

We can show you the math that proves that guessing is beneficial, but take my word for it. Guessing is like baseball. Everyone knows that Mark McGuire and Sammy Sosa used to hit home runs like Godzilla stomped on Tokyo—it looked easy. But did you know that McGuire and Sosa struck out all the time? So when you're guessing, sometimes you will get the correct answer and get lots of points, and other times you will get the wrong answer and lose a quarter of a point. But the only way to hit a home run is to step up to the plate and swing the bat. The only way to improve your GRE score is to put down answers. And good guessing is beneficial because the upside is much greater than the downside, and sometimes you will guess correctly!

One more time:

> When should you guess? (All the time.)
> When does it have the most chance of
> improving your score? (When you can
> get rid of at least one wrong answer
> choice.)

Should you guess on every problem? Guess on every problem that you work on and for which you can get rid of at least one answer choice that's wrong. Guessing randomly on problems that you don't work on and for which you can't get rid of at least one answer choice won't hurt your score, but it won't help it either—so it's probably just a waste of time.

The best guessers on standardized tests use one simple rule: get to the correct answer by getting rid of wrong answers. So if you can't do the problem, go directly to the answer choices and start crossing off answers that you know just can't be correct. If it's a volume problem but you just don't know how to do it, cross off any negative numbers (you know the volume can't be negative). As we go along, I will show you what stupid answers look like for each question type—just remember that you can often get the right answer simply by crossing off the wrong answers. In fact, this is the way I can get a 1600 without even doing many of the problems. Good guessing alone can raise your score by 100 points.

GRE Prep Tips

At some point in the middle of this book you're going to put down your #2 pencil and say, "What is all this? I didn't learn this in school!" Remember, the GRE is the evil opposite of your high school tests. So GRE prep is the opposite of normal test preparation. I'm not going to teach you math or discuss the theme of *Moby Dick*. All I'm going to

teach you is the GRE, which is one screwed-up test! So throw the idea of learning normal high-school math and English out the window. This test isn't normal, so prepping for it won't be either.

This also means that I'm going to tell you to do some things that may seem freaky: how to get the correct answer without reading the question; how to be a good guesser; how to use the weaknesses of the GRE to raise your score. Don't try to think too much about the techniques or second-guess them—just do it.

Here are a couple of important tips.

Use the Paper!

When you take the GRE, you get a few sheets of scratch paper. (You are supposed to get six pieces of paper, but you never know.) You are permitted to get more if you use all the sheets. Make sure you don't run out in the middle of a section, because if you need more paper, you'll be sitting there with your hand up while time runs out. Refresh your paper supply during breaks. When you do get more paper, the proctor will remove your used sheets of paper.

Of course, the problems and the answer choices are all on a computer screen. Some people for some reason (unknown to us) don't write on the scratch paper. This is crazy. The more you try to memorize and the more you try to work the problems on the computer, the more you will make careless errors. You paid for that scratch paper, so write all over it! No one will ever look at it, so scribble whatever you want. If you need to write down "2 + 2" for some reason, do it! No one will ever see that you needed to write this down. (However tempting it may be, I don't really encourage you to write down obscene messages to ETS.)

To prepare yourself, do not write in this book. Instead, get some scratch paper—the stuff ETS gives you will be plain, unlined copier paper. Do all your work on the scratch paper. Make notes on the scratch paper. Write the problems on the scratch paper. Write the answer choices on the scratch paper. Cross off wrong answer choices. Circle important stuff. Redraw figures in math problems. Get the idea? Once you're done with the GRE, this book should be clean and you should have 100 pages of used scratch paper. Get in the habit of rewriting problems on scratch paper.

Use Practice Tests

And finally, we're going to say something that may pain you: use all real GREs. Yes, this does help pay for ETS's duck ponds and billiard room, but there is simply no better practice for the GRE than practicing on the GRE. There are many fake GREs out there—in bookstores, at free seminars, online—but all of them are awful. I'll repeat that for you: don't use fake GREs. Always practice on the real thing. Head over to www.gre.org and order the prep software. Be sure to order the correct version: if you're taking the GRE CAT, make sure you order CAT software.

One word of warning: ETS offers a lot of "tips from the test makers." As you may have guessed, these tips are completely bogus; ETS giving you GRE tips is like the IRS giving you tax tips. Do you think ETS is really trying to help you? Do you think it's really going to give you the inside scoop on raising your score? For example, ETS's suggestion for raising your verbal score is to read more carefully. Gee, thanks. So get the real GREs and ignore the "tips."

It's you and Tom versus ETS. Are you ready? ETS works year-round to write this test, so you need to prepare for it as much as possible. Get a few pencils and a comfortable chair. With some hard work, your score can improve 100-200 points in each section. Ideally, you should work on the GRE at least two hours at a time, twice per week for seven weeks. (You should work on vocabulary all the time!) Now that you know the basics of the GRE, I'm going to teach you how to apply these basics directly to each section of the test. Your job is to learn them and apply them. I know this isn't fun. Disney is never going to have a ride called "It's a Standardized Test World." But the GRE is one of life's little necessary evils (like getting wisdom teeth pulled or listening patiently to your grandma's "The Time I Got Lost in Yonkers" story for the 700th time). So if you're ready, let's go!

Summary

If anything looks new on this summary, go back and reread this chapter. Stick it in your brain and leave it there until the GRE is over ... then forget everything we said because it's useless after the GRE.

Remember:

- ETS likes the GRE because it rakes in a big wad of cash. ETS isn't filled with brain scientists, just test-makers.

- The GRE doesn't measure anything and it won't make or break your life. It's just a little test that universities like to use because they don't trust transcripts.

- The GRE is hard only because ETS puts in tons of tricks. It's not the math or the verbal: it's the tricks! This is why the GRE is the evil opposite of your college tests.

- ETS makes the GRE for the average college student. His name is Tom. Your job is to pick Tom's answer choice on easy problems and to get rid of Tom's answer choice on hard problems.

- Your job is to pick the correct answer—it doesn't matter whether you know how to do the problem!

- Often, the quickest way to get the correct answer is simply by getting rid of the incorrect answers.

- Guessing is good. Be aggressive with the answer choices. Get rid of bad answer choices and guess!

- Don't write in this book. Get familiar with using scratch paper.

- Don't worry. If you do everything in this book, your GRE score will improve.

The Least You Need to Know

- The GRE is not about intelligence—it's about how well you take the GRE.

- Understand how Tom takes the test and how to use that to your advantage.

- Tom always picks "what looks right." Make sure you're not sucked into that kind of thinking on hard questions.

- You must write everything down on scratch paper—don't try to do it in your head.

- Develop a good-guessing strategy.

- All standardized tests boil down to your reading skills.

Chapter 2

You Are in Control

In This Chapter

- How to be successful in taking your GRE
- Pacing yourself during the test
- Practice schedules and testing

In this chapter, you'll learn the factors that will be most crucial to improving your GRE score. Take a few minutes and review this chapter. Let the advice sink in.

Key Factors to Success

First, you need to understand how GRE scores really go up. Some people think scores go up little by little—as though for each page you read of this book, your score will go up one point. Wrong. Scores improve by leaps, like 10–15 points at a time. Once you learn how to solve a particular type of problem, your score will leap higher because now you're solving a higher proportion of the problems. (For example, once you learn how to solve sentence completions, your score will increase by 10 points because you're now getting many more sentence completions correct.) So … make sure you complete every lesson in its entirety. Don't skip around and don't learn a lesson halfway. Often, a lesson learned halfway won't raise your score at all.

Next, some people think that your GRE scores will haunt you forever, as though you won't be able to apply for a mortgage 20 years from now because you didn't break 600 in the math. Your GRE scores won't be tattooed on your forehead. In fact, your GRE scores will appear only in a few places: maybe on your grad school transcript (but probably not), on your grad school applications, and in some little file in ETS's office. That's it. And after you apply to college, your GRE scores are gone, gone, gone. (And good riddance.) No one in their right mind will ever care about your GRE scores after you apply to college.

The truth is that even if your GRE scores aren't great, your life isn't ruined. In fact, nothing is ruined. Great grades and a great personal statement can help make up for mediocre GRE scores. (Of course, now that you're reading this book, you won't get mediocre GRE scores.)

Albert Einstein never took the GRE, but if he did, we wouldn't be surprised if he got a 540 in math. There is no strong correlation between your GRE score and your grades, your success in college, or how smart you are. The GRE only tests how well you take the GRE. Period. Many very smart people bomb the GRE and many people who are a little touched in the head get good GRE scores. Good GRE scores shouldn't impress you and bad GRE scores shouldn't imply anything.

Pinpoint Your Strengths

As you work through this book, it's important that you pay attention to discover your strengths, weaknesses, and needs. In Chapter 3, I'll discuss needs in the admissions process, so let's focus on strengths and weaknesses.

Verbal and math scores do not improve equally. Usually, math scores are much easier to improve than verbal scores. The two most difficult areas to improve on the entire GRE are reading skills and vocabulary, and both of those areas are tested on the verbal section. The math is comparatively easy to improve because you've probably learned all of the math in high school; improving is a matter of scraping off the rust. On average, verbal scores improve 8–15 points and math scores improve 15–18 points.

So if you want your math and verbal scores to improve equally, you'll need to spend much more time on verbal.

Pacing

Obviously you need to be able to answer the questions, but this is a timed test, so answering questions quickly is also important. As you work through problems, understand that your pacing will be important.

There are two factors to pacing. First, if you're taking the GRE CAT, you must finish each section, even if you're just making educated guesses for the last few questions. Second, pacing depends on your goal. You can move more slowly if you want to score a 500 and you must move quickly if you want to score a 650. In order to evaluate your pacing needs, you first need to know your scoring range. Take a practice GRE (a real one from ETS). Add about 60 points to your verbal and math score. That's your range.

Math

For math, you have 40 minutes to answer the questions. If you're scoring under 550, you should be moving slowly at the beginning, attempting about 7 problems in the first 15 minutes (taking a good 2 minutes per problem). This may seem slow, but this is okay as long as you're getting most of the problems correct. You should do another 7–9 problems in the second 15 minutes, once again, moving slowly enough to get most of them correct. You then have 15 minutes remaining and about 13 problems to do. Move quickly, make educated guesses, and finish the section. If your target is above 600, you should be answering 9–10 questions in the first 15 minutes.

Slowing down is often the most difficult GRE technique—but it really improves scores! Almost everyone should slow down.

Verbal

For verbal, you have 40 minutes to answer the questions. Most of the early questions will be the "short" questions: antonyms, analogies, and sentence completions. If you're scoring below a 600, you should be answering about 8 questions in the first 10 minutes. If your target is above 600, you should be pacing yourself in equal thirds, approximately answering 10 questions every 10 minutes.

Keep in mind that it's very important that you answer the first 5–10 questions in each section correctly. So regardless of the pacing recommendation above, you must work slowly enough to achieve high accuracy with those first questions. The first step to improving your GRE score is slowing down and getting the first 5–10 questions consistently correct. Do not speed through the first problems to get to the problems at the end—they aren't worth as much!

Accuracy is far more important than speed with the first 5–10 questions for each section.

Process of Elimination

One way to improve your pacing is to use the process of elimination (POE). In most cases, you have answer choices for every problem. If you get to a problem that baffles, do not stare at it for 5 minutes—that will completely ruin your pacing for the section. If a question baffles you, jump down to the answer choices. You will learn many methods for using the answer choices to your advantage, but looking at the answer choices when you don't understand the problem should be instinctive. Aggressively using the answer choices improves your odds of getting a question correct and improves your pacing.

When using POE, you need to keep Tom in mind. The wrong answer choices on medium and hard questions are "distracters." They are designed to distract Tom so he doesn't choose the correct answer. By keeping Tom in mind, you can engage in GRE judo by using the test's strengths against it. The GRE's strength in medium and hard questions is these distracters—they will draw your eye away from the correct answer. But if you keep Tom in mind, you'll know that any answer choice that simply "looks right" on the hard question must be wrong. Use your GRE POE judo and cross it off.

Establishing a Practice Schedule

The key ingredient to improving your score is time. If you have the time and you study, your score will improve. How much time do you need? Depends on what you need to improve and how much you need to improve. It's easier to improve math scores, and you can improve a math score in just two weeks. But verbal scores are more difficult to improve and it could take two to three months to improve a verbal score. So what if you're scheduled to take the GRE in two weeks? Call ETS at 1-800-GRE-CALL at least seven days before your test date and you can switch the date (it will cost you about $40).

Ideally, you have at least two months to prepare. You should buy real practice GREs from ETS (do this now!).

Real GREs

You must practice on a full-length GRE before taking the actual test. Preferably, take a few practice tests. Always take them under "actual" testing conditions (including timing yourself).

There are many fake GREs in the bookstore and online. Avoid them. Always practice on real tests, made and sold by ETS (Educational Testing Service).

Scheduling and Registering

The easiest way to get information about testing dates is to check out GRE.org. There are about 30 test dates per year, and the test is given in computer centers. GRE.org will list all the test centers and available dates in your area.

The Least You Need to Know

- Improving your GRE score is as much about how you perform as it is about what you know, so practice and pacing are important.

- Practice only on real tests, made and sold by ETS.

- Check out GRE.org to get practice tests and to register.

- Establish a practice schedule early and keep to it!

Chapter 3

The Graduate Admissions Process

In This Chapter

- ◆ The grad school search
- ◆ Admissions nuts and bolts
- ◆ Deciding between a Master's degree and a Ph.D.
- ◆ Planning ahead

Applying to graduate school is time consuming and can be frustrating. But making the decision to apply to graduate school is perhaps the easiest part of the process. There are over 400 graduate English and history programs in the United States, over 300 chemistry programs, and over 250 physics programs, and you need to choose the few programs that best suit your interests and strengths.

Grad School: The Big Picture

The amount of work required in grad school can be daunting. You'll be required to read more and read longer, more obscure books. You'll be required to write longer, more in-depth papers. You'll be required to engage in original research, to develop your own ideas, and to explore academic areas that aren't easily accessible. You will need to organize your time better, work with greater efficiency and efficacy, and set priorities.

As a graduate student, you will be asked to juggle many priorities, ranging from attending classes to teaching classes. You'll often need to teach yourself complicated concepts, and produce 50-page papers with frequency. Time management will be very important. The graduate-school classroom will also be different. Usually, the classes are small and discussion-driven. The professor won't lecture for 45 minutes, as an undergraduate professor might. You'll be expected to have read and understood complex ideas and be ready to contribute your insights to the classroom. Most graduate school students will receive "As" and "Bs" in their classes. A "C" grade in grad school is essentially equivalent to failing.

Your experience in grad school will be guided by a single advisor in your department. You'll be expected to work closely with the advisor for many years. This advisor will guide you through the maze of graduate academia; help you understand your role as a student and teaching assistant (or T.A.); and make sure you're fulfilling your requirements such as competency exams, dissertation proposals, dissertation committees, and publication. You may edit or co-author works with your advisor. Your advisor will sit on your committees, assist in finding internships, projects, grants, and jobs. In many ways, you'll be treated as a junior colleague, an apprentice professor. You'll be expected to behave as a professor would, not as a student would. You'll need to attend conferences and meetings, assist in writing grant or project proposals, read and edit others' papers, and perhaps even sit on committees. Successful graduate students go beyond what's required. As a grad student, you should find out what your advisor and other professors expect from successful students. You may not be required to teach, publish, attend conferences, or be on committees, but you'll find that the successful (and employable) grad students do those things.

You should seek as much practical experience as you can. Employers love practical experience. They want to know that you can teach or conduct research. Such practical experience may not be required to get the degree, but it is virtually required in order to get a job at another university. From the moment you step onto campus, you should seek out as much practical experience as possible: teaching, research, editing, committees, projects, grant writing, presenting at conferences. Every Ph.D. can say he or she can teach; you should have the resumé that proves it.

Your advisor and a few other professors with whom you work closely will be the gatekeepers. Their opinions of you will have significant influence with other universities, publishers, and journals. Your ability to get published and be employed will be largely determined by your reputation among a small group of professors. Whether you become a professor will depend on whether that small group of professors who really know you think you've got what it takes. So you don't just want to fulfill what's required or even meet their expectations; you should exceed their expectations.

Researching Grad Schools

You will first need to consider your intended specialization. If you want to apply to history departments, then which country, era, and topic intrigues you? If you're interested in Colonial history, do you mean North American colonial? African colonial? And are you most interested in Colonial law? Trade? Religion? (Or any number of other topics.) If you want to specialize in British Colonial Caribbean trade, there are a few graduate programs that excel in that topic and others that haven't got a single expert on their faculty.

! INFO TO GO

Start talking to people you know who have gone through grad school. They can help you better understand the experience.

Another issue with specialization is the job market. Your interests and strengths may be fascinating to you but may not be in demand. So you should consider your interests, your academic strengths, and the potential for being employed in that field. You can obtain employment information from online academic employment websites and print sources; even though you won't be on the market for many years, it's worth knowing what specializations are considered desirable. Once you've narrowed down your potential specialization, always explore a university's faculty and facilities in regards to that specialization. Not every university does everything, and no university does everything well.

Location

Geography can be an important factor. On average, you'll live in the university area for two to eight years, depending on the degree and program. You want to live in a location in which you are comfortable. Some graduate students want to be near family, while others have spouses and children to consider. Weather, crime, health issues, entertainment, and cultural events all may be important factors. Keep in mind that some graduate programs in highly desirable locations are more difficult to get into simply because of their geography, so being geographically flexible can be a competitive advantage.

Professors

The general reputation of the faculty is important, but even more important are the reputations and personalities of the professors with whom you will work. You may earn a degree from the university, but your education and your ability to get a job will come largely from your adviser and the one or two other professors with whom you will spend the vast majority of your time. The bulk of your years in a graduate program will be spent working with

a single advisor. That advisor's personality must be compatible with yours, and that advisor's connections and reputation will be very influential in opening doors to you. The academic world relies heavily on reputation and other qualitative values, so always carefully consider the advisors in a graduate program.

How can you take the measure of a program's faculty? First, talk to your college professors and ask their opinion. Next, go to the department's website. Many department websites list current students and may also list where previous students are employed. E-mail current students and ask their opinion. And try to ascertain if the program's graduates get employed at colleges where you'd like to work. Finally, meet with your potential advisor in the program to see whether his or her personality and research interests match yours.

INFO TO GO

Unlike the undergraduate admissions process, the grad admissions process can be very personal. You'll exchange e-mails with professors, interview with them, and they will directly review your application. It's important that you make personal contact early and often.

Expenses

Universities have widely varying policies regarding tuition. It's common for universities to charge full tuition for Master's degree candidates and charge little or no tuition for Ph.D. candidates (this is called "tuition remission"). In most cases, if your program charges less than full tuition, you'll be required to work, usually either teaching as a T.A. or working in a lab or on a project. It's wise to talk to both the students currently enrolled in the program and the universities to gauge exactly how much you'll be expected to pay and to learn about scholarships and grants. Finally, while visiting the school you should also investigate the cost of living near the campus. In total, the cost of attending graduate school can range from a few thousand a year (with full tuition remission and grants) to over $40,000 a year.

Ranking

Rankings are an unfortunate fact of the admissions process. While rankings rarely reflect the truth, both universities and applicants alike rely on them. In theory, you could glean some important information from rankings: library size, student-to-faculty ratio, etc. In reality, most of this information won't be relevant to your actual experience. But rankings influence reputation, and the better a program's reputation, the more employable you're likely to be. Additionally, rankings also affect applications. Top-ranked programs are often more competitive simply because they are top ranked. Rankings can artificially cause a program to be more competitive, and hence more desirable, even though the program may not be any better than lower-ranked programs. So while a higher-ranked program may be more desirable, admission will also be more competitive.

! INFO TO GO

Ask your undergraduate professors about the reputations of the programs that you're considering.

Quality of Life

You will be immersed in a gradate school and its surroundings for many years, so you need to gauge the "livability" of the area. What interests you? How do you spend your time? If you have a spouse or children, you'll need to explore the local schools, employment opportunities, and healthcare. The

weather, local cultural events, and recreational facilities may be important to you. The primary way to take the measure of a community is to spend some time there. Don't fly in, talk with a professor for an hour, and fly out. Spend a few days, including a Friday or Saturday, talk to the other students, try to spend time with them on a weekend, and see what's happening in the community. In many cases, the program secretary can be of great assistance in helping you locate information about the area.

There are many other factors that may affect your decision. Start with programs that offer you the specialization in which you're interested, and then move on to the other factors that are most important to you. Many Ph.D. students, despite their best intentions, end up staying in their program for six to eight years, so make sure it's a place in which you can be happy and successful.

X FAIR WARNING

Don't underestimate how important quality of life considerations are! It may take 8 years to finish your degree and you may teach another 2–3 years at the university, so make sure you like the surroundings!

Master's Degree or Ph.D.?

While you're searching for the right program, you should also be focusing on the school's program details specific to the degree you'll be seeking. Here are a few considerations when comparing Master's and Ph.D. programs.

In most cases, a Master's degree can be earned in two years by a full-time student. Many Master's programs are actually shorter (and still others will give you some credit for your relevant undergraduate work). If your undergraduate major is the same as your graduate concentration, you may be able to earn a Master's in as little as a year. In most cases, Ph.D. degrees take at least five years and many Ph.D. candidates will take almost ten years before completing everything. A few Ph.D. programs, most notably math programs, turn out freshly minted Ph.D. students in three years, but it's rare for a student to actually receive the degree in under five years. Do you have the time to commit yourself to a Ph.D. program?

In theory, Ph.D. programs are also more expensive because you're in school longer. In reality, the reverse is often true. It's common for Master's programs to require full tuition payment, whereas most Ph.D. programs offer partial or full tuition remission in exchange for working at the university. This explains why some Ph.D. students never leave the university: their expenses are minimal as long as they stay in the program. Often, the biggest "expense" of a Ph.D. program isn't that the university is charging you $30,000 in tuition but rather that you're not making very much money. As a teaching assistant, you may have full tuition remission but you may also be paid $15,000 per year in salary; so you won't have tuition expenses, but you're also not being paid much. Therefore, the main expense of earning a Ph.D. is most often not having regular full-time employment (which would almost certainly pay several times what a university teaching assistant earns).

In most disciplines, a Ph.D. will command a higher salary and better benefits (many Master's degree holders are never hired full time). Many universities won't consider applicants who aren't either Ph.D. holders or ABD ("All But Dissertation").

In college, you can often major in an area quite easily. Graduate school is different. The students tend to be much more competitive, each attempting to write the best paper, have the most original ideas, and be the most helpful to the advisor. Ph.D. students often will take two or three classes and teach two or three classes each semester, while attending conferences and attempting to produce (and publish) quality research. In graduate school, you'll often focus on one small area of research for months or years until you've thoroughly memorized every piece of minutia about the topic. Many students who start Ph.D. programs never finish in part because they don't have the interest required to focus on a single topic for years. Many advisors will tell you that the primary factor in earning a Ph.D. is perseverance (not intelligence). Do you have the commitment that Ph.D. programs require?

If you simply want to improve your resumé, gain additional expertise in an area, and perhaps get a raise, then you probably want a Master's degree. The Ph.D. will be too theoretical, too research oriented, and take too long for someone who wants quick, practical results. (This is why, after all, 99 percent of those going to graduate school for business degrees only earn a Master's.) The Master's degree can help you change careers, be promoted, and develop an area you ignored while in college. In many cases, the Master's degree is your ticket to being certified or licensed to practice in a particular field.

While the Ph.D. seems less practical, it's virtually required if you wish to have a full-time teaching position at the university. And most university professors who don't have Master's degrees either have significant life experiences (e.g., won a Pulitzer Prize) or were in a Ph.D. program and simply didn't earn the degree. Outside of academia, the Ph.D. can seem unimportant, but because a Ph.D. is so rare outside of academia, it may be the ideal way to set yourself apart.

Undecided?

If you truly love a specific field of study or you want to teach full-time at the college level, then the Ph.D. is probably the right choice. If you want a quick change, to improve your resumé, or learn a little more, then the Master's is probably right for you. But what if you can't decide?

In many cases, you can apply for the program's Master's degree and, after a year or so, apply again for the Ph.D. program. There are programs that forbid this and programs that don't offer Master's, so you'll need to do some research. But it's often possible to get into a Master's program first and then "trade up," and admission to the Master's program is often easier. But nothing is automatic; you will need great grades and a great relationship with a professor in the program to move up to the Ph.D. program.

But in many cases, funding (scholarships, grants, teaching assistant positions) is reserved for the Ph.D. students, so applying to the Master's program may mean taking out loans. With that in mind, if you can get admitted to the Ph.D. program, there's usually no penalty for dropping out after two years and, in most cases, you'll be awarded a Master's. So while the Ph.D. programs are more competitive, they also get the funding. In some cases, if you get rejected from the Ph.D. program, you may ask whether your application can be considered for the Master's program.

Establishing a Timeline

Planning ahead is important. This process will get complicated, so creating a schedule will be very helpful. A careful plan will help you deal with unforeseen problems when they arise (and they will arise). But a careful plan will also help your chances of being admitted because applying early almost always improves the odds. By sending everything in at the beginning of the admissions season, you will avoid the deluge of applications that admissions offices receive each December and January. If you want your recommendations and essay to be considered with the utmost care, sending your application early will be beneficial.

Most program deadlines are between December 1 and February 1. Check the program in which you're interested to confirm the deadlines you need to meet. Assume the deadline you're trying to hit is two weeks before the printed deadline, but always try to mail in your applications two months early. The following schedule assumes you're applying with a December–February deadline to attend school in the following autumn. If you have a different schedule, adjust the timeline accordingly.

April

- ◆ Start researching programs, their requirements and their deadlines. Talk to your professors and advisors about programs that may suit you.

- ◆ Register for the GRE General Test.

- ◆ Take a GRE practice test to gauge your need for preparation. Start preparing now if your score is low.

May

- ◆ Obtain a few program applications. You can usually download them online. This should help you understand what the forms are like.

- ◆ Discuss recommendations with your professors. You should secure your recommenders before school gets out for the summer.

- ◆ Plan to visit a few grad schools that you like.

- ◆ Continue with your GRE prep.

June/July

- Narrow your list of programs.
- Discuss your chances of being admitted to these programs with your advisor (if available).
- Continue visiting programs.
- Try to talk about the programs with students currently enrolled in them or who have recently attended them.
- Take the GRE.
- Begin writing your statement of intent.

August

- Your list of schools should be fairly focused now. You should know the program details, deadlines, strengths, and weaknesses. Choose one or two professors in each program and read their works. Often, professors' resumés are posted on their universities' websites.
- Request applications from all programs.
- Start to get feedback on your statement of intent.

September

- Register for the GRE General Test if you need to take it again in October.
- Register for the November GRE Subject Test if you need it. Take a practice Subject Test— some of them are brutally difficult.

October

- Complete the applications.
- Request all recommendations, transcripts, and test scores. (You should assume that it will take three to five weeks for these to be sent.)
- Finalize your statement of intent.

November

- Send the applications.
- About a week after the application has been sent, call the program secretary and confirm that everything has been received.
- If you had any meaningful contact with professors in the program, write a short note thanking them for their time and informing them that you've applied.

The Least You Need to Know

- The admissions process usually takes about a year—so start early.
- Create a timeline for the admissions process and stick to it.
- Start talking to people who have been enrolled in graduate programs and ask about their experiences.
- Learn about program strengths and the professors with whom you will be working.

Part 2

Verbal: Smorgasbord of Standardized Testing

These chapters dissect the verbal sections of the GRE. We'll start with analogies and sentence completions and then move on to long and short reading passages, and explore the new logic passages. If you've feared the GRE verbal sections, then these chapters are for you! You learn how to improve your reading skills, understand the intricacies of standardized reading, and become more comfortable with reading tests. The final chapters are verbal practice sets to help you hone your verbal skills.

4

Analogies

In This Chapter

- ◆ What analogies are
- ◆ Strategies for solving them
- ◆ What to do when you don't know the words

You've seen and used analogies before. "My sister is a monkey" or "school is a prison" are (almost) analogies. An analogy is an expression of a relationship between two words. The idea isn't strange, but doing analogies on the GRE is strange. A GRE analogy looks like this:

> LION : CAT ::
>   a. feline : cat
>   b. dog : puppy
>   c. fish : trout
>   d. oak : tree
>   e. purr : hunger

The challenge is to pick the answer choice that expresses the same type of relationship as LION to CAT. In this case, the answer is d. (We'll see why later.)

How many analogies can you expect to see? If you're taking the GRE in 2007–08, you'll usually see six to eight analogies. After 2008, the number of analogies will probably decrease. Often, several of the first questions on a verbal GRE section will be analogies, so it's very important to get these correct!

Why are you tested on these stupid things? Good question. No one studies analogies in school (unless you're preparing for the GRE). No one uses formal analogy questions in real life. Analogies (and their cousins) are standard-issue questions on intelligence tests. So the GRE analogy section is a vocabulary-based IQ test, which means it's neither a vocabulary test nor an IQ test. ETS uses analogies because they can't think of anything else to use.

Students typically get fewer analogy problems correct than anything else on the Verbal section. Why? Because it's a vocabulary test. But if you study, you can get most analogies correct. Some students improve more on analogies than any other section. Dramatically improving on analogies requires (1) studying lots of vocabulary and (2) knowing and using all the techniques I'm about to teach you.

How to Solve an Analogy

Each analogy has two parts: the stem words and the answer choices. For example,

> PEBBLE : STONE ::
> > a. banana : fruit
> > b. rock : quarry
> > c. garden : plants
> > d. water : fluid
> > e. hamlet : village

The stem words are the top two words, PEBBLE : STONE.

Following is a summary of how to solve an analogy. Later we will look at a few examples.

Step 1: Build a Bridge

The first thing you want to do is build a bridge between the two words. To build a bridge, you must create a sentence using both words. Be sure to make your sentence …

- ◆ Short
- ◆ Begin with one word, end with the other
- ◆ Sound like a dictionary definition
- ◆ Use "is defined as" between the words if needed

In the previous example, "PEBBLE is a small STONE" would be a good sentence. We'll practice making sentences later.

FAIR WARNING

> In a good bridge, the relationship is *obvious* and one word *depends* on the other.
> And remember: you're matching *relationships*, not *meanings*.

ETS has a list of analogy relationships that they like to use. They use these relationships over and over, so look out for them. Often, more than half of the analogies on a test will conform to these relationships:

- ◆ Degree or size
- ◆ "Kind of"
- ◆ "Means with"/"Using"/"Pertains to"
- ◆ "Means without"/"Lacks"
- ◆ "Purpose of"/"Used to"
- ◆ "Divided into"
- ◆ "Made of"

Degree or Size

With degree or size relationships, one word is a bigger or smaller version of another. Our example, "PEBBLE : STONE," is a degree or size relationship.

The trap: If you see two stem words and you think, "The two words mean the same thing," then you're probably looking at a degree relationship. There are no stem relationships in which one word means another; for example, you would never make a sentence like "PEBBLE is a STONE." If you're looking at the stem pair of words and you think one word simply means the other word, then you don't understand the relationship. Usually, if your first sentence is similar to "PEBBLE is a STONE," then you have a degree relationship.

Here are a few examples of words that look like they might mean the same thing but actually are degree relationships:

> FAMINE : HUNGRY
> LIVID : ANGRY
> HACKNEYED : USED
> TRIFLING : SIGNIFICANCE
> LOATHING : DISLIKE

"Kind Of"

With "kind of" relationships, one word is a type or kind of another:

> GRAPE : FRUIT

The trap: Similar to degree—don't make a lazy sentence like "GRAPE is a FRUIT." Make sure you use "kind of" in your sentence.

? BET YOU DIDN'T KNOW

Making simple "kind of" sentences works well on easy analogies.

"Means with"/"Means Using"/"Pertains To"

With these relationships, one word "means with" or "means using" or "pertains to" another word. Try

"means with" or "means using" or "pertains to" with the following:

> SUN : SOLAR
> AQUATIC : WATER
> DISHONESTY : LIAR
> WISDOM : SAGE

There are also some "pertains to" relationships that may seem weird, but ETS loves them.

> FELINE : CAT
> CANINE : DOG
> BOVINE : COW
> SIMIAN : MONKEY
> PORCINE : PIG
> EQUINE : HORSE

The trap: The problem with these kinds of relationships is that some students make sentences based on a specific aspect.

SOLAR : SUN	(don't think "energy")
AQUATIC : WATER	(don't think "sports" or "animals")

"Means Without"/"Lacks"

"Means without"/"lacks" relationships are those where one word "means without" or "lacks" the other word.

> CHAOS : ORDER
> chaos lacks order
> NAIVE : SOPHISTICATION
> naïve means without sophistication

The trap: Students often want to use the word "opposite" with these types of relationships.

> CHAOS : ORDER
> chaos is the opposite of order

Stick with the "means without" or "lacks" format for these types of analogies rather than "opposite."

"Purpose of"/"Used to"

In a "purpose of"/"used to" relationship, the purpose of one word is to do the other.

> KITCHEN : COOKING
> SHOE : FOOT

The trap:

> KNIFE : CUT

The only way to get an easy analogy like this wrong is to make a sentence that is too simple, such as "A KNIFE CUTs." Don't be lazy with easy analogies such as KNIFE : CUT. Make sure your sentence is good by using the format "A KNIFE is used to CUT" or "The purpose of a KNIFE is to CUT."

"Divided Into"

"Divided into" relationships are highly specialized, but they can be easy to solve if you see one (and ETS likes them). In these relationships, one word is divided into another:

> POEM : STANZAS
> PLAY : ACTS
> SYMPHONY : MOVEMENTS
> NOVEL : CHAPTERS
> ESSAY : PARAGRAPHS
> ARMY : BATTALION
> HOUSE : ROOMS
> CAKE : LAYERS
> BUILDING : STORIES
> YEAR : DAYS

The trap: When you see a "divided into" relationship, you may want to say "A POEM is made of STANZAS" or "There are many DAYS in a YEAR." These sentences will sometimes work on easy analogies, but as analogies get more difficult, you will probably need to use the more specific "divided into" sentence.

"Made of"

"Made of" (or "consists of") relationships are also highly specialized, but they too can be easy to spot. They look like this:

> CONSTELLATION : STARS
> ARCHIPELAGO : ISLANDS
> FLOWERS : BOUQUET

Step 2: Use That Bridge

Now put the sentence you made from the stem words into the answer choices.

> **Level: Easy**
>
> LION : CAT ::
>   a. feline : cat
>   b. dog : puppy
>   c. fish : trout
>   d. oak : tree
>   e. purr : hunger

✗ FAIR WARNING

> You must try all five answer choices!

So you make a sentence: "Lion is a type of cat." Now plug that *exact same* sentence into each answer choice.

> a. feline : cat   Is a feline a type of cat? No.

b. dog : puppy   Is a dog a type of puppy? No.

c. fish : trout   Is a fish a type of trout? No.

d. oak : tree   Is an oak a type of tree? Yes.

e. purr : hunger   Is a purr a type of hunger? No.

So the answer must be d. Notice how ETS gives you several choices that work with your sentence but not in the same order: so a trout is a type of fish, but that's not the same order that "LION : CAT" is in … so be careful.

X FAIR WARNING

> Tom will get lazy with his sentences. His sentences for the stem words will slowly mutate as he goes through the answer choices. Don't let your sentence mutate! As you go through the answer choices, make sure you're using the exact same sentence as you used with the stem words!

Step 3: Get Aggressive with the Answer Choices

The third step is to get aggressive with the answer choices. Follow these "Answer Choice Rules":

♦ Stem words: always have a certain relationship

♦ Correct answer choice: always related in the same way

♦ Some other answer choices: not related in the same way

How can you tell if a pair of words is related in the same way as the stem words? Try to make a sentence out of them using the same relationship.

Use the five-second rule!

If you know the meaning of the two words, their relationship will be clear to you—you won't need to scratch your head and try to discover some obscure relationship.

If you know the meaning of the two words, then you will see that one of the two words is dependent on the other.

Example: APPLE : FRUIT. Do you know the definitions of "apple" and "fruit"? Yes. Then can you quickly make a sentence? Of course you can—that means these words are related and are a possible correct answer.

Let's look at these answer choices for a medium analogy. Which choices are not possible correct answers?

Level: Medium

a. baby : infantile

b. flower: tulip

c. cabinet : wood

d. door : window

e. beauty : pageant

Did you make a sentence for each pair of words? (If you didn't, go back and make sentences now!) Remember to use the relationships we discussed earlier in the chapter. Your sentences should be something like this:

a. baby : infantile   infantile pertains to a baby

b. flower: tulip   tulip is a type of flower

c. cabinet : wood   a cabinet can be made of wood— no relationship

d. door : window   a door can be next to a window— no relationship

e. beauty : pageant   a pageant can judge
                       beauty—no
                       relationship

So only a. and b. are possible correct
answers.

Now try a complete analogy:

Level: Easy

HORSE : EQUINE ::
  a. baby : infantile
  b. flower: tulip
  c. cabinet : wood
  d. door : window
  e. beauty : pageant

Equine pertains to a horse and infantile
pertains to a baby, a.

Bad Answer Choices

There are four possible bad answer choices you
should be aware of:

- Weak sentences
- Common pairs
- Not a possible bridge
- Uses the same bridge

Weak Sentences

A weak sentence is one that requires you to use conditional words such as "can" or "may." For example,

cabinet : wood

A cabinet "can be" made of wood. If you need to
use conditional words, then you don't have a strong
bridge.

Common Pairs

Sometimes ETS puts together words you've seen
together often, in hopes of getting you to choose
them. For example:

beauty : pageant
climb : tree
football : practice
humorous : movie

If you've seen the two words used together often,
they probably aren't related in the ETS sense and
therefore won't be a good answer choice for an
analogy.

Not a Possible Bridge

Sometimes an answer choice makes a bridge,
but not the same bridge as the stem words. For
example:

THRONG : PEOPLE ::
  a. ---- : ----
  b. picnic : woods
  c. ---- : ----
  d. cat : kittens
  e. vase : flowers

Make a sentence with "cat : kittens"—a cat produces
kittens. Plug that into "PEOPLE" in the stem—
does something produce a people? So even if you
don't know what "THRONG" means, you know
d. can't be the correct answer. (FYI: b. and e. don't
work either, which means you should guess between
a. and c.)

Uses the Same Bridge

If you find that two of the answer choices use the same type of sentence structure, they can't both be right, so you can get rid of both and narrow your answer choices. For example,

    ---- : ---- ::

        a. ---- : ----
        b. ---- : ----
        c. hoist : elevating
        d. ---- : ----
        e. inflation : expanding

Hoist means something is elevating; inflation means something is expanding. Choices c. and e. both use the same type of sentence, so neither one can be correct—get rid of them both! Whatever the correct answer is, you know it's not c. or e.

Always get rid of any answer choice if you can only make a weak sentence (usually using words such as can, should, could, might, and may).

If you can only make an okay sentence, mark the answer choice as "weak" (perhaps just write a "W" next to it) and keep it. Remember: a weak answer choice may be correct on a hard analogy but not on easy or medium ones.

X **FAIR WARNING**

It's not easy to make good, definitional sentences. Practice makes perfect.

Practice Making Sentences

Making good sentences is harder than it seems. Not all of these will be related. Decide if each pair has a strong bridge, weak bridge, or no bridge.

1. RECUPERATE : SURGERY

_____

2. TRIAL : JURY

_____

3. STEAMROLLER : FLATTEN

_____

4. TERRESTRIAL : LAND

_____

5. DISLIKE : HYPOCRISY

_____

6. CHEESE : MILK

_____

7. COLLAGE : IMAGES

_____

8. SKETCH : ARTIST

_____

9. SECRETARY : DESK

_____

10. CREST : HILL

_____

11. PURCHASE : RENT

_____

12. DISPUTE : ARBITER

_____

13. BILLBOARD : ADVERTISE

_____

14. DRAFT : WRITER

_____

15. PRACTICE : FOOTBALL

_____

16. ANNOY : IRRITATION

_____

17. CHISEL : SCULPTOR

_____

18. ENGINE : TRAIN

_____

19. CURE : ILLNESS

_____

20. DRILL : DENTIST

_____

21. ARID : DESERT

_____

22. MEDLEY : SONGS

_____

23. ASSEMBLY : BILLS

_____

24. RUSH : PATIENCE

_____

25. FARMER : FIELD

_____

26. INVEST : GAIN

_____

27. SLEEP : INSOMNIA

_____

28. REVIVE : FAINT

_____

29. SHAMPOO : DOG

_____

30. DATABASE : INFORMATION

_____

31. SNORE : ASLEEP

_____

32. COBBLER : SHOE

_____

33. OBEY : LEADER

_____

34. TRAIL : FOREST

_____

35. TENT : CIRCUS

_____

36. STORM : THUNDER

_____

37. THEATER : PLAY

_____

38. GASP : SHOCKED

_____

39. MAGNETIC : ATTRACT

_____

40. SECRET : STRANGER

_____

41. FORT : ATTACK

_____

42. VAULT : THEFT

_____

43. LIMERICK : HUMOR

_____

44. THEATRICAL : EMOTION

_____

45. LIGHT : ILLUMINATION

_____

Answers

Your sentences should look something like these.

1. RECUPERATE is to get better after SURGERY
2. TRIAL is decided by a JURY
3. Purpose of a STEAMROLLER is to FLATTEN
4. TERRESTRIAL pertains to LAND
5. DISLIKE : HYPOCRISY (no bridge)
6. CHEESE is made from MILK
7. COLLAGE is made of IMAGES
8. SKETCH is the rough work of an ARTIST
9. SECRETARY : DESK (no bridge)
10. CREST is the top of a HILL
11. PURCHASE : RENT (no bridge)
12. DISPUTE is decided by an ARBITER
13. Purpose of a BILLBOARD is to ADVERTISE
14. DRAFT is the rough of a WRITER
15. PRACTICE : FOOTBALL (no bridge)
16. ANNOY is to cause IRRITATION
17. CHISEL is a tool used by a SCULPTOR
18. ENGINE pulls/runs a TRAIN (weak bridge)
19. CURE is to make an ILLNESS better/go away
20. DRILL is a tool used by a DENTIST
21. ARID is the climate of a DESERT
22. MEDLEY is a bunch of SONGS
23. ASSEMBLY : BILLS (no bridge)
24. RUSH means without PATIENCE
25. FARMER works in FIELD (weak bridge)
26. Purpose of INVEST is to GAIN (weak bridge)
27. Lack of SLEEP is INSOMNIA
28. REVIVE is to get better after a FAINT
29. SHAMPOO : DOG (no bridge)
30. DATABASE contains/organizes INFORMATION
31. SNORE occurs when one is ASLEEP
32. COBBLER fixes a SHOE
33. OBEY : LEADER (no bridge)
34. TRAIL : FOREST (no bridge)
35. TENT is used to hold a CIRCUS
36. STORM often has THUNDER
37. THEATER is used to hold a PLAY
38. GASP expresses that one is SHOCKED
39. MAGNETIC things ATTRACT
40. SECRET : STRANGER (no bridge)
41. FORT protects from ATTACK
42. VAULT protects from THEFT
43. LIMERICK is a poem of HUMOR
44. THEATRICAL means with EMOTION
45. LIGHT gives off/creates ILLUMINATION

When You Don't Know the Words

If you can't make a sentence out of the stem words because you don't know the definition or aren't sure of the relationship, you should go straight to the answer choices. Try this one by thinking about the top words, then working with the answer choices.

Level: Medium

INFINITESIMAL : SMALL ::

    a. feeble : weak

    b. bright : washed

    c. burned : extinguished

    d. callow : large

    e. icy : frozen

! INFO TO GO

If you don't know a word, don't eliminate it!

Solution

INFINITESIMAL : SMALL ::

We don't know what "infinitesimal" is, but we know what "small" means, so we'll start there. What kind of sentence might we have here? There are only two real possibilities: infinitesimal means very small or not very small. So we know we have a degree relationship—a degree of smallness. Now let's go to the answer choices.

    ◆ a. feeble : weak

       Can we have a degree of weakness? Yes, so this is a possible correct answer.

    ◆ b. bright : washed

       Can we have a degree of washed? No.

    ◆ c. burned : extinguished

       Can we have a degree of extinguished? No.

    ◆ d. callow : large

       Can we have a degree of largeness? Sure.

    ◆ e. icy : frozen

       Can we have a degree of frozen? No.

So now we're left with a. and d. Next question: on any medium/hard analogy, which answer choice is Tom going to choose? He's going to pick whatever reminds him of the easy stem word. In this case, Tom will pick something that reminds him of small or sizes. He'll probably pick d. because it has "large" in it. Will Tom be right? Not on a hard one, so you go the opposite way and pick a. (If you don't know what infinitesimal means, go look it up!)

! INFO TO GO

Always eliminate unrelated pairs of words and pairs whose sentence can't possibly work with the stem word you know.

Process of Elimination

For this next question, we've gotten rid of the first word—let's assume it's so hard you don't know what it means! Go straight to the answer choices, make sentences, and plug those sentences back into the word in the answer choice that you know ("fire").

Level: Medium

---- : FIRE ::

    a. disputant : argument

    b. water : wave

    c. alert : emergency

    d. criminal : crime

    e. oil : cooking

Solution

---- : FIRE ::

    ◆ a. disputant : argument

       A disputant starts an argument. Could someone start a fire? Sure.

◆ b. water : wave

No relationship.

◆ c. alert : emergency

You could be alerted of an emergency. This is a Tom answer because "fire" is an "emergency." Get rid of this.

◆ d. criminal : crime

Criminal commits a crime. Can you commit a fire? No.

◆ e. oil : cooking

You might use oil in cooking. No relationship.

INFO TO GO

You don't need to know most of the words to get to the right answer! Usually, if you know half the words, you should be able to work your way to the correct answer.

The answer must be a. (The word we got rid of is "incendiary.")

Finally, let's see how to do this one.

Level: Medium

EVICT : TENANT ::

    a. excommunicate : religion
    b. expel : student
    c. export : merchandise
    d. expunge : records
    e. exfoliate : skin

Solution

EVICT : TENANT ::
What does evict mean? To kick out a tenant. Let's use that!

◆ a. excommunicate : religion

Can you kick out a religion? No.

◆ b. expel : student

Can you kick out a student? Yes.

◆ c. export : merchandise

Can you kick out merchandise … no!

◆ d. expunge : records

Can you kick out records? No.

◆ e. exfoliate : skin

Can you kick out skin? No.

The only possible answer is a. Notice how we didn't even use any of the first words in the answer choices. Whoo!

Now try four more:

Level: Hard

1. MANUMISSION : FREEDOM ::

    a. submission : experience
    b. promotion : favor
    c. prediction : intelligence
    d. pardon : forgiveness
    e. abstention : disapproval

And try one blindfolded:

Level: Medium

2. ---- : ---- ::

    a. ceiling : top
    b. sink : water
    c. tie : silk
    d. canvas : oil paint
    e. apology : regret

And now a hard one:

Level: Hard

3. AUTOMOBILE : TRANSPORT ::

    a. house : welcome

    b. car : wheels

    c. steak : knife

    d. scissors : cut

    e. gasoline : engine

Last one!

Level: Medium

4. ADEPT : SKILL ::

    a. music : gifted

    b. professor : books

    c. intelligence : answers

    d. penchant : loathing

    e. livid : anger

Solutions

1. MANUMISSION : FREEDOM ::
   (manumission is to grant freedom)

    a. submission : experience

    b. promotion : favor

    c. prediction : intelligence

    d. pardon : forgiveness (pardon is to grant forgiveness)

    e. abstention : disapproval

2. ---- : ---- ::

    a. ceiling : top (no bridge)

    b. sink : water (weak bridge)

    c. tie : silk (no bridge)

    d. canvas : oil paint (weak bridge)

    e. apology : regret (apology is to show regret)

3. AUTOMOBILE : TRANSPORT ::
   (automobile is used to transport)

    a. house : welcome

    b. car : wheels

    c. steak : knife

    d. scissors : cut (scissors are used to cut)

    e. gasoline : engine

4. ADEPT : SKILL ::
   (adept means with a lot of skill)

    a. music : gifted

    b. professor : books

    c. intelligence : answers

    d. penchant : loathing

    e. livid : anger (livid means with a lot of anger)

Troubleshooting

"I'm on a very difficult analogy and I can only get rid of one answer choice. What should I do?"

A word of warning: many prep books and courses say that you should always pick hard/weird words on hard analogies. This is *bad* advice. Many correct answers on hard analogies are easy words! In fact, many hard analogies have only easy words in the answer choices, so there are no hard/weird words to pick! If a hard analogy has easy words in the answer choices, then you should be able to work with those words. Only when the answer choices contain several hard/weird words that you don't know should you resort to simply guessing. Guess the ugliest word!

"I made a sentence with the stem words and I know what all the words mean, but I'm still left with two possible answer choices."

First, go back to your stem words and make a more focused sentence. For example, if your stem words are "COTTON : FABRIC," your first sentence may be "COTTON is used to make FABRIC." However, a more focused sentence may be "COTTON is used to make natural FABRIC."

Summary

A quick summary for analogies:

Build a Bridge

Make a sentence from the stem words.

Make your sentence short. Begin with one word and end with the other. Define one word using the other.

Plug your sentence into each answer choice— always try every answer choice! (You never know if e. sounds better than a. if you don't try it!)

Pick the answer choice that works best with your sentence. (And remember: you're matching relationships, not meanings.)

If you can't make a sentence, you must go to the answer choices.

Get Aggressive with the Answer Choices

Always get rid of any answer choice if you know the words and can't make a sentence.

Always get rid of any answer choice if you can only make a weak sentence (usually using words such as can, should, could, might, and may).

If you can only make an okay sentence, mark the answer choice as "weak" (perhaps just write a "W"

next to it) and keep it. Remember: a weak answer choice may be correct on a hard analogy but not on easy or medium ones.

If You Can't Make a Sentence with the Stem Words

Focus on the one stem word you know best.

Make sentences with the remaining answer choices and plug those sentences back into the one stem word you know best.

Get rid of bad answer choices.

If You're Still Having Trouble

Compare remaining answer choices by making more specific sentences.

On hard analogies, get rid of any Tom-answer that has words that simply remind you of the stem words.

On hard analogies, guess the ugliest choice.

The Least You Need to Know

- ◆ Remember, analogies are about relationships between words.
- ◆ You must be able to make good sentences.
- ◆ Be aggressive with the answer choices.
- ◆ Eliminate answer choices that can't possibly work.

Chapter 5

Antonyms

In This Chapter

- ◆ What are they?
- ◆ Should you care?
- ◆ Techniques and guessing
- ◆ Typical traps for Tom

Antonyms. Nothing about them seems good. You're given a word, usually one you don't know and have never seen before, and your job is to find its opposite. Fun, huh?

The good news is that antonyms are decreasing in frequency on the GRE. ETS would like to eliminate them, but the process is slow. Until they are gone, you'll need to know how to tackle these problems. But you shouldn't be overly concerned about them. Spend most of your time studying sentence completions and reading passages, not antonyms.

Remember that on the GRE CAT, you need to answer a question before going on to the next question. So you'll probably need to answer a few antonym questions.

What Do They Look Like?

Glad you asked. An antonym question will look like this:

COMELY:
- a. Attractive
- b. Attending to
- c. Homely
- d. Taciturn
- e. Miserly

! INFO TO GO

COMELY is called the "STEM WORD."

That wasn't too bad, was it? Okay, maybe it was. Comely means "attractive," so you want to choose the answer choice that most nearly means "unattractive." The answer is c.

Most Nearly Means?

Yeah, that's the tricky part. Don't get too stuck on precise definitions. If you know the definition (or think you know the definition) of the stem word, then think broadly about that definition. Too often Tom will define a word too narrowly and talk himself out of the correct answer.

So your job seems simple: define the word and choose its opposite. The problem is that many of the words are insane, crazy, perhaps even daft. The first solution to this problem is: study vocabulary! (Now!) There's no better way to tackle an antonym than simply knowing the words. But that's not always going to happen, so you need weapons to fight this battle.

When You Kinda Know the Word

What do you do when you "know" the word but can't define it? This happens all the time. Here are the techniques.

Sentence Approach

Use the word in a sentence that (sort of) defines the word.

Bad sentence: "The dog is comely." That sentence gives no indication of the meaning of the word.

Good sentence: "The dog is comely and everyone wanted to pet it." You don't know the word, but at least you have an idea that the word "comely" is a positive word.

Once you have a semi-definitional sentence, use the same sentence (changing it to mean the "opposite") for each of the words in the answer choices and see which word gives you the opposite sense.

So if our sentence is "The dog is comely and everyone wanted to pet it," then the opposite sentence would be "The dog is _____ and no one wanted to pet it."

The word that sounds right in that blank is the best answer.

"The dog is attractive and no one wanted to pet it."
"The dog is attending to and no one wanted to pet it."
"The dog is homely and no one wanted to pet it."
"The dog is taciturn and no one wanted to pet it."
"The dog is miserly and no one wanted to pet it."

Which one sounds like it works? Once again, c. The dog is homely (sounds negative) so that would cause people to have a negative reaction. Poor dog.

Using semi-definitional sentences is a great way to leverage limited knowledge to get to the correct answer.

Phrase or Saying Approach

So what if you've heard the word in a saying or phrase? Use it.

ABOMITABLE:

    a. Atrocious

    b. Beastly

    c. Odious

    d. Facetious

    e. Commendable

You might have heard the word "abominable" in the phrase "abominable snowman." If you have, great! Let's use that.

Was the abominable snowman good or bad? Bad! So we're looking for the good snowman.

    a. Atrocious snowman?

    b. Beastly snowman?

    c. Odious snowman?

    d. Facetious snowman?

    e. Commendable snowman?

Which one of these sounds like a good snowman? Certainly e. It's the correct answer. No matter how crazy it sounds, use any information—including a saying or phrase—to help to define the words.

Vocabulary Vivisection

If you're still having trouble, then take the word apart. What's the root (the prefix or suffix)? Unfortunately, this is another plug for the vocabulary chapter (Chapter 23). Start studying it! (There are tons of great roots in there!)

So if the stem word starts with "bene," as in benefactor, you know the word means something good. So the correct answer must be a negative word, right? Similarly, "ex," as in extinguish, usually means "out," so the correct answer would probably mean "in."

Roots, prefixes, and suffixes can be a huge help on antonyms. Study them!

Answer Choice Double-Jeopardy

You should always eliminate answer choices that mean the same thing. You can also use prefixes to help you out. For example:

    a. Atrocious

    b. Beastly

    c. Odious

    d. Facetious

    e. Commendable

No matter what the stem word is, you know that a, b, and c can't be correct. That's right, no matter what the stem word is, the correct answer must be d or e. How do we know?

Because answer choices a, b, and c almost mean the same thing. If a. is the antonym of a word, then b. and c. are almost certainly also antonyms. Given that three answer choices can't all be correct, then a., b., and c. must all be wrong.

So what if you had:

    a. Beneficent

    b. Beastly

    c. Odious

    d. Facetious

    e. Benignant

Without knowing the stem at all, what's the correct answer? We already know that b. and c. mean roughly the same thing, and because they can't both be correct, they must both be wrong. What else do we know? Well, a. and e both start with the same root (bene/beni), which means "good," so they both mean something good. Get rid of those. What remains? d.! It must be correct because it's the only one left.

So if you've got multiple answer choices that use the same prefix, eliminate them both. (This technique doesn't work as well with roots or suffixes, so only apply it to prefixes.)

Traps!

ETS has a ton a great antonym traps for Tom. What are they? Hold on to your bottles of water because this gets rough.

Synonyms

Can you believe it? That crapulent test maker will put down answer choices that are synonyms of the stem word.

Be sure to quickly eliminate all answer choices that appear to mean something similar to the stem word. If your mind lapses for a nanosecond, you slip and choose a synonym—it happens all the time. So the moment you spy a synonym, eliminate it. Note in your brain that it's poison. Stay away.

✗ FAIR WARNING

Crapulent means "sick from eating or drinking too much." The latin is "crapula," which basically means drunk. No, crapulent doesn't really work in that sentence, but it's a great word!

"Typos" and Obvious Words

So what would you do if you saw this?

> FROWARD:
> a. Satiable
> b. Kind
> c. Backward
> d. Tractable
> e. Mungo

Yikes. There are no typos. None. If you see "froward," don't pick "backward" as the correct answer. Please don't. "Froward" is a real word. Well, it's a real GRE word, which probably means it's not a word in the "real" world, but you know what I mean. In fact, it's so much of a real GRE word that it's in our outrageously useful (and mungo!) vocabulary list. Learn it!

Of course, you dove into your dictionary and looked the word up—but I'll repeat it anyway—"froward" means intractable or stubborn. The correct answer is d.

So what if you saw this one?

> ENERVATED:
> a. Fatigued
> b. Confused
> c. Obfuscated
> d. Invigorated
> e. Eschewed

This is easy, right? "Enervated" is a tough word, but it's easy to figure out. It probably means something to do with energy, so the correct answer would mean something without energy. The answer must be "fatigued." This is too easy.

Yikes. If you don't know what a word means, then it's dangerous to guess. ETS has tons of words that look like they mean one thing when, in fact, they mean just the opposite. "Enervate" means to lose energy, so you want to find the word that means "to gain energy." The answer is d.

So if you know the word, have heard the word used, or can break it apart (roots, prefixes, suffixes), then dive in! Otherwise, tread carefully—there are traps in them thar words.

Guess and Go!

So what if you have no idea? The worst thing you can do is spend three minutes staring at the problem. On the GRE CAT, you must answer the question, so answer it—just don't waste time. If you're baffled, here's what you should do:

- Eliminate any answer choices that look like a synonym to the stem word.

- Eliminate any answer choices that seem similar in definition to other answer choices (start with the same prefix, for example).

- Guess a word that's not too easy and not too hard. Don't guess the simplest word in the answer choices, but don't guess the weirdest one either.

- Don't dawdle. Guess and go!

The Least You Need to Know

- Start studying the vocabulary list in Chapter 23 now! Learn the roots, prefixes, and suffixes.

- Use partial information to your advantage.

- Eliminate answer choices that mean the same thing.

- Remember: Define the word and pick its opposite.

- While you should study vocabulary, you shouldn't worry too much about antonyms. There aren't very many of them.

Chapter **6**

Sentence Completions

In This Chapter

◆ All about sentence completions

◆ How to miss them every time

◆ Mastering sentence completions

◆ Good guessing

You'll usually see five to eight sentence completions on the GRE. Several of the first questions on the GRE are usually sentence completions, so it's very important to be good at these!

What They Look Like

A sentence completion looks like this:

The student, far from being _____, showed up to class on time, listened quietly to the teacher's lectures, and politely raised his hand whenever he had a question.

    a. bored
    b. intelligent
    c. tired
    d. unscrupulous
    e. disrespectful

For every sentence completion, you'll want to start by asking yourself two questions:

> What/Who is the sentence talking about?
> And what do we know about it?

This will help find the clue and provide the answer.

How to Miss Them Every Time

The trap for every sentence completion is essentially the same: ETS wants you to plug every answer choice into the blank, and try to guess which word(s) works best. If you try to fit answer choices into the blank, you will get most of these questions wrong. The trick to getting sentence completions correct is to figure out what goes into the blank *before* you look at the answer choices.

Cover Up the Answer Choices!

Don't look at the answers until you have thoroughly reviewed the sentence and you have put your own word into the blank. In the previous example, if you tried to fit in the answer choices, you could have made an argument for many of them. However, if you worked with the sentence first, you would have said, "The student shows up to class on time, listens quietly, and is polite, so the word that goes in the blank is the opposite of this. The opposite is not polite." If you do that, the correct answer, e., is somewhat obvious.

FAIR WARNING

The answer choices are the traps! Don't look at them until you understand the sentence and the blank.

ETS puts a word or phrase into every sentence completion that describes the blank—it has to, otherwise, you couldn't tell which answers are correct.

Here's a sentence completion you would never see on the GRE:

> The car dealer was very _____ and all his customers liked him.
>
> > a. neighborly
> > b. honest
> > c. caring
> > d. hard-working
> > e. educated

Why wouldn't you ever see this question on the GRE? Because there's no clue. Most of the answer choices could work.

Here is the same sentence modified for the GRE.

> The car dealer was very _____ because he always told the truth and all his customers liked him.
>
> > a. neighborly
> > b. honest
> > c. caring
> > d. hard-working
> > e. educated

What's the clue? It's "always told the truth," so the car dealer was very "honest." Always look for the clue!

So the first step to getting a sentence completion correct is to read the sentence, find the word or phrase that holds the clue to the blank, and put your own word in the blank.

Try a Few

Read these and put your own word in the blank.

> Classic car collectors _____ old cars to their former glory instead of discarding them.
>
> *What word did you put in the blank?*
>
> Michael felt that the judge was _____ and had made up his mind before the trial even started.
> *What word did you put in the blank?*

Use the word you put in the blanks for each of these and find the correct answer.

Level: Easy

> Classic car collectors _____ old cars to their former glory instead of discarding them.
>
> > a. polish
> > b. burnish
> > c. describe
> > d. restore
> > e. paint

Level: Easy

> Michael felt that the judge was _____ and had made up his mind before the trial even started.
> > a. prudent
> > b. scholarly
> > c. capable
> > d. elected
> > e. biased

Answers

The first one is d.; the second one is e.

Strategies for Solving More Difficult Sentence Completions

There is a two-step process for solving any troubles you have with the blank. Remember: there's *always* a word or phrase that describes the blank, you just need to find it.

When You Don't Know a Word

Let's look at this one:

Level: Hard

> Jill's painting illustrated the _____, that which cannot be conveyed in words alone.
>
> > a. natural
> > b. scenic
> > c. impressionistic
> > d. ineffable
> > e. romantic

FAIR WARNING

Don't be creative on sentence completions. Just find the clue and put it (or its opposite) back into the blank.

How to do it

Ask yourself: what/who is the sentence talking about? And what do we know about it?

What is the sentence talking about? Jill's painting. And what do we know about it? It illustrates stuff you can't convey in words. So the correct answer must mean "cannot be conveyed in words."

For this question, what would Tom pick (remember him, from Chapter 1)? Anything that reminds him of painting—probably a., b., c., and e. (all painting or art words). So what's the correct answer? d. We don't know what it means but none of the other answer choices mean "cannot be conveyed in words" and the other choices are Tom choices. What does "ineffable" mean? Dunno. I guess it must mean "can't be conveyed in words." Bingo!

Try this one:

Everyone remarked on John's _____; he was easily angered and often upset.

   a. stature
   b. knowledge
   c. truculence
   d. simple-mindedness
   e. wealth

How to do it:

The correct answer must mean "easily angered and often upset." Get rid of everything that doesn't mean that and you're left with c.

"Direction" of the Sentence

One thing to keep in mind when reading a sentence is its "direction." For example, if you had the following:

Bob and Jill went to the store and …

What would you assume comes next? (Something like "they bought some mangoes.")

Although Bob and Jill went to the store …

What would you assume comes next? (Something like "they didn't find any mangoes.")

Bob went to the store but …

What would you assume comes next? (Something like "didn't buy anything" or "Jill didn't.")

In these three examples, "and," "although," and "but" are direction words, pointing you toward possible conclusions. You should also keep other direction words in mind—ETS loves to change the meaning of a sentence with one small word. Here are some examples:

ETS's Direction Word Extravaganza

Same Direction	Change Direction
and, also, furthermore, in addition, as well as, moreover	however, instead, but, although, in spite of, yet, ironically

Keep these words in mind. They either change the direction of the sentence or keep it going in the same direction—but often these little words are overlooked. The entire sentence could be positive, but if it started with "although," then the word that goes in the blank is probably negative. Watch out!

! INFO TO GO

If you're missing many sentence completions, slow down. You may just be skipping over some of ETS's small direction words.

Let's try a few examples that use direction words.

Jill thought the boy would be _____, but he was actually very sophisticated.

a. a comedian

b. a rube

c. an aberration

d. an athlete

e. a benefit

Fill in these blanks:

What/Who is the sentence talking about?

And what do we know about it?

You should have gotten the following:

What/Who is the sentence talking about? The boy.

And what do we know about him? He's sophisticated.

What word goes in the blank? Because of the direction word "but," the word we need means not sophisticated.

Answer

The answer is b. a rube.

When You Have Two Blanks

Roughly half of all sentence completion questions will have two blanks. Here's an example:

Level: Medium

Joan lived a careful and planned life, rarely engaging in _____ or _____ activity.

a. foolhardy … impromptu

b. humorous … fun

c. scholarly … capacious

d. histrionic … indifferent

e. sordid … caustic

How to do it:

The clue for the first blank is "careful" and the clue for the second blank is "planned." A key word here is "rarely." The word choices will describe something she does rarely. the word that goes in the first blank is the opposite of careful and the word that goes in the second blank is the opposite of planned. So we're looking for "not careful" and "not planned." The answer is a.

Tom tries to fill both words in at once, and then goes to the answer choices with two words swimming around in his head. He gets confused, then tries to fit some of the answer choices back into the sentence. In the end, he gives up and just picks an answer choice—the wrong choice!

Big Picture Time: How to Do Two-Blankers!

The process for solving two-blankers requires some of the same strategies you used for single blanks:

1. Ask yourself: what/who is the sentence talking about? And what do you know about it?

2. Put your own word in each blank.

3. Pick the blank you think you have the best word for, and go to the answer choices.

4. Find your word. Cross off all answer choices that don't work. You will usually be left with two or three answer choices.

5. Now go back to the sentence, fill in the second word, and return to the answer choices and choose from the remaining answer choices.

Do One Blank at a Time!

Finding it difficult to put in your own words? Try another one.

The countryside was very _____ and prone to _____, so the park service often set small, defensive fires to limit the threat.

> a. temperate … development
>
> b. apt … rain
>
> c. arid … conflagrations
>
> d. lush … overgrowth
>
> e. bountiful … agriculture

First, we know we have a relationship between the blanks: if something is very X, it is prone to Y. That's helpful, but not great.

The next clue we have is that the second blank is described as a "threat"—so the word in the second blank must be threatening. That helps a lot.

If that's all we have for clues, then let's go to the answer choices with our clue for the second blank and see what we have. Keep in mind that we're looking for a second blank word that is threatening.

> Temperate … development
> Is development threatening? No.
>
> Apt … rain
> Is rain threatening? No.
>
> Arid … conflagrations
> What's a conflagration? Dunno—leave it.
>
> Lush … overgrowth
> Is overgrowth threatening? No.
>
> Bountiful … agriculture
> Is agriculture threatening? No.

We're only left with "conflagrations"—even if we don't know what it means, we must pick it because nothing else works. So the answer is c.

Positive/Negative and Opposites

Usually, you can use the "positive/negative" strategy on two or three sentence completions. If you're having any problem putting your own word in the blank or determining the clue, ask: "Is the word that goes in the blank positive or negative?"

This doesn't always work, but when it does, it's very helpful. Sometimes, this will be all you need to know in order to get the correct answer.

Try these two questions—use positive/negative if you need to.

The politician's recent belligerent rebuttals to his critics caused people to think he was _____ fellow when, in fact, he was usually quite _____.

> a. a pugnacious … amiable
>
> b. an angry … upset
>
> c. a loud … soft-spoken
>
> d. a furtive … argumentative
>
> e. a wary … casual

Most analysts believed the company's financial statement and quarterly report would be incredibly _____ about the company's future, but to everyone's surprise, they were _____.

> a. simplistic … readable
>
> b. prodigious … replete
>
> c. roseate … pessimistic
>
> d. ambiguous … inconsequential
>
> e. upbeat … positive

How to do it:

The first example: The word that goes in the first blank must be negative (because of the word "belligerent") and the word that goes in the second blank must be positive (because "in fact" he's the opposite). Get rid of all second-blank answer choices that aren't positive. What are you left with? The answer is a.

The second example: One of these blanks must be negative and one must be positive (the direction word "but" is one clue), but you're not sure which is which. Just remember that we're looking for opposites. Get rid of everything that isn't a pair of opposites. Then guess if you must! The answer is c.

! INFO TO GO

Positive/negative is very powerful—always ask yourself if you're looking for a positive or negative word.

Avoiding the Traps

ETS plants traps on hard sentence completions for Tom. Traps on hard sentence completions are answer choices that *appear* related to the subject of the sentence, but aren't. On hard problems, avoid answer choices that *appear* related to the subject of the sentence.

Level: Medium

By passing the new law, the politicians wanted to limit _____ activity by the government and to open the state up to public scrutiny.

a. clandestine
b. domestic
c. military
d. nocturnal
e. political

How to do it:

What's the subject of this sentence? The subjects are "law," "politicians," and "government." Which answer choices will remind Tom of those subjects? "Domestic," "military," and "political." So get rid of those choices—they *can't* be right. The correct answer is a.

Here's a two-blank sentence completion that combines several of the techniques we just discussed. Try it.

Level: Medium

The designer's style was _____ and _____; his fashions have not changed in years and are always somber, full of gray and black.

a. formal … casual
b. obscure … shimmering
c. cotton … silk
d. boring … exciting
e. immutable … austere

How to do it:

Get rid of Tom choices (anything that reminds Tom of fashion). So a., b., and c. are gone! The clue for the first blank is "not changed" and the second blank is "somber." The answer is e.

Troubleshooting

Let's do some troubleshooting.

> "Is it okay to plug some of the words from the answer choices into the blank on a hard problem if I'm not sure which one is best?"

I should say "no," but the truth is that sometimes the best way to decide between two words is to plug them both back into the sentence and reread the sentence. Remember, you should only do this once you've read the sentence, put your own word in the blank, and crossed off a few answer choices. If you have done everything listed in the "Sentence Completions Summary" (following) and you still have problems picking an answer from the remaining choices, then plug the remaining answer choices back into the sentence and reread the entire sentence. Pick the word that sounds best.

> "I looked down at the answer choices and I don't know the meaning of any of the words."

First, you should always know the meaning of at least two or three of the words; if you believe this might be a problem for you, then you need to study more vocabulary before the test. If you truly don't know the meaning of any of the words—none of them— then skip the problem. This applies only if you don't know the meanings, can't guess what the meanings are, and can't even guess whether the required word is positive or negative. There's no point wasting time and guessing wildly.

! INFO TO GO

On a difficult sentence completion on the test, always guess the hardest and weirdest word (remember the "order of difficulty" concept discussed in Chapter 1—hard problems have hard, and weird, answers). The correct answer to the hardest sentence completion is never an easy word. Never!

Sentence Completions Summary

You must know the sentence *before* looking at the answer choices: read the sentence first.

Find the clue—the word or phrase in the sentence that describes the blank.

Using the word or phrase that describes the blank, fill in the blank with your own word. Often, you will fill in the blank with another word from the sentence, so you don't need to get creative; often, the correct word for the blank is right in the sentence.

Find the word in the answer choices that most closely matches your own word.

Be careful of words that may change the direction of the sentence, such as "but" and "although." For example:

> Jane was never on time, but to our surprise, she was _____ for the party.

The word/phrase that describes the blank is "never on time." However, the "but" means that the word that goes in the blank must be the opposite of "never on time." (The correct answer is "punctual.")

If you can't put your own word in, ask "What or who is the sentence talking about?" In the above example, the sentence is talking about Jane.

Second, ask "What do we know about Jane?" We know she's "never on time." Bingo. That tells us what must go in the blank. Keep in mind that "never on time" is followed by a "but," so the blank must be a word that means the opposite of "never on time."

Make sure the sentence supports your answer. In the example above, we said we know that Jane is never on time. Can we prove that? Yes, it's right in the sentence. (For example, you can't say that you know Jane is lazy or stupid. We have no idea. All we know is that she's never on time.)

If you still can't put your own word in, try to figure out if the word that goes in the blank is positive or negative. If you know the word that goes in the blank is positive, get rid of all the answer choices with negative words.

If you have two blanks, figure out the relationship between the blanks. Are they opposites or the same? If they have the same meaning, is it positive or negative?

On hard sentence completions, get rid of any "Tom" answer that has words that simply remind you of the topic of the sentence. If the sentence is talking about fashion, get rid of "cotton" and "formal … casual."

On hard sentence completions, guess the weird and ugly word.

And remember, if you don't know a word, don't cross it off!

The Least You Need to Know

♦ Understand the sentence before you look at the answer choices.

♦ Try to come up with your own word for the blank.

♦ Use positive/negative and direction words to help you understand the sentence.

♦ Eliminate wrong answer choices first, then evaluate what's left.

♦ On harder sentence completions, guess harder words.

More Sentence Completions

In This Chapter

- ◆ Practicing standard sentence completions
- ◆ Sentence completion variations
- ◆ Samples of every kind (with explanations)

Sentence completions are becoming increasingly important on the GRE. Not only will you see more of this question type, but you'll also see variations. In Chapter 6, we reviewed standard sentence completions. In this chapter, we'll practice standard sentence completions, and then we'll take a look at some new variations.

More Standard Sentence Completions

Here's a set of 20 sentence completions. Try them and check your answers at the end.

1. Jefferson's image as a skeptical but enlightened intellectual was attacked in the 1960s, when historians portrayed him as _____ thinker, eager to impart his political orthodoxies to succeeding generations but censoring those ideas he did not approve of.

    a. an adventurous

    b. a doctrinaire

    c. an eclectic

    d. a judicious

    e. a cynical

2. Dramatic literature often _____ the evolution of a culture in that it takes as its topical inspiration the guiding and shaping public events that change that culture.

    a. confounds

    b. repudiates

    c. recapitulates

    d. anticipates

    e. polarizes

3. Though the rise of historical societies to preserve sites and buildings of note is not usually perceived as _____ phenomenon, it deserves its place in the history of ideas because it launched the critique of the ideology of progress.

    a. an economic

    b. an intellectual

    c. an inconsequential

    d. a comprehensible

    e. a philanthropic

4. The ideal of self-sacrifice for a larger cause is all but unknown in this modern age, when a sense of _____ seems the most powerful predisposition shaping individual actions.

    a. entitlement

    b. ambiguity

    c. causality

    d. humanitarianism

    e. fairness

5. It is seemingly a paradox that the Amazon rainforest, one of the most lush ecosystems on the planet, supports itself on the most _____ of all soils.

    a. austere

    b. acidic

    c. coarse

    d. stark

    e. infertile

6. The menu of a restaurant is often reflected in the ambience it seeks to create; however, despite this café's _____ appearance, the offerings of its menu are rather pedestrian.

    a. elegant

    b. conventional

    c. modern

    d. traditional

    e. tawdry

7. The workings of international finance are largely incomprehensible to those uneducated in economics; hence the American media often _____ this subject, concerning itself rather with issues that make snappy headlines and are instantly accessible.

    a. neglects

    b. overrates

    c. hides

    d. criticizes

    e. repudiates

8. They were a study in contrasts: she was jovial where he was glum, loquacious where he was _____; yet as a pair they complemented each other.

    a. laconic

    b. solicitous

    c. munificent

    d. irresolute

    e. fastidious

9. Though he tried to disguise his _____ his youngest child, all of his other children foresaw that it would be the baby of the family who would inherit the family fortune.

    a. partiality for

    b. amicability towards

    c. petulance towards

    d. disinterest in

    e. attitude towards

10. Though salt may overpower the subtleties of a recipe if added in large amounts, its _____ use can greatly improve the flavor of many dishes.

    a. luxurious

    b. lavish

    c. judicious

    d. staunch

    e. occasional

11. The motivation for the senator's controversial remarks must remain _____. No conjecture as to why, if he aimed at reelection, he would risk alienating his constituents by espousing beliefs he had formerly opposed, has yet proved satisfactory.

    a. an enigma

    b. offensive

    c. a problem

    d. theoretical

    e. a necessity

12. The student's quick comprehension of all the principles involved _____ the need for further explanation.

    a. obviated

    b. necessitated

    c. extenuated

    d. evoked

    e. imputed

13. Goldenhart did not think through the full _____ of his discovery, and it remained up to future scientists to construct a theory based on his experiments.

    a. dissent

    b. extent

    c. dissemination

    d. justifications

    e. ramifications

14. To _____ the details of a fundamentally unsound proposition is akin to ignoring a flooded basement in favor of arguing over how to fix a dripping faucet.

    a. quibble over

    b. remark upon

    c. agree about

    d. ignore

    e. misconstrue

15. There is hardly a _____ of job openings for philosophy professors, which is perhaps why so many philosophy Ph.D. students end up in careers outside of academia.

    a. lack

    b. scarcity

    c. panorama

    d. plethora

    e. paucity

16. Surely we can forgive so great a leader for such a harmless _____, especially when his moral conduct is in all other respects irreproachable.

    a. merit

    b. eccentricity

    c. peccadillo

    d. phobia

    e. outburst

17. His _____ requests were met with ill-disguised resistance by his subordinates, who were accustomed to going about their business in response to gently worded suggestions.

    a. mild

    b. impromptu

    c. perfunctory

    d. peremptory

    e. angry

18. Aristotle advocated a life guided by _____: he recommended that one should be neither abstemious nor self-indulgent.

    a. hedonism
    b. temperance
    c. skepticism
    d. enquiry
    e. self analysis

19. Having publicly reneged on his promises in the past, the liar will find that his recent vows convince none but his most _____ listeners.

    a. licentious
    b. skeptical
    c. wise
    d. curious
    e. credulous

20. Although Allan's work was at best _____, he was promoted anyway, simply on the basis of seniority.

    a. forceful
    b. perfunctory
    c. concise
    d. extraneous
    e. unimpeachable

Answers and Explanations

1. b. The clue is that Jefferson's image as a skeptical but enlightened intellectual was attacked. Instead of being an "enlightened" or free thinker, he was narrow minded and followed a doctrine, or "political orthodoxy." In other words, he was doctrinarian.

2. c. The clue is that dramatic literature is often based on important events in history. Thus, it "replays" or "recapitulates" these important moments on stage.

3. b. The clue is that this phenomenon deserves a place in the "history of ideas." Therefore it must be an intellectual phenomenon.

4. a. The clue is that motivation for individual actions in the modern age is the opposite of those that motivate self-sacrifice. A sense of entitlement motivates behavior that benefits ourselves, while the ideal of self-sacrifice motivates behavior that benefits others.

5. e. The clue is that the Amazon is described as a lush forest, so we expect that it would grow in fertile soil. Therefore, it is a paradox that it grows in infertile soil.

6. a. The clue is "pedestrian," which means drab, plain, or commonplace. "Elegant" is an antonym for "pedestrian."

7. a. The clue is that the American media "does not concern" itself with this subject. Because they pay it no attention, they are neglecting it.

8. a. The clue is "loquacious," which means talkative. We need the opposite of this. "Laconic" means terse, or not given to talking.

9. a. The clue is that the youngest child, the baby of the family, will inherit all the wealth. This implies that his father loves or favors this child more than all his other children. Only "partiality for" implies in this context that the father doesn't just love this child; he loves him at the expense of his other children.

10. c. The clue is that salt can improve the flavor of many dishes, unless it is added in large amounts. "Judicious" implies a judged and well informed use of salt. A "judicious" cook would add just the right amount of salt to a dish, whether that was very little or a moderate amount.

11. a. The senator's behavior is puzzling, and no theory or guess (conjecture) about why he acted as he did can explain it. Therefore his motivations must remain an enigma, a puzzle.

12. a. Because the student understood *all* that he was told, the need for further explanation was removed, or obviated.

13. e. The clue is that Goldenhart didn't complete a theory based on his discoveries. That means he must not have understood the implications, or ramifications, of his discoveries.

14. a. Ignoring a big problem in favor of trying to fix a smaller problem is the same as "quibbling" or arguing over the small details of a proposition which is unsound, or unworkable.

15. d. The clue is that Ph.D. students can't find jobs in academia. There is hardly an abundance, or plethora, of job openings for professors.

16. c. The key is that the politician's "moral conduct" is in most respects very good. Therefore we can forgive him a small sin, or peccadillo. None of the other choices have this connotation of "moral" behavior.

17. d. We are looking for the opposite of "gently worded suggestions." The best choice is therefore peremptory, which implies a commanding and abrupt tone.

18. b. The clue is that "abstemious" and self-indulgent are two opposite extremes. Therefore, Aristotle suggests that one should seek a path of moderation, or temperance, between these two extremes.

19. e. The clue is the liar has broken his promises in the past. Therefore, only the most gullible, or credulous of his listeners will believe him this time.

20. b. "Although" implies that Allan was promoted in spite of being a mediocre employee. "Perfunctory" means that he didn't put any effort into his work and did a mediocre job.

Sentence Completion Variations

The GRE will have variations on the classic sentence-completion format. First, you'll see many sentence completions with multiple blanks. Second, you'll see more sentence completions with answer choices that are very similar, thus requiring you to make fine distinctions.

These types of sentence completion questions do not vary significantly from classic sentence completions. Every sentence has one or more clues. You must read and understand the sentence before looking to the answer choices. And you can't, ever, let the answer choices influence your understanding of the sentence.

Let's try a few. Find the word that best fits into each blank. For these new sentence completions, there may be two or three blanks. One warning: the correct answers do not need to come from the same row: the first word in column one and the third word in column two may be correct. (You'll be able to choose any combination of answers on the actual computer version of the GRE.)

Try these (answers and explanations are at the end):

1. The ＿＿＿ nature of Athenian classical tragedy belies the modern view of tragedy; according to the modern conception, tragedy is an austere and minimalist art form whose compressed representation of ideological and emotional conflicts leaves nothing ＿＿＿ for time to erode.

Blank (i)	Blank (ii)
a. unadorned	a. inalienable
b. harmonious	b. exigent
c. multifaceted	c. extraneous

2. Murray, recently acclaimed in national reviews for her autumn exhibition of paintings, has been locally celebrated for years, though often regarded by national critics with _____. However, the more _____ of these paintings must _____ all doubts.

Blank (i)	Blank (ii)	Blank (iii)
a. ostentation	a. mediocre	a. solidify
b. ambivalence	b. successful	b. confirm
c. adulation	c. pretentious	c. assuage

3. New inventions often begin by _____ what has come before; their full power to effect change is realized only after much use. Power-using companies, for example, took many years to recognize that with electricity they did not need to cluster their machinery around a power source, a necessity imposed by the use of steam power. Instead, power could be _____ their operations. Likewise, today's computer networks are still in their infancy. It remains to be seen how they will change the world.

Blank (i)	Blank (ii)
a. uprooting	a. consolidated around
b. mimicking	b. incorporated into
c. dismissing	c. transmitted to

4. Even the most cursory perusal of the manuscript version of Captain Clark's journals reveals the Captain as one of the most _____ spellers ever to write in English, but this _____ attitude towards orthographical rules never renders Clark unclear.

Blank (i)	Blank (ii)
a. indefatigable	a. cavalier
b. defiant	b. meticulous
c. fastidious	c. pretentious

5. His _____ with money was disguised by his air of propriety, especially as this behavior often encompassed impressive generosity. But in the long run _____ concerning his eventual ruin proved correct.

Blank (i)	Blank (ii)
a. temerity	a. recidivisms
b. profligacy	b. corroborations
c. prudence	c. prognostications

6. Though at first the investigation revealed no misdeeds on the part of the CEO, eventually he was shown to be _____ the scheme that _____ stockholders out of millions.

Blank (i)	Blank (ii)
a. unaware of	a. ostracized
b. complicit in	b. bilked
c. opprobrious of	c. plumbed

7. The professor's prolix and _____ style made him the _____ of popular stereotypes about intellectuals, who are often portrayed as given to long-winded and dully bookish lectures.

Blank (i)	Blank (ii)
a. pedantic	a. epitome
b. worldly wise	b. peripatetic
c. peremptory	c. contrary

8. It will long remain a _____ issue among scientists whether the results of the experiment were _____ or a meaningful aspect of larger, as yet unexplained phenomenon.

Blank (i)	Blank (ii)
a. convoluted	a. an aberration
b. pedestrian	b. an interposition
c. contentious	c. a conflation

9. He tends to hold a reverential attitude towards the stars of yesteryear, regarding any likening of those _____ to today's paler "celebrities" as _____.

Blank (i)	Blank (ii)
a. luminaries	a. reverence
b. delineations	b. propriety
c. demagogues	c. impiety

10. Had Clark not been cognizant of the _____ nature of the compliments on his new book, he would have believed in the _____ of their author.

Blank (i)	Blank (ii)
a. officious	a. mendacity
b. obsequious	b. ignorance
c. meritorious	c. perspicacity

11. Cynthia refuses to repeat a compliment if its recipient _____ the praise, believing cynically that such behavior is a _____ gambit to receive further _____.

Blank (i)	Blank (ii)	Blank (iii)
a. decries	a. disingenuous	a. commentary
b. deflects	b. innocent	b. plaudits
c. accepts	c. innocuous	c. acrimony

12. _____ her former reservations about his character, which she had suspected was somewhat timorous, she decided to support his _____ ventures.

Blank (i)	Blank (ii)
a. Accepting of	a. tentative
b. Unencumbered of	b. audacious
c. Convinced of	c. postponed

13. The scientist had a way of self-righteously correcting what he regarded as _____ remarks, and so his daughter knew she would be _____ when she mentioned how pensive the dog was looking.

Blank (i)	Blank (ii)
a. anthropomorphic	a. commended
b. anthropocentric	b. excoriated
c. animistic	c. exculpated

14. It was not a display, but rather _____ of good humor that the host put on; and although his _____ attempts to lighten the leaden atmosphere mollified the more sentimental of his guests, none but the most unobservant could help but notice how much his behavior belied his _____ temper.

Blank (i)	Blank (ii)	Blank (iii)
a. an exoneration	a. exploitative	a. irascible
b. an indication	b. light-hearted	b. placid
c. a travesty	c. mawkish	c. capricious

15. Those who believe in a liberal education hold that ignorance is _____ the development of a complete personality; that it _____ not only perceptive reasoning about the outside world, but also limits an understanding of the self.

Blank (i)	Blank (ii)
a. amicable to	a. abuts
b. inimical to	b. abets
c. crucial to	c. fetters

16. Always impressive as an insightful and persuasive debater, the celebrated professor was sought after by TV reporters, who hoped to elicit _____ and _____ opinion on whatever new issue had caught the public interest.

Blank (i)	Blank (ii)
a. an ambiguous	a. peripatetic
b. a percipient	b. tenacious
c. a pellucid	c. trenchant

17. She had almost puritanical ideas about lawn maintenance, viewing it as her mission to rid the world of _____ weeds. Needless to say, hers was a _____ manicured front yard.

Blank (i)	Blank (ii)
a. beneficent	a. mercurially
b. excessive	b. haphazardly
c. pernicious	c. meticulously

18. Tom was self-educated, having acquired a large vocabulary through reading. Though he was often embarrassed by mispronunciations, he was never guilty of a _____; though he might garble a syllable or two, the _____ of what he was saying was always understandable to his listeners.

Blank (i)	Blank (ii)
a. malapropism	a. peripherals
b. spoonerism	b. gist
c. syncopation	c. pathos

19. John's tendency to _____ his triumphs was the cause of much _____ on the part of his defeated rivals.

Blank (i)	Blank (ii)
a. underplay	a. enmity
b. gloat over	b. amicability
c. confide in	c. confusion

20. There have been many recent studies suggesting American students are unprepared for college. Graff attacks this perception, suggesting that, on the contrary, colleges are unprepared for students. According to his analysis, university culture is for the most part _____ entering students in that it fails to connect to cultural references and issues that students grasp. Understandably, many students view the college years as _____ ritual.

Blank (i)	Blank (ii)
a. opaque to	a. an arcane
b. primed for	b. a laudable
c. essential for	c. a painstaking

Answers and Explanations

1. (c. multifaceted, c. extraneous) The clue for the first blank is that Athenian classical tragedy contradicts (belies) the modern view that tragedy is an art with a single, stripped down message. Therefore the first blank is the opposite of "austere and minimalist." Multifaceted is not exactly an antonym for austere, but in this context it suggests that the Greek drama involved many "facets" such as song, dance, and costume: this is a luxurious, rather than a "stripped down" art form. The clue for blank two is "compressed representation" and the suggestion that time leaves this "compressed representation" intact. We are therefore looking for the opposite of "compressed representation." "Inalienable" means "essential," so it is the opposite of what we are

looking for, and "exigent" means "still exist-ing"; in other words, what remains *after* time has "eroded" away unimportant details. When we compress the action in a drama, we strip it down to bare fundamentals, and leave nothing *extraneous*, or unimportant, remaining.

2. (b. ambivalence, b. successful, c. assuage) The clue for the first blank is "celebrated … though." "Though" means that the word we're looking for is either less strong than "cel-ebrated" or it is the opposite of "celebrated." "Ambivalence" implies doubts about the paint-er's talents. "However" is the clue for the sec-ond and third blanks. If there are doubts, then "however" implies that they must be removed. "Assuage all doubts" means to remove all doubts, and only "successful" paintings can remove doubts about talent.

3. (b. mimicking, c. transmitted to) The clue for the first blank is that new inventions cause change *later*; that means that they start out being used in the same fashion as what has come before. "Mimicking" means "imitating." The clue to the second blank is that it must be the opposite of having machinery be clustered around, or grouped around, a power source. The opposite of grouping machines around a power source is to spread the machines out and transport the power to them (through wires). "Transmitting to" means to "transport" or "convey" to.

4. (b. defiant, c. cavalier) Start with the second blank: the "but" suggests that the Captain's attitude towards spelling *should* "render" (make) his meaning unclear, but it doesn't. A "cavalier," or careless, "high-handed" attitude towards spelling *should* make his meaning unclear. If he's a careless speller, he might also be a "defiant" speller; this is meant to be a humorous use of the word "defiant," and sug-gests that he knows the rules of spelling but chooses to ignore them.

5. (b. profligacy, c. prognostications) The clue to the first blank is "disguised by propriety": how Clark handles money must be the opposite of propriety, or correct and respectable behavior. "Profligacy" is wastefulness or mishandling of money. "Prognostications" means "predic-tions," which are only proved correct "in the long run."

6. (b. complicit in, b. bilked) The clue for the blank is that "though" at first, the CEO appeared innocent; the first blank must be the opposite of innocent. "Complicit" implies "involved in a crime." "Bilked" means "cheated."

7. (a. pedantic, a. epitome) Because "prolix" and "long-winded" are synonyms, "bookish" must be a synonym for the first blank: "pedantic." The clue for the second blank is that the pro-fessor's style agrees with popular stereotypes. So the professor must be a prime example, or epitome, of popular stereotypes.

8. (c. contentious, a. an aberration) The clue to the second blank is "or a meaningful aspect." "Or" implies that we need the opposite of a "meaningful" result, and if the results of an experiment are an "aberration," this implies that they are not meaningful, but rather the unusual or "bizarre" results of chance. Because the scientists appear not to have decided whether the results were meaningful or not, this implies they are fighting over the ques-tion: it is a "contentious" or "controversial" question.

9. (a. luminaries, c. impiety) The clue to the first blank is "reverential attitude": someone who respects the stars of the past would consider them "luminaries," or figures worth respect. The clue to the second blank is "paler celebri-ties": "paler" means "fainter," or "less colorful or interesting" in this context. "Likening" or pointing out similarities between "luminaries"

and "pale celebrities" is therefore "disrespect-ful" or "impious" toward the luminaries.

10. (b. obsequious, c. perspicacity) "Obsequious" in this context means "falsely flattering" or "seeking to please." "Perspicacity" means "perceptive judgment." So if Clark didn't know that the person who complimented him just wanted to flatter him, he would have thought this flatterer was a good judge of Clark's work. "Author" refers to the "author of the compliments," not the "author of the book," because "their" is plural, and "compli-ments" is plural, while "book" is singular.

11. (b. deflects, a. disingenuous, b. plaudits) The clue to the first blank is "repeat a com-pliment"; there is only a need to repeat a compliment if it has been shrugged off, or deflected, the first time. Cynthia believes that such behavior is not true modesty, but is a clever and deceitful, or disingenuous, attempt to receive more praise (plaudits).

12. (b. unencumbered of, b. audacious) The clue to the first blank is "former reservations." She believed he was timorous, or afraid, and now she no longer believes this. She is unencum-bered of her reservations: her doubts have been removed. The second blank must then be the opposite of "timorous": "audacious," or bold.

13. (a. anthropomorphic, b. excoriated) The clue to the second blank is "self-righteously correcting": the synonym for this is "to excoriate." The clue to the first blank is that "pensive" is an adjective that attributes thoughtful, or perhaps even troubled, qualities to a dog. In the strictest scientific sense, this might be considered an anthropomorphism, or attributing human qualities to an animal or thing.

14. (c. travesty, c. mawkish, a. irascible) The clue to the first blank is "leaden atmosphere." A "display" of good humor might make everyone happy, but a "travesty of good humor" would be an imitation of good spirits that fools no one, and therefore makes no one happy. The host's attempts to please sentimental guests are likewise "mawkish," or sickly sentimental. All these "imitations" of good humor must there-fore disguise the host's real temper, which is the opposite of good-humored: "irascible."

15. (b. inimical to, c. fetters) People who believe in, or support, education are generally against ignorance. Therefore they probably believe it is "inimical to" or the "enemy of" a com-pletely developed personality. The second blank should therefore be a synonym for "lim-its": "fetters."

16. (b. a percipient, c. trenchant) The first and second blanks should be synonyms of "insight-ful" and persuasive." "Percipient" means "insightful," and "trenchant" means forceful or relevant; a forceful remark would be one that persuades.

17. (c. pernicious, c. meticulously) "Pernicious" means "evil" or "harmful"; someone who wants to rid the world of weeds probably views them as pernicious. A lawn that is well-maintained is "meticulously" or painstakingly cared for.

18. (a. malapropism, b. gist) The clue to the first blank is that *though* Tom mispronounces words, he never misuses them: he never utters a "malapropism." Because he doesn't misuse words, his meaning, or gist, is clear.

19. (b. gloat over, a. enmity) John's boasting, or offensive delight in his triumphs, causes his defeated rivals to dislike him, or to feel enmity toward him.

20. (a. opaque to, a. an arcane). The clue to the first blank is the statement that universities fail to connect to cultural references that students grasp, or understand. Because it doesn't make these connections, it is an experience that students do not understand: it is opaque to them, or not transparent or clear to them. In the same sense, it is an "arcane" experience because it doesn't connect to their everyday lives, but rather concerns obscure knowledge.

The Least You Need to Know

- Always understand the sentence before you look at the answer choices.

- Be comfortable with variations on the classic sentence completion structure.

- If you're having problems, always try to eliminate wrong answer choices.

- Remember: hard questions have hard answers!

Chapter **8**

Long Critical Reading Passages

In This Chapter

- ◆ Read less and score more
- ◆ How Tom approaches the questions
- ◆ The trick to getting to right answers
- ◆ The ETS list of approved answer choices

You will have a series of critical reading passages on the GRE. Some will be short (usually 10–25 lines) and some will be long (usually 50–90 lines). In total, these passages will comprise half of your verbal score, so you must do well on them.

The strategy for handling the short and long critical reading passages is quite different. You should not approach them the same way. This chapter will show you how to approach the long passages. Chapter 9 shows you how to deal with the short passages.

What They Look Like

Here's a sample long passage and questions:

Questions 15–18 are based on the following reading passage:

The following is from a work by Samuel Butler on evolution.

There are few things which strike us with more surprise, when we review the course taken by opinion in the last century, than the suddenness with which belief in witchcraft and demoniacal possession came to an end. This has been often remarked upon, but I am not acquainted with any record of the fact as it appeared to those under whose eyes the change was taking place, nor have I seen any contemporary explanation of the reasons which led to the apparently sudden overthrow of a belief which had seemed hitherto to be deeply rooted in the minds of almost all men. As a parallel to this, though in respect of the rapid spread of an opinion, and not its **decadence**, it is probable that those of our descendants who take an interest in ourselves will note the suddenness with which the theory of evolution, from having been generally ridiculed during a period of over a hundred years, came into popularity and almost universal acceptance among educated people.

It is indisputable that this has been the case; nor is it less indisputable that the works of Mr. Darwin and Mr. Wallace have been the main agents in the change that has been brought about in our opinions. The names of Cobden and Bright do not stand more prominently forward in connection with the repeal of the Corn Laws than do those of Mr. Darwin and Mr. Wallace in connection with the general acceptance of the theory of evolution. There is no living philosopher who has anything like Mr. Darwin's popularity with Englishmen generally; and not only this, but his power of fascination extends all over Europe, and indeed in every country in which civilization has obtained footing: not among the illiterate masses, though these are rapidly following the suit of the educated classes, but among experts and those who are most capable of judging. France, indeed—the country of Buffon and Lamarck—must be counted an exception to the general rule, but in England and Germany there are few men of scientific reputation who do not accept Mr. Darwin as the founder of what is commonly called "Darwinism," and regard him as perhaps the most penetrative and profound philosopher of modern times.

15. The author does which of the following in the above passage?

    a. compares and contrasts two critical stances.

    b. asserts a causal relationship between the fall of a prevalent belief and the rise of a theory.

    c. describes the ascendance of a theory.

    d. refutes the importance of a figure in the rise of a theory

    e. describes the decay of a prevalent belief.

16. In the given context, "decadence" most nearly means:

    a. decay

    b. particulars

    c. corruption

    d. ascendance

    e. acceptance

17. The author mentions Cobden and Bright in order to:

    a. stress the importance of the repeal of the Corn Laws for the proglemation of the theory of evolution.

    b. compare the fame of Darwin and Wallace to that of prominent politicians of the time.

    c. stress that the theory of evolution was as well-known to the general public in England at the time as were important political issues of the day.

    d. make a connection between the repeal of the corn laws by Cobden and Bright and the recession of superstition and ignorance in the wake of Darwin and Wallace's discoveries.

    e. assert the importance of Darwin and Wallace by comparing them to prominent politicians of the time.

18. This question has no answer choice. Select a sentence in which the author provides a counterexample to a generalization.

Typically, the long passages will be 50–90 lines, followed by 6–12 questions in this format:

Level: Medium

By analyzing various forms of torture, the author of the passage concludes that the GRE is

    a. awful

    b. boring

    c. confusing

    d. stupid

    e. obnoxious

Most passages are single-passage: you have one passage and 5–12 questions about it. Each GRE usually contains one longer or double-passage: you could have two passages, each 50–80 lines in length, and 4–8 questions for each passage followed by 2–3 *compare and contrast questions*. (While many people dislike the dual-passage sections, they are often easier because each passage is shorter, making it easier to skim for clues. Usually, a dual-passage with two 55-line passages is easier than a single-passage of 90 lines.)

VEXING VOCABULARY

A **compare and contrast question** is a question that asks you to compare two components of a passage, such as the kind of evidence used in the first paragraph compared to the evidence used in the second.

Critical Reading is a hard section of the GRE to complete. What makes Critical Reading hard? The passages are long and boring. What makes Critical Reading even harder? While the questions tend to be easy, you don't have much time for them.

The secret to acing this portion of the test? The questions almost always tell you where to go for the answer.

The Subjects

There are three general types of subjects that the long critical reading passages cover: social science, science, and narrative and fiction.

Social Science

These passages are usually about sociology, anthropology, history, or government. These passages tend to be straightforward though they may contain a little jargon (and may be very boring—how would you like 80 lines on the development of hierarchical power structure among marsupials? Yuck.). The history passages are also straightforward and may not be completely boring. Humanities passages may be difficult as they concentrate on art trends about which you've never heard or literary theories you know nothing about; however, there's a chance that they might actually be interesting.

Science

Most people dislike the science passages. Few want to read about attempts to grow fungus on Mars. No matter how much you hate science passages, they are almost always the easiest passages on the entire GRE. Yes, science passages tend to be easy. Why? Because they have more straightforward questions and fewer "what does the author imply" questions than other passages. So although you may hate science passages, you should always do them.

INFO TO GO

The easiest passage on the GRE is the politically correct passage. These passages are usually social science or history passages and they are almost always about a previously disenfranchised, marginalized, or overlooked segment of the population or area of study. ETS puts this passage on the test because minority groups have complained that the GRE is biased against them; the PC passage is ETS's attempt to prove the opposite. The author's tone for the PC passage will be neutral or positive (never negative). If, for example, the author is discussing the removal of American Indians from Georgia to reservations under the Jackson administration, the author won't approve of the reservations, but ETS also won't really criticize the U.S. government. The entire tone will probably be neutral.

Narrative and Fiction

The other passage types are narrative and fiction. While these are the most interesting passages to read, they have the most difficult questions to answer. These passages have difficult questions because they often have many "What does the author imply?" and "What is Mrs. Witherspoon's tone?" type of questions. Yuck. If the easiest questions are direct, provable, specific questions, then the hardest questions are vague, implied, opinion-based questions. In addition, many of the techniques you're going to be taught don't fully work on narrative and fiction passages. Fortunately, these passages are rare. If you get one and you're aiming for a 600 or less, skip it. If you are aiming for above a 600, do it last and skim the entire passage. (More on this later.)

Reading to Improve Your Score

The most significant preparation you can do for the GRE is reading. Reading improves your math and verbal score. Some people don't believe that reading improves your math score, but most students who have high math scores are also big readers. In fact, the highest scorers on math and science tests are usually not math and science majors—they're English and history majors. Everything on a standardized test—from sentence completions to manipulating equations—starts with reading.

What should you read? Big, thick books that aren't made for the mass market. First, reading long books will acclimate you to sitting still and concentrating for long periods of time. Many college students perform poorly on the GRE simply because they can't sit still for four hours. Reading big books will help you.

And you need to read books that aren't made for the mass market. Why? Because in order to improve your reading skills—and "improve" means being challenged—you need to read stories that have some complexity. Books made for the mass market are designed to be simple so that everyone can easily understand and enjoy them. It's okay if you read a book that's very complex and that you don't fully understand. After you read it the first time, go back and read it again. The GRE is the marathon of testing. When you first start training for a marathon, maybe you don't even finish. (Who can run 26 miles?) After a few attempts, you finally finish. Then you start training for speed. After a few years, you're finishing the marathon and you've improved your time. But there's no way to improve if you don't push yourself. So reading books that you don't fully understand is good. Read them two or three times. Make notes. Look up words you don't understand. This is how you will improve your reading skills.

For pure vocabulary improvement, I would be remiss not to mention Norman Lewis's *Word Power Made Easy.* This book is somewhat boring (as any vocab book is), but it is the undisputed best book of its kind and has been since being published in 1949. Just remember that improving your vocabulary takes time, and the more time you have, the more you can improve your vocabulary. There is no useful way to cram 500 words into your head in 20 days, so start now.

How Tom Approaches His GRE Reading Passages

Here's how Tom does a GRE reading passage:

1. He reads the passage (sometimes he reads confusing parts of the passage twice).

2. He reads the first question. The first question asks about man-eating squid. He doesn't remember seeing anything about man-eating squid in the passage.

3. He goes back to the passage and reads it again. After a minute or two, he finally finds the sentence about squid.

4. He returns to question #1 and reads the answer choices. Three of them sound stupid, but the other two sound like they're saying the same thing. What's the difference between these two:

   b. The squid is angry and bites the fisherman on his gluteus maximus.

   e. The squid may get angered and bite the fisherman, causing swelling of his gluteus maximus.

   Ugh. He returns to the passage and tries to find out which answer is correct. After another minute, he gives up and picks (b).

5. Then Tom moves on to question #2 and repeats this painful process. Eventually, time is called and Tom has two to three critical reading questions unanswered.

When he gets his scores, he discovers that the correct answer to #1 was e.

Does this sound familiar? ETS designed the critical reading passages so that you do them this way, and this is how you miss half the questions.

What's wrong with the above process?

- ◆ Tom read the entire passage. Does reading the entire passage help? Not really. So we're not going to read the entire passage.

X FAIR WARNING

That's right. You should *never* read the entire passage. *Never.* The passage often contains confusing and useless information, and it's packed with so many facts that you can't remember most of it anyway.

◆ Tom wasn't very aggressive with the answer choices. You need to be very aggressive! Being "aggressive" means using the process of elimination to get rid of wrong answers, comparing the choices that remain, and finding proof in the passage for the answer you want to choose. Don't wait for the right answer to pop out at you—it won't. Attack the answer choices!

Now, we're going to approach critical reading passages completely differently.

Rather than spend most of your time reading the passage, you must spend most of your time *answering the questions*. You don't get any points for reading the passage—you only get points for bubbling in the correct oval on the screen, so we're going to concentrate on that.

The CIG Three-Step Process

Here's *The Complete Idiot's Guide* (or CIG) three-step process for acing the critical long reading passages. Carefully learn and follow these techniques and your score will improve!

The three steps are …

1. Determine the topic, tone, and location of material within the passage.

2. Answer the questions in specific, general, and weirdo order.

3. Determine the ETS-approved answer choice.

Let's look at each step in detail.

Step One: Determine the Topic, Tone, and Location of Material Within the Passage

Remember, you don't get any points for reading the passage; you get points for answering the questions.

We only use the passage as evidence—to find facts to prove our answers. We need to find out three things before we go to the questions:

◆ Topic: what the passage is about

◆ Tone: what does the author think about the topic—what's his attitude?

◆ Location: generally, where is stuff in the passage?

"How do I find this stuff?" Glad you asked. Here's what you should do with each passage before going to the questions. (By the way, do this before you look at the questions—don't read the questions first.)

◆ Read the italicized part at the top of each passage. Critical reading passages will (almost) always start with an italicized paragraph that describes the topic. One warning: usually this italicized header is vague. For example, it may say something very generic such as "The following passage is about Africa." You will need to read more to get a better idea of what the topic is, so …

◆ Also read the first one to two sentences of the passage, and …

◆ The first sentence of each additional paragraph, and …

◆ The last sentence of the passage.

This entire process should take only one or two minutes. If this process takes longer than two minutes, you are reading too much.

That's it. Read the blurb (the italicized paragraph), the first sentence of each paragraph, and the last sentence of the passage. That will give you an idea of the topic, tone, and location of material within the passage. Then go to the questions!

2 Step Two: Answer the Questions in Specific, General, and Weirdo Order

After you spend a couple of minutes finding the topic, tone, and location of information, you should go straight to the questions. At this point, you won't really understand the passage, and you won't really know any of the evidence used to support the author's thesis. That's okay. All you will know is the topic of the passage, the author's tone, and the location of evidence—and that's all you need.

There are three kinds of questions about the passage: *specific questions*, *general questions*, and *weirdo questions*

Specific Questions

Specific questions ask about specific facts in the passage:

> According to line 27, what does Dr. Huxley think of the government's planned exploration of Mars?

And you would be able to go back to the passage and find—for example—this sentence in the third paragraph (line 27):

> Dr. Huxley was shocked that the govern– ment would make such plans without him and said, "The exploration will never work like this. I doubt they know how to explore Mars as well as I do."

Obviously, Huxley is shocked, upset, annoyed, and perhaps a little arrogant.

Here's another example of a specific question:

> According to the author, which of the following must be true of space exploration (line 62)?

General Questions

General questions are more vague.

If #3 was a general question, it would look like this:

> According to the passage, what is Dr. Huxley's tone toward the government's statement?

Or, even worse, #3 could have been stated like this:

> The passage implies which of the following about Dr. Huxley?

Here's another example of a general question:

> The author's attitude toward space exploration can best be characterized as:

Weirdo Questions

Weirdo questions are hard, time-consuming, and tricky. They involve picking among three roman numeral choices, and also EXCEPT questions.

We'll look at these later in the chapter. But you'll want to do these last.

Do Specific Questions First

You should skip all general and weirdo questions and do the specific questions first. Specific questions typically come in three varieties:

1. Line reference: the question refers to a line in the passage.

2. Word reference: the question refers you to a specific word or phrase.

3. Vocabulary: the question asks you the meaning of a word.

Line Reference

A line-reference question gives a line number to refer back to and looks like this: *What does the author imply by "irresistible forces" (line 47)?* Any question that contains a line number is a line reference question, even if it asks about tone or implication. These questions should be easy for you. Here's how to solve them:

In the example above, you know you should go to line 47, but the answer probably isn't in line 47—ETS doesn't make it that easy for you.

You will need to read three to six lines above or three to six lines below the line referred to—in this case the answer is probably in lines 41–46 or lines 48–53. Immediately skim above or below the line referred to and search for the discussion of "irresistible forces."

Once you have found out what the author is implying by "irresistible forces," go back to the answer choices and find the correct answer. Remember: now you have the evidence to prove one answer correct.

Word Reference

A word-reference question refers you to a specific word or phrase—basically, it's a line-reference question without the line number. ETS will give you a specific word or phrase; your job is to go back to the passage and find that word or phrase. But you've already scouted out the basic location of information in the passage, so you should have an idea of where to look. You should not need to skim the entire passage.

What would you do if this were the question?

> The author suggests that which of the following would be compatible with Hobsen's theory of intestinal fortitude?

Here's how to solve it:

What's this about? Hobsen's theory of intestinal fortitude!

Do you know the location?

You should have a pretty good idea. But if not, you can use the chronological-order concept. If the questions are numbered 22–30, and you're looking at #29, where would you go in the passage to find the proof you need to pick an answer? You would go to the end of the passage. Hobsen's theory is probably discussed in the last paragraph.

Once you have located Hobsen's theory of intestinal fortitude, make sure you understand what the author is saying. If you don't understand, try to put the sentence into your own words—try to put Hobsen's theory into your own words.

Vocabulary

A vocabulary question asks you the meaning of a word in the context of a sentence. For example …

> In line 58, fortitude most nearly means:

What should you do? Make a Sentence Completion out of it! Here's how:

Go to line 58, find the word "fortitude," and ignore it. Now, instead of "fortitude" in that sentence, you have a blank.

Now read the sentence and put your own word in for "fortitude."

Read the surrounding sentences if you need to.

Once you have put your own word in the blank, go back to the answer choices and find the word that most nearly means your word.

Why should you solve vocabulary questions this way? Because ETS often uses the second or third definition of a word, so you must go back to the passage in order to understand which definition they're using.

Do General Questions Next

There are four main types of general questions.

1. Tone or attitude: what does the author think or feel?

2. Title or conclusion: what is the best title for this passage?

3. Implication or meaning: what is implied by a phrase or sentence?

4. Compare and contrast: what's the difference between these two ideas, paragraphs, passages?

Here's how to solve them.

Tone and Title Questions

Tone and title questions are solved the same way. These types of questions are often vague. They will ask about the author's tone, attitude, or main focus. They might ask you to name the best title for the passage or the best title of the book from which the passage was taken. Usually, there is no single line in the passage that will help you. You need to remember what you said the passage's topic and tone was from your initial skimming. To solve tone and title questions, use the "battle of the bad answers" technique.

To use this technique, instead of looking for the correct answer, look for the wrong answers first, cross them out, and then see what you have left. Often, a wrong answer is easier to find than a correct answer. What do wrong answers look like? They often have these characteristics:

- **They won't offer full coverage.** Many wrong answers give the tone or topic of part of the passage—perhaps the first paragraph—only they exclude other parts of the passage. If the first paragraph discusses the hedgehog and the third paragraph discusses the fox, the *best title* would encompass both of these topics. *The correct answer will always cover the entire passage.*

VEXING VOCABULARY

A **best title** type of question is one that asks you to choose the "best title" for the passage. It's essentially another way to ask for the passage's main idea.

- **They tend to be broad or bold.** The correct answer to a best-title question will not be "The History of Europe." Is it possible to cover the history of Europe in a 70-line critical reading passage? No. An answer choice like this is too broad. Similarly, a best title correct answer won't be "Dogs Are Bad." This is too broad ("all") and too bold; clearly, many people would be upset by this answer choice if it were correct. The correct answer to a tone question won't be bold or broad. For example, if the question asks, "What is the author's tone?," the correct answer will never be "hateful." ETS won't use critical-reading passages that claim that dogs are bad or whose author is hateful. You can get rid of answer choices that are too bold or broad. *The correct answer will rarely be too bold or broad.*

- **They won't offer proof.** After you have crossed off answer choices that don't cover the entire passage and are too bold or broad, you will have two to four remaining. The first step to deciding which one is correct is to read each answer choice and ask "Did the passage talk about that?" Often, you will have one to two answer choices that aren't even mentioned in the passage. They seem like reasonable answer choices—neither bold nor broad—but upon close inspection, you'll realize they aren't mentioned. For example, if the question asks for the main focus of the passage and an answer choice is "c. Farming is a wonderful way of life for the women of Ohio," you need to ask "Did the passage talk about women in Ohio?" You may find that the passage did talk about farming being a wonderful way of life for women, but it only referred to women in Nebraska and Kansas. ETS will often slip in one to two answer choices that sound correct but have one little word that's wrong—in this case, that word is "Ohio." *The correct answer will always be supported by proof.*

Implication Questions

Implication questions are questions that ask about something implied, instead of stated. The trap is that most people think "implication" means "the passage doesn't say it." In fact, just the opposite is true. Like all the other correct answers on critical reading, only one answer choice on an implication question is provable. If the question asks, "The author's statement that he doesn't like vegetables suggests …" then you should read each answer choice and ask, "Did the passage say that?" There will be one answer choice that you can prove.

So the key to successfully answering implication questions is to remember that just because the question is about stuff that was "implied" or "suggested" doesn't mean it's not in the passage. In fact, the correct answer is in the passage. What makes it so difficult to find? Because ETS doesn't repeat the proof from the passage in the question word-for-word. ETS paraphrases. For example, if the passage says "The Thompson Triplets always preferred to play together as a team," the correct answer might

say, "The Thompson Triplets didn't like playing alone." ETS doesn't repeat the exact same words, but the meaning is the same. For implication questions, look for the answer that paraphrases the proof from the passage.

And finally: do implication questions after you've completed the specific questions and the tone and title questions. Implication questions tend to be difficult.

Compare and Contrast

You will only find these types of questions on dual passages.

Sometimes you are asked a very general question such as, "The difference in the main focus of passage one and the main focus of passage two is that passage one …" These types of questions aren't always easy, but they could be worse. You could be asked, "Passage two differs from passage one in that only passage two mentions which of the following?" For that question, you may need to scour every corner of both passages searching for the one thing that passage two mentions that isn't mentioned in passage one. Yuck. Although that question might not be very difficult to answer, it will take a long time. This is why compare-and-contrast questions should always be attempted last.

So how do you answer a compare-and-contrast question? Usually, it just takes time. As long as you're aggressively searching for evidence for each answer choice, you will get the correct answer. But instead of searching through a single passage for evidence, you are now searching through two passages. And although compare-and-contrast questions are usually last, they often encompass the entirety of each passage, which often means you will need to skim most (or all) of each passage. If you have the time (and take your time), you can get these correct. If you don't have the time, don't worry. You can easily break 650 on the verbal while missing every compare-and-contrast question.

Do Weirdo Questions Last

There are a few types of questions, in addition to compare-and-contrast questions, that you should attempt last. There aren't too many of them, but they are nasty.

I, II, III: Roman-Numeral Questions

Roman-numeral questions take this format:

> According to the passage, the author would agree with which of the following:
>   Spaghetti is better with cheese.
>   Spaghetti should be eaten in a Ferrari.
>   Spaghetti should not be worn on your pants.
>
>   a. I only
>   b. II only
>   c. I and III
>   d. II and III
>   e. I, II and III

To answer these questions, find proof for each Roman numeral individually. If you can find proof for I, immediately get rid of the answer choices that don't have I in them. If you don't find proof for I, then get rid of every answer choice that contains I. Repeat with II, and then III.

EXCEPT Questions

EXCEPT questions look like this:

> The author supports each of the following statements about standardized tests EXCEPT:
>   a. They are stupid.
>   b. They should be replaced with pie eating contests.

>   c. The people who make them should be arrested for cruel and unusual punishment.
>   d. They should be taken underwater.
>   e. They are a communist plot.

EXCEPT questions can also come in LEAST or NOT formats.

> Which of the following is the author LEAST likely to agree with? Which of the following is NOT supported by the passage?

To tackle these questions, cross off the word "EXCEPT." Rephrase the question in your own words. Ask the question in a yes or no format for each of the questions. Do this for all five answer choices. (Make sure you try all five.) Pick the odd one.

Always do Roman-numeral and EXCEPT questions last or skip them. These are the reading questions most test takers will miss.

Step Three: Determine the ETS-Approved Answer Choice

And now, here is a checklist for determining correct answers. This list applies to the correct answer for all critical-reading question types.

In the world of ETS, correct answers …

- **Will have proof.** You can always find proof in the passage for a correct answer. Whenever you pick an answer on critical reading, always ask yourself, "Where did I find this in the passage?" If you can't find proof for an answer choice, don't pick it. It is easy to find proof for specific questions—you simply go back to the line number or the word being referred to. It's a little more difficult to find proof for general questions, which is why you should do them after completing the specific questions.

Remember, there will always be answer choices that are true but can't be proven with evidence from the passage. For example, what if a question asks "The author suggests which of the following?" and answer choice b. reads "the capital of New York is Albany"? This is true, but it's not the answer unless you can find it in the passage. Oftentimes, ETS will give you answer choices that are true, but aren't proven by the passage. If the passage doesn't say "Albany is the capital of New York" then you can't choose b.

◆ **Will match each other.** If you think you got all the other questions to a critical-reading passage correct, but the last question is stumping you, look back over your other answer choices. Correct answer choices to similarly worded questions won't contradict each other, so you can use your other answers to help you. For example, if the question is "The main focus of the passage is …" and you think the correct answer is "d. Everyone should grow their own squash," then this information can help you on a later question that asks, "What does the author think people should do?" The answer is probably something like "grow squash." This happens more often than you think. So if you're having difficulty answering a question, look back at the questions that you've already answered (and you think you got correct) and compare—that may help you choose the correct answer. Correct answers will match each other.

◆ **Will not bash America.** A correct answer won't harshly criticize Americana (democracy, capitalism, George Washington, babies, and apple pie). Why? ETS makes millions from students, so ETS won't criticize them and

anything they like. The last thing ETS wants is a lawsuit. So you know you can get rid of an answer choice that reads "c. Abraham Lincoln was an idiot."

◆ **Will correspond to the real world.** Correct answers correspond to "real life" 90 percent of the time. This means that ETS won't make this a correct answer: "d. Canada is between Honduras and Guatemala." That answer choice will never be correct because it doesn't make sense in the real world. Now more recently ETS sometimes flirts with crazy answer choices, but if an answer choice is blatantly untrue in the real world, then it won't be correct on the GRE.

◆ **Will not support radical positions.** ETS won't support a radical position or cause, so the correct answer will not be radical. For example, "a. Women are less likely to be successful entrepreneurs" is a radical position that would never be a correct answer. Once again, ETS eschews radical positions and causes because ETS doesn't want to get sued. (Go look up "eschew.")

◆ **Will not make absolute statements.** ETS won't make absolute statements unless they are clearly supported by the passage. For example, "e. Older women always make better babysitters than younger women" is an absolute statement because of the word "always." Don't pick this answer choice unless you can find clear evidence in the passage. If the passage says "older women often make better babysitters" or "older women usually make better babysitters," then you can't pick answer choice e. "Often" and "usually" do not mean the same thing as "always."

Another tricky version of the absolute answer is "a. Constant exercise is the solution to the problem." The answer is absolute because of the word "is"—"is" implies "all the time." The passage may have said "constant exercise is one good solution." This means that constant exercise is a solution, but there are other solutions, whereas answer choice a. suggests that constant exercise is the one and only solution. (See Clinton's congressional testimony for the vagaries of the word "is.")

Another way to think of it is in terms of percentages. For example, the word "always" means "100 percent" whereas the word "usually" means "less than 100 percent." If the passage says "usually" then the correct answer won't say "always." Absolute answers often contain at least one of the following words: is, always, must, only, every, never, impossible, cannot, all, totally, completely, solely.

Try a Few Blindfolded

Now I'm going to ask you to do something crazy: try some critical-reading questions without looking at the passage. You always want to go back to the passage and find proof for your answer, but this exercise will help you hone your answer-picking skills. There is no time limit; you should work on accuracy first and speed later. Try these three problems (and don't bother looking for the passages—the passages these questions ask about aren't printed in this book!):

1. According to the passage, the author suggests that the American space program can be criticized for

   a. endangering astronauts' lives for the sake of completing projects on time

   b. spending too much money for space research

   c. being too competitive

   d. making the space shuttle more complex than it needs to be

   e. proceeding in a overly cautious manner

2. The passage supports which of the following statements about the light:

   a. its properties will never be known

   b. light is the most important subject to research

   c. the Academy of Science should fund more light research

   d. the Institutes of Health is biased against light research

   e. light research can only by conducted in U.S. laboratories

3. In line 28, the author mentions "hierarchies" to support which of the following conclusions about women:

   a. women fall into clear hierarchical categories

   b. women are subjugated to clear hierarchical boundaries

   c. women are not likely to obey the fundamental requirement of society

   d. some women may be limited by hierarchical considerations

   e. hierarchies limit women

FAIR WARNING

You should always go back to the passage to find proof for your answer choice. The three questions used here are without accompanying passages to help you with your answer-choosing skills. You should never pick an answer choice without finding proof for it in the passage.

1. e. ETS won't criticize NASA, so the correct answer won't actually be a criticism. This answer choice suggests that NASA is very safe—not really a criticism.

2. c. The other answer choices contain strong wording or don't make sense. c. has weak words ("should") and could be true, so it's a good answer choice.

3. d. Any choice that starts off "some women may" could be correct. Weak words and vague assertions make for good answer choices.

More from ETS's Bag of Tricks

Here are a few passage types that ETS throws at you when it's being nasty.

Dual Passages

Dual passages are where you're given two passages instead of one. Typically, the passages are shorter and usually the last two to three questions are compare-and-contrast questions.

Do each passage separately, as if you were doing two shorter passages. Attack the first passage, and then go to the questions for the first passage. Then attack the second passage and do the questions for the second passage. Finally, do the compare-and-contrast questions. Never read both passages together and attack all the questions at once. You will waste time. Often, the dual passage is in the 15-minute verbal section at the end.

Narrative and Fiction Passages

Narrative and fiction passages are the worst. Usually, they tell a story, and often they do not follow the standard essay format. While they may be interesting to read, they usually have very hard questions.

Do these types of passages last or skip them. If you decide to do the passage, you will need to skim the entire passage instead of only reading the first sentences. So quickly skim the passage and get the topic, tone, and location of information. Remember, you still aren't trying to understand the passage (it may be impossible to understand). Quickly skim it, figure out the topic, tone, and location of information, and go to the questions. This entire process should still only take two to three minutes.

A Final Word

Critical reading is the worst part of the GRE, but you can greatly improve your performance if you do everything in this chapter. Many students improve from getting 50–60 percent of critical reading questions correct to 85–95 percent correct. And that's significant because critical reading is over half of the verbal test.

You should do the critical-reading section after completing the sentence completions and analogies because it takes more time to answer critical-reading questions and you get the same number of points for a correct answer. Most people do not finish the critical-reading section. You may leave two or three hard questions blank (Roman numeral, EXCEPT, and compare-and-contrast questions). This is okay. Take your time with critical reading. You only need to do all the questions if you're shooting for above a 650 and your analogies aren't very good. (Most people who score a 650+ on the verbal miss one or two hard analogies and a few critical-reading questions.)

So don't race to finish the critical-reading section; take your time and get all the questions you attempt right!

Summary

The most significant preparation you can do for the GRE is reading. Reading improves your math and verbal scores.

If you have three or more months before the GRE, you can significantly improve your reading skills and vocabulary by reading three books.

Read Norman Lewis's *Word Power Made Easy*.

Treat critical reading as if it were a legal case. You're the prosecutor, and you need to find out who's guilty. For each question, one answer is guilty. The passage is all your evidence. You need to go back to the passage and find evidence that convicts one answer choice.

The easiest passages are usually the science and the PC passages.

The hardest passage types are narrative and fiction.

Don't read the entire passage. Here's what you should read:

- The italicized part at the top of each passage
- The first sentence or two of the passage
- The first sentence of each additional paragraph
- The last sentence of the passage

Reading in this way will help you find out three things before going to the questions: topic, tone, and location of information.

This entire process should take only one or two minutes. If this process takes longer than two minutes, you are reading too much.

After you spend one or two minutes finding the topic, tone, and location of information, you should go straight to the questions.

Each passage's questions are not in order of difficulty; they are in rough chronological order, meaning the first question has to do with the first part of the passage, the last question has to do with the last part of the passage, and so on.

Specific questions typically come in three varieties:

- Line reference: the question refers to a line in the passage.
- Word reference: the question refers to a specific word or phrase.
- Vocabulary: the question asks you the meaning of a word.

Do general questions next!

What to look for in a good answer for general questions:

- **Full coverage.** The correct answer will always cover the entire passage.
- **No extremes.** The correct answer will rarely be too bold or broad.
- **Proof.** The first step to deciding which one is correct is to read each answer choice and ask, "Did the passage talk about that?"

Implication questions: Most people think "implication" means "the passage doesn't say it." In fact, the correct answer is in the passage. Do implication questions after you've completed the specific questions and the tone and title questions.

Compare-and-contrast questions: You will only find these types of general questions on dual passages.

Roman numeral questions (I, II, III): To answer these questions, find proof for each roman numeral individually. If you can find proof for I, immediately get rid of the answer choices that don't have I in them. If you don't find proof for I, then get rid of every answer choice that contains I. Repeat with II, then III.

EXCEPT: Cross off the word "EXCEPT." Rephrase the question in your own words. Ask the question in a yes or no format for each of the questions. Do this for all five answer choices. (Make sure you try all five.) Pick the odd one.

Dual passages: Do each passage separately, as if you were doing two shorter passages. Attack the first passage, then go to the questions for the first passage. Then attack the second passage and do the questions for the second passage. Finally, do the compare-and-contrast questions. Never read both passages together and attack all the questions at once.

Narrative and fiction passages are the worst. If you decide to do the passage, you will need to skim the entire passage instead of only reading the first sentences. This entire process should still only take two or three minutes.

Finally, remember this checklist for correct answers. ETS-approved answers …

- **Will have proof.** You can always find proof in the passage for a correct answer. Whenever you pick an answer on critical reading, *always* ask yourself, "Where did I find this in the passage?"

   Remember, there will always be answer choices that are true but can't be proven with evidence from the passage. They are wrong.

- **Will match each other.** Correct answer choices to similarly worded questions won't contradict each other, so you can use your other answers to help you.

- **Will not bash America.** A correct answer won't harshly criticize Americana (democracy, capitalism, George Washington, babies, apple pie, etc.).

- **Will correspond to the real world.** Correct answers correspond to "real life" 90 percent of the time. If an answer choice is blatantly untrue in the real world, then it won't be correct on the GRE.

- **Will not support radical positions.** ETS won't support a radical position or cause, so the correct answer will not be radical.

- **Will not make absolute statements.** ETS won't make absolute statements unless they are clearly supported by the passage. Absolute answers often contain at least one of the following words: is, always, must, only, every, never, impossible, cannot, all, totally, completely, solely.

The Least You Need to Know

- When it comes to long critical reading passages, the questions almost always tell you where to go for the answer.

- Don't read the passages unless you're answering a question.

- Passage types include social science, science, and narrative and fiction.

- Make sure you choose an ETS-approved answer choice.

- Always find proof in the passage for your answers!

- The best thing you can do to prepare for the GRE is to read.

Chapter 9

Short Critical Reading Passages

In This Chapter

 ◆ How short passages differ from longer ones

 ◆ Short-passage strategy

 ◆ Attacking the answer choices

 ◆ Short-passage practice questions

In this chapter you'll learn how to quickly identify and tackle the short passages. Short passages are becoming increasingly popular on the GRE, so you need to have a process for answering them. After looking at a few short passages, we'll look at question types and answer choices and learn how to quickly identify correct and incorrect answers.

Short and Long Passages

There are two types of critical reading passages on the GRE: short passages and long passages. There's a big difference between the two.

First, the short passages are short. (Shocking, huh?) Second, whereas the questions for long passages ask you to find specific information (and usually give you line numbers), the questions for short passages are usually more general. So while the long passages are all about hunting and gathering, the short passages are all about understanding a passage's "big picture."

A short passage question might look like this:

According to the author, ETS would better serve the world if

    a. it gave up making tests and baked pies instead.

    b. it permitted test takers to phone-a-friend.

    c. you could take the test as a group.

    d. two words: selective amnesia.

    e. Jay-Z were put in charge of making the test.

The following table sums up the differences between short and long passages:

Per Passage	Long Passages	Short Passages
# of lines	40–100	5–30
# of questions	6–13	1–2
Purpose	Tests your ability to find information	Tests your ability to grasp general ideas

So short passages are fundamentally different from longer passages because …

♦ They are short (so you can read the entire passage—time is not the major issue).

♦ They (mostly) ask about big-picture ideas, not specific info.

The "Closest Thing to Cheating" Method

Here are the steps to take for the "Closest Thing to Cheating" method for solving the short reading questions:

1. **Read the questions for the passage.** There will only be one or two questions per passage. Get an idea of what they are asking by putting the questions in your own words. Once you've clarified to yourself what they're looking for …

2. **Read the passage.** Read it carefully until you've answered the questions.

3. **Read all five answer choices.** Weed out the choices that are not possible. Pick the best choice from what remains. (Make sure you read all five answer choices—do *not* stop at choice 2 because "it seems right." Read all five answer choices every time and look for wrong answers first—they are *much* easier to spot.)

4. **Do your own victory dance here.** But don't go too far or the league may fine you. But make sure the dance is outrageous enough to make SportsCenter.

Reading the Questions

Remember: read the questions first! After you read a question, translate it into your own words. Here are the types of questions you can expect ETS to ask you.

The main point of the passage is that

What are you looking for? Where would it be in the passage? Conclusions are usually stated at the beginning or end of a short passage. (In contrast, in a long passage, the conclusion is usually at the beginning or end of the passage, or the first sentence of the second paragraph.)

The last sentence serves to

Read the last sentence in context of everything that comes before it, and look for directional words such as "therefore" and "thus" which draw a conclusion, and look for *"laundry list" sentences* that may be providing evidence or examples for a prior claim.

VEXING VOCABULARY

A "laundry list" sentence is a sentence that contains a list of items. For instance: "Bob went to the store and bought several items, including coconuts, string, a bag of hammers, lettuce, and a funnel." The list may simply serve as examples or may be evidence for an argument (in this instance, that perhaps Bob is crazy).

What would most likely be found before this passage?

What does this mean? If the passage is very specific, you'd expect a general intro before it. If the passage is very general, perhaps it is the conclusion to a more specific discussion. If the passage contains weird language or ideas, perhaps there's an explanation before the passage. The key here is to eliminate wrong answer choices first!

The primary purpose is to

This is a question asking you to determine the scope of the passage. Not too general or big—we only have 10 lines here! "Explain the history of Europe" won't be correct. Just make sure your answer is specific enough that it applies to a 10-line passage but general enough that it applies to more than any single sentence. If a passage is about cheese-eating surrender monkeys, then the passage is not about "monkeys" (too general), not about "cheese" (too general), and not about "cheese-eating surrender monkeys of nineteenth-century Marseilles" (too specific).

The passage is primarily concerned with

Another scope question. The answer will be somewhat specific, but not so specific as to exclude any of the information provided.

The author mentions monkeys in order to

Most likely in order to show, illustrate, demonstrate, indicate, support, exhibit, or help explain. The author will rarely/never challenge, shake the foundations, expose, take issue with, reveal, or thoroughly reveal. Never pick anything starting with "conclusively," "unfailingly," or "absolutely."

Let's repeat that in chart form. When it comes to choosing a correct answer for this type of question:

Be Attracted To	Be Repelled By
Show	Shake the foundations
Illustrate	Expose (the falsity, the implausibility)
Demonstrate (the possibility)	Take issue with (the claim, the assertion)
Indicate (a possible scenario)	Reveal (as false, as impossible)
Support	Thoroughly explain
Exhibit	Conclusively show/illustrate/explain
Help explain	Unfailingly support

The repellant words aren't 100 percent wrong, but they are wrong 90 percent of the time, particularly if an answer choice starts with one of the attractive words. For example, if the question asks "What is the purpose of the passage?" don't choose "Show that one can thoroughly explain the meaning of life in 20 words." "Show" is okay but "thoroughly explain" blows everything up. You can "show" something in 20 words but you can't "thoroughly explain" anything. If you're guessing, stay far away from the repellant words.

Based on this passage, monkeys can be best described as

Get rid of any answer choice that isn't supported or contradicts anything in the passage. Then see what's left. If answer A says "math abilities," get rid of it if the word "math" isn't in the passage.

The author's tone is best described as

Stay away from answers like apathetic, indifferent, hateful, full of caustic ridicule, sarcastic. Be attracted to answers like objective, subjective, ironic, doubtful, strongly opposed, neutral, questioning.

The "monkeys" (lines 4–8) are in reference to

Read those lines and match them to something else in the passage.

Dual-Passage Questions

Dual-passage questions look like this:

The author of Passage 1 mentions monkeys to suggest that

Once again, most likely to support, demonstrate, explain, etc.

The author of Passage 2 would most likely respond to the last sentence of Passage 1 by

Read the last sentence of Passage 1, then read Passage 2.

The two passages differ in that Passage 1 states that

Keep extremes and absolutes in mind here. Sometimes, both passages seem "kind of" the same. The difference could be that Passage 1 says "might be" and Passage 2 says "must be." These two passages are different because Passage 1 is less certain about something; the answer is the difference between "might" and "must."

Which conclusion is supported by both passages?

Read the answer choices and cross off any choice that isn't supported by both passages and pick what's left. Keep key words in mind—if answer choice B has the word "landscaping" in it but Passage 2 doesn't have the word "landscaping," then that's not the correct answer.

Which line from Passage 1 best supports the conclusion of Passage 2?

Find the conclusion of Passage 2 first, and then pick the answer from the choices.

Which basic assumption of Passage 1 is not assumed by the author of Passage 2?

Read each answer choice, asking yourself "Is this an assumption of Passage 1?" If no, cross it off. After you do this, go back to the choice you have left and see what isn't supported by Passage 2. That said, it's probably best to skip these kinds of questions because there probably won't be more than a couple of them and they're too time-consuming—and skip it once you've read the question, not after you've spent five minutes on the passage.

Reading the Passages

After reading and translating the questions, read the passage. Read the passage carefully, with the questions in mind. As you read the passage, you must look out for directional words. Directional words signal something important about the passage: a main point, a contrasting view, the tone, the conclusion.

For example, if you read that "It's generally accepted that pigeons are harmless creatures, but a recent study …" Where do you expect the passage to go next? It's going to say something like "but a recent study suggests that pigeons are man-eating beasts of death."

Directional words occur everywhere—in sentence completions and all types of reading passages—but they are very important in short passages because they will indicate what you need to read, as well as the structure of the argument, and they'll often signal an answer to a question. You must know these directional words! The Aztecs didn't know directional words, and look what happened to them.

Examples of directional words
"But"   "At least"
"Yet"   "Rather"
"Surprisingly"   "Therefore"
"Unfortunately"   "As a result"
"At most"
"In the end"

Questions are often asked and then answered with a contrasting position, or they may imply a contrasting position or a conclusion. For example, you might see a question such as "Is the poet insane?" The next sentence is usually a contrasting point, such as, "Some thought so, but most saw a brilliance in his seemingly irrational behavior." So questions often set up contrasting points.

Now let's put all we've learned to work.

Practice Questions Galore

Following are 10 short reading passages, each one followed by a few questions. Answers and explanations follow. Give these a try.

Passage #1

What is jazz? When asked to explain his music, Louis Armstrong is said to have responded, "If you gotta ask, you'll never know." Indeed, jazz comes in so many variants, from swing to cool school, and has informed so many other music styles, from rock and roll to modern concert music and soul, that it may well be impossible to arrive at an exclusive definition of this constantly evolving art. However, to claim that there is something inexplicable and indefinable about the heart of the music or its origins is to make a mistake; like any musical form, a specific style of jazz can be definitively described using the vocabulary of musical analysis. This concrete method allows the historian to reach conclusions about how jazz came about; what musical forms it was influenced by, what traditions shaped its character, and what geographical and social factors aided its birth and its diffusion.

In discussing the origins of jazz, therefore, it is useful to refer to the characteristics of its earliest incarnation, the so-called New Orleans, or classical, style. When one has analyzed this style, it becomes apparent that classical jazz's central characteristics—its instrumentation, rhythm, melodic and harmonic material, improvisatory and vocal nature, and social functions—are all descended from primarily three musical genres: the blues, ragtime, and the marching band. Jazz therefore represents a fusion of African American and European traditions, for each of these genres was informed by both cultures. That these three styles would be catalyzed into a totally new musical genre at the turn of the twentieth century in New Orleans would be the result of several **fortuitous** events, not the least of which would be the forced integration of black and Creole subcultures in the city.

---

1. The passage states that all are aspects of jazz EXCEPT the following:

    a. an improvisatory structure

    b. an ineffable "heart and soul"

    c. a vocal nature

    d. a style drawn from heterogeneous traditions

    e. social and historical origins in New Orleans

2. In context, the word "fortuitous" most closely means:

    a. chance

    b. serendipitous

    c. fortunate

    d. unfortunate

    e. interrelated

Passage #2

Emily Dickinson once wrote that "Biography first convinces us of the fleeing of the Biographied." Certainly, this is true of her life, which eludes easy examination. An intensely private person, Dickinson played out her life's dramas, not in actions, but in poems, essays, and correspondence. The documented specifics of her life give us nothing more than a view of a seemingly narrow existence: she never lived outside of the provincial backwater of Amherst and her father's house for any length of time, never married nor had children, and died at 56. Dickinson received the equivalent of a public high school education at Mt. Holyoke Seminary, but was never widely read. Seemingly, Dickinson's life would appear to be a progressive retreat from society after the age of 25: from a popular, outgoing student to an isolated spinster who refused visits even from intimate friends.

Under the surface of a constrained life, however, existed currents of passionate emotion, an unbearable sensitivity to the pleasures and pains of life, and an insatiable thirst for spiritual and artistic meaning: all preserved in her writings. In fact, Dickinson's inner life as an artist was closely intertwined with the intense emotional relationships that she cultivated on paper, her "avoidance" of human encounters notwithstanding. Some have suggested her withdrawal, and the years of her greatest poetic output, were the results of failed or unreciprocated love affairs. Charles Wadsworth, a married minister, appeared to have been unaware, or unresponsive, to Dickinson's feelings; and his departure from her life in 1861 coincided with, or perhaps precipitated, the years of her greatest poetic output. Indeed, according to Anderson, in avoiding human encounters, she made a flight "from the events of living into the perception of intensely felt life, a deliberate economy of thought and emotion in order to focus on her inner world of values." However, a subtler understanding of her "seclusion" reveals that it did not exclude an emotional connection to others. She maintained an intense correspondence with, among others, her sister-in-law, Susan Gilbert, though she and Susan lived but half a mile from each other for many years. In fact it was the mutual exchange of poetry between these two women that may have provided Emily with her greatest inspiration; though she might be a "nobody" escaping the presence of an "admiring bog" she needed an audience; an audience of the few friends she treasured.

---

1. Consider each answer choice separately, and select **all** that apply:

   The author suggests which of the following about Dickinson's development?

   a. Her increasing self-isolation was the result of a limited environment and education.

   b. Her increasing self-isolation may have been a conscious attempt to increase the quality of her artistic endeavors.

   c. Though Dickinson may have been increasingly isolated, she maintained emotional ties to a few close friends.

2. The author's primary purpose is to suggest that:

   a. Dickinson's most intense emotional attachments appear to have been maintained through correspondence.

   b. Dickinson's self-isolation has been misrepresented by literary scholars.

   c. The external circumstances of Dickinson's life do not add up to a complete picture of her emotional and artistic life.

   d. Dickinson avoided human contact in order to cultivate an economy of thought and emotion.

   e. Dickinson, in spite of provincial circumstances and a limited education, is one of American's most cultivated poets.

Passage #3

Though often misinterpreted, Lorraine Hansberry's *Raisin in the Sun* neither rejects integration nor denies the moral promise of the American dream. The play rather critically examines the incomplete realization of this dream, while remaining loyal to its basic premise. Recognition of this dual vision allows us to avoid attributing "unintentional" irony to the work. Instead, we can accept the work's ironic nuances as deliberate social commentary. Curiously, a resistance to crediting Hansberry with the subtlety necessary for such intentional irony has led many critics to interpret the play's thematic conflicts as mere confusion, inconsistency, or eclecticism. Isaacs, for example, refuses to find Hansberry's concerns for her own race reconcilable with ideals of human solidarity. But the play's complex view of Black self-regard and human reconciliation as compatible is no more "contradictory" than Du Bois's famous, well-thought-out ideal of an ethnic self-awareness that accommodates a sense of human unity, or Fanon's emphasis on an ideal internationalism capable of coexisting with national identities and roles.

---

1. The author's primary purpose in this passage is to:

    a. explain why certain critics refuse to consider *Raisin in the Sun* a deliberately ironic play.

    b. suggest that *Raisin in the Sun* is allied by virtue of its ironic nuances with the works of Du Bois and Fanon.

    c. analyze the thematic conflicts fundamental to *Raisin in the Sun*.

    d. emphasize the contradictory elements inherent to *Raisin in the Sun* as social commentary.

    e. affirm the thematic coherence underlying *Raisin in the Sun* as social commentary.

2. The author of the passage would probably consider which of the following statements to be most similar to the stance of the critics described in the underlined portion of the passage?

    a. Documentary filmmakers deal solely with an objective world of facts; therefore, a filmmaker who attempts to reinterpret history misleads us.

    b. The world is flat, so anyone who claims that they have sailed around it contradicts known facts and must be lying.

    c. Radioactivity cannot be detected by any of the five senses; therefore, a scientist could not possibly control it in a laboratory setting.

    d. The painter of this watercolor could not possibly have intended it to be funny; therefore the painting's humor must be the indirect result of the painter's lack of technique.

    e. Traditional social mores are what hold a culture together; therefore, anyone who deviates from them acts in a destructive manner.

Passage #4

James P. Johnson has re[ceived] consistent critical acclaim as a great early jazz pianist, originator of the 1920s Harlem "st[ride] style[,] [a]nd a jazz and blues composer of note. Johnson was also, however, an innovator in the [s]ymphonic [tradit]ion, composing "classical" music that reveals American, and especially Afric[an-American influences.]

By 1924, [both Milhaud and Gershwin had] set a precedent for incorporating elements of jazz into classical [works. Johnson, as a serious American fam]iliar with jazz, blues, spirituals, and popular music— genres [foreign to most classical musicians—was espe]cially suited to expand Milhaud's and Gershwin's effo[rts. In 192? his first large-scale work, Yamekraw, was] premiered at Carnegie Hall. A blues- and ja[zz-inspired work, Yamekraw used both spirituals and J]ohnson's own popular songs. It was an [instant success and remains one of his most frequently] [perf]ormed extended works. Indeed, *Yamekraw* [represented one of Johnson's most significant achieve]ments, vividly demonstrating the possibility of [assimilating contemporary musical music into sym]phonic traditions.

1. The passage [suggests that Johnson composed] all of the following EXCEPT:

    a. jazz works

    b. popular songs

    c. symphonic music

    d. spirituals

    e. blues pieces

2. Consider each answer choice separately, and select all that apply:

    The author suggests which of the following about most classical composers of the early 1920s?

    a. They had little familiarly with "popular" music, including jazz, blues, and spirituals.

    b. They made little attempt to innovate within the limits of the classical symphonic tradition.

    c. They were influenced heavily by Milhaud and Gershwin's experiments.

3. The author suggests that most critics:

    a. Have underrated Johnson's musical abilities

    b. Are uninterested in Johnson's influence on jazz

    c. Have little regard for classical works that incorporate popular music

    d. Neglect Johnson's contribution to classical symphonic music

    e. Have underrated *Yamekraw*'s popularity

Passage #5

Scholarship on political newspapers and their editors has traditionally maintained that, as the United States developed, the increasing influence of the press led, in the long run, to the standards of objective and neutral reporting from which we today benefit. Pasely considers this an oversimplified view, because objectivity was not a goal of early national newspaper editors, even when those editors **disingenuously** claimed that they aimed to tell all sides of a story. Instead, the intensely partisan ideologies represented in the newspapers of the infant republic led to a clear divide between traditional and republican values. Editors, charged with determining the political content of their papers—especially those editors with republican agendas—began to see themselves as central figures in the development of political consciousness in the United States.

1. Consider each of the three answer choices separately and select **all** that apply:

   The passage suggests that Pasely would agree with which of the following statements about newspapers' political role?

   a. Newspapers in the early United Sates for the most part quite openly avowed their refusal to tell all sides of most political stories.

   b. The editorial policies of some newspaper editors in the early United States became a counterweight to proponents of traditional value.

   c. Newspapers today are in many cases less neutral in their political reporting than is commonly held by scholars.

2. In this passage, the word "disingenuously" means most closely:

   a. guilelessly
   b. obliquely
   c. irresolutely
   d. pertinacious
   e. insincerely

Passage #6

The association of moral or religious values with vegetarianism is not a new one; over 2,000 years ago the secular literature of Tirukurai proclaimed: "Perceptive souls who have abandoned passion will not feed on meat … how can he practice true compassion, he who eats the flesh of an animal?" Hinduism holds that the consumption of meat promotes aggressive or unbalanced mental states, while Jainists believe in the principle of "ahimsa," or nonviolence toward all living things. Whether based on ideals of compassion, asceticism, or moderation, vegetarianism has historically had as its central assumption the power of diet to shape the spirituality, indeed the character, of the individual.

It was, however, only relatively recently that vegetarianism came to be seen as a potential political tool. Vegetarianism in the nineteenth century was associated with many social reform movements, including temperance and feminism. In the 1960s, the environmental grassroots movement recommended vegetarianism as part of a sustainable lifestyle. In *Diet for a Small Planet*, for example, Frances Moore Lappé argued that grains such as rice and soy are far more energy-efficient sources of protein than are meats such as beef and chicken. Today, some abstain from meat primarily out of a concern over the environmental impact of the meat industry, especially the impact of livestock farming in developing countries. In doing so, they transform the central tenant of vegetarianism from one of moral self-consistency to one of activism.

1. The primary purpose of this passage is to:

    a. Present a paradox about a dietary practice

    b. Argue a position about a dietary practice

    c. Examine the history of a dietary practice

    d. Make a generalization about a dietary practice

    e. Contrast possible reasons for maintaining a dietary practice

2. Which statement would the author of the passage most likely agree with?

    a. Vegetarians today mostly abstain from meat due to concerns about cruelty to animals, while in the past they did so mainly for religious reasons.

    b. Vegetarianism has historically been a vehicle for moral self-improvement, and only recently has been regarded as a political tool.

    c. Environmental activism has been responsible for a recent increase in and acceptance of vegetarianism.

    d. Vegetarianism should be practiced by all who wish to maintain their moral self-consistency.

    e. The health benefits of vegetarianism have historically been overlooked.

Passage #7

The conviction held by many linguists that each language is perfectly suited to express the thoughts and sentiments of the culture to which it is native is in some ways the exact counterpart to the belief, held by the Manchester school of economics, that supply and demand regulate everything for the best. Just as economists were blind to the numerous instances in which the law of supply and demand did not always address all actual wants, so too are many linguists deaf to instances in which the constraints of a particular language create misunderstandings in everyday conversation. "He forgot his bike—no, no, not John's, but *his own*." Thus we are often required in colloquial speech to modify and define words in order to clarify the meaning we intend. No language is perfect, and if we acknowledge this, we open our eyes to the possibility of investigating the relative merits of different languages or of the different details in languages.

1. The primary purpose of the passage is to

   a. Analyze an aspect of the English language

   b. Refute a belief held by certain linguists

   c. Show that economic theory can be relevant to linguistic study

   d. Illustrate the confusion that may result from the improper use of language.

   e. Suggest a way in which the use of language may be made more nearly perfect

2. In presenting the argument, the author does all of the following EXCEPT:

   a. Give an example

   b. Draw a conclusion

   c. Make a generalization

   d. Make a comparison

   e. Present a paradox

Passage #8

It is a frequent assumption of historians that the mechanization of work had a revolutionary effect on the social and economic position of the lives of the people who operate the new machines and on the society into which those machines are introduced. For example, it has been suggested that the role of women in European and American society was fundamentally altered beginning in the nineteenth century, when women workers first entered factories in large numbers. Friedrich Engels predicted at that time that women would be liberated from the "social, legal, and economic subordination" of the domestic sphere.

Recent historical scholarship, however, has undertaken a major revision of the theory that technology is always inherently revolutionary in its effects on society. Recast in this light, the employment of young women in textile mills during the Industrial Revolution was not an exodus from an established place in family hierarchy, but largely an extension of an older pattern of employment of young, single women as domestics. Some historians now believe that such dramatic innovations as the sewing machine, the typewriter, and the vacuum cleaner in no way resulted in an equally dramatic change in women's social and economic position, either at home or at work. It was not, for example, the change in office technology, but rather the segregation of secretarial work, previously considered an apprenticeship for beginning managers, from administrative work that led in the 1880s to a new class of "women's work." In other words, by becoming a "dead-end job," secretarial work automatically became the province of women. Fundamentally the conditions under which women work has changed little: segregation of work by gender, lower pay for women, and unskilled work with little chance of advancement all persist, while the demands of the domestic sphere remain a pressing factor in the lives of most women.

1. Which of the following statements best summarizes the primary idea of the passage?

    a. The effects of mechanization of women's work have not borne out the commonly held notion that new technology is intrinsically revolutionary.

    b. Recent studies suggest that mechanization revolutionizes the traditional values and gender roles of those societies into which it is introduced.

    c. Mechanization has changed the nature of women's work since the Industrial Revolution.

    d. The mechanization of work creates whole new classes of jobs, which previously were nonexistent.

    e. The mechanization of women's work has not, on the whole, resulted in the sort of deleterious effects predicted by traditional historical scholarship.

2. It can be inferred from the passage that the author would consider which of the following an indication that the nature of women's work has undergone a fundamental alteration?

    a. Statistics showing that the majority of women now have white-collar jobs.

    b. Surveys of married men showing that husbands now do some household tasks.

    c. Census results showing the recent creation of a new class of jobs in electronics in which women workers outnumber men six to one.

    d. Analysis of the labor market showing that, on average, the wages and salaries offered to women are as high as those of working men.

    e. Enrollment figures from universities showing that increasing numbers of women are obtaining Master's and Ph.D. degrees.

Passage #9

A photograph depicts objective reality, but only as much as a camera is capable of capturing it. It depicts as well the photographer's temperament, implicit in the selection and framing of his or her subject. To take a picture is to simultaneously annex the objective world and to express the singular self. Thus two antithetical ideals arise from the camera's ability to capture a slice of reality: in the first, photography is about the world, the photographer merely its passive recorder. In the second, photography is the instrument of an expressive, searching subjectivity, and the photographer's decisions as artist and chronicler count for everything.

The conflict between these ideals arises from a fundamental uneasiness on the part of both photographers and viewers towards the aggressive component inherent in "taking" a picture. Hence the ideal of the photographer as observer: such an ideal implicitly denies that picture-taking is an aggressive act. The issue, however, is not so clear-cut. Photographers can neither be characterized as aggressive predators, nor as simply, and essentially, as benevolent artists. Consequently, one ideal of picture-taking or the other is always being rediscovered and championed.

---

1. According to the passage, the two conflicting ideals of photography differ primarily in the

    a. Means with which each requires that photographers work.

    b. Value that each places on the beauty of the finished product

    c. Way in which each defines the photographer's role.

    d. Level of skill required of each of the photographers

    e. Emphasis that each places on the psychological impact of the finished product

2. In context, "essentially" means most closely:

    a. significantly

    b. basically

    c. importantly

    d. pressing

    e. interestingly

Passage #10

The crash of 1929 and Great Depression marked the transition from an American governmental policy guided by the ideals of rugged individualism to a new era of expanded federal powers. While Roosevelt's New Deal failed in its central goal of relieving economic depression, it increased the role of the federal government in the lives of individuals and communities and provided the framework for a later welfare system.

During the first few years of the Depression, the Hoover administration did little to assume a federal role in relief efforts, a policy reflecting the belief that the "boom and bust" cycle was a natural part of the capitalist system, and that the economy and its attendant social problems should right themselves without government help. Instead, Hoover focused on "restoring business confidence" through aid to corporations, privatized and government industries. As conditions worsened, however, public opinion shifted against Hoover, and Roosevelt's platform of economic reform was eagerly embraced in the election of 1932. In contrast to Hoover's policies, Roosevelt's efforts, collectively known as the "New Deals," reflected a belief in the power of the government to set the economy right and to aid individuals in distress. In attempting to turn the Depression, a barrage of reform measures passed during the first "Hundred Days" of Roosevelt's term marked the beginning of a new role for government in social affairs.

---

1. Which of the following would have likely been a part of Hoover's relief efforts?

    a. Government credit to failing banks and railroad companies

    b. The creation of public jobs for the unemployed

    c. Funds to provide public housing and improve slums

    d. Relief funds for the disabled and elderly

    e. Government assistance of private and religious charities

2. Which of the following would most likely follow this passage?

    a. A discussion of the causes of the Depression

    b. A discussion of how the reform measures passed by Roosevelt differed from the policies of his predecessors

    c. A discussion of the impact of the Depression on American businesses.

    d. A discussion of the failures of Roosevelt's New Deals to address the structural causes of economic problems

    e. An analysis of the efficacy of Hoover's policies in comparison to Roosevelt's

Answers and Explanations

Here are answers and explanations to the example passages.

Passage 1

1. b. An "ineffable heart and soul" means an "inde-scribable heart and soul," and the passage states: "to claim that there is something inexplicable and indefinable about the heart of the music ... is to make a mistake."

2. a. "Fortuitous" implies coincidence or chance; it doesn't have a positive or negative connotation.

Passage 2

1. c. The clue is that "In fact, Dickinson's inner life as an artist was closely intertwined with the intense emotional relationships that she cultivated on paper, her 'avoidance' of human encounters notwithstanding."

2. c. The clue is that "her life ... eludes easy exam-ination. An intensely private person, Dickinson played out her life's dramas, not in actions, but in poems, essays, and correspondence." The rest of the passage supports and elaborates upon this statement.

Passage 3

1. e. The clue is that the passage, in numerous sentences, seeks to contradict the following "misinterpretation": "a resistance to crediting Hansberry with the subtlety necessary for such intentional irony has led many critics to inter-pret the play's thematic conflicts as mere confu-sion, inconsistency, or eclecticism." Instead of confusion or inconsistency, the passage stresses that Hansberry maintained thematic coherence.

2. d. The author of the passage counters the claim that Hansberry lacks the skills to create intentional irony. The claim that a painter cre-ates a humorous effect unintentionally because he lacks skills is very similar to the claim made by Hansberry's critics.

Passage 4

1. c. The passage says that Johnson "quotes" spirituals, not that he composes them.

2. a. The passage states that jazz, blues, spiritu-als, and popular music were "genres foreign to most classical musicians."

3. d. The author notes that Johnson is respected as a jazz musician and composer, but that he was also, "however," an innovator in the sym-phonic tradition. "However" suggests that the author is pointing out a fact not commonly recognized.

Passage 5

1. b. The only statement supported by the pas-sage is that some newspapers were proponents of progressive, republican values, which were opposed to proponents of traditional values.

2. e. The editors claimed that they told all sides of a story, but instead of doing so, they repre-sented "intensely partisan ideologies" in their newspapers. Therefore their claims were insin-cere, or deceitful.

Passage 6

1. e. The passage compares two broad categories of reasons for vegetarianism: those associated with individual morality, and those associated with political activism.

2. b. The passage seeks to contrast two different broad categories of reasons for being a vegetarian: those reasons associated with morality, and those associated with political activism.

Passage 7

1. c. The clue is that theories of linguists and of economists directly contradict each other. Wherever we have a contradiction between theories, the contradiction is relevant because it supplies opposing arguments with which to evaluate the respective theories.

2. e. A paradox is something that is self-contradictory. The fact that two theories contradict each other is not a paradox; it would be a paradox only if one theory contradicted itself. The fact that a particular theory does not address all the instances of a phenomenon is also not a paradox, it simply reveals the limits of the theory.

Passage 8

1. a. The main point of the passage is summed up in the first sentence: scholars are finding evidence against the theory that "technology is always inherently revolutionary in its effects on society."

2. d. The author cited inequality of pay as one of the reasons that women's work has not changed fundamentally, so evidence against this assumption might change his opinion.

Passage 9

1. c. The two conflicting ideals define the role of the photographer: according to one, he is a passive recorder, according to the second a subjective artist.

2. b. "Essentially" refers, in this context, to the mistake of reducing a complex role to its "essentials" or basics.

Passage 10

1. a. The clue is that Hoover focused on "restoring business confidence" by helping businesses, rather than fixing "attendant social problems," i.e., problems of joblessness, hunger, and so forth.

2. b. Because the emphasis of the passage is on how Roosevelt's New Deal ushered in a "new era of expanded federal powers," one would expect in the next paragraph to find out how his reform measures were revolutionary, i.e., how they differed from all that had gone before.

Reading Usage Questions

The GRE will have a few reading questions that ask about "reading usage." For these questions, you'll be asked to identify certain usage techniques. Often, you won't be given answer choices. Rather, you'll be asked to highlight the portion of the passage that answers the question.

For example, a reading usage question may ask you to select a sentence that quotes an authority, suggests an alternative approach, or asks a question. These would be fairly easy usage questions.

The more tricky usage questions will require you to interpret the question and the sentence in the passage to which it refers. Such a question may ask you to identify the sentence that "implies an error" or "contradicts a previous statement."

Here's the quick guide to what you need to know about usage questions.

1. Usage questions often simply restate something from the passage. For example, the question might ask you to choose the sentence where ideas "converge." You need to find a synonym for "converge" in the passage. Often, it's simply a matter of translating the question into something that was mentioned in the passage.

2. You need to carefully read and fully understand the question before going to the passage. ETS counts on you reading the question too quickly and only having a vague idea of what it's asking. If you go to the passage without a clear understand of what the question asks, you're doomed.

3. As with all short passages, read the question first, and then read the entire passage. It's very important that you read the entire passage before choosing an answer. Often, a sentence near the beginning of the passage will "almost" answer the question. Don't be fooled by choosing it! Read the entire passage, then choose the best answer.

Reading Usage Practice

Here are three reading usage questions based on the short passages we read earlier in this chapter. Answers and explanations are at the end of this chapter.

Reading Usage Question #1

Though often misinterpreted, Lorraine Hansberry's *Raisin in the Sun* neither rejects integration nor denies the moral promise of the American dream. The play rather critically examines the incomplete realization of this dream, while remaining loyal to its basic premise. Recognition of this dual vision allows us to avoid attributing "unintentional" irony to the work. Instead, we can accept the work's ironic nuances as deliberate social commentary. Curiously, a resistance to crediting Hansberry with the subtlety necessary for such intentional irony has led many critics to interpret the play's thematic conflicts as mere confusion, inconsistency, or eclecticism. Isaacs, for example, refuses to find Hansberry's concerns for her own race reconcilable with ideals of human solidarity. But the play's complex view of Black self-regard and human reconciliation as compatible is no more "contradictory" than Du Bois's famous, well-thought-out ideal of an ethnic self-awareness that accommodates a sense of human unity, or Fanon's emphasis on an ideal internationalism capable of coexisting with national identities and roles.

This question has no answer choices. Select a sentence in the passage in which the author uses examples to argue against a stance taken by critics cited earlier in the passage.

Reading Usage Question #2

It is a frequent assumption of historians that the mechanization of work had a revolutionary effect on the social and economic position of the lives of the people who operate the new machines and on the society into which those machines are introduced. For example, it has been suggested that the role of women in European and American society was fundamentally altered beginning in the nineteenth century, when women workers first entered factories in large numbers. Friedrich Engels predicted at that time that women would be liberated from the "social, legal, and economic subordination" of the domestic sphere.

Recent historical scholarship, however, has undertaken a major revision of the theory that technology is always inherently revolutionary in its effects on society. Recast in this light, the employment of young women in textile mills during the Industrial Revolution was not an exodus from an established place in family hierarchy, but largely an extension of an older pattern of employment of young, single women as domestics. Some historians now believe that such dramatic innovations as the sewing machine, the typewriter, and the vacuum cleaner in no way resulted in an equally dramatic change in women's social and economic position, either at home or at work. It was not, for example, the change in office technology, but rather the segregation of secretarial work, previously considered an apprenticeship for beginning managers, from administrative work that led in the 1880s to a new class of "women's work." In other words, by becoming a "dead-end job," secretarial work automatically became the province of women. Fundamentally the conditions under which women work has changed little: segregation of work by gender, lower pay for women, and unskilled work with little chance of advancement all persist, while the demands of the domestic sphere remain a pressing factor in the lives of most women.

This question has no answer choices. Select a sentence in the passage in which the author gives a counterexample to the assumptions about the impact of technology on society now questioned by historians.

Reading Usage Question #3

A photograph depicts objective reality, but only as much as a camera is capable of capturing it. It depicts as well the photographer's temperament, implicit in the selection and framing of his or her subject. To take a picture is to simultaneously annex the objective world and to express the singular self. Thus two antithetical ideals arise from the camera's ability to capture a slice of reality: in the first, photography is about the world, the photographer merely its passive recorder. In the second, photography is the instrument of an expressive, searching subjectivity, and the photographer's decisions as artist and chronicler count for everything.

The conflict between these ideals arises from a fundamental uneasiness on the part of both photographers and viewers toward the aggressive component inherent in "taking" a picture. Hence the ideal of the photographer as observer: such an ideal implicitly denies that picture-taking is an aggressive act. The issue, however, is not so clear-cut. Photographers can neither be characterized as aggressive predators, nor as simply, and essentially, as benevolent artists. Consequently, one ideal of picture-taking or the other is always being rediscovered and championed.

This question has no answer choices. Select a sentence that best expresses the dualistic nature of photography.

Answer for Reading Usage Question 1

But the playwright's complex view of Black self-regard and human reconciliation as compatible is no more "contradictory" than Du Bois's famous, well-thought-out ideal of an ethnic self-awareness that accommodates a sense of human unity, or Fanon's emphasis on an ideal internationalism capable of coexisting with national identities and roles.

Explanation

The critical stance cited earlier is that Hansberry's play is full of self-contradictions and unintentional irony. The sentence cited claims that Hansberry's complex views are not self-contradictory, and supports this claim by giving examples of similarly well-thought-out, complex views.

Answer for Reading Usage Question 2

It was not, for example, the change in office technology, but rather the segregation of secretarial work, previously considered an apprenticeship for beginning managers, from administrative work that led in the 1880s to a new class of "women's work."

Or:

Recast in this light, the employment of young women in textile mills during the Industrial Revolution was not an exodus from an established place in family hierarchy, but largely an extension of an older pattern of employment of young, single women as domestics.

Explanation

Both of these sentences show that new jobs for women, supposedly created by technological innovations, did not fundamentally change the position of women in society. The women factory workers continued a pattern of work established as domestics, while the women secretaries took on work in the office that men no longer considered worthwhile because it no longer led to advancements.

Answer for Reading Usage Question 3

To take a picture is to simultaneously annex the objective world and to express the singular self.

Explanation

The dualistic nature of photography is that it is both subjective and objective; in other words, it captures or claims the "objective world" but it is also a means of expressing the artist's—the individual's—subjective opinions.

The Least You Need to Know

◆ Whereas the questions for long passages ask you to find specific information (and usually give you line numbers), the questions for short passages are usually more general.

◆ To ace the shorter critical reading passages, read the questions before reading the actual passage.

◆ Read the passage carefully until you've answered the question.

◆ Read all five answer choices. Weed out the choices that are not possible. Pick the best choice from what remains.

◆ Make sure you read all five answer choices— do *not* stop at choice 2 because "it seems right." Read all five answer choices every time and look for wrong answers first—they are *much* easier to spot.

10

Short Logic Passages

In This Chapter

- ◆ Quick logic review
- ◆ Identifying the facts and the conclusion
- ◆ Ten passages to practice on
- ◆ Answers and explanations

Mixed in with your sentence completions and short and long reading passages will be a few "logic" passages. These passages are usually also short. They ask questions about the logic of the passage, usually an argument or analysis. The questions will focus on the passages' implications, assumptions, and conclusions.

Logic Review

An argument or analysis is based on three components: the data (or facts), the assumptions, and the conclusions or implications. The data is the starting point of an argument or analysis and the conclusion is the end. You link data to a conclusion or to implications by making assumptions. You can either make those assumptions explicitly or implicitly.

Here's an example:

> Four out of five dentists recommend this chewing gum.

That's an argument. The data or fact is the survey of dentists. The conclusion or implication is that you should consider chewing the gum (think of this argument as an advertisement). The assumption is that the survey is valid and represents more than just the opinion of four dentists.

Your job with any logic passage is to identify the "facts" and the conclusion. Usually, that's fairly easy. The more difficult part is to identify the assumptions. Remember: the assumption links the facts to the conclusion. So when you're trying to find the assumptions, just ask yourself "How do I get from the facts to the conclusion?"

Logic questions won't always ask you to find the assumptions, but finding the assumptions will be helpful in many regards. First, if you want to weaken or strengthen an argument, you're usually weakening or strengthening the assumptions. Second, if you're looking for "implications," then often you're trying to find the assumptions.

But don't overthink "implication" questions. Usually, an "implication" is just another way to state the conclusion. And keep in mind that no matter what the question is asking, the information is always in the passage. Unless the question explicitly asks you to add new information, you must work only with the information in the passage.

Ten Practice Passages

Now let's try ten logic passages. Answers and explanations are at the end of the chapter.

Passage 1

Warm-blooded animals maintain a constant body temperature through an elaborate system of physiological controls. Why should body temperature rise during sickness, a response to infection, which would apparently increase stress on the infected organism? Garibaldi was the first to suggest a relationship between fever and serum iron, which is known to fall in animals during infection. He discovered that microbial synthesis of siderophores—iron-binding substances—in the bacteria *Salmonella* declined at environmental temperatures above 37 degrees Celsius and stopped altogether at 40.3 degrees Celsius. To Garibaldi this suggested that fever made it more difficult for an infecting bacterium to acquire the iron it needs in order to multiply. Cold-blooded animals were used in an experiment to test this hypothesis, because their body temperature can be easily controlled in a laboratory setting. Kluger reported that iguanas infected with the potentially lethal bacterium *A. hydrophilia* were more likely to survive at temperatures of 42 degrees Celsius than at temperatures of 37 degrees Celsius, which is the environmental temperature healthy iguanas prefer. When animals at 42 degrees Celsius were injected with an iron solution, mortality rates were found to increase significantly. Research to investigate whether similar phenomena occur in warm-blooded animals is sorely needed.

Select the best answer choice:

1. Given the above information, what can be inferred about warm-blooded animals?

   a. The body temperature of warm-blooded animals is not easily controllable in the laboratory.

   b. Warm-blooded animals are more comfortable at an environmental temperature of 37 degrees Celsius than are cold-blooded animals.

c. In warm-blooded animals, bacteria are responsible for the production of siderophores, which in turn provide iron to the animal.

d. In warm-blooded animals, bacterial infections are responsible for most fevers.

2. If experimentation determined that "similar phenomena occur in warm-blooded animals," which of the following, assuming each is possible, would likely be the most effective treatment of bacterial infections in warm-blooded animals?

a. Administration of a medication to lower the body temperature of an infected animal.

b. Injection of an iron solution into infected animals.

c. Administration of a medication that renders serum iron unavailable to bacteria.

d. Reduction of the amount of iron in an infected animal's diet.

e. Exposure of the animal to an environmental temperature higher than 37 degrees Celsius.

Passage 2

It has been the policy at AnyInc to advertise job openings to current employees, and to refuse outside applicants if a suitably qualified AnyInc employee applies for the job. Strict adherence to this rule has been observed in the last two years, yet during that time, some entry-level jobs have been filled by people from outside the company, though numerous AnyInc employees have been qualified for these positions.

Select the best answer choice:

1. If the information provided is true, which of the following **must** also be true about AnyInc during the past two years?

a. Some entry-level positions were open, for which no qualified AnyInc employee applied.

b. Some entry-level positions were open, but were not advertised to AnyInc employees.

c. The total number of employees at AnyInc has gone up.

d. AnyInc hired certain people for jobs for which they had no qualifications.

e. All job openings at AnyInc in the last two years have been for entry-level positions.

Passage 3

How does sap move through a tree's circulatory system? A tall tree can transport hundreds of gallons of water a week from its roots to its highest twigs. Is this water somehow pulled from above, or is it propelled from below? Over the last century, most scientists have suspected the former: that the water is somehow "pulled." This theory of a "pull mechanism," first proposed in the late 1800s, relies on a property of water not commonly associated with liquids: its tensile strength. Water that evaporates from treetops actually "tugs" on the remaining water molecules, rather than breaking off cleanly, and this tug extends from molecule to molecule all the way down to the roots. The tree is actually a passive conduit in this system; all the work involved in the upward transportation of water comes from the sun, which provides the energy necessary for evaporation.

Select the best answer choice:

1. The passage's primary purpose is to:

   a. Refute a hypothesis supported by scientists

   b. Discuss the importance of a phenomenon

   c. Present a possible explanation of a phenomenon

   d. Contrast two schools of thought

   e. Discuss the origins of a theory

Consider **each** answer choice separately and select **all** that apply.

2. Which of the following statements is supported by the passage?

   a. The pull theory is not universally accepted by scientists.

   b. The pull theory depends on one of the physical properties of water.

   c. The pull theory was proposed at an earlier date than the push theory.

Passage 4

Biodiesel is a fuel derived from cultivated rapeseed. Production and use of biodiesel causes 35 percent less air pollution per gallon than does the production and use of regular diesel fuel. Replacing regular diesel with biodiesel would seem to be the obvious way to meet the government's plan to reduce diesel-related air pollution by 25 percent over the next decade. However, the greatest possible production of biodiesel would amount to only one percent of all diesel fuel production projected during the next 15 years.

Select the best answer choice:

1. This passage implies which of the following conclusions?

   a. Over the next 15 years, the use of biodiesel will increase by less than one percent.

   b. The production of biodiesel will be increased as fast as it is possible to increase it during the next 15 years.

   c. During the next 15 years, it will be impossible to meet the government's goal with respect to reducing air pollution solely by switching to biodiesel.

Passage 5

The discovery of distinctively shaped ceramic pots at various prehistoric sites scattered over a large geographic region has led archaeologists to question how the pots were spread. Some believe the pot makers migrated to the various sites, carrying the pots along with them; others believe that the pots were spread by trade, while their makers remained in one place. Now, analysis of the bones of prehistoric human skeletons has led some scientists to believe that high concentrations of a certain metallic element in the human skeleton is indicative of migration to a new location after childhood. Many of the bones found near the pots at a few sites showed high levels of this metallic element. Therefore some scientists conclude that the pots were spread by migration.

Select the best answer choice:

1. Which of the following could be inferred from the passage?

   a. Archaeologists now suspect that the pots in question were spread by trade.

   b. Archaeologists assume that the distinctive shape of the ceramic pots is indicative of their common cultural origin.

c. The sites in question were probably centers of trade.

d. Archaeologists believe that the pots were manufactured in order to store supplies during migration.

e. The high levels of the metallic element found in prehistoric skeletons of people who migrated are not to be found in the bones of modern people.

2. Which of the following facts would most directly weaken the conclusion that the pots were spread by migration?

   a. The style of the pots at the various sites was found to be uniform.

   b. The style of the pots at the various sites was found to differ subtly from site to site.

   c. Analysis of the pots revealed that the clay from which they were made came from a common source hundreds of miles away from the sites in which they were found.

   d. Comparably high levels of the same metallic element found in the prehistoric skeletons were also found in modern people who had lived their entire lives in the same regions as the sites where the pots were found.

   e. Ceramic pots of the same style were found at a new site that predated the sites analyzed by several thousands years.

Passage 6

Better Books is a newly opened bookstore in competition with Books&Breakfast, a combination café-and-bookstore in operation for twenty years. Better Books hires a consultant to find out why Books&Breakfast has a larger customer base than Better Books. The consultant recommends that Better Books open a café inside its bookstore in order to better compete with Books&Breakfast. To make space for the café, Better Books will have to discontinue the children's section, which will narrow its already-limited selection. The consultant, however, reasons that the children's books section will become less profitable in coming years, given that the last national census indicated a significant decline in the percent of the population who are under age 10.

Select the best answer choice:

1. Which of the following statements would most directly undermine the consultant's assumptions about Books&Breakfast's competitive edge over Better Books?

   a. Statistics indicate that book sales are declining nationwide.

   b. Studies show that customers are more likely to spend a significant amount of time in a bookstore if beverages are available for purchase.

   c. Books&Breakfast was suffering from declining sales before it opened its café.

   d. Books&Breakfast has a large customer base because it is well known for a wide selection of books on a variety of subjects.

   e. Better Books' customer base includes a high percentage of parents of teens.

2. Which of the following statements can be inferred from the passage?

   a. Better Books should open a café if it wants to attract as many customers as Books&Breakfast.

b. Books&Breakfast should hire a consultant to deal with the new competition offered by Better Books.

c. Better Books has a less-established client base than Books&Breakfast.

d. Better Books has suffered a recent decline in its customer base.

e. Books&Breakfast has a larger children's section than Better Books.

Passage 7

How did the earth acquire its oceans? According to one theory, water in the earth's oceans originated from comets. As the earth was being formed out of the collision of space rocks, the energy from those collisions and from the increasing gravitation of the planet made the entire planet molten, including the surface. Any water on the planet's surface would have evaporated and been released into space. As the planet approached its current size, its gravitation became strong enough to hold an atmosphere of gases and water vapor around the planet. Because comets are mostly ice made up of frozen water and gases, a comet striking Earth then would have vaporized. The water vapor that resulted would have been retained in the atmosphere, eventually falling as rain on the now cooled and solidified surface of Earth.

Select the best answer choice:

1. Which of the following would most directly undermine the theory discussed above?

a. Of all comet impacts with the earth, the vast majority occurred while the planet still had a molten surface and no atmosphere, while only a small number of relatively tiny comets have struck since the earth acquired an atmosphere.

b. As the planet approached its current size, volcanic activity increased, releasing steam and other gases into the atmosphere.

c. The atmospheric pressure increased as the earth cooled, slowing the rate of evaporation of water.

d. The earth's moon has no water, although it too has been struck by comets.

e. An analysis of a sample of water taken from a comet showed that it had a similar composition to the water found in the earth's oceans.

Consider **each** answer choice separately and select **all** that apply.

2. Which of the following statements is supported by the passage?

a. Earth's early atmosphere was probably formed largely by comets.

b. Earth's gravitation was weaker when it was first forming.

c. The space rocks which formed the body of Earth probably held very little water.

d. The comets which impacted with Earth were probably very large.

e. The atmosphere of early Earth was made up of gases released by volcanic activity.

Passage 8

In recent years, the music publishing industry has suffered tremendous loss of sales. One possible explanation is that performers, educational institutions, and nonprofit organizations have come to rely on copies of music scores, rather than originals.

As an example of the devastation wrought on the music publishing industry by the photocopier, one publishing executive noted that for a recent music festival involving 1,300 instrumentalists, the festival's coordinator purchased only 10 copies that were published by the executive's company of the music to be performed at the festival.

Select the best answer choice:

1. Which of the following would most directly weaken the support the example lends to the executive's claim that music publishers suffer a loss of sales because of the photocopier?

     a. Only one fourth of the 1,300 instrumentalists were involved in performing the music published by the executive's company.

     b. Over two thirds of the instrumentalists had already listened to the music they were expected to perform before they began to practice for the festival.

     c. Because of limited funding, the coordinator of the festival required instrumentalists to buy their own copies of the music performed at the festival.

     d. Each copy of music that was performed at the festival was shared by three instrumentalists.

     e. Publicity generated by the performance of the music at the festival bolstered public awareness of this type of music.

Passage 9

Studies have shown that over 65 percent of all traffic accidents occur within a 10-mile radius of the home of at least one of the drivers involved. This statistic indicates that drivers drive incautiously when they are close to home, perhaps because the familiarity of their surroundings gives them a false sense of security.

Select the best answer choice:

1. Which of the following might explain the above statistic without necessitating the assumption that drivers are more incautious near home?

     a. The places where people feel safest are actually the very places where they are at greatest risk of serious injury.

     b. 90 percent of drivers spend 90 percent of their total driving time within a 10-mile radius of their home.

     c. Less than 45 percent of traffic accidents occur outside of a 10-mile radius from the home of at least one of the drivers involved.

     d. Drivers in familiar surroundings are less likely to come to a complete halt at stop signs.

     e. Of the 65 percent of all traffic accidents occurring within a 10-mile radius, at least one of the drivers had been involved in a previous accident within the last 6 months.

Passage 10

The mental-health movement in the United States began when Dorothea Dix successfully campaigned for the national establishment of asylums where the mentally ill could be cared for. By the early 1900s, however, asylums were underfunded by the government, and became places where overcrowding, neglect, the use of force, and abuse were common. After World War II, however, new medications were discovered for some major mental illnesses previously thought untreatable (penicillin for syphilis of the brain and insulin treatment for depression and schizophrenia); newspaper exposés and books focused public attention on the plight of the mentally ill; and Dr. David Vai's Humane Practices Program was founded, becoming a model program for future efforts to reform other asylums. But substantial change took place only in the 1960s, when the civil-rights movement led lawyers to investigate America's disproportionately high population of black prisoners in jails and asylums. Patients' rights groups, formed by these lawyers, successfully lobbied for reform in the state legislatures.

Select the best answer choice:

1. It can be inferred from the passage that which of the following factors contributed to post–World War II reform of state mental institutions?

   a. An increase of funding provided by state legislatures to rehabilitate asylums.

   b. The invention of drugs to sedate and otherwise render passive mental patients.

   c. The discovery of effective treatments for illnesses that were previously considered untreatable.

   d. Realization that some criminal behavior is due to mental illness.

   e. Advances in penology that discredited the effectiveness of incarceration.

2. The passage provides information that would help answer all of the following questions EXCEPT:

   a. Who are some of the influential figures in the history of the public health movement in the United States?

   b. What were some of the mental illnesses that went untreated before the 1950s?

   c. What were some of the more influential legal cases that shaped the legislation of patients' rights?

   d. How did the civil-rights movement help to bring about the legislation of patients' rights?

Answers and Explanations

Here are the answers and explanations to the above passages.

Passage 1

1. a. The clue is the line "cold-blooded animals were used … because their body temperatures can be easily controlled." This implies that warm-blooded animals would have been used, were it not for the fact that their body temperature is not as easily controlled. Also, the fact that no experiments have been performed on warm-blooded animals to this date suggests there is some obstacle in undertaking such experiments.

2. c. The clue is that Garibaldi suspected that "fever made it more difficult for an infecting bacterium to acquire the iron it needs in order to multiply." So, according to Garibaldi, temperature only indirectly reduces mortality rates. Therefore a medication that had the same effect as fever without changing body temperature, namely reducing the availability of iron to pathogens, would be most effective if Garibaldi's hypothesis is true.

Passage 2

1. a. The clue is that "strict adherence to this rule has been observed, but some entry-level jobs

have been filled with people from outside the company." The only circumstance that they could have been hired in, according to the policy, is if no AnyInc employee had applied.

Passage 3

1. c. The clue is that only one explanation of the mechanism of sap circulation is described; therefore the purpose of the article can't be to contrast two different schools of thought. Although a brief mention is given of the theory's origin, it doesn't go into specifics and isn't the main point of the passage.

2. a. and b. There is no evidence in the passage that the pull theory was proposed at an earlier date than the push theory.

Passage 4

1. c. The clue is that "the greatest possible production of biodiesel would amount to only one percent of all diesel fuel production projected during the next 15 years." This means that biodiesel use cannot reduce total emissions by 35 percent.

Passage 5

1. b. The key is that archeologists wonder how the "pots were spread." They present two alternative theories: either, that the "pot makers" migrated, or that they sold the pots, which were then carried to distant locations. Both theories assume that the pots were made by "pot makers" of a specific culture, rather than theorizing that this unique shape could have been common to many different settled peoples over a wide geographic range.

2. d. If high levels of this metallic element are endemic to the regions where the bones were

found, then we **cannot** assume that these high levels are indicative of migration.

Passage 6

1. c. The consultant assumes that Books&Breakfast has a larger customer base because it has a café. Answer c directly contradicts this assumption: Books&Breakfast has a larger customer base because it is known for its wide selection of books.

2. c. The only thing that we can safely assume is that Better Books has a "less-established" client base, because it is "newly opened," while Books&Breakfast has a "larger" customer base and has been in operation for 20 years.

Passage 7

1. a. If the vast majority of comet impacts occurred when the earth had no atmosphere, this means they occurred when the earth was not large enough to retain an atmosphere. Consequently the water contained in the comets would have escaped into space. It seems likely that a "small number of tiny comets" whose water would have been retained in the atmosphere would not account solely for Earth's oceans.

2. b. The clue is that "as the planet approached its current size, its gravitation became strong enough … to hold an atmosphere." This means that while it was smaller, the earth had a weaker atmosphere than at present.

Passage 8

1. c. The executive assumes that photocopies were made from the 10 copies sold to the festival and then distributed to the instrumentalists. However, if each instrumentalist had bought an original copy of the music from

the publisher, then the music company may have sold 1,310 copies of music to the festival, instead of only 10.

Passage 9

1. b. The explanation offered by the passage is that drivers are less cautious when close to home. However, if the majority of drivers spend the majority of their time driving close to home, then this could be an explanation for why the majority of traffic accidents occur close to home, and does not necessarily imply that the drivers are less cautious.

Passage 10

1. c. The clue is that the word "however" contrasts pre-World War I conditions with post-World War II conditions, "when new medications were discovered for some major mental illnesses." This suggests that the medications helped lead to changes in care of the mentally ill.

2. c. There are no examples given of specific legal cases that were fought on behalf of the mentally ill.

The Least You Need to Know

◆ Logic questions focus on the passages' implications, assumptions, and conclusions.

◆ Your job with any logic passage is to identify the "facts" and the conclusion.

◆ Don't overthink "implication" questions.

◆ Keep in mind that no matter what the question is asking, the information is always in the passage.

Putting It All Together: Verbal Practice Set 1

28 Sentence Completion and Reading Questions

28 Questions. 40 minutes.

Each of the following questions includes a sentence with a blank indicating that something has been omitted. Select the answer choice that best completes the sentence.

1. Scientific studies suggest that the canine sense of smell is incredibly _____, capable of distinguishing between thousands of subtly differing chemical compounds.

   a. caustic
   b. keen
   c. sullied
   d. cavalier
   e. blunted

2. Writer William Faulkner was widely acclaimed for his experiments with the first-person narrative; in his books, the main characters' ability to relate the details of their stories in a unique manner is compelling enough to render any further commentary _____.

   a. inarticulate
   b. superfluous
   c. uncontestable
   d. subjective
   e. intransigent

Each of the following questions includes a sentence with a blank indicating that something has been omitted. Select the two answer choices that best complete the sentence.

3. A decision made before all the relevant factors have been considered could be seen as _____ _____.

    a. premature

    b. wise

    c. draconian

    d. impetuous

    e. just

    f. parsimonious

4. Famously reclusive, Jane Austen's isolation may have reflected her dedication to her _____ _____; some scholars hypothesize that she avoided conventional society, and even marriage, in order to concentrate on writing poetry.

    a. sabbatical

    b. vocation

    c. dowdiness

    d. craft

    e. ostracized

    f. music

5. Though lionized at the time by the press, the leader of the arctic expedition was later revealed to be not nearly as _____ _____ as he had been portrayed; in fact he vacillated over several essential decisions.

    a. heroic

    b. decisive

    c. resolute

    d. domineering

    e. indecisive

    f. irresolute

Questions 6–8 are based on the following reading passage:

The life of Lucy Terry, considered the first African American poet ever to be published, and that of her husband, Abijah Prince, can without hyperbole be described as extraordinary. Sold into slavery at age five in 1730, at age sixteen Terry achieved fame in the state of Massachusetts by writing a ballade about an Indian attack on the town in which she lived, Deerfield, Massachusetts. Abijah Prince's achievements were equally unusual for the time; by the time of his marriage to Terry, he had served in the state militia, bought his own freedom and that of his wife, and acquired farmland in Vermont and Massachusetts. So prominent was he in Vermont that he petitioned King George III to be recognized as a founder and grantee of the newly formed township of Sunderland. A patriotic family, the Princes sent two of their sons to fight for the colonies during the Revolutionary War.

The true test of the Prince family's mettle came not with war, but with attacks by Caucasian neighbors on the family's rights and property. In 1785 one of the family's farms in Guildford, Vermont, was destroyed by a wealthy neighboring farmer. In 1794, the boundaries of the family's Sunderland property were contested by the owner of a bordering farm. As Abijah was by that time incapacitated by old age, Lucy fought successfully for the rights of the family, in the first instance before the governor's council, and in the second before the Vermont Supreme Court. In the words of the judge presiding over the Sunderland case, Lucy "made a better argument than he had heard from any lawyer at the Vermont bar." It was the first time in the nascent country's history that a Black woman had wielded the tools of argumentation in order to win legal justice for herself and her family.

6. The author's tone can be described as:

    a. indignant over the social injustices suffered by the Prince family.

    b. reservedly optimistic about the future of race relations in the United States.

    c. lauding of Lucy and Abijah's achievements.

    d. confident that the examination of early American history reveals precedents for the Civil Rights movement.

    e. objective about the prosaic nature of the Princes' story.

7. The passage suggests that Lucy Terry was admired at every stage of her life for her:

    a. determination to reveal social injustice.

    b. mastery of the English language and of rhetoric.

    c. talents as a writer and as a literate Black woman.

    d. facility for speaking extemporaneously in public.

    e. ability to effectively organize people around a cause.

8. The passage states that Abijah did all of the following except:

    a. help to found a small Vermont community.

    b. fight the British in the American Revolution.

    c. own multiple plots of farmland.

    d. purchase his wife's freedom from slavery.

    e. join a militia during wartime.

Select the answer choice that best completes the sentence:

9. It would be methodologically _____ to assert that Neolithic peoples perceived costal areas as locales ideally suited for settlement given the _____ of sites from which to garner evidence.

    a. unsound … paucity

    b. insane … completion

    c. suspect … uperabundance

    d. inexorable … imperfection

    e. sound … dearth

10. That scientific advancement shapes daily life in contemporary culture is admitted by even its most vitriolic critics, but surprisingly, its ameliorative effects on society are frequently _____, even by its _____.

    a. recognized … partisans

    b. comprehended … benefactors

    c. questioned … apologists

    d. erased … detractors

    e. acquiesced to … detractors

11. It is only on the rarest of occasions that the athlete allows herself even minor indulgences; indeed, her adherence to her training regime is almost _____.

    a. languid

    b. sporadic

    c. corrosive

    d. efficacious

    e. obsessive

12. While female chimpanzees abandon their natal troops upon maturation, it has been observed that such defections rarely affect the overall size and composition of the troop because departed chimpanzees are _____ by young females from other troops.

    a. impugned

    b. rebuffed

    c. replaced

    d. bound

    e. reinstated

13. Immersed in unfamiliar culture settings, where rigid prices are _____, a nod can mean "no," and a smile can be a sign of _____, Canadian tourists may well react with "culture shock."

    a. autonomous … glee

    b. innumerable … agreeableness

    c. negotiable … anger

    d. mutable … happiness

    e. intransient … rancor

14. C. S. Lewis, Christian allegorist and author of *The Lion, the Witch and the Wardrobe*, would surely have disagreed with Anthony Burgess's statement that a novelist ought not _____, for the best fiction rarely has room for preaching.

    a. adjudicate

    b. patronize

    c. sermonize

    d. distend

    e. enlighten

Questions 15–18 are based on the following reading passage:

The following is from a work by Samuel Butler on evolution.

There are few things which strike us with more surprise, when we review the course taken by opinion in the last century, than the suddenness with which belief in witchcraft and demoniacal possession came to an end. This has been often remarked upon, but I am not acquainted with any record of the fact as it appeared to those under whose eyes the change was taking place, nor have I seen any contemporary explanation of the reasons which led to the apparently sudden overthrow of a belief which had seemed hitherto to be deeply rooted in the minds of almost all men. As a parallel to this, though in respect of the rapid spread of an opinion, and not its **decadence**, it is probable that those of our descendants who take an interest in ourselves will note the suddenness with which the theory of evolution, from having been generally ridiculed during a period of over a hundred years, came into popularity and almost universal acceptance among educated people.

It is indisputable that this has been the case; nor is it less indisputable that the works of Mr. Darwin and Mr. Wallace have been the main agents in the change that has been brought about in our opinions. The names of Cobden and Bright do not stand more prominently forward in connection with the repeal of the Corn Laws than do those of Mr. Darwin and Mr. Wallace in connection with the general acceptance of the theory of evolution. There is no living philosopher who has anything like Mr. Darwin's popularity with Englishmen generally; and not only this, but his power of fascination extends all over Europe, and indeed in every country in which civilization has obtained footing: not among the illiterate masses, though these are rapidly following the suit of the educated classes, but among experts and those who are most capable of judging. France, indeed—the country of Buffon and Lamarck—must be counted an exception to the general rule, but in England and Germany there are few men of scientific reputation who do not accept Mr. Darwin as the founder of what is commonly called "Darwinism," and regard him as perhaps the most penetrative and profound philosopher of modern times.

———————————————————

15. The author does which of the following in this passage?

    a. compares and contrasts two critical stances.

    b. asserts a causal relationship between the fall of a prevalent belief and the rise of a theory.

    c. describes the ascendance of a theory.

    d. refutes the importance of a figure in the rise of a theory

    e. describes the decay of a prevalent belief.

16. In the given context "decadence" most nearly means?

    a. decay

    b. particulars

    c. corruption

    d. ascendance

    e. acceptance

17. The author mentions Cobden and Bright in order to:

    a. stress the importance of the repeal of the Corn Laws for the promulgation of the theory of evolution.

    b. compare the fame of Darwin and Wallace to that of prominent politicians of the time.

    c. stress that the theory of evolution was as well-known to the general public in England at the time as were important political issues of the day.

    d. make a connection between the repeal of the Corn Laws by Cobden and Bright and the recession of superstition and ignorance in the wake of Darwin and Wallace's discoveries.

    e. assert the importance of Darwin and Wallace by comparing them to prominent politicians of the time.

18. This question has no answer choices. Select a sentence in which the author provides a counterexample to a generalization.

Question 19 is based on the following reading passage:

> Until recently, most inhabitants of Sedentaria made most of their purchases by driving to large commercial malls and chain stores. As most households now own one or more computers, however, the majority of inhabitants have switched to shopping on the Internet. Now, most purchases in Sedentaria are delivered by mail from companies well outside the Sedentaria metropolitan area. For many purchases, therefore, Sedentarians no longer need to drive to and from malls.

19. Which of the following conclusions is suggested by the passage?

    a. There will be an overall reduction in the consumption of vehicle fuel in the region of Sedentaria, as inhabitants no longer need to drive in order to shop.

    b. The commercial malls in the Sedentaria area have probably experienced a loss of sales from the inhabitants of Sedentaria.

    c. The rate of computer ownership in Sedentaria has risen as the demand for online shopping has risen.

    d. Commercial centers in Sedentaria have adapted to the change in shopping habits of consumers by offering delivery options and online purchasing.

e. The inhabitants in Sedentaria are able to find more competitive prices online than those offered by local stores.

Select the answer choice that best completes the passage:

20. Adhering to his altruistic principles, Greg _____ the _____ conviction of his business partner that a client is a simple source of revenue, whose needs are best approached as an opportunity to improve one's professional status.

    a. praised … diligent
    b. questioned … mercurial
    c. rejected … mercenary
    d. exonerated … lamentable
    e. lauded … questionable

21. The scientific community attempts to expose internal error through such self-corrective mechanisms as peer review. Thus it is appropriate for qualified readers of prestigious scientific journals to _____ work that seems based on _____ interpretations of experimental results.

    a. champion … flawed
    b. ignore … precise
    c. question … oblique
    d. honor … improbable
    e. criticize … improbable

22. Well aware that _____ was frowned upon in some circles, gallery owner Miranda Gomez was _____ to convey her elation at the success of her recent painting auction.

    a. ebullience … eager
    b. self-control … obliged
    c. enthusiasm … unashamed
    d. etiquette … forewarned
    e. impulsiveness … prepared

23. Although not uncritical of the proposed design of the art gallery, the planning committee eventually gave the architect's designs its _____ approval.

    a. unqualified
    b. qualified
    c. critical
    d. hesitant
    e. delayed

Question 24 is based on the following reading passage:

Milk and dairy products are good sources of phosphorus, vitamin D, and calcium, substances essential for bone growth and maintenance. It is therefore commonly believed that a diet rich in dairy products can help to prevent osteoporosis, a multifactorial disorder in which nutrition plays a significant, but not exclusive, role. Osteoporosis is associated with a high rate of bone fractures, because the disorder weakens the bones as a person ages. Recently a long-term experiment involving a large number of participants found that those participants who consistently consumed the recommended amount of dairy products or of calcium supplements throughout the years of the study had a higher rate of bone fractures than any other participants in the study. The experiment design carefully regulated and observed the dairy or calcium intake of the participants: some patients were assigned to consume a calcium supplement daily, others were assigned to consume the recommended amount of dairy servings daily, and others were assigned to eat less than the recommended amount of calcium supplements or dairy servings daily. The experiment therefore concluded that a diet rich in dairy products or calcium may actually increase the risk of osteoporosis, rather than decreasing it.

24. Which of the following would most directly undermine the design of the experiment, and therefore its stated conclusion?

   a. Dairy sources of calcium are at least as efficacious in protecting against osteoporosis as are calcium supplements.

   b. The protein and sodium contents of dairy foods do not adversely affect the bone benefit of the dairy package of calcium, phosphorus, protein, and vitamin D.

   c. The principal reason for failure to find an association in most observational studies is the weakness of the methods available for estimating long-term calcium intake.

   d. The participants in the study who regularly consumed the recommended amount of calcium supplements or dairy products were also those patients already at high risk or suffering from bone fractures and osteoporosis.

   e. Of 52 other investigator-controlled calcium intervention studies, all but two showed reduced bone loss in the elderly, or reduced fracture risk for those patients who ate recommended amounts of dairy products.

Questions 25–27 are based on the following reading passage:

The dominant image of Benny Carter as a big-band arranger and jazz composer is belied by his multifaceted talents and his chameleon-like career changes. For example, it is little known that Carter was a virtuosic improviser on the alto saxophone, well respected by colleagues. His innovative solos on the instrument featured long, sinuous melodic lines and a rhythmic vitality which eschewed clichéd "arpeggio work" and technically tortuous scale runs. He also taught himself to play trumpet, did recording work on five other instruments, sang, and occasionally wrote song lyrics. Perhaps emblematic of his versatility was the aplomb with which he met the shift from swing to bebop. It was a shift that left many of his contemporaries, among them Benny Goodman, playing for the "nostalgia market"; Carter chose instead to adopt bebop's offbeat rhythms and dissonant harmonies. It is hardly surprising, then, that Carter's recording career spanned almost three quarters of a century, from 1928 to 1996.

25. What is most probably meant by the "nostalgia market"?

   a. members of the public still enamored of the swing style

   b. audience members attracted to melancholy songs about the past

   c. musicians still selling the big-band music of the "jazz 20s"

   d. members of the public still enamored of the bebop style

   e. members of the public still enamored of the alto saxophone

26. Which of the following is Carver best known as by the public?

    a. big-band arranger

    b. virtuosic soloist

    c. versatile instrumentalist

    d. lyricist

    e. "bebop" composer

27. This question has no answer choices. Select a sentence in which the author provides an example refuting a commonly held view.

Question 28 is based on the following reading passage:

GenericInc is a large, highly diversified company. Seven years ago, it built two new office buildings in two different regions, region Alpha and region Beta. GenericInc hired two different construction companies to complete the two buildings: Dieser and Jener. Jener has a stable workforce with little employee turnover, while Dieser is a relatively new company started only 15 years ago. The two buildings had virtually identical floor plans, yet the building constructed by Dieser in region Alpha cost 40 percent more to build than the building constructed by Jener in region Beta. Furthermore, the building constructed by Dieser cost 50 percent more to operate over the last seven years, both in terms of maintenance and in terms of energy consumption. The president of GenericInc therefore recommends that GenericInc discontinue its contract with Dieser and use Jener for all future construction needs.

28. Which of the following would most directly undermine the conclusion of the president?

    a. Jener recently constructed a building in region Beta that cost 30 percent less to operate than the building constructed there by Dieser, but which cost 10 percent more to construct.

    b. Dieser must have constructed its building less efficiently in terms of heat insulation and the durability of building materials than Jener.

    c. Because Dieser is a new company, it is bound to have increased its efficiency since its operation seven years ago.

    d. A study suggests the difference in cost of construction and maintenance of the two buildings is due to regional differences and the diversified nature of the operations of GenericInc.

    e. Jener has recently undergone a shift in management and will be increasing its operational costs by 2 percent.

Answers

1. b. keen

2. b. superfluous

3. a. premature, d. impetuous

4. b. vocation, d. craft

5. c. resolute

6. c. lauding of Lucy and Abijah's achievements

7. b. mastery of the English language and of rhetoric

8. b. fight the British in the American Revolution

9. a. unsound … paucity

10. c. questioned … apologists

11. e. obsessive

12. c. replaced

13. c. negotiable … anger

14. c. sermonize

15. c. describe the ascendance of a theory.

16. a. decay

17. b. compare the fame of Darwin and Wallace to that of prominent politicians of the time.

18. France, indeed—the country of Buffon and Lamarck—*must be counted an exception to the general rule*, but in England and Germany …

19. b. The commercial malls and stores in the Sedentaria area have probably experienced a loss of sales from the inhabitants of Sedentaria.

20. c. rejected … mercenary

21. e. criticize … improbable

22. c. enthusiasm … unashamed

23. b. qualified

24. d. The participants in the study who regularly consumed the recommended amount of calcium supplements or dairy products were also those patients already at risk or suffering from bone fractures and osteoporosis.

25. a. members of the public still enamored of the swing style.

26. a. big band arranger.

27. For example, it is little known that Carter was a virtuosic improviser on the alto saxophone, well respected by colleagues.

28. d. A study suggests the difference in cost of construction and maintenance of the two buildings is due to the difference in region and the diversified nature of the operations of GenericInc.

Putting It All Together: Verbal Practice Set 2

28 Sentence Completion and Reading Questions

28 Questions. 40 minutes.

Each of the following questions includes a sentence with a blank indicating that something has been omitted. Select the answer choice that best completes the sentence.

1. Rarely remaining at a given site for more than two days, the paleobotanist enjoyed the decidedly _____ life she led while collecting specimens.

    a. erratic
    b. insidious
    c. nomadic
    d. cacophonous
    e. imperceptible

2. Though scientists have shown that time and space are relative, most people continue to believe that a ticking clock measures _____ phenomenon.

    a. an illusory
    b. a tentative
    c. an absolute
    d. a caustic
    e. an extraordinary

Each of the following questions includes a sentence with a blank indicating that something has been omitted. Select the two answer choices that best complete the sentence.

3. Though the head injury permanently disrupted his capacity for rational thought, John's memories and moral sensibility miraculously remained _____ _____.

    a. intact

    b. preternatural

    c. inaccessible

    d. consistent

    e. impassive

    f. impetuous

4. Her disarmingly forthright demeanor and the fearlessness with which she faced the consequences of her words marked her as an unusually _____ _____ candidate.

    a. discreet

    b. amenable

    c. blunt

    d. candid

    e. judicious

    f. politic

Questions 5–7 are based on the following reading passage.

Rivers are boundaries, regions of flux in the physical, biological, and cultural landscape. A river may divide politically, may serve as the cartographer's handiest means of separating one political state from another. But in the natural world, static "divisions" do not exist; fluid "edges" do. And "edges" are by no means tidy places; they are zones of activity where trade and collision and all imaginable forms of interactions ferment. In short, "edges" are in the biological sense as vibrant as humanity's urban "centers" are in the cultural sense. The melting pot of New York has its counterpart in the mudflats of the Mississippi. Both are crowded, raucous, and wild. Expect the unexpected on a river.

Furthermore, rivers have a destination. They lead us seaward, they invite us to that greatest of all boundaries—the distant horizon where sea meets sky. But cloud-watching is not the province of river travelers; for meditation, the **pilgrim** must journey to the plains, those oceans of grass ascending into the highlands. The river carves out its lowest possible course, but the plains direct our gaze upward. Rivers turn corners, wear down banks, treacherously hide shallows and shoals; in short demand attention. The plains expand lazily, featureless and grand, inspiring contemplation of the unhindered and the immutable. A river defines the edges of a space, but a plain reveals infinity.

5. How is a river an "edge" in the biological sense, according to this passage?

    a. It is a place in which groups intermingle.

    b. It is a barrier set up between different types of people.

    c. It is a place of refuge in contrast to metropolitan areas.

    d. It is a topological feature of the landscape that is always in flux.

    e. It represents conflict between two irreconcilable modes of life.

6. In the passage, the author suggests that perspectives facilitated by plains and rivers are similar in that plains:

    a. are crammed with the occurrence of the unexpected.

    b. manifest various ecological changes.

c. provide an unhindered and pristine understanding of Nature.

d. are not themselves objects of reflection, but instead inspire reflection.

e. direct our gaze upward.

7. In context, **pilgrim** means most closely which of the following?

    a. puritan

    b. traveler

    c. priest

    d. disciple

    e. cloud-watcher

Questions 8–9 are based on the following reading passage.

Taken from a book by Clement A. Miles.

A carol, in the modern English sense, may perhaps be defined as a religious song, less formal and solemn than the ordinary Church hymn—an expression of **popular** and often naîve devotional feeling, a thing intended to be sung outside rather than within church walls. There still linger about the word some echoes of its original meaning, for "carol" had at first a secular or even pagan significance: in twelfth-century France it was used to describe the amorous song-dance which hailed the coming of spring; in Italian it meant a ring- or song-dance; while by English writers from the thirteenth to the sixteenth century it was used chiefly of singing joined with dancing, and had no necessary connection with religion. Much as the mediaeval Church, with its ascetic tendencies, disliked religious dancing, it could not always suppress it; and in Germany, there was choral dancing at Christmas round the cradle of the Christ Child. Whether Christmas carols were ever danced to in England is doubtful; many

of the old airs and words have, however, a glee and playfulness as of human nature following its natural instincts of joy even in the celebration of the most sacred mysteries. It is probable that some of the carols are religious **parodies** of love-songs, written for the melodies of the originals, and many seem by their structure to be indirectly derived from the choral dances of farm folk, a notable feature being their burden or refrain, a survival of the common outcry of the dancers as they leaped around at Christmastide to drink a cup and take a gift, and bring good fortune upon the house—predecessors of those carol-singers of rural England in the nineteenth century, whom Mr. Hardy depicts so delightfully in "Under the Greenwood Tree." On the whole, in spite of some mystical exceptions, the mediaeval English carol is somewhat external in its religion; there is little deep individual feeling; the caroller sings as a member of the human race.

8. All of the following are mentioned as original meanings of the word "carol" EXCEPT:

    a. a celebration of the changing of the seasons.

    b. a dance or song to be performed in a circle.

    c. the connection of song and dance.

    d. a song or dance with pre-Christian religious significance.

    e. a religious parody of love songs.

9. In the context in which it appears, **parodies** most closely means:

    a. profanes

    b. imitations

    c. denunciations

    d. ersatz

    e. sources

10. This question has no answer choices. Select a sentence in which the author hypothesizes about the possible origins of the <u>melodic and structural components of English carols.</u>

Select the answer choice that best completes the sentence:

11. As a young man, Jean Toomer fiercely resisted the _____ facets of his racial heritage, seeking to integrate them until they might _____, rather than battle one another.

    a. disparate … admonish

    b. contrary … complement

    c. divergent … dispel

    d. inexplicable … surpass

    e. inverted … induce

12. Respiration—the process of oxygen consumption—produces such _____ byproducts that almost all organisms that breathe have evolved elaborate mechanisms to counter the effects of such metabolic waste.

    a. inefficient

    b. erratic

    c. indispensable

    d. toxic

    e. compounded

13. It is somewhat farcical that a new book tracing the cultural history of cartoons should approach its subject matter with such gravity, as if its subject matter were indeed _____.

    a. droll

    b. morbid

    c. pedantic

    d. weighty

    e. ludicrous

14. In his seminal watercolors James Audubon united art and _____, an approach that subsequent guides to birds have often adopted.

    a. anthropology

    b. topology

    c. science

    d. ornithology

    e. entomology

15. Donkeys are not usually known for docility; indeed their famous _____ is reflected in the expression, "as stubborn as a mule."

    a. optimism

    b. complacency

    c. intractability

    d. tameness

    e. laziness

16. Introspective by nature and reclusive by force of habit, the author _____ public appearances and conducted all interviews and contacts through correspondence.

    a. eschewed

    b. enforced

    c. overcame

    d. endorsed

    e. relished

17. Her drab attire, nondescript features, and retiring attitude made her the perfect spy, so _____ with her surroundings that she was nearly impossible to _____.

    a. vexed … dislodge

    b. blended … discern

    c. harmonized … interrupt

    d. impatient … distinguish

    e. integrated … classify

18. The phrase "too much of a good thing can kill you" is certainly applicable to the world of medicine, where substances that are _____ in small doses can be _____ in large.

    a. malignant … beneficent
    b. neutral … benign
    c. curative … toxic
    d. useless … effective
    e. beneficial … miraculous

Questions 19–20 are based on the following reading passage.

Taken from a book by Thomas Troward.
It is an old saying that "Order is Heaven's First Law," and like many other old sayings it contains a much deeper philosophy than appears immediately on the surface. Getting things into a better order is the great secret of progress, and we are now able to fly through the air, not because the laws of Nature have altered, but because we have learnt to arrange things in the right order to produce this result—the things themselves had existed from the beginning of the world, but what was wanting was the introduction of a Personal Factor which, by an intelligent perception of the possibilities contained in the laws of Nature, should be able to bring into working reality ideas which previous generations would have laughed at as the absurd fancies of an unbalanced mind. The lesson to be learnt from the practical aviation of the present day is that of the triumph of principle over precedent, of the working out of an idea to its logical conclusions in spite of the accumulated testimony of all past experience to the contrary; and with such a notable example before us can we say that it is futile to enquire whether by the same method we may not unlock still more important secrets and gain some knowledge of the unseen causes which are at the back of external and visible conditions, and then by bringing these unseen causes into a better order make practical working realities of possibilities which at present seem but fantastic dreams?

19. The author would likely consider which of the following most representative of the process by which "progress" is made?

    a. A child rebels against his mother's advice, but later comes to see the mother was right.
    b. A president relies on the advice of his predecessors and wins a political battle.
    c. An architect builds a bridge which other architects are certain will fall; however, it stands.
    d. A philosopher writes a treaty that brilliantly defends the work of a previous philosopher against a new, critical attack by a rival scholar.
    e. A chemist discovers by accident that a certain substance can protect against skin cancer.

20. In context, what does the author mean by the phrase "it is futile to enquire whether by the same method we may not unlock still more important secrets and gain some knowledge of the unseen causes which are at the back of external and visible conditions"?

    a. It is useless to predict what future advances may be made in science, because we have already exhausted the limits of the possible.

b. It is frivolous to speculate about the future, because such speculations have always proven false.

c. It is useless to question the idea that the future will bring progress, because experience shows that it will.

d. It is advantageous to enquire into the hidden causes of things, because this is how the fantasies of a previous generation turn into the realities of the present.

e. Future progress will be made by those who question the worth of previous inventions.

Question 21 is based on the following reading passage.

Tree-ring dating, or dendrochronology, is based on the scientific analysis of tree-ring growth patterns. Most trees in temperate zones grow a new layer of tissue under the bark each year, which in cross-section appears as a "ring" delineated by darker tissue. The width of this ring is subject to climate variation: a wide ring results from adequate rainfall and sunlight, a narrow ring from drought. In a process known as cross-dating, dendrochronologists compare tree-ring growth patterns from many trees of various species in a given geographic region and from this build up an average chronology of the region. Thus, dendrochronologists can match known historical changes in the climate in a region with the pattern of an individual tree's growth rings and determine the age of the wood precisely. Curiously, trees growing in semiarid, adverse conditions are the most sensitive to climatic changes and often live the longest, providing the most reliable dating.

21. The process of cross-dating relies directly on which of the following assumptions?

a. Patterns of narrow and wide tree ring growth will tend to be similar for trees growing in the same region and subject to the same climatic conditions.

b. Trees growing in a semiarid environment will respond differently to climatic change than trees growing in more temperate zones.

c. Patterns of tree ring growth vary widely between species of trees within a given geographic region.

d. Recent tree ring samples are less reliable than tree ring samples collected over a period of many years.

e. Most species of trees growing in temperate and semiarid zones will respond similarly to periods of drought and to periods of heavier rainfall.

Select the answer choice that best completes the sentence:

22. In the preindustrial world, an education in a particular craft would serve a skilled worker his entire life, but in industrialized countries today, the _____ rate of technological progress means that certain skills may unexpectedly be rendered _____ overnight.

a. vertiginous … obsolete

b. capacious … ineffective

c. unpredictable … useful

d. proscribed … antiquated

e. deregulated … irrelevant

23. The widespread sales of "true crime" novels, which typically include a tabloid writing style and _____ depiction of criminal activities, directly reflect the reading public's attraction to _____ violence.

    a. prurient … abridged

    b. austere … underestimated

    c. lurid … sensationalized

    d. sordid … glamorous

    e. enigmatic … explicit

24. The professor critically examined the arts of almost every West African nation in only six lectures, which compensated for their occasional lack of _____ with their remarkable _____.

    a. loftiness … inaccessibility

    b. discontinuity … concreteness

    c. profundity … inclusiveness

    d. levity … detail

    e. analysis … comparability

Question 25 is based on the following reading passage.

Earth's crust, the surface layer of rocks extending 6–35 km beneath our feet, is by no means homogenous. In contrast to Earth's continental crust, whose formation was largely the result of vertical tectonic activity, oceanic crust appears to be the result of sustained horizontal tectonic movement. By measuring the refraction of seismic waves through rock and soil layers with a seismograph, scientists have been able to characterize the subsurface geologic structure and composition of the oceanic crustal areas. They have found that oceanic crust has a much simpler structure than continental crust, suggesting a more rapid formation. In fact, continental crust contains rocks as old as 3 to 4 billion years, while oceanic crust contains no regions older than 200 million years. Oceanic crust contains a high percentage of dense basalt, while continental crust is less dense, containing a higher proportion of silicon and other, lighter minerals. Seismic refraction reveals the oceanic crust to be comparatively thin—only 6 or 7 kilometers deep, as opposed to the average thickness of 35 km in continental crustal zones.

Select all that apply:

25. The conclusion suggests which of the following:

    I. The present oceanic crust was formed over a longer period of time than the continental crust.

    II. The total mass of the continental crust is heavier than that of the oceanic crust.

    III. The present-day oceanic crust was not formed when the oldest regions of present-day continental crust were first formed.

    a. I only

    b. II only

    c. III only

    d. I and II only

    e. II and III only

Questions 26–27 are based on the following passage.

From Goethe's "Sufferings of Young Werther." That the life of man is but a dream, many a man has surmised heretofore; and I, too, am everywhere pursued by this feeling. When I consider the narrow limits within which our active and inquiring faculties are confined; when I see how all our energies are wasted in providing for mere necessities, which again have no further end than to prolong a wretched existence; and then that all our satisfaction concerning certain subjects of investigation ends in nothing better than a passive resignation, whilst we amuse ourselves painting our prison-walls with bright figures and brilliant landscapes,—when I consider all this, Wilhelm, I am silent. I examine my own being, and find there a world, but a world rather of imagination and dim desires, than of distinctness and living power. Then everything swims before my senses, and I smile and dream while pursuing my way through the world.

All learned professors and doctors are agreed that children do not comprehend the cause of their desires; but that the grown-up should wander about this earth like children, without knowing whence they come, or whither they go, influenced as little by fixed motives, but guided like them by biscuits, sugar-plums, and the rod,—this is what nobody is willing to acknowledge; and yet I think it is palpable.

26. In the given context, *palpable* means most nearly:

    a. oppressive

    b. inconceivable

    c. apparent

    d. limiting

    e. deceptive

27. The difference between adults and children, according to the author, is that:

    a. children do not know that they are governed by the simplest of external incentives, whereas adults are aware of the shallowness of their own desires.

    b. while children are at liberty to pursue a variety of activities, adults are bound by necessity to a very narrow range of activities.

    c. children are unaware of the cause of their desires, while adults are aware of the cause of their desires but are powerless against them.

    d. children experience the world as it truly is, while adults concoct fantasies of how their lives should be without actually acting to fulfill those dreams.

    e. Children unquestioningly act on their desires or are restrained by external forces, while adults choose to ignore the equally capricious nature of their own desires and limitations.

Question 28 is based on the following passage.

The University of Woebegon recently changed its hiring policy for Spanish language instructors: now, it will only hire nonnative speakers to teach Spanish. In a statement to the school newspaper, the university president justified the change in policy by reasoning that the nonnative speakers learned later in life themselves, and so they had a better understanding of how to teach the language effectively. In fact, in a recent survey, most students who were studying beginning Spanish gave higher course-evaluation ratings to classes taught by nonnative speakers than to classes taught by native speakers.

28. All of the following would further support the university president's position EXCEPT:

    a. In Woebegon, it is extremely hard to find native speakers of Spanish, whereas nonnative speakers are easily found.

b. Students in higher level Spanish courses gave higher course-evaluation ratings to native speakers than nonnative speakers.

c. Nonnative speakers receive training in language pedagogy more often than native speakers.

d. In the last ten years, the proportion of native to nonnative Spanish instructors has decreased, and during that time, a higher proportion of students have continued with Spanish courses after the first year.

e. Native Spanish speakers rarely stay at a post at the University of Woebegon for more than two years, whereas nonnative speakers are often willing to stay for more than five years.

Answers

1. c. nomadic

2. c. an absolute

3. a. intact, d. consistent

4. c. blunt, d. candid

5. a. it is a place in which groups intermingle.

6. d. are not themselves objects of reflection, but instead inspire reflection.

7. b. traveler

8. e. a religious parody of love songs

9. b. imitations

10. It is probable that some of the carols are religious **parodies** of love-songs, written for the melodies of the originals, and many seem by their structure to be indirectly derived from the choral dances of farm folk, a notable feature being their burden or refrain, a survival of the common outcry of the dancers as they leaped around.

11. b. contrary … complement

12. d. toxic

13. d. weighty

14. d. ornithology

15. c. intractability

16. a. eschewed

17. b. blended … discern

18. c. curative … toxic

19. c. An architect builds a bridge which other architects are certain will fall; however, it stands.

20. c. It is useless to question the idea that the future will bring progress, because experience shows that it will.

21. a. Patterns of narrow and wide tree ring growth will tend to be similar for trees growing in the same region and subject to the same climatic conditions.

22. a. vertiginous … obsolete

23. c. lurid … sensationalized

24. c. profundity … inclusiveness

25. c. III only

26. c. apparent

27. e. Children unquestioningly act on their desires or are restrained by external forces, while adults choose to ignore the equally capricious nature of their own desires and limitations.

28. b. Students in higher level Spanish courses gave higher course-evaluation ratings to native speakers than nonnative speakers.

Math: All Bark, No Bite

In these chapters, we'll cover all the math you need to know for the GRE. If you miss eighth grade, then our arithmetic chapter will take you back. What took you a year to learn is crammed into one arithmetic-packed chapter. Then if you miss high school, we have algebra and geometry. These chapters are great if you want to improve once-great math skills or recover from mathophobia. We'll also explore charts, graphs, tables, and other random GRE math. The final chapter offers several practice sets covering every math concept you need to know for the GRE.

Chapter 13

Arithmetic: Yes, This Was Easier in Middle School

In This Chapter

- Scope of GRE math
- Math basics review
- Solving every kind of arithmetic problem

You know far more math than is actually tested on the GRE. Even if you're scoring below a 150, you still know more math than is actually tested on the GRE. It's important to keep this in mind: what makes hard GRE math problems hard isn't the math!

GRE Math: An Overview of What You Need to Know

Arithmetic: That's right, seventh-grade stuff. That's the subject of this chapter. Division, multiplication, fractions, percents, averages, ratios, proportions, and a few oddities. Some of these problems are easy and some are very difficult—but it's not about the math!

Algebra: Chapter 14 covers simple Algebra I stuff (ninth or tenth grade for most students): simple equations, simultaneous equations, maybe an inequality if you're lucky. In most cases, we're going to avoid algebra—so you can safely assume that there's no algebra on this test. Whoo hoo.

Geometry: Chapter 15 covers geometry. Think back to the first six to eight weeks of your geometry class—area of squares, circles and triangles, Pythagorean theorem, slope, and maybe a little surface area of volume of a cube if things get scary. Geometry on the GRE doesn't go much beyond this—there's no distance formula, no midpoint formula, no SOHCAHTOA, no law of cosines, and no proofs.

You need to know exactly what is and what isn't on this test because many students look at the "hard" math problems and think of every math concept they've ever learned, but 90 percent of the math you've ever learned won't be on this test. Once you know the scope of what's tested, most math problems become a little easier.

It's not the math. Most hard math problems aren't about the math, so whenever you miss a hard problem, your first step shouldn't be to redo the math. Your first step should be to carefully reread the problem, make sure you understand the problem, and be sure your answer is what they're asking for—did the problem ask for $2x$ and you just solved for x?

Basics of CIG Arithmetic

Test-taker Tom does every problem the same way. Regardless of whether it's easy or difficult, Tom attempts every problem like it's the first one.

If you get the first four to six math problems correct, you'll start hitting difficult math problems. After you learn the CIG techniques, many very hard questions will suddenly be very easy, so don't let the order-of-difficulty hold you back from trying the most difficult math problems.

Process of Elimination

Our old friend process of elimination keeps coming back. It's important that you remember to apply it aggressively to math problems. What's the first thing you should do if you don't understand the problem? Look at the answer choices! Sometimes you can get

rid of a few that are simply impossible (a negative answer if the question asks you to find the area of something—there are no black holes on this test).

Get in the Ballpark!

Make sure the answer you choose is possible. Sometimes there will be answer choices that aren't even possible. Try this one and watch out for impossible answer choices!

Level: Easy

Line segment L contains points A, B, and C, in that order. If AB is three times the length of BC and AC is 28, what is the length of BC?

    a. 3
    b. 5
    c. 7
    d. 21
    e. 28

So what's impossible here? First, BC must be the shorter length, so BC can't be 21 or 28. Even if you're not sure how to do it, guess one of the smaller numbers. Common sense goes a long way on the GRE.

X FAIR WARNING

> Unfortunately, you can't use a calculator on the GRE. So don't use one as you try these problems. Instead, prepare yourself for test conditions by working problems out on scratch paper.

To solve this problem, you might want to set up an equation: if BC = x, then AB is $3x$. So the equation would be $3x + x = 28$. Combine like terms, so you get $4x = 28$. So x must be 7. The answer is c. Don't worry too much about equations now, just understand that you should always use common sense on math problems.

Vocabulary and Numbers

Here's the math vocabulary you need to know for the GRE. There may be other terms on the test, but knowing these is mandatory! This list is in order of least to most complicated.

- *Integer.* A whole number—anything that isn't a fraction or decimal, including negative numbers. Example: 2, 87, -14.

- *Negative.* Anything less than zero, including any fractions or decimals less than zero. Example: –.23, –47.

- *Positive.* Anything greater than zero, including fractions or decimals. Example: .23, 47.

- *Negative/positive rules.* Make sure you know the following rules:

  Positive multiplied by a positive is positive. Example: 2 × 3 = 6.

  Negative multiplied by a negative is positive. Example: –2 × –3 = 6.

  Positive multiplied by a negative is negative. Example: 2 × -3 = –6.

- *Distinct.* Representing different values. So 2 and 3 are distinct numbers, but .25 and ¼ are not distinct.

- *Even.* Numbers evenly divisible by 2, including negative numbers. Examples: 0, 2, 4, –8.

- *Odd.* Any number that isn't even. Examples: 3, 27, –5.

- *Even/odd rules.* Zero is even. Fractions aren't even or odd. Even/odd is determined by the units/ones digit, so if the units/ones digit is even, the entire number is even. There are rules regarding even/odd addition and multiplication that you absolutely do not need to memorize. But you should know that rules exist.

Because you currently can't use a calculator on the test, the fine folks at GRE love problems that aren't so much about math as they are about reading and vocabulary. Try this one:

Level: Medium

The product of the number of prime factors of 30 and the number of prime factors of 32 is

    a. 3

    b. 6

    c. 15

    d. 30

    e. 960

Solution

How many prime factors does 30 have? Three: 2, 3, 5. How many prime factors does 32 have? One: 2. So what's the product of the number of prime factors of 30 and the number of prime factors of 32? It's 1 × 3 = 3. The correct answer is a. 3. (See the following section if you've forgotten what a prime factor is.)

Addition

even + even = even

odd + odd = even

even + odd = odd

Multiplication

even × even = even

odd × odd = odd

even × odd = even

Again, no need to memorize these rules. Just remember these rules exist, and if you need to figure them out on the test, just give yourself an example: 2 × 3 = 6, therefore an even multiplied by an odd must always give you an even number!

♦ *Difference.* The difference between two numbers is what you get when you subtract them. Also, the "difference" is that space between two numbers on a number line.

♦ *Sum.* The sum of two numbers is the result of addition.

♦ *Product.* The product of two numbers is the result of multiplication.

♦ *Quotient.* The quotient of two numbers is the result of division.

♦ *Absolute value.* This value of a number is equal to its distance from 0 on the number line. So the absolute value of 3 and −3 is the same, because both are 3 away from 0 on the number line.

♦ *Numerator.* In a fraction, the number on top. So in ¼, the 1 is the numerator.

♦ *Denominator.* In a fraction, the number on the bottom. So in ¼, the 4 is the denominator.

♦ *Consecutive.* In a row and increasing, so 2, 3, 4 and −4, −3, −2 are both groups of consecutive numbers. Keep in mind that −2, −3, −4 are

not consecutive because they aren't increasing in value. On the GRE, consecutive numbers will always be integers, so .1, .2, .3 are not consecutive. But there can be variations of consecutive integers. For example, you could have consecutive even integers (2, 4, 6).

♦ *Remainder.* What's left over after you divide. Remainders are always integers. Example: 2 goes into 6 an even number of times (three times). So there's no remainder (or you could say the remainder is 0). But 2 goes into 7 three times with a remainder of 1. What's the reminder of 9 divided by 5? Hopefully you said 4 because 5 goes into 9 once and 4 is left over.

INFO TO GO

Remember, 1 is not a prime number!

♦ *Prime.* Any number only divisible by two numbers, one and itself. Examples: 2, 3, 5, 7, 11, 13, 17, 23. The prime rules are:

> 0 is not prime.
>
> 1 is not prime.
>
> 2 is the lowest prime number and the only even prime number.
>
> All prime numbers are positive integers—they can't be negative or a fraction.

INFO TO GO

Numbers only have a few factors. But any number will have many multiples.

♦ *Factor/divisor.* A factor or divisor is a number that evenly goes into another number (divides into it). So 2, 3, 4, and 6 are all factors and divisors of 12 because they all evenly go into 12.

- *Multiple.* The multiple of a number is that number multiplied by an integer. So 100 is a multiple of 2, 5, 10, 20, 25, and so on.

- *Rules of zero.* Zero is an even integer, but it is neither positive nor negative.

- *Unit/ones.* Both are the first digit to the left of the decimal place. In the number 237.548, the 7 is the units or ones digit.

- *Digits.* The numbers on your phone (0–9). The digit places in the number 237.548 are as follows: 2 is the hundreds, 3 is the tens, 7 is the units or ones, 5 is the tenths, 4 is the hundredths, and 8 is the thousandths. It's worth knowing that mathematically, the number 237.548 is shorthand for:

  > 2 hundreds, plus
  >
  > 3 tens, plus
  >
  > 7 ones, plus
  >
  > 5 tenths (which is equal to five divided by ten, or one half), plus
  >
  > 4 hundredths (or four divided by 100), plus
  >
  > 8 thousandths (or 8 divided by 1,000).

- *Mean.* By "mean," the GRE usually means "arithmetic mean," which is the same as the average. An average of a set of numbers is derived by adding the numbers in the set and dividing by the number of items in the set. (We'll be exploring averages a little later in the chapter.) You can always find the average of a set of numbers. The mean of a set of numbers may or may not be one of the numbers, but if the set contains a sequence of an odd set of numbers, the mean will be in the set of numbers and will be equal to the median. For example, in the set {2, 3, 4, 5, 6} the mean and the median is 4.

- *Median.* The middle number in a set of numbers. If there's an odd number of items in the set, the median is the "middle" number. For example, in the set {2, 3, 4, 5, 6} the median is 4 (the middle of the five numbers). In the set {1, 2, 6, 18, 234] the median is 6. If your set has an even number of items, the median is the average of the middle two numbers. For example, in the set {2, 3, 4, 5} the median is the average of the middle two numbers. So average 3 and 4 and you get the median, 3.5. You can always find the median of a set of numbers.

- *Mode.* The mode of a set of numbers is the number that appears the most often. The mode of the set {2, 4, 8, 8, 9} is 8. The mode of the set {2, 3, 15, 23} is {0} or "empty set." So there may not be a mode for a set of numbers.

Translating Vocabulary into Math

Sometimes, the GRE will simply want you to translate a word problem back into math. This stuff is easy. Just remember:

The Vocab	The Math
Is, are, were	=
What, how much	x, y, or z
Of	× (multiply)
Percent (%)	Divided by 100

Try these:

Level: Easy

1. Seventy percent of 70 is what percent of 196?
   - a. 7%
   - b. 20%
   - c. 25%
   - d. 70%
   - e. 196%

2. Ten percent of 40 percent of what number is equal to 60 percent of 200?

> a. 8
>
> b. 60
>
> c. 120
>
> d. 600
>
> e. 3,000

Solutions

Math translation #1:
> $.7 \times 70 = y\% \times 196.$
>
> $49 = y\% \times 196.$
>
> $49/196 = y\%.$
>
> $.25 = y\%.$

Answer: c. 25%.

Math translation #2:
> $.1 \times .40 \times (y) = .60 \times 200.$
>
> $.04y = 120$
>
> $y = 3,000$

Answer: e. 3,000.

Order of Operations

You must follow the order of operations to solve an expression or equation. You're probably thinking "This is easy stuff," but most test-takers scoring below a 650 on math make at least one order of operations mistake. In long form, the order of operations is …

1. Parentheses or brackets first (starting with the innermost).

2. Exponentials or powers next.

3. Multiplication and division next.

4. Addition and subtraction last.

5. If an expression involves three or more operations at the same level of priority, those operations are done from left to right.

These rules are important. If you don't obey them when evaluating expressions or when manipulating algebraic expressions, you will get a wrong answer.

In short: the order is known as PEMDAS (parentheses, exponentials, multiplication, division, addition, subtraction).

Try this one:

> $5 - 3 + 6 =$

Did you did get -4? If so, you got the wrong answer! Adding the 3 to the 6 to get 9 violates the fifth rule of PEMDAS. The subtraction and addition are at the same level of priority, so the subtraction, being the leftmost of the two operations, is done first. Thus, 5 - 3 gives 2. Therefore 2 + 6 = 8. The correct answer is 8.

X **FAIR WARNING**

Test-taker Tom loses points because he doesn't apply the order of operations to every problem. Don't lose points! Know PEMDAS!

Here's a problem with no apparent multiplication operator. Give it a try:

> $3 + 5(10 - 6)$

Did you do this?

> $8(10 - 6)$
>
> $8(4)$
>
> 32

If you did, you got the wrong answer. Instead, you should have done the parentheses first (the highest priority) and followed these steps:

$$3 + 5(4)$$

Then do the multiplication—it has higher priority than the addition:

$$5(4) = 20$$

Finally, do the remaining addition:

$$3 + 20 = 23$$

The correct result is 23.

FAIR WARNING

Tom's most common mistake is to overlook higher priority operations that may not be obviously present. This often happens when multiplications are overlooked, because no specific multiply operator is present.

Try this one:

$$35 \times 16 - 96 + 14$$

Do the single multiply first—it has the highest priority present.

$$35 \times 16 = 560$$
$$560 - 96 + 14$$

Now do the left-most of the two add/subtract operations. They have the same level of priority, so the left-most one is done first:

$$464 + 14$$

Finally, do the remaining addition, to get the correct result of 478.

Try this one:

$$3 - 5(4 - 6 \times 2 - 5 + 7) + 8 \times 3$$

We need to start with the expression inside the parentheses, which has the highest priority. Inside the parentheses, the multiply operation has the highest priority.

$$3 - 5(4 - 6 \times 2 - 5 + 7) + 8 \times 3$$
$$3 - 5(4 - 12 - 5 + 7) + 8 \times 3$$

Now, do the leftmost subtract inside the brackets, because the two subtracts and one add are at the same priority level.

$$3 - 5(-8 - 5 + 7) + 8 \times 3$$

Again, leftmost subtract inside the brackets.

$$3 - 5(-13 + 7) + 8 \times 3$$

And the last add in the brackets.

$$3 - 5(-6) + 8 \times 3$$

Both of the multiplies are at the same priority level—here they don't interfere with each other, so we can do both at the same step. We can regard the first one as being –5 times –6, giving the positive result 30.

$$3 + 30 + 24$$

Now the remaining two adds can be done to get the final answer.

$$33 + 24 = 57$$

The correct answer is 57.

Try this one:

$$2 - 5(6 - 9)^3$$

Evaluation of the bracketed expression takes priority over every other operation present.

$$2 - 5(-3)^3$$

The exponentiation is done next, because it is the highest priority of the remaining operations. The power 3 is applied to the entire contents of the brackets:

$$(-3) \times (-3) \times (-3) = -27$$

$$2 - 5 \times -27$$

The multiplication has the next highest priority.

$$-5 \times -27 = 135$$

Then do the addition.

$$2 + 135 = 137$$

The answer is 137.

Fractions

Fractions are simply another way to write a division problem. So $\frac{1}{4}$ is the same as 1 divided by 4, which is the same as .25. So any fraction is also a division problem and a decimal.

Reducing

You can reduce a fraction by dividing both the top and the bottom (numerator and denominator) by the same number. So $\frac{4}{16}$ can be reduced by dividing the top and bottom by the same number (and,

of course, a number that goes into both the top and bottom). In the case of $\frac{4}{16}$, you could reduce it by dividing it by 2 or 4. If we divide it by 2, you'll get $\frac{2}{8}$, which can still be reduced (by dividing by 2 again). If you divide $\frac{4}{16}$ by 4, you'll get $\frac{1}{4}$, which is reduced.

Multiplying

Multiplying fractions is easy: you just multiply straight across. You can (and should) reduce first. For example:

$$\frac{8}{10} \times \frac{20}{24}$$

You can multiply 8×20 and 10×24, but it's much easier to reduce first. Keep in mind that you can reduce the individual fractions and you can reduce across the multiplication sign. In this example, $\frac{8}{10}$ reduces to $\frac{4}{5}$ (divide both by 2), and $\frac{20}{24}$ reduces to $\frac{5}{6}$ (divide both by 4). So we have,

$$\frac{4}{5} \times \frac{5}{6}$$

You can now reduce across the multiplication sign. The 4 and 6 each divide by 2 and the 5s each divide by 5, so you get:

$$\frac{2}{1} \times \frac{1}{3}$$

So the answer is $\frac{2}{3}$.

Dividing

You probably remember this from grade school: "Flip the second and multiply." And that's all you need to know. If you're dividing two fractions, flip the second one and then follow the rules for multiplying. For example, if you want to divide $\frac{1}{2}$ by $\frac{1}{4}$, you would multiply $\frac{1}{2}$ by 4 because when you flip $\frac{1}{4}$, you get $\frac{4}{1}$, which is just 4.

If you are dividing more than two fractions, just work with them two at a time.

The one oddity that you may encounter is an integer being divided by a fraction or a fraction whose top or bottom number is also a fraction. For example, what do you do with a fraction whose top number is 7 and bottom number is $\frac{1}{4}$?

Remember, fractions are another way of writing a division problem. So you could do this:

$$\frac{7}{\frac{1}{4}} =$$

Flip the second and multiply, and you'll get $7 \times 4 = 28$.

Adding/Subtracting

Adding and subtracting fractions that have the same bottom number is easy—just add or subtract the top numbers and write the result of the common bottom number. For example:

$$\frac{2}{17} + \frac{11}{17} = \frac{13}{17}$$

If the bottom numbers aren't the same, you need to perform a bowtie. For example,

$$\frac{2}{5} + \frac{3}{7} =$$

The two steps to perform the fraction bowtie:

1. Cross multiply. So you multiply 2×7 and 3×5, which gives us 14 and 15. Because we're adding, you would add those two results $(14 + 15 = 29)$. That result (29) is the top number in your answer!

2. Multiply the bottom numbers. $5 \times 7 = 35$. That result (35) is the bottom number in your answer.

Therefore,

$$\frac{2}{5} + \frac{5}{7} = \frac{29}{35}$$

Notice how we never found "common denominators"? If you use the bowtie, you can skip ever finding common denominators. Try this one:

$$\frac{7}{9} - \frac{5}{6}$$

Do the bowtie. $7 \times 6 = 42$. Write that number above the 7. Knowing $9 \times 5 = 45$. Write that above the 5. Now subtract $42 - 45$, and you get -3. That's the top number for your result. Now multiply the bottom numbers: $9 \times 6 = 54$. That's the bottom number for your result. So the answer is:

$$\frac{7}{9} - \frac{5}{6} = \frac{-3}{54}$$

Reduce that to $-\frac{1}{18}$.

Comparing

Comparing fractions is easy. You may need to know which fraction is bigger, especially for quantitative-comparison questions. So which one is bigger?

$$\frac{7}{9} \text{ or } \frac{5}{6}$$

Use the bowtie again. $6 \times 7 = 42$. Put that number above the 7. Knowing $9 \times 5 = 45$. Put that number above the 5. Which fraction has the bigger number above it? Because 45 is bigger than 42, $\frac{5}{6}$ must be bigger than $\frac{7}{9}$. Cool, huh? Try this one:

$$\frac{2}{7} \text{ or } \frac{11}{33}$$

$33 \times 2 = 66$. Put that above the 2. And $7 \times 11 = 77$. Put that above the 11. Because 77 is bigger than 66, $\frac{11}{33}$ must be bigger than $\frac{2}{7}$.

Mixed Numbers

A mixed number is a number represented by a fraction and an integer. For example:

$$3\frac{5}{6}$$

You can convert this to a fraction by multiplying

3 by 6 and adding that to the 5. So $3 \times 6 = 18$. $18 + 5 = 23$. That 23 becomes the new top number. (The bottom number always stays the same.) Therefore,

$$3\tfrac{5}{6} = \tfrac{23}{6}$$

Exponent Rules

Powers, or exponents, begin as shorthand notation for repeated multiplication. For example, we write:

$$2^5 = 2 \times 2 \times 2 \times 2 \times 2$$

Here, 2 is called the base and 5 is called the power or exponent. We describe 2^5 as meaning "2 raised to the power 5."

The exponent applies only to the quantity to its immediate lower left. Be careful indicating powers of negative numbers. Brackets must be used:

$$(-3)^4 = (-3) \times (-3) \times (-3) \times (-3) = +81$$

But without the brackets

$$-3^4 = -3 \times 3 \times 3 \times 3 = -81$$

Without the brackets, the power of 4 in -3^4 applies only to the 3, and does not include the minus sign.

FAIR WARNING

Exponents are becoming increasingly popular on the GRE. You will probably see many exponent problems, so read this section carefully!

Root Rules

Because $3^2 = 9$, we say that 3 is the square root of 9, written

$$\sqrt{9} = 3$$

Thus $\sqrt{9}$ is defined as the number whose square is 9. Now, you may recall that $(-3)^2 = 9$ as well. Thus, it would appear that every positive number has two square roots—a positive number and the same number with a minus sign. The square root symbol, $\sqrt{}$, without an explicit sign is reserved for the positive square root. To indicate the negative square root, you need to have a minus sign:

$$\sqrt{9} = 3 \quad \text{but} \quad -\sqrt{9} = -3$$

In symbols, then, for any positive number b, the symbol $\sqrt{b}$ has the meaning

$$\left(\sqrt{b}\right)^2 = b \quad \text{and} \quad \left(-\sqrt{b}\right)^2 = b$$

Some numbers, such as 1, 4, 9, 16, 25, etc., are the squares of whole numbers, so their square roots are whole numbers:

$$\sqrt{1} = 1 \quad \sqrt{4} = 2 \quad \sqrt{9} = 3 \quad \sqrt{16} = 4$$

For this reason, the numbers 1, 4, 9, 16, 25, etc., are said to be perfect squares. Numbers that are not perfect squares still have square roots, but their square roots are not whole numbers.

BET YOU DIDN'T KNOW

To the horror of the ancient Greeks who first discovered this, all simple whole numbers (2, 3, 5, etc.) that aren't perfect squares not only don't have whole number square roots, but their square roots also have an infinite number of decimal places. They are an example of what mathematicians (and other cool people) call irrational numbers.

So, for example, your calculator will tell you that

$$\sqrt{2} = 1.414213562$$

But, if you were to carefully multiply

$$(1.414213562)^2 = 1.414213562 \times 1.414213562$$

without any error, you would get something like 1.999999998944727844. That's because 1.414213562 gives only the first nine decimal places of the actual value of $\sqrt{2}$, and so is only just quite a good approximation to the exact value of the square root of 2. We will use the symbol $\sqrt{2}$ to represent the exact value of the square root of 2, even if we can never write this number down exactly in decimal form. For the GRE, you can usually just use 1.4 for $\sqrt{2}$.

Just as any positive number can be considered to be the square of other numbers (its square roots), so it is possible to express numbers as the third power, the fourth power, etc., of other numbers. So, for example,

$$64 = 4^3$$

In this case, we would say that 4 is the cube root of 64.

What Are Roots Good For?

Low-order roots occur commonly in basic geometry problems.

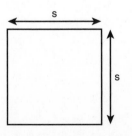

For example, in the accompanying figure, the formula for the area, A, of a square with sides of length s, is

$$A = s^2$$

But, this means that the length of the side, s, is equal to the square root of the area, A:

$$s = \sqrt{A}$$

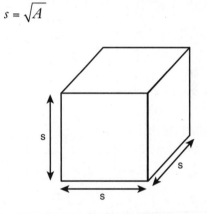

A second similar example—in the accompanying figure, the volume, V, of a cube which has edges of length s is

$$V = s^3$$

Thus: $s = \sqrt[3]{V}$

Radicals

Radical is used to refer to roots or expressions involving roots. Thus $\sqrt{2}$, $\sqrt[3]{17}$, and $\sqrt[5]{28}$ are called *radicals*.

You may have noticed that all scientific calculators have a built-in function labeled $\sqrt{}$ for calculating square roots of numbers. On many, you must press the 2nd Function or INV key first, before pressing the $\sqrt{}$ key. Of course, you don't have a calculator on the GRE, so practice this without using your calculator and memorize these very common roots:

$$\sqrt{2} = 1.414213562$$

For the GRE, 1.4 is good enough.

$$\sqrt{3} = 1.732050808$$

For the GRE, 1.7 is good enough.

Cube Roots

"Cube root" is often expressed like this: $\sqrt[3]{}$. To calculate cube roots ($\sqrt[3]{}$), recall that

$$\sqrt[n]{x} = x^{\frac{1}{n}}$$

That is, the $\frac{1}{n}$ power is the same as the nth root of a number. For example,

$$\sqrt[3]{17} = 17^{\frac{1}{3}} \cong 2.571281591$$

rounded to nine decimal places. Think about it like this: what number times itself 3 times results in 17? Essentially, 2.57 cubed is about 17. You need to be careful to think about the exponent $\frac{1}{3}$ as accurately as possible. If you approximate $\frac{1}{3} \cong 0.33$ you will get this:

$$\sqrt[3]{17} = 17^{\frac{1}{3}} \cong 17^{0.33} = 2.547112599$$

But 2.54 is already wrong in the second decimal place. This is more than you need to know for most GRE math problems—but it's good to keep in mind if you're aiming for 750+.

Sums and Differences of Square Roots

Sums and differences of square roots are often fairly ugly expressions to deal with algebraically, but sometimes we can use the methods for simplification of single square roots to help get lengthier expressions with two or more square root terms into a more compact form.

To illustrate ways to simplify a sum or difference of terms containing square roots, consider the following very simple example:

$$9\sqrt{2} + 3\sqrt{2} - 4\sqrt{2} = (9 + 3 - 4)\sqrt{2}$$
$$= 8\sqrt{2}$$

The grouping together of the *coefficients* 9, 3, -4 in brackets as shown above makes use of the distributive law for multiplication, which we described earlier in the discussion of the use of brackets.

VEXING VOCABULARY

A **coefficient** is a number or symbol (such as x or z) multiplied by a variable or an unknown quantity, such as 8 in $8x$, or z in $z(a + b)$. Eight and z are coefficients.

Alternatively, you could regard

$$9\sqrt{2} + 3\sqrt{2} - 4\sqrt{2}$$

as saying: "we have 9 of these $\sqrt{2}$'s , and another 3 of these $\sqrt{2}$'s , and we've taken away 4 of these $\sqrt{2}$'s. That means we have, on balance, $(9 + 3 - 4)$ = 8 of these $\sqrt{2}$'s left." But "8 of these $\sqrt{2}$'s" is written mathematically as $8\sqrt{2}$. (Substitute "jelly donut" for the symbol $\sqrt{2}$ in the sentences above if you're having trouble understanding the logic of this method.) We can regard this method as collecting together all terms that have identical square root parts.

Now, when the expression involves square roots of different numbers, we first need to simplify each square root as much as possible before collecting the terms with identical square root parts.

Try this one:

Simplify: $2\sqrt{75} - 7\sqrt{3} + 5\sqrt{12}$

Solution

We first check the square roots in each of the three terms to see whether any of them by themselves can be simplified:

$$\sqrt{75} = \sqrt{5^2 \times 3} = \sqrt{5^2}\sqrt{3} = 5\sqrt{3}$$

so

$$2\sqrt{75} = 2 \times 5\sqrt{3} = 10\sqrt{3}$$

then

$\sqrt{3}$ is as simple as possible.

Finally,

$$\sqrt{12} = \sqrt{2^2 \times 3} = \sqrt{2^2}\sqrt{3} = 2\sqrt{3}$$

so

$$5\sqrt{12} = 5 \times 2\sqrt{3} = 10\sqrt{3}$$

thus, our original expression becomes

$$2\sqrt{75} - 7\sqrt{3} + 5\sqrt{12}$$
$$= 10\sqrt{3} - 7\sqrt{3} + 10\sqrt{3}$$
$$= \left(10 - 7 + 10\right)\sqrt{3} = 13\sqrt{3}$$

and this is its simplest form.

Try this one:

Simplify $8\sqrt{12} + 7\sqrt{20} - 6\sqrt{45} + 9\sqrt{48}$

Solution

First simplify each square root part as much as possible:

$$\sqrt{12} = \sqrt{2^2 \times 3} = 2\sqrt{3}$$

therefore

$$8\sqrt{12} = 16\sqrt{3}$$

$$\sqrt{20} = \sqrt{2^2 \times 5} = 2\sqrt{5}$$

therefore

$$7\sqrt{20} = 14\sqrt{5}$$
$$\sqrt{45} = \sqrt{3^2 \times 5} = 3\sqrt{5}$$

therefore

$$6\sqrt{45} = 18\sqrt{5}$$
$$\sqrt{48} = \sqrt{4^2 \times 3} = 4\sqrt{3}$$

therefore

$$9\sqrt{48} = 36\sqrt{3}$$

thus:

$$8\sqrt{12} + 7\sqrt{20} - 6\sqrt{45} + 9\sqrt{48}$$
$$= 16\sqrt{3} + 14\sqrt{5} - 18\sqrt{5} + 36\sqrt{3}$$
$$= \left(16 + 36\right)\sqrt{3} + \left(14 - 18\right)\sqrt{5}$$
$$= 52\sqrt{3} - 4\sqrt{5}$$

This is as simple as we can get the original expression because there is no simple way to combine terms involving $\sqrt{3}$ with terms involving $\sqrt{5}$.

Multiplying and Dividing Square Roots

The rules for doing arithmetic with square roots are quite simple:

Multiplication

$$\sqrt{a} \times \sqrt{b} = \sqrt{a \times b}$$

"The product of square roots is the square root of the product."

Division

$$\frac{\sqrt{a}}{\sqrt{b}} = \sqrt{\frac{a}{b}}$$

"The quotient of square roots is the square root of the quotient."

For example:

$$\sqrt{3} \times \sqrt{5} = \sqrt{3 \times 5} = \sqrt{15}$$

$$\frac{\sqrt{32}}{\sqrt{8}} = \sqrt{\frac{32}{8}} = \sqrt{4} = 2$$

$$\frac{\sqrt{27}}{\sqrt{12}} = \sqrt{\frac{27}{12}} = \sqrt{\frac{\cancel{3} \times 9}{\cancel{3} \times 4}} = \sqrt{\frac{9}{4}} = \frac{\sqrt{9}}{\sqrt{4}} = \frac{3}{2}$$

> **! INFO TO GO**
>
> You can always multiply and divide square roots, but you can only add or subtract them if they are the same.

Addition and Subtraction of Roots

There is *no* simple relationship between the square roots of a sum or a difference and the square roots of its terms. You *must* know this!

$$\sqrt{a+b} \neq \sqrt{a} + \sqrt{b}$$

$$\sqrt{a-b} \neq \sqrt{a} - \sqrt{b}$$

It's easy to see why these prohibitions apply. For example:

$$\sqrt{9+16} = \sqrt{25} = 5$$

but

$$\sqrt{9} + \sqrt{16} = 3 + 4 = 7$$

Thus $\sqrt{9+16}$ does not give the same value as $\sqrt{9} + \sqrt{16}$. In conclusion:

$$\sqrt{9+16} \neq \sqrt{9} + \sqrt{16}$$

Because the two forms are unequal in this specific example, we have demonstrated that you cannot assume that $\sqrt{a+b}$ equals $\sqrt{a} + \sqrt{b}$. (These two forms are only equivalent when a or b or both are equal to zero!)

Percents

Percent simply means "out of 100" (per means "out of" and cent means "100"). You can also think of percent as meaning "divided by 100."

> **✗ FAIR WARNING**
>
> Some test-takers find percents difficult, but they are all over the GRE and not that bad if you practice. Master percents and you'll pick up some points.

Part of Whole and Rate of Change

Percents express part of a whole:

- ◆ A shirt is 80 percent cotton.
- ◆ Fifteen percent of all high school students have part-time jobs.

◆ Construction of the new school building is 80 percent complete.

Percents express a rate of change:

◆ Woody received a 5 percent salary increase.

◆ The number of cases of serious skateboard accidents reported this year is down 30 percent from last year.

◆ The price of beer has increased by 12 percent over the last year.

The thing to remember is that percents represent the numerator of a fraction that always has a denominator of 100. So, when we say, for example, 25 percent, we are really speaking of the fraction $^{25}/_{100}$ or 0.25 in decimal form.

So conversion between a percent, an actual fraction with a numerator and denominator, and a decimal fraction is very easy to do.

If you start with the percent then to get the fractional equivalent, just write a fraction with the percent in the numerator and a denominator of 100. For example:

$$37\% = {}^{37}/_{100}$$

To get a decimal fraction equivalent, just divide the percent by 100 (which is the same thing as moving the decimal point two places leftwards). For example:

$$37\% = 0.37$$

If you start with a proper fraction *or* a decimal fraction, just multiply by 100. For example:

$$^{37}/_{100} = (^{37}/_{100} \times 100)\% = 37\%$$

$$0.37 = (0.37 \times 100)\% = 37\%$$

This rule also works if the starting fraction has a denominator which is not equal to 100. For example:

$$^{19}/_{76} = (^{19}/_{76} \times 100)\% = 25\%$$

It may be that this conversion results in digits to the right of the decimal point. For example:

$$^{25}/_{55} = (^{25}/_{55} \times 100)\% = 45.45\%$$

(rounded to two decimal places.) The number of decimal places should be retained in the final percent that depends on the question.

Finally, notice that percents can be (and often are) larger than 100. Such percents just correspond to fractions and decimal numbers that are bigger than 1. For example:

$$^{14}/_{8} = (^{14}/_{8} \times 100)\% = 175\%$$

and

$$5.72 = (5.72 \times 100)\% = 572\%$$

✗ FAIR WARNING

It is vital that you work all of these problems out on scratch paper. Do not try to work these problems in your head!

The meaning of percents bigger than 100 percent will depend on the situation. When a percent is expressing a part or fraction of a whole, it makes no sense to have a value bigger than 100 percent (because then the part would be more than the total stuff that it is part of). However, if the percent is referring to a rate of increase, values bigger than 100 percent just mean that the quantity has more than doubled in size.

Percent Increase and Decrease

The language of percents is frequently used to indicate a degree of change. For percent increase/decrease, you have the following parts:

♦ Original value: what number or amount did we start with? Change to refer to the actual amount of change, the amount by which the "base" quantity either increases or decreases.

♦ Rate or percent change: this is the actual percent value, in this situation representing a percent increase or decrease. In the arithmetic calculations, the decimal equivalent of the percent increase or percent decrease is always used.

Keep in mind that with percent increase/decrease, everything is positive (it doesn't matter if the amount is decreasing!).

Try these. First, an easy one. Then the same problem with one of the GRE's nasty variations.

Level: Easy

A television is priced at $329.50. If the retailer offers a 30 percent discount, what would be the new price of the item?

Level: Medium

How much does Woody pay for a television that is originally priced at $329.50, but then discounted 30 percent, and sold in a state that charges 8.5 percent sales tax?

Solutions

Level: Easy

$$= (\$329.50)(1 + [-0.30])$$
$$= (\$329.50)(0.70)$$
$$= \$230.65$$

Thus, with the 30 percent discount, the new price of the item will be $230.65.

Level: Medium

$$= (\$230.65)(1 + 0.085)$$
$$= (\$230.65)(1.085)$$
$$= \$250.26 \text{ (rounded to the nearest cent)}$$

Thus, the actual amount of money Woody would pay for the item (including sales tax) would be $250.26.

The work we did above to come up with the final cost of $250.26 is correct—this is the way the calculation would be done in the store. The sales representative would first apply the 30 percent discount to the original price, to obtain the discounted price of $230.65. Then, the 8.5 percent sales tax would be applied to this discounted price, resulting in the final cost to you.

FAIR WARNING

What you *absolutely cannot do* is to combine two rates. You might think that a 30 percent decrease followed by an 8.5 percent increase amounts to an effective rate of change of 21.5 percent (30 percent − 8.5 percent). But this will get you the wrong answer! The source of the error here is that the two rates in the problem do not refer to the same base values! The 30 percent discount is 30 percent of the original price of $329.50, whereas the 8.5 percent sales tax is 8.5 percent of the discounted price of $230.65. So you can't simply add percents together!

In order to avoid error in percent problems, always make sure you have correctly identified the base values to which *each* percent refers, and also that you correctly distinguish between new values and base values.

Try this one:

Woody buys a stereo, paying a total of $982.35, which includes 6.5 percent sales tax. What was the store's price for the stereo?

   a. $917.35

   b. $919.50

   c. $922.39

   d. $982.35

   e. Cannot be determined

Obviously, the rate of change here is the 6.5 percent rate of paying sales tax. This rate is applied to the original price of the item, which is what we are asked to determine. This results in a new value, the $982.35 actually paid. So,

   $982.35 = original price + original price × 6.5 percent

or

   $982.35 = original price × 1.065

Therefore,

   $982.35/1.065 = $922.39

rounded to the nearest cent. Thus, we conclude that the original stated price of the item was $922.39. The answer is c.

You can double-check our answer to the last example by computing the total cost of an item after 6.5 percent sales tax is added to its labeled price of $922.39. We should end up with the value $982.35, as stated in the problem. So:

   assumed original price: $922.39

   plus 6.5 percent sales tax
   (= 0.065 × $922.39) $59.956

   total cost = $982.35

Test-taker Tom often makes the error of subtracting 6.5 percent of the final cost of $982.35 from that final cost, thinking this will give the original price:

   $982.35 − ($982.35)(0.065) → $982.35 − $63.85 → $918.50

But you know this is incorrect, because when you buy an item in a store, the sales tax is always computed with the original price, whereas this incorrect calculation applies the sales tax to the final cost which already includes the sales tax.

One more!

Woody buys a house for $212,500, and later sells it for $243,700. By what percent did the price of the house change from when he bought it to when he sold it?

   a. 12.8

   b. 14.68

   c. 15.1

   d. 20.12

   e. 21

Start by sorting out the numbers. We have

   original price = "original value" = $212,500

and

   selling price = "new value" = $243,700

We are asked to find a rate, the percent by which the house price increased between these two transactions. There are at least two ways to do this:

1. Find the "amount" or increase in the house price

   = new value - original value

   = $243,700 - $212,500 = $31,200

   Then, using

   amount = base × rate

   we have

   $31,200 = $212,500 × rate

   so that

   $$rate = \frac{\$31200}{\$212500} \cong 0.1468$$

   (rounded to four decimal places.) Thus, the house price increased by 14.68 percent. The answer is b.

2. Or we could also begin with

   new value = base × (1 + rate)

   Rearrange that equation to look like this:

   $$1 + rate = \frac{new\ value}{base}$$

   so that

   $$rate = \frac{new\ value}{base} - 1$$

   Putting the numbers in gives

   $$= \frac{\$243700}{\$212500} - 1$$

   1.1468 − 1 = 0.1468

   again rounding to four decimal places where necessary. This is, of course, exactly the same answer of a 14.68 percent increase obtained with the first method.

Averages

All averages have three components:

- The average
- The number of things you're averaging
- The total amount

For example: if Woody buys three shirts and he spends $210 total, then his average per shirt is $70. Here, we have

- The average: $70
- The number of things you're averaging: three shirts
- The total amount: $210

How do you find an average? Think of averages like this:

$$\frac{Total\ Amount}{\#\ of\ Things\ \mid\ Average}$$

Think of the big horizontal line as a division line. Think of the smaller vertical line as a multiplication line.

- *To find the total amount*: multiply the # of things and the average.
- *To find the # of things*: divide the total amount by the average.
- *To find the average*: divide the total amount by the # of things.

So for our problem above, you would have this:

$$\frac{\$210}{3\ Shirts\ \mid\ ???}$$

So to solve for this, simply divide the *total amount* ($210) by the *# of things* (three shirts) and you get $210.

You always have two of the three components in every average problem. Which two components do you have? Well, if you're being asked for the average, you *must* have the total amount and the # of things. If you're being asked to find the # of things, then you *must* have the other two components.

If you don't have two components, you can make up the components you need. (We'll see this later.)

Try this one:

Level: Medium

Woody buys three apples for a total of $1.24 on Tuesday and four apples for a total of $1.46 on Wednesday. Rounded to the nearest whole cent, what is the average amount Woody paid for apples on these two days?

    a. $.17
    b. $.18
    c. $.21
    d. $.39
    e. $1.35

Solution

We need to plug our problem into this formula:

$$\frac{\text{Total Amount}}{\text{\# of Things}} = \text{Average}$$

What's the total amount Woody spent?
$1.24 + $1.46 = $2.70.
How many things did he buy? 7.

Now divide:

$$\frac{\$2.70}{7 \text{ apples}} = .3875$$

Round .3857 to the nearest cent and you get 39 cents. The answer is d.

Try this one:

Level: Hard

The average of 24 numbers is 134. One number is removed and the new average is 130. What number was removed?

    a. 6
    b. 24
    c. 130
    d. 134
    e. 226

Solution

We need to plug our problem into this formula:

$$\frac{\text{Total Amount}}{\text{\# of Things}} = \text{Average}$$

What's the total amount here? We can find out by plugging our two numbers in like this:

$$\frac{???}{24 \text{ numbers}} = 134$$

Now multiply 24 and 134.

$$\frac{3216}{24 \text{ numbers}} = 134$$

So 3,216 is the total amount. Now 1 number is removed and the new average is 130. Let's find the new total. Keep in mind that if 1 number is removed, we now must have 23 numbers instead of 24 numbers.

$$\frac{2990}{23 \text{ numbers} \mid 130}$$

We multiplied 234 and 130 and got 2,990. So what number was removed? Our first total was 3,216 and our second total was 2,990, so the difference between the totals must be the number that was removed. So 3,216 - 2,990 = 226. The answer is e.

Try this one:

Level: Hard

The average of 9 numbers is 70. Four numbers are removed and the new average is 84. What is the average of the numbers that were removed?

    a. 7.78

    b. 9.33

    c. 52.5

    d. 70

    e. 84

Solution

We need to plug in the # of things (nine numbers) and the average (70) in order to determine the total:

$$\frac{630}{9 \mid 70}$$

So the total is 630 (9 × 70).

Now if four numbers are removed, that leaves five numbers. If five numbers are left and their average is 84, then we can find their total.

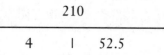

$$\frac{420}{5 \mid 84}$$

Because the total of all nine numbers is 630 and the total of five of the numbers is 420, then the total of the remaining four numbers must be 210. Now divide that total (210) by the # of things.

$$\frac{210}{4 \mid 52.5}$$

So the average of the four numbers that were removed must be 52.5. The answer is c.

Try this one:

Level: Medium

Four different positive integers average 6. What is the greatest possible value of one of these integers?

    a. 1

    b. 2

    c. 6

    d. 18

    e. 24

Solution

We need to plug in the # of things (four numbers) and the average (6) in order to determine the total:

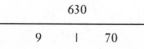

$$\frac{24}{4 \mid 6}$$

The total is 24 (4 × 6). So what we know is this:

___ + ___ + ___ + ___ = 24

If we want to make one of the numbers as big as possible, we want to make the other three numbers as small as possible. Because the numbers must be positive integers, the smallest possible number is 1. Because they must all be different, then the lowest three numbers must be 1, 2, and 3. So we have:

1 + 2 + 3 + ___ = 24

The missing number is 18. So the biggest possible number must be 18. The answer is d.

Try this variation:

Level: Hard

A teacher is in a classroom with 11 students. The teacher's age is five times the average age of the students. What fraction is the teacher's age of the combined age of all 12 people in the classroom?

    a. $\frac{1}{16}$

    b. $\frac{1}{12}$

    c. $\frac{1}{11}$

    d. $\frac{5}{16}$

    e. $\frac{5}{12}$

FAIR WARNING

Did you try to work that problem in your head? Use your scratch paper! Write everything down! Don't lose points because of careless mistakes.

Solution

First, make up numbers for the age of the teacher and the average age of the students. Any numbers will work, as long as the teacher's age is five times the age of the students. Let's say the teacher is 50 years old and the average age of the students is 10.

Now, let's work with the student numbers. Let's plug in the # of things (11 students) and the average age (10) in order to determine the total:

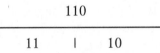

So the total age for the 11 students is 110. Now simply create a fraction by dividing the teacher's age (50) by the total age (50 + 110 = 160). You get this:

$$\frac{50}{160}$$

Reduce, and you get $\frac{5}{16}$. The answer is d.

Simultaneous Equations

Here's a quick rule for simultaneous equations (anytime you see 2 equations): stack them, and try to add or subtract them.

Should you add or subtract? You should do whichever leaves you with only one variable. If you're not sure whether to add or subtract, just jump in and try one—if it doesn't work, try the other.

For example:

If $7x + 4y = 20$ and $2x + 4y = 10$, what is x?

Just stack them (bigger numbers on top) and because we're trying to get rid of y, let's subtract.

$$7x + 4y = 20$$
$$2x + 4y = 10$$
$$\overline{}$$
$$5x + 0 = 10$$
$$5x = 10$$
$$x = 2$$

Try this one:

Level: Easy

If $x - 19y = 32$ and $2x + 19y = 7$, what is the value of x?

a. 1

b. 2

c. 3

d. 13

e. 39

Solution

$$2x + 19y = 7$$
$$+ \ x - 19y = 32$$
$$\overline{}$$
$$3x + 0 = 39$$
$$3x = 39$$
$$x = 13$$

The answer is d.

D = RT

Distance = rate × time is one of the two formulas that the GRE doesn't give you (the other is slope, covered in Chapter 15). You won't see more than one of these questions, but if you know the formula, they're usually quite easy.

Try this one:

Level: Medium

If Woody finished a 50-yard race in 7 seconds and his fat dog finished the race in 9.3 seconds, in yards per second, the dog's rate was approximately how much less than Woody's rate?

a. 1.76

b. 2.3

c. 2.51

d. 115

e. Cannot be determined

Solution

Because D = R x T, we can find the rates. Woody's rate

$$50 = R \times 7$$
$$50/7 = R$$
$$7.14 = R$$

Fat Dog's Rate

$$50 = R \times 9.3$$
$$50/9.3 = R$$
$$5.38 = R$$

Answer: 7.14 - 5.38 = a. 1.76

Ratios

You've seen ratios before. For example, the ratio of boys to girls at a school is three to four. Ratio problems all work the same way. Every ratio problem has three components: the ratio, the actual numbers, and the multiplier.

Here's an example. Let's say we have a ratio of boys to girls, and the ratio is three to four. And let's say we actually have 90 boys. You can plug this information into a grid like this:

	Boys	Girls	Total
Ratio	3	4	
Multiplier			
Actual #	90		

Now, we can find out everything we need to know. The multiplier is how we get from the ratio number to the actual number. If the ratio number for "boys" is three and the actual number is "90," then what was the "3" multiplied by to get "90"? Yes, 30. Let's plug that in.

	Boys	Girls	Total
Ratio	3	4	
Multiplier	30		
Actual #	90		

Now here's the trick. The multiplier is the same all the way across. So now that we know what the multiplier is, we can plug it in everywhere, like this:

	Boys	Girls	Total
Ratio	3	4	
Multiplier	30	30	30
Actual #	90		

Now we can find any number we want by simply multiplying it by the multiplier (makes sense, doesn't it?). If you quickly wanted to find the total, just add the ratio numbers (3 + 4 = 7), put the 7 into the ratio/total box, and multiply, like this:

	Boys	Girls	Total
Ratio	3	4	7
Multiplier	30	30	30
Actual #	90		210

Of course, to find the actual number of girls, you can just multiply the ratio by the multiplier (4 × 30) and get 120. Easy stuff, eh?

Try this one:

Level: Easy

Four partners share the profits of their business in a ratio of four to three to three to two. The total profits for the year were $228,000. What is the largest share?

    a. $19,000

    b. $57,000

    c. $76,000

    d. $114,000

    e. $228,000

Solution

First, fill in the information you know. We have the ratio and the total amount. From that, we can also find the ratio total (12) by simply adding the ratio. This tells us the total number of parts we're dealing with.

Partners	#1	#2	#3	#4	Total
Ratio	4	3	3	2	12
Multiplier					
Actual #	$228,000				

Next, find the multiplier by dividing the total actual number by the total ratio.

Partners	#1	#2	#3	#4	Total
Ratio	4	3	3	2	12
Multiplier					$19,000
Actual #					$228,000

Finally, put the multiplier ($19,000) under the ratio number we're trying to solve. In this problem, we want the largest share, which will be the largest ratio number. So we put the multiplier under 4 and multiply. This gives us the correct answer ($76,000).

Partners	#1	#2	#3	#4	Total
Ratio	4	3	3	2	12
Multiplier	$19,000				$19,000
Actual #	$76,000				$228,000

Proportions

Proportions are just two ratios set equal to each other. For example: if 3 pounds of flour makes 150 cupcakes, how many pounds of flour are needed to make 450 cupcakes? You can set the problem up like this:

$$\frac{3\ lbs/flour}{150\ cupcakes} = \frac{Y\ lbs/flour}{450\ cupcakes}$$

Now cross-multiply.

$$3 \times 450 = Y \times 150$$
$$1,350 = 150Y$$
$$9 = Y$$

Now try one:

Level: Easy

If Woody reads 320 pages in 50 minutes, how long will it take him to read 400 pages?

    a. 47 minutes

    b. 50 minutes

    c. 62.5 minutes

    d. 70.5 minutes

    e. 98 minutes

Solution

$$\frac{320\ pages}{50\ minutes} = \frac{400\ pages}{Y\ minutes}$$

Now cross-multiply.

$$320 \times Y = 50 \times 400$$
$$320Y = 20,000$$
$$Y = 62.5$$

The answer is c.

Now try this one:

Level: Medium

If Woody reads 320 pages in 50 minutes and his friend Reggie reads at twice this rate, how long would it take Reggie to read 400 pages?

    a. 28.25

    b. 30

    c. 31.25

    d. 62.5

    e. 125

Solution

You might be tempted to set it up like this:

$$\frac{320\ pages}{50\ minutes} = \frac{400\ pages}{Y\ minutes}$$

If you did, then you set it up incorrectly. Remember, Reggie reads at twice this rate. So he reads twice as fast. Set up the ratio, then make Reggie's reading twice as fast. You could set it up like this:

$$\frac{320\ pages}{50\ minutes}$$

So twice the rate is

$$\frac{640 \text{ pages}}{50 \text{ minutes}}$$

Or like this:

$$\frac{320 \text{ pages}}{25 \text{ minutes}}$$

In both cases, the second ratio is "twice as fast" as the first rate. We'll use the top example (640 over 50). So let's use that ratio to solve for the question.

$$\frac{640 \text{ pages}}{50 \text{ minutes}} = \frac{400 \text{ pages}}{Y \text{ minutes}}$$

Now cross-multiply and solve for Y.

$$640 \times Y = 50 \times 400$$
$$640Y = 20{,}000$$
$$Y = 31.25$$

The answer is c.

Now for a very hard one. Try this one:

Level: Hard

Woody can make 300 cupcakes with 8.5 pounds of flour and Billy can make 700 cupcakes with 7 pounds of flour. If Woody pays $3.50 per pound and Billy pays $2.65 per pound for flour, what is the approximate positive difference in the cost in flour it takes Woody to make 1 cupcake and the cost in flour it takes Billy to make 1 cupcake?

a. $.01
b. $.055
c. $.065
d. $.073
e. $.25

Solution

First, solve for the amount of flour needed to make one cupcake. We'll start with Woody.

$$\frac{300 \text{ cupcakes}}{8.5 \text{ pounds}} = \frac{1 \text{ cupcake}}{Y \text{ pounds}}$$

Now cross-multiply and solve for Y.

$$300 \times Y = 8.5 \times 1$$
$$300Y = 8.5$$
$$Y = .02833$$

Second, solve for the amount of flour needed for Billy to make one cupcake.

$$\frac{700 \text{ cupcakes}}{7 \text{ pounds}} = \frac{1 \text{ cupcake}}{Y \text{ pounds}}$$

Now cross-multiply and solve for Y.

$$700 \times Y = 7 \times 1$$
$$700Y = 7$$
$$Y = .01$$

We know the amount of flour Woody and Billy need to make one cupcake. Now find Woody's flour cost per cupcake. Multiply the number of pounds needed to make one cupcake by the cost per pound of flour:

$$.02833 (\$3.5) = \$.099155$$

Now find Billy's flour cost per cupcake. Multiply the number of pounds needed to make one cupcake by the cost per pound of flour:

$$.01 (\$2.65) = \$.0265$$

Now subtract the larger number by the smaller number to find the positive difference.

$$\$.099155 - \$.0265 = \$.072655$$

The answer is d. $.073.

Tables and Charts

You will probably see one to three table/chart problems on the GRE. Usually, each math section has one table or chart and two to three questions about that table or chart. The key to answering these questions correctly is to understand that ETS doesn't use charts/tables to help you understand information. On the contrary, ETS uses charts/tables to hide information or make it more difficult to understand.

Most charts and tables only require basic arithmetic skills. You'll be required to do ratios, percents, proportions, and other basic operations. The key will be finding the information you need and using it correctly. Here is what's important on charts and tables:

- **Titles and labels:** Make sure you read, understand, and keep track of all titles and labels. Don't mix up two labels or confuse a label with the wrong data. ETS will often make titles and labels confusing, so don't take anything for granted.

- **Footnotes and small print:** What's written below the table or chart? Are there any asterisks or parenthesis? Are there any footnotes or small print written below the chart or table? ETS likes to hide crucial information, so make sure you are fully aware of everything included in the chart or table.

- **Units:** You need to make sure you are fully aware of the units involved. Are the numbers "in hundreds" or "in thousands"? Are all the same numbers in the same units?

- **Estimating:** Estimating will be important. Usually, you won't need to get precise answers. If you ever see "approximately" or

"about" in a question, you should estimate—don't do all the math. If you think that the math will take a long time, then you're probably right: skip all the details and estimate. Finally, if the values in the answer choices are far apart, then you can and should estimate. So always take a look at the answer choices; they will let you know if estimating is possible.

Let's try a bit of estimating. Quickly, what is 9.7 percent of 65? It's a little less than 10 percent of 65, so it's a little less than 6.5. Now what's 19.9 percent of 202? Well, 10 percent of 200 is 20, so double that to 40 and you're very close.

Charts and tables usually depend on carefully surveying all the information provided and being organized.

Try this one:

Education Expenditures

Year	Amount (Millions)
1990	2.3
1991	3.1
1992	5.3
1993	6.7
1994	7.5
1995	9
1996	11.8
1997	14
1998	19
1999	23.2

The following questions refer to the chart above, which lists the education expenditures of country X.

Level: Easy

Which year had the greatest growth, in millions, in the amount spent?

- a. 1992
- b. 1995
- c. 1997
- d. 1998
- e. 1999

Level: Medium

The amount spent in 1991 was what percent greater than the amount spent in 1990?

- a. .8
- b. 1
- c. 25.8
- d. 34.7
- e. 49.2

Level: Hard

What was the ratio of growth in millions from 1993 to 1994 and 1995 to 1996?

- a. .8 : 2.5
- b. .8 : 2.8
- c. 2.5 : 2.8
- d. 6.7 : 9
- e. 7.5 : 11.8

Solutions

Easy problem: The growth from 1997 to 1998 is 5 million. (1998 to 1999 is 4.2 million.) So the answer is d.

Medium problem: 1991 saw an increase of .8 million over 1990, so .8 is what percent of 2.3? Make this easy: 8 is what percent of 23? Well, 8 is about ⅓ of 23,

right? So we're looking for an answer choice that's close to ⅓ (or 33 percent). And d. is the closest to 33 percent—it's correct.

Hard problem: The growth from 1993 to 1994 was .8 and the growth from 1995 to 1996 was 2.8, so the ratio is simply .8 to 2.8. That's easy as long as you understand the problem and are careful. The answer is b.

If you're having trouble with these, move on to Chapter 14, which contains a more in-depth review of charts, tables, and data interpretation.

The Least You Need to Know

- ◆ Math vocabulary is important. Be sure you know what integers, prime numbers, and so on mean.
- ◆ Know basic math rules such as PEMDAS.
- ◆ You can't use a calculator.
- ◆ You must write everything down on scratch paper—don't try to do it in your head.
- ◆ Averages and exponents will be tested, so be sure to review both.

Chapter 14

Algebra

In This Chapter

◆ Solving for variables

◆ Plugging in your own numbers

◆ Factoring

There are two kinds of algebra problems on the GRE: equations and everything else. Most GRE algebra problems fall into the "everything else" category and they are easy to solve. But first, we'll look into the equation category.

Equations

Usually, the only time you want to deal with an equation on the GRE is when you're given one. You don't want to be in a habit of setting up equations or trying to write equations—there's *always* an easier way to solve the problem.

Solving for One Variable

The kind of equation problems you're given are usually fairly easy. You know the routine: get the letters (or variables) on one side and the number(s) on another. Let's try one.

Level: Easy

If $5d + w = 7$, and $w = 7$, what is the value of d?

    a. 0

    b. .2

    c. .4

    d. 1

    e. 2.8

Solution

Plug w into the equation and you get $5d + 7 = 7$.

Subtract 7 from both sides and you get $5d = 0$.

Divide both sides by 5 and you get $d = 0$. The answer is a.

> **! INFO TO GO**
>
> You must always do the same operation to both sides of an equation—if you subtract 7 from one side, you must subtract it from the other, too.

Solving for Multiple Variables and Equations

Now for something more difficult. Whenever you have two equations, think: add or subtract them. You can also solve for the appropriate variables and set them equal to each other. Try this one:

Level: Medium

If $5n + p = 3$ and $2m - 10n = 2$, what is the value of $10(m + p)$?

    a. 4

    b. 20

    c. 40

    d. 70

    e. 80

Solution

You can solve this problem two ways: either stack the equations or solve for m and p separately and add them. We'll stack the equations first.

> **✗ FAIR WARNING**
>
> Again, use your scratch paper! Write everything down! Don't lose points because of careless mistakes

We want to get rid of the n variable, because we don't need it for our answer (our answer is about m and p). We have $5n$ on one side and $10n$ on the other. In order to get rid of n, it'll need to have the number. So let's make the $5n$ a $10n$ by multiplying the first equation by 2, so we'll get: $10n + 2p = 6$. Now we can stack them, lining up similar variables:

$$10n + 2p = 6$$
$$2m - 10n = 2$$

Because n is the only similar variable, it's the one that needs to be lined up—and now we have $10n$ and $-10n$. In order to get rid of this pesky n, we'll add them (because $10n$ plus $-10n$ equals nothing). When we add, we'll get:

$$10n + 2p = 6$$
$$\underline{+\ \ 2m - 10n = 2}$$
$$2m + 0 + 2p = 8$$

So now we have $2m + 2p = 8$. Or, $2(m + p) = 8$. To get the $10(m + p)$, we need to multiply by 5, so the answer is 40.

Another way to solve it is to solve for m and p, then add them. Here we go:

$$5n + p = 3$$
$$p = 3 - 5n$$
$$2m - 10n = 2$$
$$2m = 2 + 10n$$
$$m = 1 + 5n$$

Now add m and p.

$$3 - 5n + 1 + 5n$$

The two $5n$s cancel (because one is positive and one is negative) and you're left with $3 + 1 = 4$. Since $m + p$ is 4, then $10(m + p)$ must be 40. The answer is c.

Everything Else

But much of the algebra on the GRE doesn't involve solving given equations. Much of it is goofy and looks like this:

> **Level: Medium**
>
> Seven years ago, Jane was y years old and Woody was x years older than Jane. In terms of y and x, how old will Woody be 12 years from now?
>
> a. yx
> b. $y + 7$
> c. $y + x + 12$
> d. $y + x + 19$
> e. Cannot be determined

You can set up an equation and solve it, but that's more work than you need to do (and why would you want to do more work than necessary—you don't get more credit if you do more work!). And keep in mind that this is a fairly easy problem—they get much more difficult.

Plugging In Your Own Numbers

The easy and foolproof way to solve this problem is just to plug in your own numbers. Let's just make up a number for Woody: how old was Woody seven years ago? Let's say W was 10 years old. Now make up a number for x—let's say 2. So we have:

> 7 years ago: Woody was 10 years old
> $x = 2$, so Woody was 2 years older than Jane
> So J was 8 years old
> So $y = 8$

Now we can complete the chart:

	7 yrs ago	Now	12 yrs from now
W	10	17	29
J	8	15	27

The question asks how old will Woody be 12 years from now. The answer, given our numbers, is 29. So plug in our numbers, $x = 2$ and $y = 8$, and see which answer gives us 29.

> a. $yx = 16$
> b. $y + 7 = 15$
> c. $y + x + 12 = 22$
> d. $y + x + 19 = 29$
> e. Cannot be determined

So the answer must be d., since it's the one that gives us Woody's age in 12 years.

Plugging in Rules

If that was hard, then here are the rules to make it easier.

1. Plug in easy numbers. Always think of plugging in 2. There's no reason to plug in a number like 3.7.

2. Plug in numbers that work. If you're dealing with ⅓ and ½, plug in a number that can be divided by 3 and 2 (such as 6 or 12). If you're subtracting something from the number, then plug in a large number (10 or 100). If you're dealing with hours in a day, plug in 24.

3. Percents = 100. If you're dealing with percents, plug in 100.

4. Don't use 0, 1, or any numbers in the problem. If the problem has a bunch of 2s and 3s in it, plug in 5.

5. Use all different numbers. Make sure that your numbers are all different—different from each other and different from the numbers in the problem.

6. If you're not sure if you did it correctly, go to the answer choices and plug in your numbers. If only one answer choice works, you probably did the problem correctly. If no answer choice works, you messed up. If multiple answer choices work, then you need to plug in new numbers, but the answer choices that didn't work don't need to be tried again—if it didn't work once, it isn't correct!

7. Get rid of "in terms of blah." Most algebra problems have extra words in them that make the problem a little hard to read—the most common extra words are "in terms of"—just cross that phrase out, and reread the problem. Don't let ETS's extra word tricks get you down!

Try this one:

If w gallons of chocolate fill the candy vat in t hours, and the chocolate costs $20 per gallon, in terms of w and t, what is the cost of the chocolate that will fill the vat in $t + 7$ hours?

    a. $wt20$
    b. $w(t + 7)20$
    c. $20(t + 7)$
    d. $20(w/t)(t + 7)$
    e. $20(t/w)(t + 7)$

! INFO TO GO

If there are variables in the problem or the answer choices, you can make up your own numbers!

Solution

This one is easy if you assigned numbers to the variables. Let's assign the following numbers:

    w = 10 gallons
    t = 2 hours

Now if chocolate flows in at a rate of 10 gallons in 2 hours, that means it's flowing in at a rate of 5 gallons in one hour. If it's flowing at 5 gallons in 1 hour, how many gallons will flow in $(t + 7)$ hours? Well, $(t + 7) = 9$ (we made $t = 2$). So 5 gallons in 1 hour would become 45 gallons in 9 hours. At $20 per gallon, that would cost $900 ($45 \times 20$). Our answer is 900.

Now plug in our variable (w = 10 and t = 2) into the answer choices and find the one that gives us 900. The answer is d.

You can plug in on simple equations too. Take a look at this one:

Level: Easy

$2(3x + 5x) - 2(x + 3x) =$

   a. x

   b. 3x

   c. 5x

   d. 8x

   e. 27x

Solution

Would you like to make this one easy? Just make up a number for x! Let's keep this easy, so make $x = 2$. If $x = 2$, then we have:

$$2(3x + 5x) - 2(x + 3x) =$$
$$2(6 + 10) - 2(2 + 6) =$$
$$2(16) - 2(8) =$$
$$32 - 16 =$$
$$16 =$$

Now just find the answer choice that equals 16. Plug in 2 for x for every answer choice and pick the once that gives you 16.

   a. $x = 2$

   b. $3x = 6$

   c. $5x = 10$

   d. $8x = 16$ (right answer!)

   e. $27x = 54$

Using the Answer Choices

You can also use the answer choices to help you solve the problem. Try this one:

Level: Medium

Bob's age is twice Jim's age and three times Jane's age. Together, their three ages add up to 55. What is Bob's age?

   a. 6

   b. 10

   c. 15

   d. 30

   e. 36

Solution

It doesn't mater whether you can set up an equation for this problem. There are answer choices, and we can simply use them. Whenever you're using the answer choices, it's best to start in the middle, then work your way up or down depending on whether you believe you need a bigger number.

So let's start with c. 15. We know that Bob is twice as old as Jim and three times as old as Jane. So if Bob is 15, Jim is 7.5 and Jane is 5. If 15 is the correct answer, those three numbers would add up to 55 (the total age). But we're not even close to 55, so the correct answer cannot be c. 15 and we know we need a bigger number. So let's try d. 30. If Bob is 30, then Jim is 15 and Jane is 10. Do those add up to 55? Yes, so d. is the correct answer. Easy!

! INFO TO GO

Stuck on a problem? If there are numbers in the answer choices, plug them back into the problem in order to solve it!

You want to see the "algebra" solution? Okay, but it's harder and takes more time! We know that Jim = $\frac{1}{2}$ Bob and Jane = $\frac{1}{3}$ Bob. Therefore, $B + \frac{1}{2}B + \frac{1}{3}B = 55$. Add together those Bs and you get $1\frac{5}{6}B = 55$. Solve, and $B = 30$. You don't need to know any of that to get the correct answer!

Let's try another:

Level: Hard

> A salesman's salary is equal to 20 percent of his sales plus a $1,500 base salary. If he made $4,300 one month, what was his total amount of sales for that month?
>
> a. 560
> b. 860
> c. 2,800
> d. 14,000
> e. 150,000

! INFO TO GO

Use common sense on math. Think: should my answer be bigger or smaller than the numbers in the problem?

You can set up an equation. But if you understand that his salary is a small fraction of his sales, you know that his sales must be more than his salary, right? So his sales must be more than $4,300. Look at the answer choices: that only leaves d. and e. as possible correct answers. If you had to guess, which would you guess? Probably d., right? $150,000 just seems too big. If you guessed d., you were correct. Often, all you need to do is understand the basic logic of the problem and then use the process of elimination in order to guess the best answer.

If you want to set up an equation, you need to translate the words in that problem into math. We have:

> salary is 20 percent of sales plus a $1,500 base salary

The math translation:

> salary = .20x + 1,500

And because his salary for one month is 4,300, plug that in. So we get:

> 4,300 = .20x + 1,500

Subtract 1,500 from both sides.

> 2,800 = .20x

And divide by .2.

> 14,000 = x.

Inequalities

Inequalities can be intimidating, but as long as you know the lingo and the rules, you'll be fine. There usually aren't more than two to three of these on the GRE, so you can skip these if they freak you out.

Know the Lingo

Here's the lingo you need to know:

What It Looks Like	What It Means
$\neq$	not equal to
$<$	less than
$\leq$	less than or equal to
$>$	greater than
$\geq$	greater than or equal to

If you see any of these symbols, you have an inequality. What should you do with it? Solve it just like an equation, but with these special rules.

Know the Rules

Inequality rules are easy. First, solve inequalities like an equation, but keep the inequality symbols intact—don't change them!

The second rule is the exception: if you multiply or divide by a negative number, you must "flip" the sign (for example, a < would become a >).

Try this one:

$3x + 3 > 24$

FAIR WARNING

Inequalities are all about intimidation. Don't let them intimidate you—follow the rules and you'll get them right.

How would you solve it? Just like an equation! Subtract 3 from each side and divide by 3. So you get:

$3x + 3 > 24$
$3x > 21$
$x > 7$

So $x > 7$ is the answer. Easy, right? And because we didn't multiply or divide by a negative number, we didn't need to flip the sign. Try this one:

$-3x + 30 \leq 39$

First, subtract 30 from both sides and you should get

$-3x \leq 9$

Now divide by -3.

$x \leq -3$

But because we divided by a negative number, we must flip the sign. So the answer is:

$x \geq -3$

Must Be/Could Be

You need to be alert if a problem uses the words "must be" or "could be." If a problem asks "Which one of these could be the answer?" then you only need to find one answer that works. Usually, this means you only need to plug in once. But if a problem asks something like "Which one of these must be the answer?" then you need to choose the answer choice that will work every time. To make sure an answer choice will work every time, you need to plug in more than once.

If you see "must be" in a question, make sure you try at least two different numbers. If any answer choice doesn't work for the first number you plug in, then you never need to try that number again. But you may have multiple answer choices that will work for the first number you plug in. In this case, you must try each of those answer choices with a second number. Try this one:

Level: Medium

If x is a positive, odd integer, for which of the following must y be negative?

a. $xy = 0$
b. $x - y = 0$
c. $x(2y) = 2$
d. $-2xy = 1$
e. $x + y = -3$

Solution

If you make $x = 1$, plug that into each answer choice, and see what you get for y.

a. $1y = 0$
$y = 0$
b. $1 - y = 0$
$y = 1$

c. $1(2y) = 2$

$y = 1$

d. $-2(1)y = 1$

$y = -1/2$

e. $1 + y = -3$

$y = -4$

So d. and e. work. You don't need to try a., b., or c. again, but I'll work them out in the next example. We need to plug in another number for d. and e. to find out which one must be odd every time. Let's make $x = 5$.

a. $5y = 0$

$y = 0$

b. $5 - y = 0$

$y = 5$

c. $5(2y) = 2$

$y = 1/5$

d. $-2(5)y = 1$

$y = -1/10$

e. $-5 + y = -3$

$y = 2$

So we know only d. works, and that must be our answer.

Standard Deviation

You probably won't encounter standard deviation on the GRE, but if you do, you'll usually just need to have a basic understanding of it. Simply put, standard deviation is the distance between members of a set of numbers. Remember this: a set that contains numbers that are all close together in value will have a smaller standard deviation than a set that contains numbers that are very different in value. So the set {3, 4, 4} will have a smaller standard deviation than the set {0, 9, 14}. Sometimes, that's all you need to know. So you usually don't need to know how to calculate standard deviation—you just need to know what it means.

Take a look at this one:

Level: Hard

If the mean of a set of numbers is 20 and standard deviation is 3, which of the following represents two standard deviations from the mean?

a. 14 to 26

b. 15 to 25

c. 17 to 23

d. 20 to 26

e. 20 to 60

Solution

Test-taker Tom would be intimated by the big words, but this is really quite easy. Each "deviation" from the mean must have a value of 3, so you're looking for the answer that moves away from the mean in intervals of 3—and because we need two deviations, we need a total distance of 6 on each side of the mean. Only a. satisfies these requirements. That really wasn't so hard.

Factoring and FOIL

Factoring is simply another way to write an expression. For example, $xy + xz$ can also be written $x(y + z)$. When you rewrite that expression, you have factored it (factored out the x, to be exact). This is often helpful because $x(y + z)$ may be easier to deal with than $xy + xz$. Often, GRE math problems are easier to solve after you factor. Sometimes a GRE math problem is actually easy to solve, if only you realize that it can be factored.

It's worth noting that you can "unfactor" an expression. So you may decide that $x(y + z)$ is easier to deal with if you rewrite it as $xy + xz$. In this case, you have distributed the x. "Unfactoring" isn't usually helpful, but you should keep in mind that factoring works both ways.

CIG Fast Factor Tips

If you see an expression that can be factored, you should always factor it and see what happens. Usually, the result will quickly lead you to the answer. So if you see "$3z + 3y$," you should instantly think "$3(z + y)$."

Similarly, if you see "$3(z + y)$," distribute that 3 and see what happens. Often, simply factoring or distributing will lead you to a correct answer.

Factoring can work with many kinds of numbers. For example, what would you do with this:

$$(7^5 + 7^4)/8$$

You could factor out a 7^4, and you would have this:

$$7^4(7^1 + 1)/8$$

Now simplify by adding $7^1 + 1$:

$$7^4(8)/8$$

Because $(8)/8 = 1$, we can simplify $7^4(8)/8$ to $7^4/1$ or just 7^4. So by using factoring, we can determine that $(7^5 + 7^4)/8$ is the same as 7^4.

When you see two sets of parentheses, you need to multiply every term in the first set by every term in the second set. This process is known as FOIL: first, outer, inner, last. So if you see $(y + 2)(y + 3)$, you would multiple $y \times y$, then $y \times 3$, then $2 \times y$, then 2×3. So you would get:

$$(y \times y) + (y \times 3) + (2 \times y) + (2 \times 3)$$
$$= y^2 + 3y + 2y + 6$$
$$= y^2 + 5y + 6$$

You can also do this in reverse. If I gave you $y^2 + 5y + 6 = 0$, you should immediately think that it could be written as this:

$$()()$$

Now you know the variable must be y (it's the only variable in the problem). So you would have this:

$$(y)(y)$$

Now everything in $y^2 + 5y + 6 = 0$ is positive, so we must have plus signs:

$$(y +)(y +)$$

Now focus on the "$5y$" in our expression. What 2 numbers add up to 5? Obviously, 2 and 3. So our two "numbers" are 2 and 3. Hence,

$$(y + 2)(y + 3) = 0 \text{ or } (y + 3)(y + 2) = 0$$

So you have 2 numbers: $(y + 2)$ and $(y + 3)$. According to the equation, when you multiply them, you get 0. What do you know about two numbers that, when multiplied, equal 0? You know that at least one of them must be 0. So either $(y + 2)$ or $(y + 3)$ must equal 0, so y must be either -2 or -3 (because $-2 + 2 = 0$ and $-3 + 3 = 0$). So your answer is $y = -2$ or -3.

> ! **INFO TO GO**
>
> Whenever you see anything that can be factored, factor it! Whenever you see anything that can be distributed (or unfactored), distribute it!

The Quadratics

Quadratic equations are common versions of the foiling we just did. There are three common quadratic equations that you should memorize and be able to quickly recognize. Usually, problems involving these equations involve nothing more than recognizing the equation. Once you recognize which equation you're dealing with, the problem solves itself.

Quadratic #1: $x^2 - y^2 = (x + y)(x - y)$

Quadratic #2: $(x + y)^2 = x^2 + 2xy + y^2$

Quadratic #3: $(x - y)^2 = x^2 - 2xy + y^2$

Level: Hard

If $x^2 - y^2$ is 18 and $x - y$ is 2, what is $x + y$?

a. 1

b. 4

c. 5

d. 9

e. 20

Solution

You know we're dealing with Quadratic #1, so $x^2 - y^2 = (x + y)(x - y)$. And we know that $x - y$ is 2. Plug that in and we get:

$x^2 - y^2 = (x + y)(x - y)$

$(x + y)(x - y) = 18$

$(x + y)2 = 18$

So $(x + y)$ must equal 9. d. is the correct answer.

The Least You Need to Know

♦ Know how to manipulate a basic equation.

♦ If you have two equations, stack them and add or subtract them.

♦ You can plug in your own numbers for any problem that has a variable in the question or answer choices.

♦ Always plug in numbers that are easy to work with.

♦ Stuck on a problem? Use the answer choices to help you solve it.

♦ Memorize FOIL and the three quadratics.

Chapter 15

Geometry: The Closest Thing to Cheating

In This Chapter

- ◆ Geometry basics
- ◆ Figures and formulas
- ◆ Solving hard problems without doing much math

Before we get into geometry problems, you'll need to understand the basic concepts—geometry terms and formulas. The first step to understanding GRE geometry is to understand what it's not. Almost all GRE test-takers know far more geometry than is actually tested on the GRE. There's no midpoint formula. No distance formula. No trig. GRE geometry stops at the Pythagorean theorem and basic slope problems. That's it.

First we'll take a look at the formulas and lingo you'll need to know. Then we'll go through the basics of solving geometry problems. Finally, we'll get into some amazing techniques and tips.

The Basics

Here are the terms and formulas you need to know. Memorize this stuff!

Circles

Area and circumference of a circle are fairly easy (circumference is the perimeter of a circle). Just remember that in order for the radius or diameter to be useful, it must go through the center of the circle. Here are the two circle formulas you need to know:

$$A = \pi r^2$$
$$C = 2\pi r$$

The diameter is the longest line you can draw in a circle. Finally, $2r = d$ (the diameter is twice as big as the radius).

> **! INFO TO GO**
>
> Pi (π) goes on forever, and you probably remember using 3.14 for pi in school. But on the GRE you can usually just use 3 (and remember that it's a little bigger). For some problems, you can keep things in terms of pi—so you don't need to use any number.

Try this one:

> **Level: Medium**
>
> A circular piece of cardboard with a radius of 2 is cut into two equal pieces. What is the perimeter of one of the pieces?
>
> a. 4
> b. 10
> c. $2\pi + 2$
> d. $2\pi + 4$
> e. $4\pi + 4$

> **Solution**
>
> Draw this if it helps. We started with a circle, and then we cut it in half. The perimeter of a piece includes half of the circumference and the diameter. The circumference is $2\pi r$, or $2\pi 2$, which is 4π. We only need half of the circumference, so that's 2π.

Add the diameter to that, and we've got the perimeter of the piece. So the answer must be $2\pi + 4$. The answer is d.

> **! INFO TO GO**
>
> If the problem describes a figure, draw that figure on your scratch paper.

Quadrilaterals

Any four-sided figure is a quadrilateral. A parallelogram is a special quadrilateral: its opposite sides are parallel. A rectangle is a special quadrilateral: it's a parallelogram with right angles. A square is a special quadrilateral: it's a rectangle with sides of equal length (so a square is a rectangle, a parallelogram, and a quadrilateral).

Regardless, all quadrilaterals (four-sided figures) have two things in common:

1. The area can always be found by multiplying the length and the width. Super-important rule: the length and width must always be perpendicular! In a square and rectangle, this means you can just use any two perpendicular sides. But in a quadrilateral that doesn't have right angles, you can use any side for the width (or base) and then you must use a line dropped from the opposite-side perpendicular to the width. Got it? *Your length must always be perpendicular to your width!* ETS will try to snag you on that!

2. When you add up all four interior angles, you always get 360 degrees—that's with squares, rectangles, or any other four-sided figure (with or without right angles).

Solids (Cubic or Rectangular)

Solids are rare on the GRE, so don't worry too much about them. Their volumes are easy to find: just multiply all the numbers. The formula is $V = lwh$.

Cylinders

The formula for finding the volume of a cylinder is:

$$V = \pi r^2 h$$

You'll almost never need to know this—in the past ten years, ETS has only asked a cylinder question two or three times—that's it! Most of the time, if you see a cylinder, the question is about something else (such as a right triangle within the cylinder).

Surface Area

Surface area is the two-dimensional area of a three-dimensional figure (or the area of its surface). This doesn't come up too often and usually it's not too bad. The only trick to know is this: the surface of a cube can be written SA = $s^2$6. Why? Because all of the sides of a cube are the same, the area of any one side is s^2, and there are six sides. There are a few hard problems where it will be helpful to know this surface-area shortcut.

Points and Lines

Here are some basic concepts and terminology that you must understand. These are such basic ideas that it is sometimes difficult to come up with a clear definition in words.

- **Point**—basically a location, represented by a dot in diagrams. Points have no size. Generally, we label points with uppercase alphabetic characters.

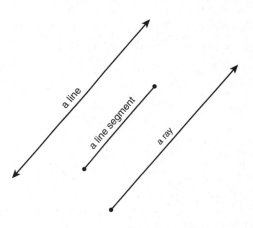

- **Line**—or "straight line." When we say "line," we mean "straight line." If the figure is not straight, we call it a curve. Lines are determined by specifying exactly the location of two points through which the line passes. Lines are considered to extend indefinitely in either direction.

- **Line segment**—a finite-length part of a line, generally bonded by two specific points on the line.

- **Ray**—the part of a line on one side of a specified point on that line. Rays extend indefinitely in one direction.

- **Plane**—a plane is what we recognize as a flat surface. Two of the ways that planes are determined are, 1, by giving the exact locations of any three points through which the plane passes; and 2, by specifying two lines that lie in the plane. Like lines, planes are considered to extend indefinitely in all directions.

Parallel Lines and Their Angles

Two lines are parallel if …

- They both lie in the same plane.

- They do not intersect (or cross each other).

Because a line is considered to extend indefinitely in both directions, this definition really means that parallel lines never cross no matter how far you check in either direction.

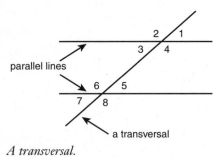

A transversal.

A transversal is a third line that crosses a pair of parallel lines on a slant, as shown in the accompanying illustration. As the transversal crosses the two parallel lines, eight angles are formed, numbered 1 through 8 in the illustration. You can see that four of the angles are quite large, and four of them are quite small. A very important set of properties of these angles is that the angles that appear to be the same in the illustration really are exactly the same. The properties of parallel lines can be summarized in these three easy rules:

- Two kinds of angles are created: big ones and small ones.

- All big angles are equal to each other and all small angles are equal to each other.

- Any big angle plus any small angle equals 180 degrees.

Got it? That's easy to remember. If you want the more complicated version (which you don't need unless you're aiming for 750+), here it is …

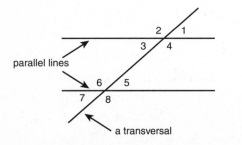

Given this figure, we can conclude that

$$\angle 1 = \angle 3 = \angle 5 = \angle 7$$

and

$$\angle 2 = \angle 4 = \angle 6 = \angle 8$$

Also pairs of adjacent angles always add up to 180°, as you can easily see from the figure. Thus $\angle 1 + \angle 2 = 180°$, $\angle 2 + \angle 3 = 180°$, $\angle 3 + \angle 4 = 180°$, $\angle 5 + \angle 6 = 180°$ and so forth.

Now for the terminology:

- Angles in the same relative position around the two intersection points are called corresponding angles. Thus $\angle 1$ and $\angle 5$ are corresponding angles, as are $\angle 4$ and $\angle 8$, $\angle 2$ and $\angle 6$, and also $\angle 3$ and $\angle 7$. Corresponding angles are equal.

- $\angle 3$ and $\angle 5$ are called alternate interior angles. $\angle 4$ and $\angle 6$ are also alternate interior angles. Alternate interior angles are equal.

- $\angle 2$ and $\angle 8$ are called alternate exterior angles. $\angle 1$ and $\angle 7$ are also alternate exterior angles. Alternate exterior angles are equal.

These properties of parallel lines are important in understanding and exploiting the properties of similar triangles.

These properties also work both ways. For instance, all it takes to determine that two lines are parallel is to demonstrate that when a transversal is drawn across them, one of the pairs of corresponding angles formed is equal.

! INFO TO GO

Figures in multiple-choice problems are drawn to scale unless the instructions say otherwise. So an angle that *looks* bigger *is* bigger.

Try this one:

Level: Easy

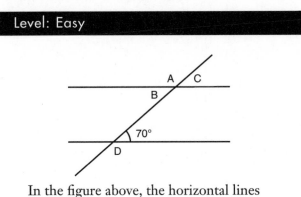

In the figure above, the horizontal lines are parallel. What is the sum of angles A, B, C, and D?

    a. 180

    b. 250

    c. 290

    d. 360

    e. 430

Solution

Because angle B is the alternate interior partner of the given angle of 70°, and alternate interior angles are equal, we know immediately that

$$B = 70°$$

Angle C and the given angle of 70° are corresponding angles, and corresponding angles are equal, so

$$C = 70°$$

Angles A and B are adjacent, so they must add up to 180°. Thus

$$A + B = A + 70° = 180°$$

so

$$A = 180° - 70° = 110°$$

Similarly, angle D is adjacent to the given angle of 70°, so the two must add up to 180°. That is

$$D + 70° = 180°$$

so

$$D = 180° - 70° = 110°$$

Thus, our solution is ...

$$A = 110°, B = 70°, C = 70°, \text{ and}$$
$$D = 110°.$$

Therefore, the sum is 360° and the correct answer is d.

Vertical Angles

When two lines cross, as shown in the accompanying diagram, they form four angles.

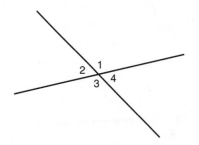

Four angles formed by two crossing lines.

∠1 and ∠3 are said to be vertical angles (or sometimes vertically opposite angles, though the word "opposite" is a bit redundant).

∠2 and ∠4 also form vertical angles.

As is fairly obvious from the diagram, vertical angles are equal. Thus

$$∠1 = ∠3$$

and

$$∠2 = ∠4$$

Angles

When two lines or line segments intersect in a plane, they form angles. The following figure shows such a situation. The lines forming the angle are called its sides, and the point at which the lines meet is called the vertex of the angle.

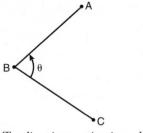

Two lines intersecting in a plane.

Angles are normally drawn as arcs, sometimes with arrowheads to indicate direction. The GRE usually refers to the angle in the figure using the notation ∠ABC or ∠CBA. Sometimes the GRE will refer simply to "angle B." Without a labeled figure, these notations can be ambiguous because even in the simple situation shown in the figure above, there are two possible angles to which the symbols "B" or "∠ABC" could be referring: the smaller angle shown, and the larger angle formed by thinking of the rotation being clockwise from BC to BA.

Angle Measurement

The most common unit of measurement for angles is degrees. In the degree system, 1 complete revolution = 360 degrees or 360°.

Parts of a degree are indicated by digits to the right of the decimal point as is done for other quantities in life. Thus, the angle 72.53° has 72° plus 0.53 of a seventy-third degree. Because 72/360 = ⅕, the angle 72.53° is just slightly more than one fifth of a complete revolution.

Special Angles

The GRE loves special angles. A right angle corresponds to ¼ of a complete revolution. Right angles are denoted by small boxes rather than circular arcs.

Lines that meet at right angles are said to be perpendicular. Obviously, the measure of a right angle is 90°.

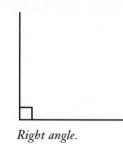

Right angle.

A straight angle looks like no angle at all, but corresponds to one half rotation or 180°.

Straight angle.

Acute angles are angles that measure between 0° and 90°. They are narrower than a right angle.

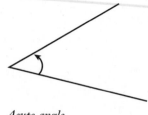

Acute angle.

Obtuse angles are angles that measure between 90° and 180°. They are broader than a right angle, but not as broad as a straight angle.

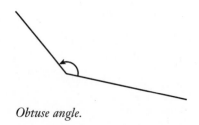

Obtuse angle.

Two angles are said to be complementary if they add up to 90° or a right angle. In the following figure, angles A and B are complementary.

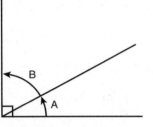

Complementary angles.

Two angles are said to be supplementary if they add up to 180° or a straight angle. In the following figure, angles A and B are supplementary.

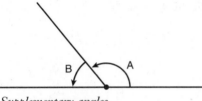

Supplementary angles.

Triangles

Triangles are plane geometric figures with three straight sides and three angles (*tri*-angles). Typically, the three angles are labeled with uppercase characters from the beginning of the alphabet, and the sides opposite each angle are labeled with the corresponding lowercase letters.

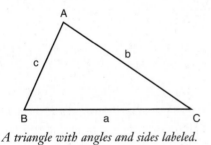

A triangle with angles and sides labeled.

Sometimes, the symbol Δ is used for the word "triangle." (Oddly, the GRE doesn't use the Δ symbol very often.)

Special Triangles

There are quite a number of terms to describe triangles of various special types. You need to know the following types:

- ◆ **Equilateral triangles**—all three sides have the same length and all three angles are the same size: 60°. Notice how sometimes small cross-lines are used to indicate which sides of the triangle have equal lengths.

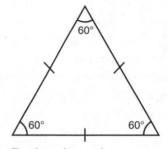

Equilateral triangle.

- ◆ **Isosceles triangles**—two of the three sides have the same length. The two angles opposite the equal-length sides have the same measure.

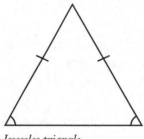

Isosceles triangle.

- ◆ **Scalene triangle**—this term is used to refer to a general triangle, having no specific relationships between the lengths of any sides.

! INFO TO GO

Big important triangle rule: one thing we can say about the lengths of the sides of any triangle in general is that no one side can be longer than the sum of the lengths of the other two sides.

The most important special triangle is the …

◆ **Right triangle**—has one angle which forms a right angle (90°). The vertex with the right angle is conventionally labeled C. The two shorter perpendicular sides are called legs of the right triangle. The longest side, opposite the right angle, is called the hypotenuse.

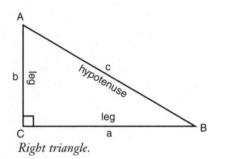

Right triangle.

FAIR WARNING

Don't assume triangles are right or equilateral just because they look like right or equilateral. Can you tell the difference between a 59° and 60° degree angle? Probably not.

The folks who make the GRE love right triangles because they love the *Pythagorean theorem*. If fact, 60–70 percent of *all* medium to hard GRE problems are Pythagorean theorem problems! In order to employ Pythag's theorem, you must have a right triangle. The GRE usually does not ask you to use the Pythag theorem or even give you a right triangle. The GRE will often simply give you a right angle and you need to find the right triangle, then deduce that the Pythag theorem should be used. So, on medium-hard geometry problems, you should investigate the problem carefully for right angles or right triangles. If you have a right angle but no triangle, draw a right triangle. Now ask: "How can I use the Pythag theorem?"

You'd be surprised at how often this leads to the correct answer.

VEXING VOCABULARY

What is the **Pythagorean theorem?** If you never studied it or have forgotten, review this carefully. Pythagoras's theorem is:

$$c^2 = a^2 + b^2$$

We'll look at the various uses of this theorem after we've spent a little more quality time with triangles.

Properties of Triangles

For every triangle, the angles *always* add up to 180°:

$$A + B + C = 180°$$

Try this one:

Level: Easy

Two angles in a triangle are 63.6° and 42.10°. What is the measurement of the third angle?

a. 42.1

b. 63.6

c. 74.3

d. 105.7

e. Cannot be determined

Solution

Okay, so this one is easy. It's designed just to get your brain going. Let x be the third angle which we are to determine. Then, because all three angles must add up to 180°, we must have that

$$x + 63.6° + 42.1° = 180°$$

So

$$x = 180° − (63.6° + 42.1°) = 74.3°$$

The third angle must be 74.3°. The answer is c.

Try this one:

Level: Easy

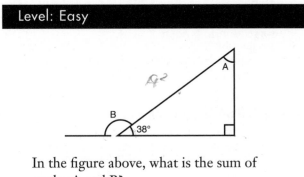

In the figure above, what is the sum of angles A and B?

    a. 52

    b. 128

    c. 142

    d. 180

    e. 194

Solution

The three angles inside the triangle must add up to 180°. The angle at the lower right is indicated to be a right angle, so it must measure 90°. Thus

$$38° + 90° + A = 180°$$

Therefore,

$$A = 180° − (38° + 90°) = 52°$$

Angle B, together with the 38° angle, form a straight angle which has a measure of 180°. Thus

$$B + 38° = 180°$$

So

$$B = 180° − 38° = 142°$$

So angle A (52°) plus angle B (142°) equals 194°. The correct answer is e.

Here's a fun angle fact. For any right triangle, C = 90°, so A + B = 90°—the two acute angles are complementary.

In any triangle, the longest side is always opposite the largest angle, and the shortest side is always opposite the smallest angle.

Perimeter of a Triangle

The perimeter, P, or distance around any triangle, is simply the sum of the lengths of its sides:

$$P = a + b + c$$

Try this one:

Level: Easy

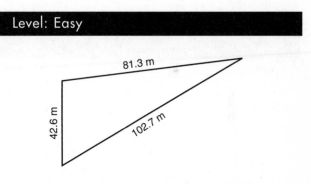

A triangular plot of land is sketched as shown in the figure above. What is the cost, in dollars, of putting a fence around the perimeter of this plot of land if the fence material costs $15.95 per meter?

    a. 226.6

    b. 679.47

    c. 1,296.74

    d. 1,638.07

    e. 3,614.27

X FAIR WARNING

Don't lose points because you didn't sketch this on your scratch paper!

Solution

The perimeter is just the sum of the lengths of the three sides:

$$P = 42.6 \text{ m} + 81.3 \text{ m} + 102.7 \text{ m}$$
$$= 226.6 \text{ m}$$

To get the cost of the fence, just multiply the number of meters of fence required (the perimeter of the triangle) by the cost in dollars per meter. Thus

$$Cost = 226.6 m \times \left(15.95 \, \frac{\$}{m} \right) = \$3614.27$$

Now the GRE is having some fun (at your expense). Try this one:

Level: Medium

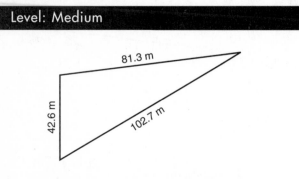

A man wants to fence in his triangular plot of land, as shown in the figure above. What is the cost, in dollars, of putting a fence around the perimeter of this plot of land if the fence material costs $15.95 per meter for the first 100 meters, $12 per meter for the next 100 meters, and $8 per meter for each meter after that, and the fence company charges a $75 installation fee in addition to the per-meter cost?

    a. 226.6

    b. 1,812.80

    c. 2,719.20

    d. 3,082.80

    e. 3,614.27

Solution

As before, the perimeter is just the sum of the lengths of the three sides:

$$P = 42.6 \text{ m} + 81.3 \text{ m} + 102.7 \text{ m}$$
$$= 226.6 \text{ m}$$

To get the cost of the fence, multiply the number of meters of fence by the corresponding cost:

    First 100 meters: $100 \times 15.95 = 1,595$
    Second 100 meters: $100 \times 12 = 1,200$
    Remaining meters ($226.6 - 200 = 26.6$): $26.6 \times 8 = 212.8$

Include the $75 installation fee and add it all together:

    $1,595 + 1,200 + 212.8 + 75 = 3,082.80$

The answer is d.

Base and Height of a Triangle

Any side of a triangle can be the base. Often, the "bottom" side is chosen as the base—but sometimes you need to choose another side to make the problem easier. Once you've chosen the base, you can draw a height (or altitude). The rule for heights is this: the height of a triangle is a line dropped from the angle opposite the base perpendicular to the base. This is important: the base and the height are always perpendicular!

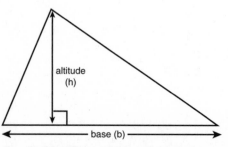

Base and height are always perpendicular.

Area of a Triangle

Area of the triangle is

$$A = \frac{1}{2}bh \quad \text{(one half base times height)}$$

You will get exactly the same answer if you use any of the three sides of the triangle as the base. In some tricky cases, the altitude may not be inside the triangle. Instead, it may have to be a vertical line from the top vertex drawn to intersect an extension of the base, as shown below. The base is still just the actual horizontal side of the triangle and not its extension.

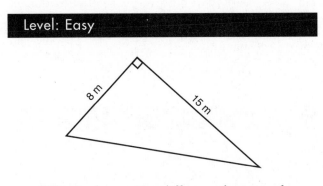

Altitude as a vertical line from the top vertex drawn to intersect an extension of the base.

Try this one:

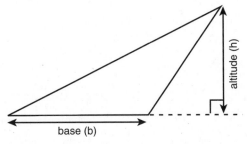

What is the positive difference between the perimeter and the area of the figure above?

a. 20
b. 40
c. 60
d. 100
e. 120

Solution

This triangle is a right triangle with the length of the two legs given. To calculate the perimeter, we need the lengths of all three sides. Fortunately, because this is a right triangle, Pythag's theorem applies, giving us a way to calculate the length of the third side (in this case, the hypotenuse).

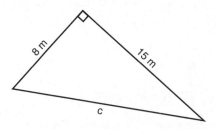

So, letting c stand for the length of the longest side of this triangle, we have by Pythagoras that

$$c^2 = (8 \text{ m})^2 + (15 \text{ m})^2$$
$$= 64 \text{ m}^2 + 225 \text{ m}^2 = 289 \text{ m}^2$$

Therefore,

$$c = \sqrt{289 \text{ m}^2} = 17 \text{ m}$$

So,

perimeter = p = sum of the lengths of the three sides

$$= 8 \text{ m} + 15 \text{ m} + 17 \text{ m}$$
$$= 40 \text{ m}$$

To calculate the area, imagine rotating the triangle so that the side of length 15 m is on the bottom, horizontal. Then the side of length 8 m will be vertical (because it is perpendicular to the side of length 15 m).

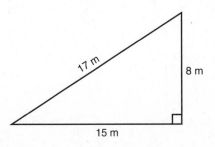

In this orientation, the side of length 15 m forms a base of the triangle (so $b = 15$ m) and the side of length 8 m forms the corresponding altitude of the triangle ($h = 8$ m). Thus, we get

$$Area = A = \frac{1}{2}bh$$

$$= \frac{1}{2}(15\,\text{m})(8\,\text{m}) = 60\,\text{m}^2$$

The perimeter is 40 and the area is 60, so the positive difference is 20. The answer is a.

The Geometry Goldmine: Pythagoras's Theorem

The so-called theorem of Pythagoras states that for a right triangle, it is always true that:

$$c^2 = a^2 + b^2$$

Recall that in a right triangle, the longest side, opposite the right angle, is called the hypotenuse. Thus Pythag's theorem states that for right triangles the square of the length of the hypotenuse equals the sum of the squares of the lengths of the other two (shorter) sides. If the lengths of any two sides of a right triangle are known, then the length of the remaining third side can be computed using this formula.

Try this one:

Level: Easy

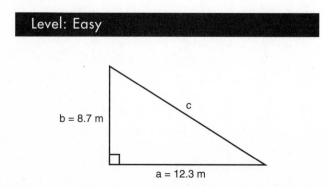

In the previous figure, the two perpendicular sides of a right triangle have lengths 12.3 m and 8.7 m, respectively. What is the length of the hypotenuse (round your answer to the nearest tenth)?

    a. 8

    b. 8.7

    c. 12

    d. 15

    e. 15.1

Solution

We are asked to determine the value of c (the hypotenuse). Applying Pythag's theorem directly gives

$$c^2 = a^2 + b^2$$

$$= (12.3\ \text{m})^2 + (8.7\ \text{m})^2$$

$$= 226.98\ \text{m}^2$$

Therefore,

$$c = \sqrt{c^2} = \sqrt{226.98\ \text{m}^2} \cong 15.0659$$

Because we are asked to round the tenth's place (first place after the decimal), the length of the hypotenuse of this right triangle is 15.1 m. The correct answer is e.

Try this one:

Level: Easy

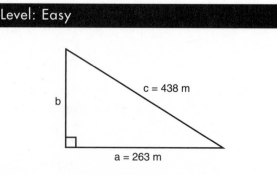

A plot of land in the shape of a right triangle has a hypotenuse of length 438 m, and one of the other sides is 263 m long. At a cost of 20 cents per square meter, what will it cost, in dollars, for farmer Woody to plant grass on this entire plot of land (1 dollar = 100 cents)?

    a. 9,211.58

    b. 11,519.40

    c. 18,423.15

    d. 23,038.80

    e. 921,157.50

Solution

The goal is to compute the area of this triangular region. With a right triangle, the two perpendicular sides can be considered to form a base and the corresponding altitude of the triangle. So, for this specific triangle, we have that

$$Area = \frac{1}{2}\ base \times altitude = \frac{1}{2}\ ab$$

Thus, to calculate the area, we need to calculate the length b of the side oriented vertically in the figure. But by Pythagoras's theorem

$$c^2 = a^2 + b^2$$

we can write

$$b^2 = c^2 - a^2$$
$$= (438 \text{ m})^2 - (263 \text{ m})^2$$
$$= 122{,}675 \text{ m}^2$$

Thus

$$b = \sqrt{b^2} = \sqrt{122675 \text{ m}^2} \cong 350.25 \text{ m}$$

Now we can calculate the area:

$$Area = \frac{1}{2}\ ab \cong \frac{1}{2}\big(263 \text{ m}\big)\big(350.25 \text{ m}\big) = 46057.875 \text{ m}^2$$

Because the area is 46,057.875, we can figure out the cost per meter. Because 20 cents is equal to .20, we can simply multiply: 46,057.875 × .20 = 9,211.575.

Round the answer using normal rounding rules, and you get a. 9,211.58.

Try this one:

Level: Medium

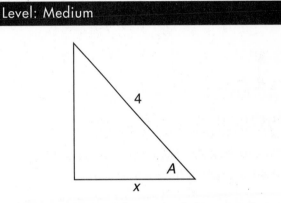

In the right triangle pictured above, angle A is 45 degrees and the hypotenuse is 4. What is x?

    a. $\sqrt{2}$

    b. 2

    c. $\sqrt{4}$

    d. 4

    e. $\sqrt{8}$

Solution

This is part vocabulary question, part Pythagorean Theorem question. First, you need to recognize that the hypotenuse is the longest side, opposite the right angle. Next, by definition, if a right triangle has one 45 degree angle, then they must both be 45 degrees, so we have a 45-45-90 triangle. You don't need to memorize any fancy rules, just apply the Pythagorean Theorem:

$$a^2 + b^2 = c^2$$

You know that c is 4 (the problem tells us) and, because sides opposite equal angles are also equal, we know that a and b are both the same. That's all we need to solve it!

$$a^2 + b^2 = c^2$$
$$a^2 = b^2$$
$$c^2 = 4^2 = 16$$
$$2(a^2) = 16$$
$$a^2 = 8$$
$$a = \sqrt{8}$$

When you have a 45-45-90 triangle, you only need to know the length of one side to solve for everything else! The answer is e.

If we know the lengths of the three sides of a triangle, Pythagoras's theorem can also be used to determine whether that triangle is a right triangle.

Try this one:

Which of the following can be the lengths of the sides of a right triangle?

(i) 8, 19, 13
(ii) 13, 12, 5
(iii) 7, 42, 9

    a. i only
    b. ii only
    c. i and ii
    d. all
    e. none

Solution

In each case, the longest side must be the hypotenuse (because the hypotenuse is always the longest side of a right triangle). If the given triangle is really a right triangle, then the square of the length of the longest side must be exactly equal to the sum of the squares of the lengths of the other two sides.

So, for case (i), the length 19 must be the length of the hypotenuse. Here,

$$19^2 = 361$$

But

$$8^2 + 13^2 = 64 + 169 = 233$$

Because $233 \neq 361$, these three numbers do not satisfy Pythagoras's theorem, and so they cannot represent the lengths of the three sides of a right triangle.

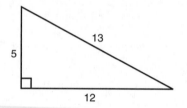

For case (ii), the length 13 must be the length of the hypotenuse. Then

$$13^2 = 169$$

and

$$5^2 + 12^2 = 25 + 144 = 169$$

Because these two results are equal, we conclude that these three lengths do form a right triangle, as sketched in the figure.

For case (iii), the length 42 would have to be the length of the hypotenuse. Then, checking, we find that

$$42^2 = 1,764$$

and

$$7^2 + 9^2 = 49 + 81 = 130$$

Because $1,764 \neq 130$, we know that these three lengths cannot form a right triangle. In fact, because 42 is greater than 7 + 9 = 16, it turns out that these three lengths cannot even form a triangle of any shape!

The answer is b. ii only.

Slope

Slope is the rate of change of a line on a graph. The formula for slope is Δy divided by Δx in which

Δy = the change in y

Δx = the change in x

So if you're given two points, you subtract the two y points and you subtract the two x points, then divide what you got for the y points by the x points. Here's an example:

What's the slope of a line that passes through points (2,3) and (4,7)?

Points on an x,y graph are always given in the order x,y. So pick either y point and subtract it from the other y point. *Hint: it's easier to pick the larger points, if possible, and subtract the smaller points because then you're only dealing with positive numbers.* In this case, let's do this:

Δy = the change in y = 7 − 3 = 4

Δx = the change in x = 4 − 2 = 2

Now divide our Δy (4) by our Δx (2) and we get 4 / 2 = 2.

So our slope is 2.

Try this one:

Level: Medium

A line passes through points (7,3) and (z,8) and has a slope of 2. What is the value of z?

　a. 7

　b. 7.5

　c. 9.5

　d. 12

　e. 17

Solution

Δy = the change in y = 8 − 3 = 5

Δx = the change in x = z − 7

Now divide our Δy (5) by our Δx (z − 7) and set it equal to the slope, 2.

$5/z − 7 = 2$

Multiple both sides by z − 7.

$5 = 2 (z − 7)$ which equals

$5 = 2z − 14$

Add 14 to both sides.

$19 = 2z$

Divide by 2.

$9.5 = z$

The answer is c.

Try this one:

Level: Medium

What is the slope of a line that passes through point (−2,4) and the origin?

　a. −2

　b. −1

　c. 0

　d. 1

　e. 2

Solution

The origin is (0,0). So we'll use (−2,4) and (0,0) as our two points.

Δy = the change in y = 4 − 0 = 4

Δx = the change in x = −2 − 0 = −2

Now divide our Δy (4) by our Δx (−2).

$4/−2 = −2$

So our slope is −2. The answer is a.

Tricks and Tips

Now that you have the basics, you'll need a few tricks to get you out of trouble spots. What if you can't quite do a problem? What if you don't think you have enough information? We're here to help.

Plug in the Answer Choices

Whenever you have a tricky geometry question, particularly one that involves measurements of angles, you can plug in the answer choices if the answer choices are numbers. (If the answer choices are variables, then they won't help much.) Often, you can plug in numbers even if you don't understand the problem (or how to set it up).

Try this one:

Level: Hard

If the length of the edge of a cube is increased by 2, then the surface area is increased by 192. What is the original length of the edge of the cube?

a. 96
b. 32
c. 24
d. 8
e. 7

Solution

Remember that surface area is the two-dimensional area of a three-dimensional figure (or the area of its surface). The surface of a cube can be written $SA = s^2 6$. Why? Because all of the sides of a cube are the same, the area of any one side is s^2, and there are six sides.

For this problem, instead of trying to write an equation, simply go to the

answer choices. Find the surface area for each of the answer choices, then find the surface area for each answer choice increased by two.

Answer Choice	SA	+2	New SA	Increase of
a. 96	55296	98	57624	2328
b. 32				
c. 24				
d. 8	486	10	600	114
e. 7	294	9	486	192

First, try choice A. You're looking for a new surface area (SA) that's 192 more than the old SA. Once you realize that choice (a) is way too big—it gives us a new SA that's 2328 bigger—skip down to the smaller numbers: d. or e. Choice d. gives us an increase of 114, so try e.—it's the correct answer.

Make Up Your Own Numbers

If you're stuck on a problem and there aren't nice numbers in the answer choices, make up your own. Don't ask questions about whether it will work—just try it and see (it usually works). Parallel lines are a great example of a problem type for which making up numbers is key! In the following problem, just make up numbers!

FAIR WARNING

With geometry, you can usually make up any numbers you wish, but it's best to make up numbers that look right—if an angle looks like it's 45 degrees, call it 45 degrees.

Another warning: make sure you follow the rules of geometry (if two angles make a straight line, make up two numbers that equal 180).

Level: Hard

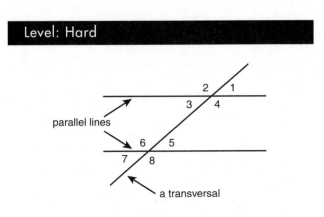

parallel lines

a transversal

In the figure above, angle 7 must be equal to

   a. the sum of angle 3 and angle 1

   b. the sum of angle 6 and angle 8 minus angle 1

   c. the sum of angle two and angle 4 minus 50 degrees

   d. angle 6 minus angle 5

   e. the sum of angle 2, angle 3, and angle 4 minus the sum of angle 6 and 8

Solution

Just make up a number for angle 7—anything you want. We'll call it 30. Now, using what we know about parallel lines, let's figure out what all the other angles will be.

   Angles 1, 3, 5, and 7 will be 30.
   Angles 2, 4, 6, and 8 will be 150.

Now go through the answer choices, plug in these numbers, and see what you get. We're looking for angle 7, which we called 30.

   a. the sum of angle 3 and angle 1 equals 60

   b. the sum of angle 6 and angle 8 minus angle 1 equals 270

   c. the sum of angle 2 and angle 4 minus 50 degrees equals 250

   d. angle 6 minus angle 5 equals 120

   e. the sum of angle 2, angle 3, and angle 4 minus the sum of angle 6 and 8 equals 30—bingo.

So the answer is e. Plugging in numbers works every time!

Draw and Redraw

When the GRE gives you a figure that's labeled "Not drawn to scale," you must wonder: *why isn't it drawn to scale? Did the folks at ETS lose their protractors?* Of course, it's not drawn to scale just to fool you. Pay attention: there's something messed up about the figure. Here are the rules for figures not drawn to scale:

♦ Redraw the figure, making it to scale. If one side is bigger than the other, make one side look bigger. If you're not sure what it's supposed to look like, then sketch a few different figures to help you understand the different possibilities.

♦ If you got your answer from the figure, then you got the wrong answer. The figure is giving you bad information. You must work with the information in the problem, not with the info from the figure.

♦ Sometimes the figure isn't drawn to scale because if it were, the answer would be obvious. So always redraw and keep an eye out for the answer—sometimes the correct answer is in a good drawing.

Measure It!

Finally, any figure that doesn't have "Not Drawn to Scale" below it is drawn to scale. So if all else fails, measure the sides or angles you are trying to find.

For example:

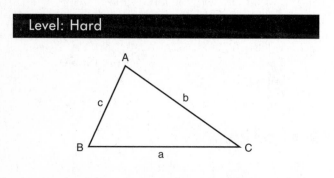

Level: Hard

In the figure above, side a is 7, side b is 6.25, and the measure of angle B is 55. What is the closest approximation of the measure of side c?

a. 2.4

b. 3.75

c. 4.5

d. 5.25

e. 5.75

Solution

Could you whip out some trig and solve this? Perhaps, but who cares? Just take your pencil or your answer sheet and mark off either 7 or 6.25, then measure side c. If you measured carefully, you'll find that side c is a little more than half 7—so pick the answer that's a little more than half of 7 (that is, a little more than 3.5). The answer is b.

You'd be surprised by the number of GRE problems that are solvable simply by measuring!

The Least You Need to Know

- ◆ Memorize geometry formulas.
- ◆ Know the rules of triangles and quadrilaterals.
- ◆ Draw figures on your scratch paper.
- ◆ Measure any figure that's drawn to scale.
- ◆ When all else fails, make up your own numbers to help solve the problem.

Chapter 16

Quantitative Comparisons

In This Chapter

- ◆ Understanding the directions
- ◆ Strategies and tips
- ◆ Tricks for getting them right!

Quantitative comparisons are a disappearing problem type—you won't see too many. But they can be easy with a little practice and are certainly worth reviewing.

Understanding Quantitative Comparisons

Quantitative comparisons are those problems that ask you "Which side is bigger, Column A or Column B?" Some of your math problems will be in quant comp format. There are only four answer choices for quant comp questions (instead of five) and every quant comp question has the same four answer choices:

a. The quantity in Column A is greater.
b. The quantity in Column B is greater.
c. The two quantities are equal.
d. The relationship cannot be determined from the information given.

Make sure you understand the answer choices:

Pick a. if A is *always* bigger.
Pick b. if B is *always* bigger.
Pick c. if they are *always* equal.
Pick d. if you get more than one answer or you can't tell.

Always is italicized because it's the most important word in the answer choices. If you get Column A is bigger, it doesn't mean that a. is the correct answer. In order for a. to be correct, column A must *always* be bigger.

But if you get A is bigger just once, that does mean that b. and c. are not possible answer choices. If A is bigger just once, then B can't always be bigger and they can't always be equal. Makes sense, doesn't it?

Also keep in mind that e. is not an answer choice. So unlike every other type of multiple choice question, e. is not possible. This means that you only have four answer choices and your chances of guessing the correct answer are higher, so be aggressive!

QC Tricks

Here are the six tricks to getting quant comps correct:

1. A problem must have variables in order for d. to be a possible answer choice—if there are no variables, d. isn't correct. So if you're looking at a bunch of numbers, the correct answer is a., b., or c.

2. If you have variables, you must plug in at least twice. First, plug in a "normal" number (such as 2 or 3), then plug in a weird number (such as 0, 1, fractions, negative numbers, and negative fractions). Keep in mind that the second time you plug in, your goal is to get an answer other than what you got the first time. If you got A is bigger the first time, try to make B bigger the second time.

3. Whatever you get the first time will eliminate two answer choices. If you get A is bigger the

first time, then you don't know if A is always bigger until you plug in at least one more time. But you do know that if A is bigger once, then B can't always be bigger and they can't always be the same, so you can get rid of b. and c.

4. On hard quant comps, simply get rid of whichever side looks bigger. Test-taker Tom is attracted to the bigger side, and you know it must be wrong. If the two sides look equal, c. can't be the correct answer. If you have a ton of variables and the problem seems to be unsolvable, get rid of d. Whatever Tom would pick is wrong on a hard question.

5. There are always two or three quant comp problems where you're given two variables (sometimes three), and a little information (x and y are positive, or integers, or they add up to 20). The correct answer is always D. You should try them to make sure, but don't fall into the trap. It's easy to plug in once to these problems and get a. or b., but that's the trap! Whenever you see two variables (x and y) and a little information ($x + y = 7$ and xy is positive), then look for d.—it's probably correct.

6. Take it easy. Your job isn't to calculate the exact value of Column A and Column B. Your job is simply to figure out which one is bigger. Often, you can do that without actually calculating exact values. In fact, usually the most frustrating quant comps are the ones that don't give you much information. Just keep in mind that you only need to determine which is bigger.

Try a few!

Now let's try a few quant comps for practice.

Example #1

Level: Medium

Material Y contains less than 1 percent of chemical X.

Column A	Column B
The total percentage of chemical X in material Y	The total percentage of all other chemicals in material Y

Example #2

Level: Medium

Column A	Column B
$x + 7 + y$	$x + 7 - y$

! INFO TO GO

Remember to plug in twice if you have variables.

Example #3

Level: Medium

Column A	Column B
The circumference of a circle with a radius of 2	The diameter of a circle with a circumference of 2

Solutions

Example #1: If material Y contains less than 1 percent of chemical X, then we can deduce that all the other chemicals must be more than 99 percent. Column B is always bigger.

Example #2: We have no idea whether x and y are positive or negative numbers. In fact, x and y could both be 0. So the answer is D.

Example #3: Circumference = $2\pi r$, so the circumference for Column A is 4π, or about 12. For Column B, $2 = \pi d$, so the diameter must be $\frac{2}{\pi}$, or about $\frac{2}{3}$. So Column A is always bigger.

The Least You Need to Know

- Quant comps are mixed into multiple-choice problems.
- Know the answer choices before you take the test.
- No variables means D isn't correct.
- Plug in twice if you have variables.

Chapter 17

More Charts, Tables, and Data (Oh, My)!

In This Chapter

◆ The layout of chart/table/data questions

◆ Ways to get them all correct!

◆ Practice questions

The fine folks at ETS have decided that the GRE should contain more chart, table, and "data interpretation" questions. All of these question types are quite easy, if you know how to gather and interpret data. Each of these questions will present you with information, and the questions will ask you to find that information. The trick, of course, is to make sure you know what the question is asking and where to find it.

Getting Them Correct

The first step is to read these questions slowly; often, people miss chart/table questions simple because they misread them. This is important because fine differences in how you read a question can cause major differences in the answers you get.

Data interpretation questions are questions that ask you to understand and use some bit of information. Such questions may range from interpreting data on a chart or table to following a set of instructions. The set of instructions may look like this:

$$x\$y = (x + y)/(x - y)$$

Don't freak out. You may think, "But I've never seen this before!" That's okay, no one has! ETS has simply invented a set of instructions for you to follow. In the above, it just means that when you see this: $x\$y$, you do this: $(x + y)/(x - y)$. So if you saw 3\$4, you would plug 3 in for x and 4 in for y and get this: $(3 + 4)/(3 - 4)$, which results in 7/-1, or -7. Just remain calm, read the question carefully, and proceed methodically.

Here are the steps to follow for all chart, table, and data questions:

1. **Read and interpret the question.** The first step in interpreting the data correctly is making sure you fully understand the question!

2. **Explore all the information in a chart.** Make sure you read every label, every title, and every number. Are the numbers in millions or billions? Does each entry cover a single year? Is everything in the same units? Don't assume anything.

3. **Read all the answer choices.** And be wary of any answer choice that simply repeats the information from the table or chart.

4. **Most importantly: practice a little.** Most students can get fairly good at these question types with a little practice.

So here are a few practice questions!

Practice Question #1

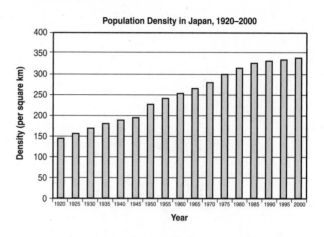

Population Density in Japan, 1920–2000

1. By what percentage did the population density of Japan increase between 1920 and 2000?

   a. 30 percent

   b. 57 percent

   c. 130 percent

   d. 200 percent

   e. 300 percent

Solution

(340 - 147)/147 = 130%

The correct answer is c.

2. What were the average rates of increase in the population density from 1920 to 2000, and from 1975 to 2000, respectively, in people per square km per decade?

   a. 2.4, 1.6

   b. 35, 16

   c. 24, 16

   d. 12, 8

   e. 1.2, .8

Solution

For 1920 to 2000: (340 - 147)/8 decades = 24 (people/sq km)/decade.

For 1975 to 2000: (340 - 300)/2.5 decades = 16 (people/sq km)/decade

The correct answer is c.

Practice Question #2

The following chart shows the distribution of representatives by party in a hypothetical parliament:

Party Name	Number of Representatives
A	116
B	220
C	125
D	35
E	4

1. Which two parties, when combined, could form a majority in the parliament?

    a. A and C

    b. C and D

    c. B and E

    d. D and E

    e. B and D

Solution

Total number of members of people in parliament = 500

The only two groups from the above choices which total more than 250 are B and D.

The correct answer is e.

2. How many different such two-party majority coalitions are possible?

    a. 1

    b. 2

    c. 3

    d. 4

    e. 5

Solution

B and A have 336 members, B and C have 345 members, B and D have 255 members.

The correct answer is c.

Practice Question #3

The table below shows the results on a high school final, where the grades are out of 100:

Grade Range	Number of Students
0–60	1
61–70	5
71–80	12
81–90	16
91–100	8

    a. At least 44

    b. At most 47

    c. At most 35

    d. 55

    e. 58

Fill in two of the answer choices above to make the following sentence true, based only on the information given in the table:

1. If the lowest score on the test was _____ then the difference between the highest and lowest score was _____.

Solution

91 – 47 = 44, so if 47 is the upper limit for the lowest grade on the test, then the highest grade is at least 91, so the difference between the two is at least 44.

The correct answers are b. and a.

2. What would have to have been the worst grade on the test so that the average of the students' scores was 77?

    a. At most 53

    b. 77

    c. At least 55

    d. At least 77

    e. Cannot be determined

Solution

Clearly it is not b., c., or d. If 5 students got 61, 12 students got 71, 16 students got 81, and 8 students got 91, then the final grade would have to be 53 to make the average 77.

The correct answer is a.

Practice Question #4

Percentage of World Population by Continent in 1750 and 2000

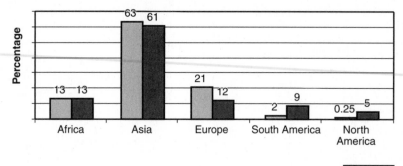

Africa   Asia   Europe   South America   North America

☐ 1750
■ 2000

1. If the population of the world was 790 million in 1750, and was 7.7 times larger in 2000, then which area had the largest net increase in <u>total population</u>?

    a. Africa

    b. Asia

    c. Europe

    d. South America

    e. North America

Solution

Calculate the population in 2000, then take percents to get actual value for populations in 1750 and 2000.

Net increase of Africa is 690 million
Net increase of Asia is 3.2 billion
Net increase of Europe is 565 million
Net increase of South America is 504 million
Net increase of North America is 314 million

The correct answer is b.

2. How many of the areas shown had fewer than 10 million people in 1750?

    a. None

    b. 1

    c. 2

    d. 3

    e. 4

Solution

Similarly, multiply the percent for the region by the total population, and we see that the total population of North America is only 2 million in 1750. All the others have populations above 10 million.

The correct answer is b.

3. How many of the areas shown had more than 600 million people in 2000?

    a. None

    b. 1

    c. 2

    d. 3

    e. 4

Solution

Again, we have already found the world population in 2000, so we simply multiply the percents. Africa, Asia, and Europe qualify.

The correct answer is d.

Practice Question #5

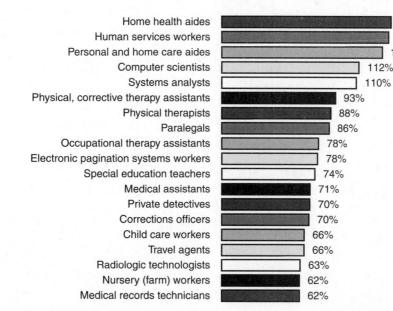

**Fastest Growing Occupations
1992-2005**

Occupation	Percent
Home health aides	138%
Human services workers	136%
Personal and home care aides	130%
Computer scientists	112%
Systems analysts	110%
Physical, corrective therapy assistants	93%
Physical therapists	88%
Paralegals	86%
Occupational therapy assistants	78%
Electronic pagination systems workers	78%
Special education teachers	74%
Medical assistants	71%
Private detectives	70%
Corrections officers	70%
Child care workers	66%
Travel agents	66%
Radiologic technologists	63%
Nursery (farm) workers	62%
Medical records technicians	62%

1. What additional information would suffice to determine the ratio between the number of home health aides to the number of child care workers in 2005?

   a. The number of home health aides in 1992

   b. The number of child care workers in 2005

   c. The ratio between the number of home health aides and child care workers in 1992

   d. None of the above is sufficient

   e. No additional information is needed

Solution

If given the ratio in 1992, we can simply add the percent increase to each number in the ratio to get the ratio in 2005.

The correct answer is c.

2. Which of the following conclusions can be derived from the information in the chart:

   a. There were more home health aides than travel agents in 2005.

   b. The number of human service workers in 2005 exceeds the sum of the numbers of child care workers and travel agents in 2005 combined.

   c. The number of nursery (farm) workers and medical records technicians was approximately the same in 2005.

   d. The increase in the number of home health aides between 1992 and 2005 was greater than the increase in the number of travel agents in the same period.

   e. The ratio between number of child care workers and travel agents stayed the same between 1992 and 2005.

Solution

This chart does not tell anything about actual numbers of workers, but only gives ratios between the two years. Hence, choices a. through d. cannot be supported by the chart. Choice e. is true because the two job categories increase by approximately the same ratio between 1992–2005.

The correct answer is e.

Practice Question #6

Define the operation ~ as follows:

$$@(x) = \text{minimum } (x^2, 1)$$

1. Which of the following properties are true:

   I) For all real numbers x, y,

   $$@(x - y) \geq 0, \text{ and } @(x - y) = 0$$
   when $x = y$

   II) For all real numbers x, y,

   $$@(x - y) = @(y - x)$$

   III) For all real numbers x, y, z,

   $$@(x - y) + @(y - z) > @(x - z)$$

   a. I

   b. II

   c. III

   d. I, II

   e. I, II, III

Solution

I is true, because $(x - y)^2$ is always positive, unless $x - y$ is zero, in which case $@(x - y) = 0$

II is true, because $(x - y)^2 = (-1(y - x))^2 = (y - x)^2$

III is false, because if $x = \frac{1}{2}$, $y = \frac{1}{3}$, and $z = \frac{1}{4}$, then

$$@(x - y) = \min\left(\frac{1}{36}, 1\right) = \frac{1}{36}$$
$$@(y - z) = \min\left(\frac{1}{144}, 1\right) = \frac{1}{144}$$
$$@(x - z) = \min\left(\frac{1}{16}, 1\right) = \frac{1}{16}$$

and $\frac{1}{36} + \frac{1}{144} = \frac{5}{144}$, which violates property III, because $\frac{5}{144} < \frac{1}{16}$

The correct answer is d.

! INFO TO GO

$|x|$ is defined as the absolute value of x. Absolute value is always positive. So the absolute value of 2 is 2, and the absolute value of −2 is 2.

2. If we redefine $@(x)$ to be minimum$(|x|, 1)$, then which of the three properties are true?

   a. I

   b. II

   c. III

   d. I, II

   e. I, II, III

Solution

Now III is true, we have removed the complications which arise from squaring numbers less than 1.

The correct answer is e.

Practice Question #7

The two tables below give values for functions $f(x)$, and $g(x, y)$ for x and y from 0 to 5.

x	f(x)
0	0
1	1
2	4
3	3
4	4
5	1

$g(x,y)$

x	y 0	1	2	3	4	5
0	0	0	0	0	0	0
1	0	1	2	3	4	5
2	0	2	4	0	2	4
3	0	3	0	3	0	3
4	0	4	2	0	4	2
5	0	5	4	3	2	1

1. For which values of x does $g(x, f(x)) = x$?

   a. 0,1 only

   b. 0,1,5 only

   c. 2,4 only

   d. 0,3 only

   e. 0,1,2,3,4,5

Solution

Simply plug in numbers into the two charts, and we see that this formula works for all values of x.

The correct answer is e.

2. For which values of x does $g(x,x) - f(x) = 0$?

   a. 0,1 only

   b. 0,1,5 only

   c. 2,4 only

   d. 0,3 only

   e. 0,1,2,3,4,5

Explanation

Plug in the numbers—we see that the numbers along the diagonal in the second chart represent $g(x,x)$, and these numbers are 0,1,4,3,4,1—same as in the chart for $f(x)$.

The correct answer is e.

The Least You Need to Know

- Charts, graphs, and tables are increasingly popular on the GRE—so practice!

- Read these problems slowly. Half the challenge is understanding all the information presented.

- ETS likes to insert weird symbols as variables, so don't freak out when you see strange symbols.

- Make sure you completely understand the question before you go back to the figure to find the answer.

Chapter **18**

Random Math You Last Saw in Eleventh Grade

In This Chapter

◆ Random bits of GRE math

◆ Hard and (somewhat) rare problems

◆ Making the difficult and obscure easy

You're about to learn funky stuff that's on the GRE math section. The probability that all of these concepts will be on one test is zero. Nada. Won't happen. In fact, you probably won't even see most of these concepts on any single test. At most, you may see three to four "hard" questions, most of which will test the following concepts.

The point? Prepare to be disappointed. If you know how to do everything in this chapter, you'll know stuff that won't be tested. This means that (1) you won't find many examples of these concepts on real tests, and (2) if you don't understand any single concept, don't worry. There's a good chance it won't be on the GRE.

Finally, if you're aiming for a GRE math score below 600, then reading this chapter probably isn't necessary. If you're scoring below 550, then you probably won't be asked these kinds of questions. Then again, if you want to find out how a very intimidating math problem is, in fact, very easy, then read on.

Exponential Growth

An exponential growth question will look like this:

Level: Hard

If the first term in a geometric sequence is 4, and the fifth term is 64, what is the eighth term?

 a. 76

 b. 512

 c. 864

 d. 1,024

 e. 1,245

Solution

Remember, this is a hard question, so the answer will never be anything easy.

Test-taker Tom gets past a.—he figures if it takes 60 to go from the first to the fifth term, the eighth term is at least 35 or so away. No go on 76.

Tom also thinks that 1,245 isn't likely because it's not divisible by 4. Smart thinking—it's also wrong.

But he doesn't know where to go from there. He could, sort of, just figure it out. Or he could use this formula:

 $A(n) = A(1)\, r^{n-1}$

♦ $A(n)$ is the nth term in the sequence.

♦ $A(1)$ is the first term.

♦ r is the "ratio"—no need to understand it.

Plug the problem into this formula and you'll get the answer. Memorize this formula and you'll get the answer every time.

(The answer is b.)

Sets

Here's a set question:

Level: Easy

If set W contains six distinct numbers and set Q contains five distinct letters, how many elements are in the union of the two sets?

 a. 1

 b. 5

 c. 6

 d. 11

 e. Cannot be determined

Solution

Tom knows it isn't 5 or 6, because numbers in the problem that appear in the answer choices are wrong! And "Cannot be determined" is for chumps on any hard question. That only leaves 1 and 11 as possible answers. "Union" ought to tip you off, oughtn't it? (Correct answer is 11.)

Absolute Value

Absolute value isn't a vodka, but instead is the distance between a number and zero on a number line. The AbVal of 7 is 7. The AbVal of –7 is 7. Both are 7 away from 0. Easy stuff. AbVals are always positive.

Level: Hard

If $|r + 7| < 2$, which of the following must be true?

 I. $r < -9$

 II. $r < -5$

 III. $r > -9$

 a. I

 b. II

 c. III

 d. I and II

 e. II and III

The problem says that "the absolute value of some number is less than 2." So any number that, when added to positive 7, gives us an absolute value less than 2 is an answer. Stop thinking about this and go to the answer choices.

! INFO TO GO

Usually, you can solve inequalities the same way you would solve an equation: variables on one side, numbers on the other.

I. $r < -9$. Remember, less than -9 means numbers like -20, not -2. So plug in -20. Does it work? No, because $-20 + 7 = -13$, and the absolute value of that (13) is greater than 2.

II. $r < -5$. Plug in -6: $-6 + 7 = 1$. That works.

III. $r > -9$. Plug in -8: $-8 + 7 = -1$. That works too.

The answer is e.

Rational Equations and Inequalities

Example problem:

Level: Hard

For all values of x not equal to -2 or 3, what is the value of

$$\frac{x^4 - 5x^3 - 2x^2 + 24x}{x^2 - x - 6}$$

a. $x^2 - 4x$

b. $x^2 - 5x - 2$

c. $x + 24$

d. x

e. $x - 4$

Solution

After your headache subsides, you've got a shot at getting this. How? Because whenever you see a mangy thicket of variables, you must plug in numbers. And you should love the number 2. So plug in 2. You get -4. Plug 2 into each answer choice and A also gives you -4. You got the correct answer in about 25 seconds!

! INFO TO GO

A key ingredient to GRE math is intimidation. Don't let these problems scare you—they are far easier than they look!

Radical Equations

Here's an example:

Level: Hard

$4 - \sqrt{n} = -1$, what is the value of n?

a. 3

b. 5

c. 9

d. 25

e. Cannot be determined

Solution

Do it like any ordinary equation. So,

$$4 - \sqrt{n} = -1$$
$$5 = \sqrt{n}$$
$$5^2 = n$$
$$25 = n$$

Integer and Rational Exponents

Here's an example:

Level: Hard

If $x = \frac{1}{4}$, then $x^{-4} =$

 a. $\frac{1}{256}$

 b. $\frac{1}{16}$

 c. 4

 d. 16

 e. 256

Solution

Tip: the negative sign simply means you've got a positive exponent all under one, like this: $3^{-2} = \frac{1}{3^2}$ which is $\frac{1}{9}$.

So x^{-4} is $1/x^4$, which is $1/(\frac{1}{4})^4$, which equals $1/\frac{1}{256}$, which is e. 256.

Direct and Inverse Variation

Here's an example:

Level: Medium

If the height of a tree is directly proportional to its age, and a 6-month-old tree is 14.1 inches tall, how many feet tall is an 80-year-old tree?

 a. 160

 b. 188

 c. 376

 d. 1,128

 e. 2,256

Solution

Set up a proportion: $6/14.1 = 80/x$. Make sure you put age on top and height on the bottom for both. Before you do anything,

check that the units are all the same. Are they? Nope. We have months in one numerator and years in another, so change that 6 to $\frac{1}{2}$ (or .5). So you have: $.5/14.1 = 80/x$. Solve this by cross-multiplying and you get $x = 2,256$. But that's not the correct answer (and part of the reason why this is difficult). "2,256" is in the same units as the original number, which is 14.1 inches. We need to convert that to feet. So $2,256/12 = 188$. b. is correct.

X FAIR WARNING

Often, ETS will not present proportion information in the same order you need to set up the proportion. So read proportion problems carefully and make sure you arrange the information correctly.

Function Notation

Functions can look scary, but they are usually quite tame. Take a look at this problem:

Level: Hard

If $g(a) = (a + 4)^2$ and $h(b) = 2b - 7$, then what is the value $h(g(2))$?

 a. 1

 b. 36

 c. 45

 d. 65

 e. 79

Solution

It's all about substituting. Here we go …

They want to know the value of $h(g(2))$, so we need to plug 2 in for a. So plug 2 in for a in that first equation, and you get $g(2) = (2 + 4)^2 = 36$.

So $g(2) = 36$.

ETS wants to know the value of $h(g(2))$, and $g(2)$ is simply a substitution for the b in $h(b)$. So plug in g(2), which is 36, for b in the second equation and you get $h(36) = 2(36) - 7 = 72 - 7 = 65$. So the answer is d.

Domain and Range

Domain is the set of possible outcomes for a function. For example, what's the domain of

$$f(x) = \frac{1}{1-x^2}$$

x could be anything except 1 or –1, because that would make the denominator 0, and if have a denominator of 0, the math gods will descend upon your house and curse your dog. Now we wouldn't want that, would we?

Try this one:

Level: Hard

If $(a) = a^2 + 7$ for all real values of a, then $f(a)$ could be

    a. -2

    b. 0

    c. $\sqrt{5}$

    d. $\sqrt{7}$

    e. $100\sqrt{3}$

Solution

a^2 must be positive or 0. It can't be negative. (Square any number other than 0 and you'll get a positive number. 0^2 is 0.) So $f(a)$ must be 7 or greater because the least a^2 could be is 0. Don't bother trying to solve it. Just pick e. and move on (it's the only one that's 7 or more).

Functions of a Line

This stuff is a little difficult and very boring. Here we go:

Level: Hard

Which of the following describes a line perpendicular to the line $y = 7x + 49$?

    a. $y = -7x - 49$

    b. $y = -\frac{1}{7}x + 10$

    c. $y = \frac{1}{7}x + 7$

    d. $y = 7x - 49$

    e. $y = 7x + 14$

Solution

If two lines are perpendicular, the slope of one must be the negative reciprocal of the slope of the other. You need to know that $y = mx + b$ is the equation for a line, and m is the slope (b is the y-intercept). The negative reciprocal of 7 is $-\frac{1}{7}$, and the only equation with this number is b., so it must be correct.

Quadratic Functions

Putting the funk into functions, we have these parabolic functions. They are just like linear functions, except that they're not linear. (That's all.)

! INFO TO GO

A parabolic function, when graphed, creates a parabola. A linear function, if graphed, would just be a line. You don't really need to know that! There are other kinds of functions that graph all kinds of waves. Mathematicians are working hard on a smiley face function. (Joke!)

The form of a quadratic function is $f(x) = ax^2 + bx + c$. Memorize that if you want to be a math stud. Here's a quad-func problem:

Level: Hard

If $x^2 - 7x + 12 = 0$, what is the sum of the two possible values of x?

    a. −4

    b. −1

    c. 3

    d. 4

    e. 7

Solution

Factor that bad boy:

$$x^2 - 7x + 12 = 0$$
$$(x - 4)(x - 3) = 0$$
$$x = 4 \text{ or } x = 3$$
$$4 + 3 = 7$$

The answer is e.

FAIR WARNING

It's much more important that you understand the arithmetic, algebra, and geometry chapters than the material presented here. Don't spend too much time on this chapter if you still need to work on those chapters.

Harder Geometry Problems

Here's the stuff from the geometry chapter that has a high probability of showing up on hard problems:

FAIR WARNING

Review geometry words: segment, line, ray, tangent, congruent, inexorable—oh wait, that last one's from verbal ... Hard geometry problems sometimes just contain a lot of big words, so you need to know your geometry vocabulary.

Special right triangles:

45-45-90: ratio of sides is $1 : 1 : \sqrt{2}$

30-60-90: ratio of sides is $1 : \sqrt{3} : 2$

INFO TO GO

Memorize this: $\sqrt{2}$ is about 1.4 and $\sqrt{3}$ is about 1.7.

A few coordinate geometry concepts (most of which are drawable): For example:

What's the midpoint of PQ if P is (8,10) and Q is (0,4)?

If you want to be extra cool, you may want to memorize these:

Midpoint:

$$\frac{x_1 - x_2}{2}, \frac{y_1 - y_2}{2}$$

Distance formula: $\sqrt{(x_2 - x_1)^2 + (y_2 - y_1)^2}$

Yes, that whole thing is under the rad sign. And yes math geeks, that is just a screwed-up Pythag theorem.

The answer to that midpoint problem is (4,7).

The Least You Need to Know

- At most, you may see three to four "hard" questions on the GRE.

- Plug in your own numbers on the answer choices.

- A key ingredient to GRE math is intimidation. Don't let these problems scare you—they are far easier than they look.

- Read proportion problems carefully and make sure you arrange the information correctly.

- Hard geometry problems sometimes just contain a lot of big words, so you need to know your geometry vocabulary.

- You won't see everything in this chapter on a single test.

Math Practice Sets

Set 1

25 Multiple Choice Questions. 40 minutes.

1. Which of the following numbers could have been rounded to 56.7?

    a. 56.6

    b. 56.4

    c. 56.785

    d. 56.695

    e. 57

2. A large piece of land with a total area of 169 square miles is going to be divided into 13 sections. What is the average (arithmetic mean) area, in square miles, of each section?

    a. 13

    b. 14

    c. 15

    d. 16

    e. 17

3. If $4x + 2x = 3x + x + 10$, then x equals which of the following?

    a. 10

    b. –5

    c. 2

    d. 20

    e. 5

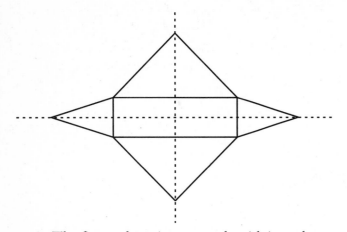

4. The figure above is a rectangle with isosceles triangles attached to each edge. That figure has two axes of symmetry, as shown by the dotted lines. Which of the following letters has at least two axes of symmetry like the figure above?

    a. A

    b. H

    c. E

    d. Y

    e. Z

5. If x is a positive integer, what is 40 percent of $20x$?

    a. $10x$

    b. $2x$

    c. 10

    d. 8

    e. $8x$

6. In a fish store, a tank has 10 fish in it. If 6 of the fish are female, what is the probability that a fish selected at random will be female?

    a. $\frac{3}{5}$

    b. $\frac{1}{6}$

    c. $\frac{2}{3}$

    d. $\frac{2}{5}$

    e. $\frac{4}{10}$

7. When k is divided by 4, the remainder is 1. What happens to the remainder when $k + 2$ is divided by 4?

    a. nothing

    b. It increases by 1

    c. It is multiplied by 3

    d. The remainder is 0

    e. Cannot be determined by the information given

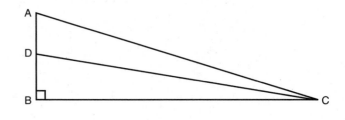

Note: figure not drawn to scale

8. In right triangle ABC shown above, ∠BAC is 60° and CD bisects ∠ACB. What is the value of ∠BDC?

    a. 30°

    b. 60°

    c. 75°

    d. 80°

    e. 90°

9. The average (arithmetic mean) of 3, 6, 7, 14, 20, and x is equal to x. What is the value of x?

    a. 7

    b. 8

    c. 9

    d. 10

    e. 11

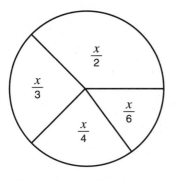

Note: figure not drawn to scale

10. The circle above has been divided into sectors with angles as shown. What is the value of x?

    a. 144

    b. 168

    c. 200

    d. 256

    e. 288

11. Nathan can run 2 miles in 1 hour and 15 minutes. How long will it take Nathan to run a 26-mile marathon?

    a. 15 hours

    b. 16 hours 15 minutes

    c. 16 hours 20 minutes

    d. 16 hours 45 minutes

    e. 17 hours

12. If n and s are positive integers, let n ★ s be the sum of all the integers between and including n and s. For example, $n ★ s = 3 + 4 + 5 = 12$. If $3 ★ s = 18$, what is s?

    a. 3

    b. 4

    c. 5

    d. 6

    e. 7

13. A store bought an item for $200. The store increased the item's price by 30 percent to sell it. Two months later, the store has a sale, discounting the item by 30 percent. What is the price of the item during the sale?

    a. $182

    b. $198

    c. $200

    d. $230

    e. $260

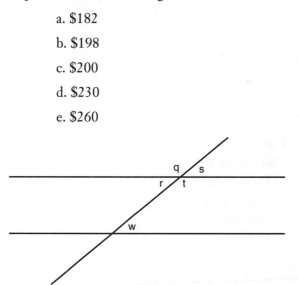

Note: figure not drawn to scale

14. If $r + s = q$, what is w equal to?

    a. $r - s$

    b. $r + t$

    c. $2t$

    d. $2s$

    e. ½

15. Mr. Wallace averages 60 miles per hour for the first t hours on an 800 mile trip. If $t < 13$, in terms of t, how many miles does Mr. Wallace have left?

    a. $60t - 800$

    b. $48,000 - 60t$

    c. $800 - 60t$

    d. $\dfrac{800}{t} - 60$

    e. $\dfrac{3}{40} - t$

16. If x is a positive integer and $\dfrac{2\sqrt{x}}{\sqrt{2}} = 0.5 \times \dfrac{\sqrt{2}}{\sqrt{x}}$, then $x =$

 a. 2

 b. 2.5

 c. $\sqrt{2}$

 d. 4

 e. 0.5

17. If $0 < a < b < c$ and the average (arithmetic mean) of a, b, and c is equal to the median of the three numbers, then which of the following is equal to b?

 a. $\dfrac{a+c}{3}$

 b. $\sqrt{ac}$

 c. $\dfrac{a+c}{2}$

 d. $\dfrac{c-a}{3}$

 e. $a + c$

18. If a circle with a radius of 8 inches is cut in half along the diameter, what is the perimeter of the resulting semicircle?

 a. 16π

 b. 8π

 c. $16\pi + 8$

 d. $8\pi + 8$

 e. $8\pi + 16$

19. If $8x + y = 3$ and $2z - 16x = 2$, what is $y + z$?

 a. 4

 b. 5

 c. 6

 d. 7

 e. 8

20. If $2^{x+1} = y$, which of the following is equal to y?

 a. 2^x

 b. 2^y

 c. y^2

 d. $y - 1$

 e. $y - 2$

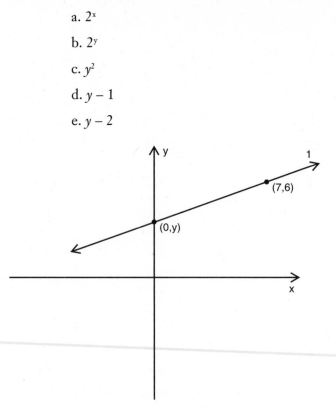

Note: figure not drawn to scale

21. If the slope of the line l above is $\frac{1}{3}$, what is y?

 a. $\frac{17}{3}$

 b. $\frac{7}{3}$

 c. 3

 d. $\frac{7}{6}$

 e. $\frac{11}{3}$

22. How many positive 4-digit integers start with 3 and end with either 3 or 6?

 a. 100

 b. 144

 c. 169

 d. 200

 e. 256

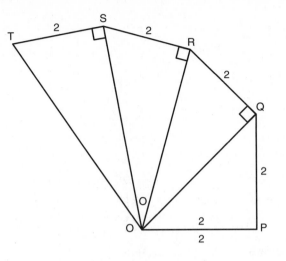

Note: figure not drawn to scale

23. What is the length of OT in the figure?

    a. 8

    b. $2\sqrt{3}$

    c. $2\sqrt{5}$

    d. $\sqrt{10}$

    e. 20

24. The average (arithmetic mean) of three distinct positive integers is 12. The second integer is 9 times the first one. What is the least possible value for the third integer?

    a. 16

    b. 20

    c. 26

    d. 12

    e. 2

25. If $3xy = 4$ and $x - 2y = 7$, what is $3x^2y - 6xy^2$?

    a. 3

    b. 12

    c. 28

    d. 42

    e. 60

Set 2

25 Quantitative Comparison and Student-Produced Questions. 40 minutes.

Questions 1–15—Quantitative Comparison. Choose the column that represents the greater value. Choose a. if Column A is greater. Choose b. if Column B is greater. Choose c. if the two columns are equal in value. Choose d. if there is not enough information to make a determination.

Column A	**Column B**

1.

The cost of 3 candy bars at $0.90 a piece	$3.00

2. 5 more than x is 3

x	-2

3.

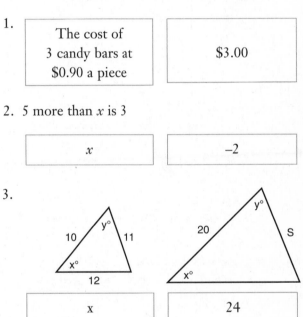

x	24

4. Triangle ABC is a right triangle. $\angle A$ is 90°.

The measure of $\angle B$	90°

5. p and q are 4-digit numbers greater than 2,000 but less than 8,000.

   The tens digit of p is 3.

   The tens digit of q is 7.

p	q

	Column A	Column B

6. The average (arithmetic mean) price of Nathan's baseball cards is twice the average price of Mac's baseball cards.

The price of Nathan's most valuable card	The price of Mac's most valuable card

7.

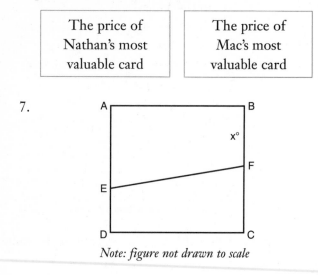

Note: figure not drawn to scale

ABCD is a square

$x = 90°$

The length of AD	The length of FE

8. r, s, and t are integers.

$r \times s < 0$

$r \times s \times t > 0$

t	0

9. A car factory made 100 cars in 8 hours.

The number of cars made in the last 2 hours	20

10. Lines l and m are $\perp$ to each other.

The number of lines $\perp$ to m but not $\parallel$ to l	0

	Column A	Column B

11. $5x - 3y = 5$

$x + y = 3$

x	6

12. Greg teaches a class of p students, and q of them are male. Four of the students are female.

$p - q$	4

13. $x > 0$

The result when x is increased by 70 percent	$0.7x$

14. $\left(q^4\right)\left(q^r\right) = q^{6s}$

r	s

15. $0 < x < y < 5$

x^y	y^x

Student Produced Questions.

For each of the following questions, you must produce and enter your own response. 10 questions.

16. What is $(x + y)^2$ if $x = 3y$ and $y = 2$?

17. On an hour-long drive, 40 minutes were spent in traffic. What fraction of the drive was *not* in traffic?

18. The first term of a sequence is 3. Each term after the first is 5 less than three times the term right before it. What is the fourth term of the sequence?

19. If the quotient when 0.56 is divided by an integer is $\frac{7}{25}$ (0.28), what is the integer?

20. In any triangle ABC, if the lengths of the sides are a, b, and c, what could be a value of $\frac{b}{a+c}$?

21. A polling firm surveyed 3,500 people on the street. On a specific question, the possible answers were yes, no, or undecided. Only 90 percent of the people asked answered that particular question. If 30 percent of the people who answered said "yes," and 37 people said "undecided," how many people said no?

22. If $50x(x^2 + \frac{1}{2}x + \frac{1}{5} + \frac{1}{x}) = ax^3 + bx^2 + cx + d$, what is the value of $\frac{a+d}{2b+5c}$?

23. A plane ticket bought more than one month in advance costs $500. If the ticket is purchased less than a month in advance, it costs $750. The total amount collected is as if each ticket had cost $600. If 50 tickets were purchased in advance, how many tickets were sold total?

24. Seven people were asked to pick a random positive integer. If the average of these numbers is 7, what is the highest possible value for one of the numbers?

25. x, y, and z are three distinct prime integers greater than 2. If $r = x \times y \times z$, then how many factors, including 1 and r, does r have?

Set 3

10 Multiple Choice Questions. 15 minutes.

1. 52.3

   Moving the decimal point to the left one place in the number above could result from which of the following?

a. Multiplying 52.3 by 10

b. Multiplying 52.3 by 100

c. Dividing 52.3 by 10

d. Dividing 52.3 by 100

e. Adding 10

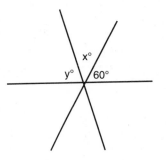

Note: figure not drawn to scale

2. In the figure above, if $2x = y$, what is the value of x?

   a. 40°

   b. 45°

   c. 50°

   d. 55°

   e. 60°

3. Greg and Nathan are racing. Nathan goes 120 miles in 6 hours. Greg manages to cover the same distance in half the time. Greg's average speed for the race is

   a. 20 miles per hour

   b. 40 miles per hour

   c. 60 miles per hour

   d. 80 miles per hour

   e. 100 miles per hour

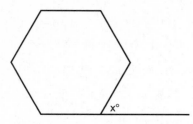

Note: figure not drawn to scale

4. In the figure above, all of the internal angles are equal. What is the value of x?

    a. 30

    b. 45

    c. 60

    d. 90

    e. 120

5. Mac answered every question on his math test. He got 70 percent of them right. He answered 12 questions incorrectly. How many questions were there on the test?

    a. 30

    b. 40

    c. 50

    d. 60

    e. 70

6. Which is the diameter of a circle with an area of 9π?

    a. 3

    b. 4

    c. 5

    d. 6

    e. 9

7. The percent decrease from 20 to 13 is equal to the percent decrease from 34 to what number?

    a. 13

    b. 15.2

    c. 18

    d. 22.1

    e. 34

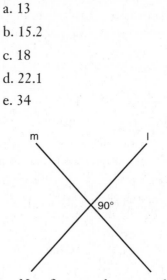

Note: figure not drawn to scale

8. Line *l* has a slope of $\frac{1}{2}$. What is the slope of line *m*?

    a. –2

    b. $-\frac{1}{2}$

    c. 0

    d. $\frac{1}{2}$

    e. 2

9. How much did Michelle weigh last year if she now weighs *p* pounds, but immediately gained 10 over last year's weight?

    a. $p + q + 10$

    b. $p - q - 10$

    c. $p - q + 10$

    d. $q - p - 10$

    e. $p + q - 10$

10. $x - y = 3x + 9y$

How many ordered pairs (x,y) are solutions to the equation above?

   a. 0

   b. 3

   c. 4

   d. 100

   e. More than 100

Answers for All Sets

Set 1:

   1. d
   2. a
   3. e
   4. b
   5. e
   6. a
   7. c
   8. c
   9. d
   10. e
   11. b
   12. d
   13. a
   14. e
   15. c
   16. e
   17. c
   18. e
   19. a
   20. c

21. e

22. d

23. c

24. a

25. c

Set 2:

Quantitative Comparison Questions

   1. b
   2. c
   3. b
   4. b
   5. d
   6. d
   7. c
   8. b
   9. d
   10. c
   11. b
   12. c
   13. a
   14. a
   15. b

Student-produced questions

   16. 64
   17. $\frac{1}{3}$
   18. 16
   19. 2
   20. $0<x<1$
   21. 2168

22. 1

23. 33.33333

24. 43

25. 8

Set 3:

1. c

2. a

3. b

4. c

5. b

6. d

7. d

8. a

9. e

10. e

Part 4

Analytical Writing: First Impressions Are Everything

These chapters will give you the details of what the two essay sections test and how they're scored. The two essay types require very different approaches. After reviewing the requirements of these different approaches, we'll review essay structure. Finally, you can read through some sample GRE essays.

HERE ARE SOME *SAMPLE* ESSAYS FOR YOU.

Chapter 20

Analytical Writing: An Overview

In This Chapter

◆ What you'll write and how it's scored

◆ Why the essays are important for you

◆ Essentials for approaching any essay topic

◆ The secret to getting a great essay score

Up until June 2002, the GRE included a multiple-choice "Analytical" section that contained logic questions and games (similar to the LSAT). In October 2002, ETS eliminated this section and replaced it with an "Analytical Writing" section. So instead of gauging your ability to analyze logical situations in a multiple-choice format, the GRE now assesses your ability to write about them. The writing portion is a single, 75-minute section composed of two writing exercises, and this section is always first.

Why Did ETS Decide to Include These Essays?

The official ETS party line is that graduate schools wanted a better way to measure an applicant's writing ability. ETS further claims that scores on the writing section correlate strongly to grades in undergraduate writing courses. While this may be true of some graduate admissions programs, many simply wanted something more useful than the current verbal section, which is largely a vocabulary test. Think about it: a graduate program in public policy, nursing, or hotel management probably isn't incredibly interested in whether you know the definition of "inexorable," but they are all somewhat interested in whether you can write.

And still other graduate programs wanted a better assessment of an applicant's fluency in English. As international applications to graduate schools increase, universities want a standardized way to test an applicant's English communication skills. It's possible to score well on the verbal section of the GRE and lack fluency in English, so admissions offices wanted a more accurate test of an applicant's English skills.

> **! INFO TO GO**
>
> If your undergraduate degree is from a college that does not conduct its courses in English, you may be required to take the TOEFL (Test of English as a Foreign Language) or other English proficiency exam. Check with the graduate department's requirements.

ETS, of course, had no problem adding a writing section because it had been giving an SAT II writing and GMAT (with a writing assessment) for many years. So ETS could add a scored essay to the test fairly easily. The fact that the GRE is (mostly) given on computer sealed the deal. It's very easy to manage an essay program and grade those essays when they are all typed into computers (instead of hand-written or scanned into computers). So universities wanted it, ETS had it, and now you get it.

Some complain that if universities really just want to assess your writing ability, why don't they (1) read your application essays or (2) consider your grades in undergraduate writing classes? The answers reveal a bit about all admissions processes. First, although admissions readers will carefully review your application essay(s), they are acutely aware that you had somewhat unlimited time and probably somewhat unlimited editorial assistance.

So admissions readers are not so much assessing your writing skills when they read your admissions essays as they are taking the measure of your ideas. Admissions readers know that Microsoft Word and the Writing Center at your college are capable of solving the riddle of your grammar but usually don't add substantively to your ideas. The writing section of the GRE gives them a standardized and fast measure of your writing skills.

So why don't they simply look at your grade in an undergraduate composition class? Because chances are you don't have one. Undergraduate composition classes are not uniformly required and are certainly not uniformly graded. Some are pass/fail. In many cases, even if your college did require a composition class, you could have tested out of it with a high score on the SAT II writing or a good score on a placement test. Is that information on your transcript? Maybe. Admissions offices aren't particularly interested in running investigations, but they are interested in admitting a wide range of the best applicants from many different colleges. In order to assess writing skills across a broad range of colleges and disciplines, they asked for a writing section on the GRE. Voilà.

What Are Readers of Your Essays Looking For?

Well, perhaps ending that header with a preposition isn't a good start. (English majors are thinking, "I can't believe he did that." Engineers are thinking, "Did what?" And math theoreticians are trying to write an algorithm for my placement of vowels.) So back to the now grammatically correct question: for what are admissions readers looking? (Sounds awkward, doesn't it?)

And the answer is: depends.

If you are applying to a math program, your essay score may matter for little apart from letting the admissions readers know whether you're fluent in English. But unless you're applying to be a math teacher, most math programs really care about one thing: whether you know math. That's it.

If you attended college in a non-English speaking country, the admissions office will take a greater interest in your essay score.

If you are applying for a writing-intensive program, your essay score may matter greatly. If you are applying for a communications program, your essay score may matter greatly. If you have no under-graduate grade in a composition course, or if you attended a college with which the graduate school has no experience, your essay score may matter greatly.

FAIR WARNING

> Your recommendations and test scores should agree with each other. If you are getting a recom-mendation from a history or English professor who will (presumably) remark on your wonderful writing skills, your GRE essays must reflect these great writ-ing skills. If they don't, then the graduate admissions office may disregard that recommendation.

If you have an undergraduate composition grade, particularly from a well-known school, and that grade isn't very good (B- or lower), your essay score may matter greatly.

But if you're applying for a physical therapy pro-gram, and your well-known undergraduate college gave you an A in Advanced Freshman Composition, there's still a good reason to score highly on the GRE Writing section. The admissions readers are human, and while they may not need a score from you, they will still be influenced by a ridiculously

low score. Just as when a lawyer gets something "inadmissible" thrown out in court which neverthe-less influences a jury (even if it's stricken from the record), a low GRE Writing score will be seen and considered, even if not officially. A 1.5 score on the writing section means, according to ETS's official guide, that your essay "demonstrated fundamen-tal deficiencies in analysis and writing skills." And before you know it, the jury will be reading that guilty verdict and you'll be saying to yourself "I thought they weren't supposed to consider that."

How the Essays Are Scored

The first of the two exercises is a 30-minute "Analyze an Issue" essay. The second exercise is a 30-minute "Analyze an Argument" essay. I will start beating the dead horse now: these are two different kinds of essay. If you write the same kind of essay for both questions, you will score poorly on at least one of them. Before we get to the details of how to write great essays, let's first look at how these essays are scored.

FAIR WARNING

> For many test-takers, the most difficult part of the writing section is the timing. You will need to outline and write a 400–700 word essay in 30 minutes. You should practice writing essays (from start to finish!) in 30 minutes or less.

Two readers score each essay on a 1–6 scale. If the two scores are within 1 point of each other, those two scores are averaged, and that average is your essay score. If the two scores differ by more than 1 point, a third reader scores your essay, and, assuming that score is within a point of one of the two original scores, that third score is averaged into the original score. So each of your essays receives a 1–6 score, which is the average of 2 (or possibly more) readers. Your two essay scores are then averaged together, producing your overall essay score. Your overall essay score will be 1–6, rounded to the nearest half point. That overall essay score will be reported to you a few weeks after you take the test.

Your Official GRE Scoring Guide

So what exactly do the numerical scores mean? Well, here are summaries of ETS's descriptions of each score for the "Issue" and "Argument" portions.

"Analyze an Issue" Scoring

The Official GRE Scoring Guide for the "Analyze an Issue" essay looks like this:

- Score 6: a cogent, well-articulated analysis of the complexities of the issue that conveys meaning skillfully. A typical paper in this category presents an insightful position on the issue, develops the position with compelling reasons or persuasive examples, and sustains a well-focused, well-organized analysis.

- Score 5: a generally thoughtful, well-developed analysis of the complexities of the issue that conveys meaning clearly. A typical paper in this category presents a well-considered position on the issue, is focused and generally well organized, and demonstrates facility with the conventions of standard written English but may have minor errors.

- Score 4: a competent analysis of the issue that conveys meaning adequately. A typical paper in this category presents a clear position on the issue, and generally demonstrates control of the conventions of standard written English but may have some errors.

- Score 3: demonstrates some competence in its analysis of the issue and in conveying meaning but is obviously flawed. A typical paper in this

category may be vague or limited in presenting or developing a position on the issue, may be weak in the use of relevant reasons or examples, and may have problems in language and sentence structure that result in a lack of clarity and contain occasional major errors or frequent minor errors in grammar, usage, or mechanics that can interfere with meaning.

- Score 2: demonstrates serious weaknesses in analytical writing. A typical paper in this category may be unclear or seriously limited in presenting or developing a position on the issue; may provide few, if any, relevant reasons or examples; may have serious problems in the use of language and sentence structure that frequently interfere with meaning; and may contain serious errors in grammar, usage, or mechanics that frequently obscure meaning.

- Score 1: demonstrates fundamental deficiencies in analytical writing skills.

- Score 0: off topic, in a foreign language, or blank.

I've abbreviated these descriptions, but you get the idea. Your logic and your writing count.

"Analyze an Argument" Scoring

The Official GRE Scoring Guide for the "Analyze an Argument" essay is similar. In short, it looks like this:

- Score 6: a cogent, well-articulated critique of the argument that conveys meaning skillfully.

- Score 5: a generally thoughtful, well-developed critique of the argument that conveys meaning clearly.

- Score 4: a competent critique of the argument that conveys meaning adequately.

- Score 3: has some competence in its critique of the argument and in conveying meaning but is obviously flawed.

◆ Score 2: demonstrates serious weaknesses in analytical writing.

◆ Score 1: demonstrates fundamental deficiencies in both analysis and writing.

Once again, your logic and writing skills determine your score. We will get into the details of what a "well-articulated critique of the argument" looks like (and how to write one) in Chapter 21.

The Essay Scoring Process: Who and How?

Most likely, your freshman composition course was taught by a graduate teaching assistant (T.A.) who was paid around $12,000 to teach three or four classes. That person is (most likely) grading your essay. They typically do it online from their home, and are paid per essay. (Try not to envy them.)

The essays are graded "holistically," which is Latin for "in under one minute." Okay, it's not Latin, and they may take an extra 30 seconds, but the essay graders are reading these essays quickly, and they are reading a lot of them. That means that small errors in spelling and grammar don't make a huge difference. Technically, grammar and spelling mistakes aren't taken into consideration, but because these are college T.A.s, a terrific number of grammatical errors will annoy them just as they would annoy your sixth grade grammar teacher. And because their time is limited, they aren't going to spend five minutes attempting to decipher an incomprehensible sentence. If the reader can't understand something the first time, he or she probably will just keep reading, ignoring what they can't understand and trying to make sense of the rest. So don't fret about a single, small error. Fret large if your subjects and verbs tend not to agree.

Fairness and Standardized Writing

Can you grade writing on a standardized test? Is it fair? For every person who decries the inherent unfairness of grading standardized essays, there are two people bemoaning a poor grade in college because "the teacher didn't like me." So in some ways, this is fairer than a college composition course because the grader doesn't know you; there's no personal side.

While grading an essay "holistically" (in a minute) seems ridiculous, there is a surprising level of consistency in the grades. Bad writers almost always get low scores (1–2.5). Good writers usually get high scores (4.5–6). Everyone else scores in the middle (3–4). The debate is usually about whether a particular essay should have scored a 5 or 6, but such an essay would almost never score a 2 or 3. It may be disturbing to have your 75 minutes of essay-writing graded in the same amount of time that it takes McDonald's to make a Big Mac Value Meal (a "holistic" amount of time). But in the end, it's probably about as accurate and fair as a grade you would receive in a freshman composition course.

ETS has this to say about fairness:

> "To ensure fairness and objectivity in scoring, responses [essays] are randomly distributed to the readers, all identifying information about the test takers is concealed from the readers, each response is scored by two readers, readers do not know what other scores a response may have received, the scoring procedure requires that each response receive identical or adjacent scores from two readers; any other score combination is adjudicated by a third GRE reader."

This basically means that a rogue grader giving 1s to everyone won't last long.

What Are the Essay Topics?

You will write two essays, an "Issue" and an "Argument" essay. I cannot stress enough that these are different kinds of essays; if you write the same kind of essay twice, you will receive at least one very low score. The "Issue" essay is a discussion and defense of your position on an issue; your opinion matters. The "Argument" essay is an analysis of the logic and evidence of a particular argument; your opinion is not relevant.

Issue Essay

ETS says: "The Issue task states an opinion on an issue of broad interest and asks test takers to address the issue from any perspective(s) they wish, so long as they provide relevant reasons and examples to explain and support their views."

ETS means: Here is an issue. What is your position and how do your evidence and logic support your position?

Argument Essay

ETS says: "The Argument task presents a different challenge: it requires test takers to critique an argument by discussing how well reasoned they find it. Test takers are asked to consider the logical soundness of the argument rather than agree or disagree with the position it presents."

ETS means: Here is someone else's opinion or conclusion about an issue. Does his or her evidence and logic support the opinion/conclusion?

ETS says some more: "Thus the two tasks are complementary in that one requires test takers to construct their own argument by making claims and providing evidence supporting their positions on the issue, whereas the other requires them to critique someone else's argument by assessing its claims and evaluating the evidence it provides."

That last part is a great example of poor writing: don't say something, and then say it again. If you have something to say, say it once. If you keep saying the same thing, people will get bored. Are you getting bored? It's because I just said the same thing three times. (And it's also because you're reading about the GRE, but there's nothing I can do about that.)

Once again, in the Issue essay, you are defending your own position with your own evidence and logic. In the Argument essay, you are critiquing someone else's position by analyzing their evidence and logic. Got it?

So what exactly are the topics? The fine folks at ETS actually provide a list of every possible topic, which you can find at www.ets.com.

So what do GRE Issue-essay prompts look like? Here are some examples:

- "Unconventional pursuits such as astrology, fortune-telling, and psychic and paranormal interests play a vital role in society by addressing human questions that are not addressed by mainstream media and the sciences."

- "Education is not a solitary activity but rather one that requires the cooperation of many people; therefore, all students will benefit academically if they work frequently and successfully in groups."

- "Politicians must maintain high ethical and moral standards in order to be effective leaders."

- "Government or their related organizations should never fund research that has unclear ethical consequences."

- "Civilization will better prepare its children to be leaders if these children are raised with a strong sense of cooperation, despite the fact that some leaders in government, sports and industry believe that their success was borne of fierce competition."

And here are a few samples of Official GRE Argument-essay prompts:

- "The following appeared in the editorial section of a weekly newspaper.

  Many states are creating new laws that restrict the use of hand-held cell phones by automobile drivers. Such restrictions are ridiculous. Some drivers with phones certainly cause accidents, but most drivers with hand-held cell phones cause no problems at all. Careless drivers are often distracted by many activities, including changing the radio station, putting on makeup, and eating/drinking. Since it would be ridiculous to restrict these activities—can you imagine a law forbidding touching your radio while driving?—it follows that it is ridiculous to forbid the use of hand-held cell phones while driving."

- Until recently, residents of Town X did most of their shopping at malls, most of which are located several miles outside of Town X. But increasingly they are ordering from mail-order catalogs and the Internet. These purchases are delivered to them by mail. For many purchases, residents of Town X no longer need to drive to and from shopping malls; there will therefore be a resulting reduction in the consumption of vehicle fuel in Town X."

You can obtain a copy of the entire pool of possible analytical writing questions from ETS's website. I'd give you the exact web address, but they keep changing it. Go to www.ets.com and search for "The Pool

of Argument Topics" or "The Pool of Issue Topics" and you'll be in essay prompt heaven.

FAIR WARNING

The pool of issue topics is 29 pages long and the pool of argument topics is 68 pages long, so you really shouldn't spend your time devising and memorizing responses to every possible topic. Instead, you should learn and practice our system for answering any topic.

Dress for Success

The first step in getting a great analytical writing score is to understand that 50 percent of a good score is a good-looking essay. That's right: an essay that looks good is usually mistaken for an essay that is good. The single greatest determining factor for high scores is appearance.

So what does "appearance" mean for the essay? It means that these qualities are vital to a great score (in order of importance):

- Length (each essay should be 400+ words)
- Indentations (four to seven indented paragraphs)
- Varied sentence length (use colons, semicolons, dashes, etc.)
- Grammar/spelling (too many basic errors mar the appearance of an essay)

Think of it this way: a "good-looking" essay is given the benefit of the doubt and must work its way down from a high score. A messy, short, unkempt essay must work its way up from a low score. In Chapter 21, we'll discuss the basics of great content—which is the other 50 percent of getting a great score.

The good news is that you get to type the essay. Because neatness counts for so much, those with poor penmanship would suffer greatly if the essay had to be hand-written (as it does on the SAT).

ETS and CAT

ETS first wanted the GRE to go to the computer-adaptive (CAT) version in 1995. But ETS had a big problem: a significant number of GRE test-takers couldn't take a test on computer—their scores on the paper-and-pencil version of the test were consistently higher. GRE test-takers often wrote papers on computer, but taking a test on computer seemed to be something completely different. So for years ETS offered the CAT and paper-and-pencil version to all test-takers.

Now that the pool of potential graduate students is more computer savvy, ETS expects (nearly) everyone to take the CAT version. But the fact remains: GRE test-takers often find navigating the computer version of the test more difficult than the actual content of the test.

! INFO TO GO

The paper-and-pencil version of the GRE is only offered in places where "computer-based testing is not available," which, according to ETS, includes such remote locations as New York University (in New York City) and the University of California at Los Angeles. Anyone can take the GRE paper version, but the test dates are few and far between (typically in November and April) and it takes longer to get your score. More info can be found at www.ets.com. Go to "Get Test Details" and scroll down to "Where Do People Take It?" Click on the link in that paragraph; you will be magically transported to the secret list of paper test locations.

ETS's Computer Program

ETS gives you a very basic word processor to type your essay. The ETS word processor has no spell- or grammar-check features. None. You should start using your word processor without automatic spell- and grammar-check just to see how good (or bad) your spelling and grammar really are. The ETS word processor doesn't even have auto-indent; you must hit the space bar a few times to achieve an indentation. (Hitting the space bar five times will achieve a standard indentation.)

The ETS word processor is similar to Microsoft's Notepad program. You can move the cursor with the arrow keys, and you can delete, cut, copy, and paste text. (So you can move around whole paragraphs if you decide that something is in the wrong place.) The backspace key moves the cursor back, and pointing/clicking the mouse also moves the cursor.

! INFO TO GO

All PCs running Microsoft Windows have Notepad included with the system. Macs have a similar program called TextEdit. You should practice with these programs because they do not correct spelling or grammar.

The essay prompt will always appear at the top of the computer screen, so you don't need to memorize it or write it down; you can keep referring back to the top of the screen to ensure that you're still on topic.

If you are comfortable with computers and regularly use word processors, the next few paragraphs will cause excruciating boredom. Skip them. If you aren't very comfortable with word processors, I will go into great detail about how to use ETS's writing program. But it's imperative that you compose a few essays on a practice computer GRE regardless of your computer proficiency. More on practice GREs later; first, the innards of ETS's computer program.

How to Use the Program

The essay is the first section of the GRE. When the test begins, the screen will automatically take you to the essay section. The essay prompt will appear at the top of the screen and will stay there for the duration of the allotted time. A clock will appear next to the prompt and will begin counting down your time (30 minutes for the Issue essay and 30 minutes for the Argument essay). A window will open below the essay prompt; this is where you will write your essay. To the right of this window will be icons allowing you to cut, paste, and undo (delete), and the icons will be marked thusly.

Keyboard keys (aside from the numbers and letters) that you may find useful include …

- "Home"—relocates the cursor to the beginning of the line.
- "End"—relocates the cursor to the end of the line.
- "Enter"—relocates the cursor to the beginning of the next line.
- "Page Up"—relocates the cursor up one page.
- "Page Down"—relocates the cursor down one page.
- "Delete"—removes the text to the right (in front) of the cursor.
- "Backspace"—removes the text to the left (behind) the cursor.

Arrow keys move the cursor up, down, left, and right, without deleting any text.

Once again, if you aren't completely familiar with word processing, you must practice on a computer version of a practice GRE.

Basic Essay Structure

The essay readers are given very specific scoring guides. I'm going to tell you exactly what they are looking for and how to prepare ahead of time. You will not know the essay prompt ahead of time, but you can plan and practice now in order to minimize thinking on test day. When you minimize thinking on test day, you also minimize potential error and risk. Chapter 21 will teach you how to build a great essay framework now so that you can write a great essay on test day, regardless of the prompt.

Remember that half of your essay score is appearance; the other half is content. It's very important that you build an essay that progresses from thesis, through evidence, and to conclusion. The basic framework you should use for both of your GRE essays is a fairly simple five-paragraph essay modified for the GRE reader's scoring guidelines. The framework looks like this:

> Paragraph one: Thesis
> Paragraph two: Evidence
> Paragraph three: Evidence
> Paragraph four: Antithesis/Evidence
> Paragraph five: Conclusion

Advanced Essay Planning

Let's modify the essay outline above for the GRE.

- **Thesis.** State your thesis clearly. The essay readers are moving quickly, so you don't earn any points by being subtle. Be direct and firm. Avoid broad generalizations (which are generally not provable anyway) and absolute statements. Introduce your evidence.

- **Evidence.** This is where you will earn most of your points. If the reader sees a clear and convincing connection between your thesis in your first paragraph and evidence in your second paragraph, you will probably get a good score.

- **Evidence.** Either add additional examples to the evidence offered in the second paragraph or introduce new, complementary evidence.

- **Antithesis/Evidence.** This is the variable paragraph: you may either introduce and refute a counterargument (antithesis) or you may provide additional evidence. You should avoid introducing completely new evidence at this point. Only add new examples of previously offered evidence. Otherwise, introduce (by stating clearly and concisely) the opposing argument and gently but effectively refute it. Because there is no "right" answer to a GRE essay prompt, all refutations should be "gentle," which means dismiss the counterargument with respect and without using absolutist verbiage (e.g., "Anyone who believes the other argument is a complete idiot!").

- **Conclusion.** Restate a modified version of your thesis by including the evidence that you introduced. These two components of conclusion-writing are important. Many writers think they are restating their thesis without actually checking it and don't realize that, in fact, they have changed their thesis. Essay readers are trained to read the conclusion and then reread the thesis (or first paragraph—some writers don't have a thesis). If the idea to be proven in the first paragraph doesn't match the idea proven in the last paragraph, the essay will receive a lower score. But the second component of conclusion-writing is also important. You cannot simply write your thesis statement again. That's not a conclusion. A conclusion restates the thesis and incorporates

the evidence offered in support of it. So when you are writing the conclusion, make sure you first reread your thesis, quickly consider your evidence, and write something that includes both without introducing anything new.

In Chapter 21, we will explore how this outline fits into the Issue and Argument essay prompts, and you will learn how to memorize and adapt a detailed version of the outline to any essay prompt. Finally, you'll learn how to construct your argument for the Issue essay (words to use and avoid, logic structure, etc.) and how to disassemble any argument for the Argument essay (basic argument structures, common assumptions, effective criticisms).

Seven General Ways to Most Assuredly Earn a Low Writing Score

The following are guaranteed to get you a low score:

1. Write a short essay. Fewer than 200 words and your score probably won't break a 2.

2. Don't use paragraphs/don't indent. If the essay appears disorganized in appearance, the readers will assume that it's disorganized in ideas. Messy essays don't score highly. Worth noting: essays with fewer than four paragraphs usually don't score well either. So not only should you use paragraphs, but you should also have at least four of them.

3. Write on another topic. You may love your cat, but an essay on your cat won't score well. (No, cat lovers, "Write about your cat" is not on ETS's list of possible essay topics.)

4. Insert your opinion into the Argument essay. The Argument essay is your analysis of someone else's opinion. Write about your own opinion, and you'll earn a sub-2 score.

5. Write the same thing over and over and over. Some people write a great first paragraph, then repeat the same idea for three more paragraphs. Your essay must move forward, developing its ideas with each sentence.

6. Don't provide evidence. You cannot simply provide an opinion, observation, or conclusion without providing evidence. Essay readers will score your essays based on your ability to link your observations to evidence that supports your observations.

7. Use excessively poor grammar, spelling, or punctuation. This may not matter much if you are applying for a math or math-based science program. But your essays will be read by graduate students who have experience grading college essays, and such readers are notorious sticklers for grammar, spelling, and punctuation. Minor mistakes won't be taken into consideration, but persistent errors will prejudice the readers against your essay.

One More Time: Why You Should Care

If you're applying to a writing-intensive program, your essay score may matter. If your undergraduate college isn't in the United States, your essay score may matter. If you have no undergraduate composition grade, your essay score may matter.

But perhaps most importantly, all graduate programs have access to your GRE essays. They can and may read these essays. Many programs will not officially consider your essays in the admissions process, but they can and often will review your essays to confirm your application essays (Did you really write them? How much editing was done to them?) and evaluate your communication skills.

The essay is increasingly a variable in the admissions process: great essays can put a mediocre application into the admit pile while awful essays can put the same application into the reject pile.

The Least You Need to Know

- Timing is often the most difficult part of the essay.

- You must practice writing good essays under pressure.

- The two GRE essays require fundamentally different responses.

- Colleges will see your actual essays (along with the essay score).

- An essay must look good in order to be good.

- Follow a basic, straightforward essay format.

Chapter 21

The Foolproof Way to Sound Intelligent

In This Chapter

- ◆ Building an Issue essay
- ◆ Building an Argument essay
- ◆ Tips for improving your writing
- ◆ Going for the perfect score

After reading Chapter 20, you know how the essays are scored and how they should appear. Here, we're going to explore strategies for building essays. Because you need to organize and write each essay within 30 minutes, it's important to have a plan of attack.

The Issue Essay

In the Issue essay, your job is to take a stand. The Issue prompt may be something like "Children learn most from praise and least from criticism." Which side should you argue? Recall the standard essay format:

> Paragraph one: Thesis
> Paragraph two: Evidence
> Paragraph three: Evidence
> Paragraph four: Antithesis/Evidence
> Paragraph five: Conclusion

In an Issue essay, your score is going to be largely determined by your evidence. So once you read the Issue prompt, consider all the evidence you have for either side of the issue. Argue for the side that has the most evidence, even if you don't really agree with it. This essay is not a personal litmus test but rather a test of your ability to buttress an argument with evidence, so go with whichever side has the most evidence.

Once you've decided which side has the most evidence, consider the two or three strongest pieces of evidence; you'll use those in your essay. If the other side has a strong piece of evidence, remember that, too.

Thesis

Start your essay with a clearly written thesis. That is, state within the first one to two sentences exactly what you're going to argue. It should be very clear which side you're on. Your thesis paragraph should also broadly introduce your evidence. By the end of your first paragraph, the reader should have a clear idea about which side of the issue you're on and how you're going to support your argument.

Evidence Paragraphs

You should have two to three evidence paragraphs. Each paragraph should focus on a specific piece of evidence. Evidence can be facts, points of logic, or examples. Don't list three or four examples in a paragraph. Instead, choose your best example and analyze it. If you want to analyze a new example, you should start a new paragraph, introduce the example, then analyze it.

In each instance, when you analyze evidence, you are isolating the aspect of that evidence that is related to the issue and then stating why that aspect supports your side of the issue. Never let the reader

assume how a piece of evidence supports your side of the issue. In summary, an evidence paragraph should look like this:

> Introduce the evidence. What is the evidence's source? Who said it? When did it happen? State the evidence. Whether you're using a quote, a fact, or an example, state your evidence clearly. Analyze the evidence. Precisely what aspect of the evidence is related to the issue and how does that aspect support your side?

Antithesis

If you have the time and space, you should write an antithesis paragraph. Thus far, you've spent all your time stating your argument and giving evidence for your side of the issue. Now you can bring up evidence for the other side of the issue and either attack it or incorporate it into your own argument (sort of like rhetorical judo).

Examine all the evidence that you considered before you took a side on the issue. What's the best evidence for the other side? If there's a problem with that evidence, attack it. If that evidence is convincing, use it. Here's how:

◆ **Attacking the evidence.** If the evidence for the other side has a weakness, exploit it. First, introduce your antithesis paragraph by stating what you're going to do: analyze the opposing position's primary evidence. Then state and analyze the evidence as if you were arguing the other side (just as you've done for the previous two to three paragraphs). Then state why this analysis is faulty. Often, the most obvious way to state why this analysis is faulty is to point to the evidence you've already marshaled in earlier paragraphs. When attacking the evidence, it's important to never stridently denigrate the other side; remember, there is no "right" answer to these questions. So while you don't want to completely agree with the other side, you also don't want to label them idiots.

◆ **Using the evidence.** What if the other side has a great piece of evidence that really supports their side of the issue? Find a way to incorporate it into your argument. It's the exception to the rule. You should be clear that your position is correct most of the time; you can't introduce evidence that contradicts your previous arguments without stating that your position is correct most of the time and this evidence points to a minor exception. It's best to both begin and end this paragraph with a disclaimer that this evidence is the exception to your otherwise powerful argument.

Conclusion

You need to make sure to do two things when you write a conclusion.

First, go back and reread your thesis paragraph. Points are often lost because the conclusion doesn't conclude what the thesis stated. Sometimes a thesis undergoes a mild transformation as the evidence is argued and eventually mutates into something else. So go back and reread your thesis paragraph and make sure you're going to restate your thesis, not a slightly different version thereof.

Second, you need to make sure you restate your thesis and incorporate your evidence. You cannot simply restate your thesis and ignore all the evidence. So your conclusion ought not to say anything other than your thesis, but also cannot simply be your thesis statement alone. Usually, two to three sentences summarizing your evidence, along with your thesis statement, make for a great conclusion.

The Argument Essay

In the Argument essay, you don't take a side on an issue. Rather, you analyze an argument presented to you. To understand how to best analyze an argument, let's look at how a basic argument is constructed.

Evidence

All arguments have evidence. The evidence may be stated or implied. Evidence often includes facts, testimonials, opinions from "experts," surveys, or studies. The difference between an argument and an opinion is that an argument has evidence. You may opine that "Blue is the best color." You could convert that into an argument by saying "Blue is the best color because …" After reading an argument, you must identify the evidence. You can't analyze an argument without understanding the evidence used to support it.

Conclusion

All arguments also have conclusions. What is the argument saying? What is the argument trying to convince you of or trying to get you to do or think? An argument exists to support a conclusion. Sometimes the conclusion is obvious; such a conclusion may be set off by conclusion trigger words (therefore, in conclusion, as a result). Other times, conclusions are implied. For example, nearly all advertisements have implied conclusions. They may not explicitly say "Buy this product," but that's the conclusion.

If you're having problems locating the conclusion, look at the evidence and ask, "What conclusion does this support?" If you're having problems finding the evidence, read the conclusion and ask, "What evidence does this need?" Either the evidence or the conclusion is obvious in every argument; use one to find the other.

Assumptions

So an argument has evidence and a conclusion, but what glues those two things together? Assumptions! Every argument has assumptions that make the evidence relevant to the conclusion. Assumptions aren't stated and sometimes aren't obvious, but it's imperative that you know the assumptions of an argument.

Let's look at a few simple arguments to illustrate how assumptions work.

> It's rained the last three Mondays.
> Tomorrow is Monday.

The conclusion in this simple argument is implied, not stated. The conclusion is "It's going to rain tomorrow." The evidence is stated: it's been raining on Mondays and tomorrow is Monday. The assumption is that the evidence about prior rainy Mondays somehow predicts rain on future Mondays.

Here's another:

> Four out of five dentists prefer
> SuperWhite toothpaste.

This sounds like an advertisement, doesn't it? And the conclusion for all advertisements is "Buy this." So the conclusion here is "Buy SuperWhite toothpaste." The evidence is the survey. What's the assumption? It's that the survey is somehow representative of the whole.

Attacking an Argument

The mistake that most writers make when attacking an argument is that they attack the conclusion. But attacking the conclusion should be a by-product of attacking the evidence and the assumptions. Never attack a conclusion before addressing the evidence and the assumptions.

First, you should attack the evidence if you can. It's not always possible to attack evidence, but it's usually the starting point. Next, attack the assumptions. You can and should always attack the assumptions of an argument. How would we attack the two simple arguments below?

> It's rained the last three Mondays.
> Tomorrow is Monday.

- **Attack #1:** The evidence doesn't state whether it has rained on all days over the prior three weeks (it implies that there's something specific with the Mondays, but we really don't know).

- **Attack #2:** What if it has rained the last three Sundays and didn't rain "today" (presumably a Sunday in the argument)? Once again, the evidence could be highly selective.

- **Attack #3:** The idea that rain only occurs on specific days is not logically or scientifically valid, so even if the evidence isn't selective, this argument presents a coincidence, not a valid pattern.

And now for the second one:

> Four out of five dentists prefer SuperWhite toothpaste.

- **Attack #1:** The evidence—the survey information—may have only surveyed five dentists.

- **Attack #2:** The assumption that the survey represents the sentiment among all dentists may be wrong—we simply don't know.

- **Attack #3:** Did the dentists prefer SuperWhite to all other toothpastes or just a single inferior product? (It's possible that the dentists were asked if they prefer to brush their teeth with SuperWhite or charcoal briquettes, in which case the conclusion shouldn't be "Buy SuperWhite" but rather "Don't brush your teeth with charcoal.")

> **! INFO TO GO**
>
> If you're attacking the evidence, it's a good idea to provide counterexamples, such as the "charcoal briquettes" example. Just don't make the essay about your counterexamples: toss out the counterexample, and then redirect your attention back to the argument you're analyzing.

In order to analyze an argument, you need to focus on the validity of the evidence and the assumptions that tie that evidence to the conclusion. In every argument, you need to identify the evidence and the conclusion, and then determine the assumptions that link them. Your analysis should focus on the strengths and weaknesses of the evidence and the assumptions.

Advanced Writing Techniques

Here are a few tips for improving your writing for either essay.

> **✗ FAIR WARNING**
>
> Absolute statements are easy to attack, so you should always attack them in arguments and never make them yourself. (That was an absolute statement!) Always leave room for an exception, and always suggest an exception if someone makes an absolute statement.

Avoid Absolutes

Don't make statements that state or imply that something is the case 0 percent or 100 percent of the time. For example, don't say something "never happens" or there is "no evidence." Instead, qualify your statement by saying "it usually never happens" or "it appears that there is no evidence." Similarly, don't say something is "always the case" or "must be true." Temper such absolute statements in your

own writing and attack such absolute statements in arguments.

> **! INFO TO GO**
>
> Be careful: "is" is an absolute word. "It is going to rain later today" means you're 100 percent sure it's going to rain. Avoid such statements. Rather, say "It is likely to rain later today."

Write Clearly

Don't try to be subtle. These essays are read quickly. Simple, direct statements are your friend.

Link Your Paragraphs

Writing good transition sentences can be difficult. Don't worry about it when you're first writing your essay. Just write five to seven great paragraphs. Afterward, go back and make sure that each paragraph is linked to the next with a good transition sentence. The last thing you should do with an essay is check the transition sentences and make sure all your paragraphs are solidly linked together. If you find it impossible to link two paragraphs, one of them should probably be moved. The computer GRE has a cut/paste function, so cut that paragraph out and paste it where it will make more sense. A problem with a transition sentence is usually a sign that the logic of the paragraphs is off, and sometimes it's easier to move the paragraphs than force in a transition sentence.

Address the Issue or Argument

A mistake writers make is that they sometimes alter the issue or argument presented and then attack that new issue or argument. It's also a mistake to attack the writer of the argument and not the argument itself. Always address the issue or the argument, not the writer.

Don't Use Slang

This is difficult because slang easily slips past writers—you don't even realize you're using it. The essay graders are not grading on diction, grammar, or spelling, but if you use slang, the grader may think you're less capable of putting together a great essay.

INFO TO GO

The GMAT has very similar essays, but those essays are graded by computers that aren't influenced by potentially negative writing habits, such as using slang. The problem is that if you use slang or misspell a word, the computer may not understand what you're writing at all. For now, the GRE is graded by humans.

Spelling Doesn't (Technically) Count

But, once again, graders can be negatively influenced by many misspelled words. So only use big words if you know how to spell them.

Don't Say the Same Thing Three Times

Probably the biggest mistake writers make is that they write an entire five- to seven-sentence paragraph and really only make one minor point. Make sure every sentence adds something new: introduce new information, analyze the evidence, offer new evidence, tie evidence together.

The Least You Need to Know

◆ For the Issue essay: choose the side with the most evidence.

◆ For the Argument: attack the evidence and assumptions.

◆ Stay focused on the issue or argument, and address the idea, not the writer.

◆ While diction, grammar, and spelling technically don't count, stick with what you know so you don't negatively influence the readers.

Chapter 22

Sample Analytical Essays

In This Chapter

- ◆ Sample Argument essay prompts and responses
- ◆ Sample Issue essay prompts and responses
- ◆ Real essays so you know how to score your practice essays

Here's your chance to practice writing essays and then compare your response to actual responses. We have three Argument and three Issue essay prompts below. Don't look at them until you're ready to start writing. Time yourself! You have 30 minutes to write each essay.

The sample responses are actual, unedited responses (complete with some grammar and spelling errors). These responses all received a score of 6 (the highest possible score).

Argument Essay Prompt #1

The following appeared in a newspaper article published in the United States.

> "Only two decades ago, nearly one half of the population in the United States met the standards for adequate physical fitness as then defined by the national council of health. Today, the national council reports that slightly less than one quarter of the population is adequately fit, and reports that increased usage of computers might be the reason for the decline. But since average fitness levels are actually highest in those geographic regions where levels of computer ownership are also highest, it's certain that computer usage

is not a significant factor in the decline of physical fitness. Indeed, this year's unusually low expenditures on fitness-related products and services suggest that the recent decline in the economy is a more likely cause. Fitness levels will therefore improve when the economy rebounds."

Sample Response #1

The reasoning for the claim that a decline in the economy is responsible for low physical fitness is rife with logical fallacies, and it is far more likely that other factors, such as changing work-place conditions over the last twenty years, the changed dietary habits of Americans, and the association between level of education and income with fitness play a much larger role. First, the author neglects to address the larger issue of computer usage: its role in a sedentary lifestyle. Secondly, he claims that a positive correlation between computer ownership and physical fitness implies a non-causal relationship (correlation does not imply causation or non-causation), third, he makes the assumption that low fitness-product sales is an reliable indicator of the economy as well as of people's physical activity without offering any supporting evidence, and lastly, he claims that this supposed correlation of depressed economy and lowered fitness levels implies a causal relationship.

In the first place, the author confuses the issues of sedentary life style with that of computer ownership. In the past twenty years, as throughout the century, Americans have adopted an increasingly sedentary lifestyle, both at the workplace and in the home. Computer usage is undeniably a factor in this overall lifestyle shift. However, it has also been shown that people with a high education and income level are more likely to be fit, perhaps because they have the leisure and disposable income to pursue physical activity and make healthy life style choices. Therefore, it is likely that high income is a more powerful factor in physical fitness than computer usage, which may still play a role in lower-income areas. Since a high level of computer ownership implies a high income-area, it may be income and education level that is responsible for the lack of correlation in the US. Meanwhile, for all we know, computer usage in the workplace may be having a powerful effect on the physical fitness of people in lower-income areas.

Secondly, the assumption that lowered fitness services sales must mean a depressed economy and lower levels of fitness is by no means supported in the passage. Different sectors of the economy might have fared differently; there is no indication that a decrease in treadmill sales should mean the same as a lowered stock market. Likewise, perhaps the market for fitness equipment and services was saturated last year, and people were exercising with equipment they bought in previous years, or at home instead of the gym. And most importantly, even if we were to accept the claim that last year, the economy was depressed and this correlated to a lower level of fitness, we have no context in which to judge whether a true correlation is taking place: to reference only one year is to fall prey to problems that "small sample size" poses to statistical analysis. A sample size of one is no sample at all. If our author had claimed that, twenty years ago, the economy was much better, and that it has declined to the present day, coinciding with a decline in fitness levels, we would have a basis to claim correlation—but still not causation!

In conclusion, the author fails to address those factors that may play a more powerful role in the decline of fitness levels which has been evident over the past *century*, not just the last two decades:

namely, the gigantic shift in dietary and work habits that Americans have experienced. Today, most people work in sedentary jobs and drive everywhere. Pursuing fitness costs time and money. Secondly, American's eating habits have changed radically: today, many people habitually eat out rather than at home, and are accustomed to huge serving sizes as a result. Americans also have fallen prey to "snack food" and the concept of "meal time" has all but fallen by the wayside. These changes in lifestyle are probably the most important factors contributing to low levels of physical fitness today.

Argument Essay Prompt #2

The following appeared in a letter to the editor of a newsletter on health issues:

"For the past ten years, most doctors have cautioned teenagers against eating greasy foods in the belief that dietary fat contributes to acne and related skin conditions. However, the number of teenagers who have sought medical help for these skin problems has actually increased over the same period of time. A recent study reported that teenagers who avoided eating greasy foods for a month had about the same number of outbreaks of acne and related skin conditions as those who ate an average of two servings of greasy food per day. Such results show that greasy food is probably not a contributing factor in acne outbreaks. Doctors therefore should no longer direct people to avoid such foods."

Sample Response #2

The claim that greasy food does not cause acne is not supported by the statistic that the number of teenagers seeking medical help has increased since this recommendation started circulating. The study that suggests that teenagers who avoid greasy food for a month have the same average number of outbreaks as teenagers who eat greasy food regularly could be more convincing, but suffers two flaws that render it unconvincing as support: first, since it was conducted only for a month, it is inconclusive (dietary changes usually take longer than a month to have their full effect), and second, too little is reported about the study for us to be able too judge its methodological validity. Given the information at hand, then, the conclusion that this paragraph draws is unsupported.

The fact that the number of teenagers seeking medical help for acne has increased does not necessarily imply that the proportion of teenagers in the general population suffering from acne has increased. Confounding factors include population growth, which increases the number of patients anyway. More importantly, it may be that many acne sufferers went untreated in the past; the increase could be due to any number of factors, including better health care coverage for acne treatment, improved treatments that motivate previously untreatable sufferers to seek a solution; less of cultural emphasis on medical treatment for cosmetic issues, and so forth. In sum then, the opposite of the claim made in this statement may be true: it may be that the number of people suffering from acne because of diet has decreased, while the overall number of patients has increased due to other factors.

Additionally, the study cited is unconvincing. No one would claim that a low-fat diet reduces cholesterol levels simply because a one-month study failed to find any reduction in cholesterol levels; dietary changes, like many lifestyle changes, make take years to have their full effect. That is one methodological flaw; there may be others, but we simply don't know from the information given.

How many teenagers were involved in the study? A small sample size renders statistical analysis suspect. Who conducted the study? If it were funded by McDonald's, say, we might reasonably suspect that there could be a structural bias of some sort built into the study.

In conclusion, it is probable that many lifestyle choices as well as genetics and environment influence acne outbreaks. It is entirely possible that, for some people, greasy food is a significant factor, while for others, it is significantly less so.

Argument Essay Prompt #3

The following appeared as an editorial in a newspaper:

"The Heatherly county school district should cut its music education programs. The music program is unpopular with our students: only 10 percent of high school students participated in a music program last year. Moreover, only a tiny percentage of the Tolland county's college-bound students are interested in pursuing music as their major at the university level. Consider a town in our neighboring school district of Courtmanch: there, Bender High school cut its music programs three years ago, and the overall GPA in the high school increased by 10 percent the next year. It seems obvious that the money spent on Heatherly music programs would be better used if spent on improving the quality of our core academic areas, especially math and science."

Sample Response #3

Music is an integral part of any education, and to do away with it would be a grave disservice to our students. The two reasons for canceling the music program in the editorial (that the program is unpopular, and that grades have improved since it was canceled) are unconvincing. In direct contradiction to the editorial's claims, proponents of music education often argue that music programs improve individual's discipline (through practicing), team work (through collaboration in ensembles), performance anxiety-management techniques (through competitions and auditions) and overall academic performance (nationwide, there is a strong correlation between high grade point average and participation in music programs.) However, these reasons, though valid, are all indirect benefits of music. The fundamental reason that music programs should be encouraged is that music is in and of itself a worthwhile, indeed a necessary, human activity.

In the first place, the reasoning presented in the editorial is unconvincing. Numerous studies have shown a correlation between high academic performance and participation in musical activities. The statistic cited in editorial sent to the Solano newspapers seem in this context aberrant. Were other changes made in the curriculum coinciding with the cut, which could be responsible for the improvement in grades? The fact that the music program's participation is not very high is not a sign to cut the music program; it is a sign to investigate the quality of the music teacher and of the resources available to him or her. Maybe the music program was unpopular because it was so severely underfunded that the students could be presented with neither quality instruments nor motivating opportunities to perform at festivals and competitions.

To address the "side" benefits of music—which are extremely important in the overall scheme of education—music does indeed foster self-discipline, community, and intellectual development. All students of music must devote considerable time to practicing, an endeavor that involves patience, confidence, and a result-oriented outlook. Students learn that their teachers have expectations for them, and every week, they are responsible for meeting those expectations. At a higher level, dedicated practice involves the sort of life lessons that anyone who pursues a high-level skill will recognize: self-analysis, constant self-criticism balanced with a belief in one's own abilities; strengthening of *attention* and *concentration* over long periods of time, and above all, perseverance. But music making is not all about solitary discipline and self-development; it is about learning to play as a group, to listen to one another, to work towards a goal together. It is through rehearsing, performing, and competing together that students come to understand their part in creating a larger artistic endeavor, as well as the responsibility they have towards both their classmates and their director to ensure that the concert is a success.

Finally, music is in and of itself a worthwhile human activity, one common to all cultures and all levels of civilization. In the US, a lifelong comprehension, practice, and enjoyment of music is historically often begun in the public schools (in contrast to other countries; for example in France, most music education occurs outside the context of public schools. In the USA, public education, for better or for worse, is the one chance most people get to explore their potential as musicians.) And though most students do not go on to become professional musicians, most professional (wind and string) musicians in this country got their start in forth grade, with their elementary school band. Canceling a music program does more than rob those few students of the crucial opportunity to get started at an early age; it robs our culture of an educated and culturally active population, of the "intelligent listener"; the "classical concert-goer"; the community chorister and church pianist. And with that, we lose opportunities for community; for lifelong learning; for the support of the public institutions that make up the arts.

Issue Essay Prompt #1

"All college professors should be required to have work experience in a field relevant to their discipline, in order to become better teachers."

Sample Response #1

Should college professors be required to work in a field relevant to their subject? The question rests on the assumption that "those that can, do. Those who can't, teach." I would argue that requiring college professors to have "work experience" is too general a recommendation to be useful in all cases. In the world of academia, the dichotomy between "teaching" and "doing" is at best an overgeneralization, at worst a fallacy. In particular, there are disciplines in which an academic education is intended to prepare one for an academic career; others where an academic career represents one of the highest "levels of achievement" of the field, and others where *teaching* is truly *doing*, in that teaching is accomplished by modeling the skills involved. In these cases it would be counterproductive to require professors to acquire "work experience."

The central object that the requirement of working in a field is meant to address is the divorce between theory and practice. Certainly addressing this divorce is appropriate in those disciplines where it exists. However, in considering those fields where an academic education is intended to prepare one for an academic career, we come to see that there is no practical disjunct between the two. In astrophysics, non-applied branches of math, and particle physics, the "work world" is primarily centered within universities. Academic theory is directly relevant to "field work, because each informs the other constantly; graduate students are expected to "work" and to shape theory, even as their professors do. Asking an astrophysicists to acquire "work experience" outside the environs of the academic research facility might be entirely misguided, because "industry jobs" might be nonexistent for the professor's particular subfield of research. Forcing him to find work in a more general category of research might involve for him years of personal frustration and wasted opportunity.

Likewise, artists usually instruct by modeling the "real life" activity that constitutes the craft of their art: painters demonstrate a brushstroke, violinists a bow stroke, photographers the choosing of a shutter speed. Thus, in an academic environment the student of art learns, not theory, but direct, "real-world" skills: instruction and practice are one.

In other fields, the most highly successful career is an academic one. It's a rare poet who lives on his poetry alone; rarer still the poet laureate who has not had 'professor' attached to his or her name. For most artists, growth and skill takes place precisely when they are not "at work": it takes place in the practice room, over a cup of coffee staring at the inevitable blank page. It is an private pursuit that involves confrontation with the self, and it cannot be taught in the classroom. For artists, "work in a field relevant to their discipline" is, de facto, teaching. In fact, any work other than teaching for an artist might constrain the artist's originality. Gesualdo wrote some of the most bizarrely chromatic and avant guarde music of any era at the very beginning of the Baroque period; he was privately wealthy and had no need of a patron's approval. Likewise, the "patrons" of today are the demands of mass media. And if we hired only musicians with "real life success"—that is, those who had garnered recognition outside of the academic world—we would have had no Schoenberg teaching in the United States after WWII, no John Cage revolutionizing the philosophy of music through the aesthetics of aleatorism in the 1950s—in short, no "art" or "concert" music during this century.

Argument Essay Prompt #2

> "Competing for grades degrades the quality of education for students; this is as true at the university level as it is in the kindergarten classroom."

Sample Response #2

To claim that competition for grades harms quality of learning is to claim two things. Firstly that 'competition', to the extent of comparing one's achievements to those of others, somehow impedes the highest goal of education, namely that of imparting a love of learning and the skills necessary for self-education later in life, and secondly, that "grades" are not a valid benchmark for measuring 'true learning'. I take issue with both claims; though it can be abused, competition, in its purest sense, implies an orientation towards results, towards achievement, that need not imply antagonism towards other students. Likewise, grades, in the hands of a skilled teacher, can be a useful tool for conveying feedback about the quality of those results, without which a student can have little motivation to improve, indeed no notion that improvement is an objective.

In the first place, 'competition' need not be a negative word. Properly channeled, competition can imply the creation of standards, through comparison with one's peers. More than that, it can imply inspiration. Competition among the Bronte sister led to the fine works of literature; competition among Russian ballet dancers led to fine dancers (whereas a lack of competition, in, say, Jamaica does not lead to the creation of fine ice hockey players). "Competition" between nations and scientist racing to get to the Moon led to the historic first steps of Armstrong. The key to these disparate examples is that intellectual movements, national sports and arts, and scientific achievements are characterized by groups of people, working on a goal, mutually inspired through their "race" towards a goal; not through working together, but concurrently.

Secondly, 'grades' are a worthy goal. They are non-exclusive; just because I got an "A" doesn't mean you can't too. In this, grades avoid engendering the antagonism that comes with competition over limited resources (such as entrance to an elite college). Grades orient a student towards results; studies show that the single most important factor in effective learning is neither now the material is explained, nor the use of pedagogical techniques such as repetition or the presentation of material visually or aurally, but rather whether the students were expected to achieve or produce something given the material they had learned. "Grades" are, in the hands of a skilled instructor, merely a short hand for constructive criticism of results, and used properly they can show where improvement needs to be made. An anecdote about the motivating power of grades seems appropriate at this point: an English teacher once related the story of taking a course in college where the idealistic professor assigned everyone an automatic "A" at the start of the course in the hopes that this would inspire free discussion, learning for the sake of learning, and a true love of the literature being discussed. Instead, no one, including the English teacher, showed up to class.

It is only after we have strived as students, after we have been pushed, through competition with others, that we acquired the discipline of thought and the methodology of self-education to enjoy competition with ourselves. One read Jane Austen for pleasure in one's 30s because one had to struggle with Shakespeare, with guidance and criticism, as a freshman in high school; one know how to 'compete' with oneself, to strive with one's own inadequacies, because one has 'competed' with others.

Argument Essay Prompt #3

> "The purpose of art is to upset us; the purpose of science is to reassure us. It is in doing so that both are of value to us."

Sample Response #3

If we assume that the quote refers to "reassuring" and "upsetting" in regards to humankind's deeply held convictions about ourselves and our place in the universe, then there can be no legitimate dichotomy between science and art, in Western culture at least. Science reassures us that we can "know" things—that we, as well as the world, are quantifiable. Art reassures us that there is beauty in "being" as well as knowing. But both science and art—by teaching us what it is to know and what it is to be—tell us things about ourselves that unsettle us, that shake our deepest beliefs about ourselves.

At a deep level, science in the Western intellectual tradition has always been a pursuit that implicitly demands a certain "human confidence" in the face of the unknown. The earliest science was about taming the mystery of observable natural phenomenon; by taking thunder and lightening and putting Zeus's face behind them, we actually put a god in the shape of a man behind a frighteningly uncontrollable world. Thunder might not be controllable in any way, but a God is reassuringly controllable, or at least appeasable. Though in the modern world chaos theory and astronomy have turned the natural world into a far more unknowable, grand, and mysterious place than the ancient Greeks could ever have conceived, yet we persist in the face of the unknown. Every fifty years or so for the last two hundred years, some eminent old scientist or another announces the "end of science": whether on the grounds that chaos theory renders particle physics unknowable, or that impossibly of human flight. All that can be enquired into has been enquired into; we have reached the end of progress, they say. And yet in the face of chaos, scientists persist: it was the greatest leap of faith that the Western world took in the transition from the middle ages to the Renaissance, when we assumed that the outside world could be transformed into quantifiable representations; that time could be measured in constant units, instead of letting the hours stretch or compress with the summer and winter daylight hours; that experimentation, not just observation, could not just reveal the world, but shape it. It's a leap of faith that we have not yet abandoned.

In a similar vein, the arts, at least since the Renaissance in the western world, have been a humanistic endeavor that have at their base a similar confidence in human capacities. Though the goal of arts changes—be it to portray the vagrancies or the virtues of human character; the sublime and romantic or the orderly and composed in nature; the emotions of the artist; the impressions that light made on the retina—the fundamental confidence that the goal can be conveyed, that some truth, whether objective or subjective, can be portrayed, remains a constant. At times the arts have set themselves up in imitation of or drawn their insights from the sciences: visual artists discovering perspective in the Renaissance concurrent with advances in engineering; Virginia Woolf seeking to portray the human mind as the science of the time—Freud—understood it. At others, they have actively opposed the sciences: the expressionists in the time of the Weimer Republic rejecting all notions of progress and technology, expressed a longing for "Der Untergang" of the modern world; "Les sixes" of French impressionistic music adopted a whimsical, dada-ist approach to music and reality. Always, however, they have complemented the sciences in their search for some sort of "truth", and in their confidence that they have "found" it.

But both science and the arts pay a price—or is it the reward?—of confidence. We learn things about ourselves that we didn't want to know; we learn things about the world that shake our central place in it. Nothing was more upsetting to the Catholic Church than the "heresies" of Galileo, that the world was not the center of the universe, and nothing was more upsetting to the Victorians than Darwin's notion that humans might be descended from apes. Science upsets our world order; with the atomic age, humans had reason during the Cold War to fear—for the first time in human history—that they might destroy civilization and bring about the end of the world as we know it. And however frightening the outside world may be, science shows us the frightening world inside our head—a world full of subconscious motivations, a world in which ordinary people can be led to commit horrible acts, given the right circumstances. (Who will forget the Stanford prison experiments, when students assigned to be "guards" quickly demonstrated abusive behavior?) And art reflects an understanding of what it is to be alive—an understanding that, in the symphonies of Mahler or the literature of Joseph Conrad, is the "heart of darkness."

Ultimately, at the deepest level, both teach us things about ourselves—and since humankind is both reassuring and upsetting, science and art alike are but the mirrors of our own natures.

The Least You Need to Know

◆ Keep in mind that length, and minimal spelling and grammar errors, are all important.

◆ Your argument should address all sides of an issue or argument.

◆ Focus on the gaps in logic.

Chapter 23

Vocabulary: The Necessary Evil

In This Chapter

- How to improve your vocabulary
- Your GRE vocabulary assessment
- *The CIG to Acing the GRE* Master Vocabulary List
- *The CIG to Acing the GRE* Roots and Prefixes List
- Progress quizzes

A poor vocabulary can be a big impediment to improving your GRE score. It will take longer to read passages, and you'll read with less comprehension. And just because some of the more "vocab-based" questions are now gone (analogies, for example), that doesn't mean that having a great vocabulary is no longer important. "College-level" vocabulary is used throughout the reading passages. So improving your vocabulary is germane to improving your overall verbal score.

Studying vocabulary is both the most boring and most useful part of GRE prep. It's boring because it's vocabulary. If you don't have a great vocabulary, that probably means that you don't read much (or, possibly, English is not your first language). So studying a list of words isn't going to be fun. But this is also the most useful part of GRE prep because a good vocabulary is valuable in the real world. Techniques for solving math problems without knowing how to do the math aren't very helpful in the real world—you can't plug in a number on your taxes and work backward! But in graduate school and beyond you will be reading, writing, and speaking, and your vocabulary will be obvious to everyone.

Improving Your Vocabulary

In this chapter is our list of words that have appeared multiple times on the GRE. If you learn all of these words, your score will improve. Our list isn't very long (much shorter than most other lists) because we really focus on the words that ETS loves. You should make flash cards (if they work for you) and start learning them now. You will know some of these words, but the more you learn, the better these verbal techniques will work!

In addition to improving your verbal score, an improved vocabulary will certainly improve your writing skills and essay scores. This doesn't mean you should force a big word into a sentence where a small word will do. But writing with greater precision and variety certainly produces better essays.

So what are the best ways to improve your vocabulary?

Learn *The CIG to Acing the GRE* Master Vocabulary List. Most people find that making flash cards is the most useful way to learn words. Usually, the act of making the cards—writing the words and their definitions—is what helps students remember the words. So if you don't think flash cards help you, I encourage you to rewrite our list, because the act of writing the words and definitions is conducive to remembering them.

Get in the habit of looking up new words. Too many people are comfortable with ignoring words they don't know or assuming they know what they mean from context. If you don't know a word, look it up and write it down. But when you "write it down," you should always convert dictionary-speak into your own language; don't simply repeat a dictionary definition that you don't understand. Keep in mind that the first definition may not be the one ETS uses. Scan all the definitions and make sure you're

not using an archaic or obscure one. ETS generally uses commonly used definitions of hard words. Eventually you should have a "new word" list.

Use your new words. When you look up a new word, say it out loud. Pronounce it correctly. Then after you write it down, use it during the day, in your papers, at the dinner table. You may sound funny saying "soporific" at dinner, but daily use is the best method for acquiring a new and improved vocabulary.

> **INFO TO GO**
>
> Try to learn 5–10 new words every day.

Four-Step CIG Vocabulary Method

Follow these four steps to get the most out of your vocabulary building.

Step 1: Take the Introductory Quizzes

First you'll find two general quizzes of words chosen randomly from the list. We suggest that you take both quizzes now and then grade them by comparing your answers to the vocabulary list. *Be tough on yourself* (don't give yourself partial credit!). Then study the words and quiz yourself again until you know most of the definitions. Quizzes are great for one reason: most people think they know more words than they really do.

Each quiz has 40 words on it. Allow yourself about 10 minutes per quiz. For each quiz, compare your score to this chart:

# Correct	Your Performance
Fewer than 20	Your poor vocabulary is hurting your verbal score (and probably your essay score)—start studying!
20–29	Good score—your vocabulary is neither hurting nor helping your score. A little studying should go a long way.
30–40	You have a very good vocabulary—learn a few more words and practice verbal techniques and your score should be very good.

Step 2: Study the Vocabulary List

Make flashcards. Start today. There are 1,370 words on our list, so if you have four months until the GRE, you need to learn almost 12 words each day. You may already know some of these words, so perhaps you only need to learn 8–10 words each day. Regardless, start now!

> **INFO TO GO**
>
> Roots and prefixes are a very efficient way to unlock the meaning of thousands of words.

Step 3: Study Roots

After the life-changing *The CIG to Acing the GRE* Master Vocabulary List, we've included a list of commonly occurring roots and prefixes. Much of the English language is built on Latin and Greek roots and prefixes. Learning these will certainly improve your reading comprehension skills and reading speed.

> **FAIR WARNING**
>
> Start improving your vocabulary now!

Step 4: Wrap It Up with Progress Quizzes

After spending much time studying the vocabulary and roots lists, try taking the introductory quizzes again. Once you think you've got the GRE vocabulary mastered, take the two progress quizzes at the end of the chapter and see if you've improved.

Assessment Quizzes

Take about ten minutes and write down as many definitions as you can. Then check your definitions against the definitions included in *The Complete Idiot's Guide* list or in a dictionary. Don't give yourself half-credit for "sort-of" close answers.

Quiz 1

abjure _____

accolade _____

aggravate _____

animosity _____

apropos _____

arrant _____

astringent _____

auxiliary _____

bedizen _____

bilk _____

bolster _____

cacophony harsh sound

catholic Universal, comprehensive

chastisement Castigation

chromatic color.

cloture _____

cognizant _____

condense make thick

convoke _____

cower to hide

immaculate Clean

implicit precise

incredulous _____

insipid _____

ire _____

levee _____

lucubrate _____

maleficent _____

mesmerize _____

revere _____

sash _____

secular _____

shiftless _____

slate _____

sophisticated _____

squat _____

striated _____

suffocate _____

sybarite _____

vigilance _____

Quiz 2

brittle _____

centurion _____

coalescing _____

contentious _____

crease _____

dormant _____

effete _____

engrossing _____

epitome _____

exacerbate _____

extinct _____

fecund _____

florid _____

foster _____

garner _____

grave _____

hallow	_____
hermetic	_____
homiletics	_____
hoodwink	_____
impiety	_____
indistinct	_____
inter	_____
irate	_____
libel	_____
luminary	_____
meretricious	_____
mollify	_____
nervy	_____
nibble	_____
obtrusive	_____
ostracism	_____
pedantic	_____
perish	_____
pied	_____
polemic	_____
primp	_____
pugnacious	_____
racy	_____
reprobate	_____

The CIG to Acing the GRE Master Vocabulary List

abate	to lessen; to subside
abdication	giving up control, authority
aberration	deviation from the norm
abeyance	suspended action
abhor	to hate; to detest
abide	to be faithful; to endure
abjure	to promise or swear to give up
ablution	washing or cleansing
abnegation	self-denial
abrogate	to repeal or annul by authority
abscond	to go away suddenly (to avoid arrest)
abstemious	practicing restraint, especially from indulging in food and alcohol
abstruse	difficult to comprehend; obscure
abut	to border on, be next to
abysmal	bottomless; extreme
acarpous	effete; no longer fertile; worn out
acclaimed	to praise enthusiastically
accolade	praise; approval
accretion	the growing of separate things into one
adamant	kind of stone; inflexible
addle	to become rotten; to become confused
adduce	to offer as example, reason, or proof
adjudicate	to settle judicially
adjunct	something added; assistant
adjure	to beg
admonitory	containing warning
adorn	to add beauty; to decorate
adulteration	making impure, poorer in quality
adumbrate	to suggest or hint; to overshadow

adventitious	coming from another source and not innate
affable	polite and friendly
affinity	close connection relationship
aggravate	to make worse
agile	active; quick-moving
agnostic	doubtful or noncommittal
agog	eager; excited
ail	to trouble; to be ill
alacrity (+celerity)	eagerness and cheerful readiness; speed
alcove	recess; partially enclosed place
allegiance	duty; support; loyalty
alleviate	to make (pain) easier to bear
alloy	to debase by mixing with something inferior
ally	to place in a friendly association
aloof	reserved; indifferent
altercate	to dispute angrily or noisily
amalgamate	to mix; to combine
ambidextrous	able to use the left hand or the right equally well
ambiguous	doubtful; uncertain
ambivalent	having both of two contrary meanings
amble	leisurely walk
ameliorate	to improve; to make better
amorphous	shapeless
amortize	to end (a debt) by setting aside money
anathema	something loathed; curse
anguish	severe suffering
animosity	strong dislike
antebellum	existing before a war
antediluvian	made a long time ago, old
anthropomorphic	having human characteristics
antidote	medicine used against a poison or a disease

antithetical	direct opposing
apartheid	brutal racial discrimination
aphasia	loss of the power to use or comprehend words
aphorism	concise statement of a principle
aplomb	self-confidence
apostasy	renunciation of a religion
apostate	one who abandons long-held religious or political convictions
apotheosis	deification; glorification to godliness
appease	to make quiet or calm
appellation	identifying name or title
apprehensive	grasping; understanding; unhappy feeling about future
apprise	to give notice; to inform
approbation	approval
apropos	appropriate to the situation; apt
apt	well-suited; quick-witted
arabesque	a complex ornate design
arboreal	pertaining to with trees
ardor	devotion or enthusiasm
arduous	steep; difficult; ascent; laborious
argot	jargon; slang
arrant	in the highest degree
arrogance	proud superior manner of behavior
articulate	to speak distinctly; to connect by joints
ascend	to go or come up
ascendancy	dominance
ascertain	to get to know or understand
ascribe	to consider to be the origin of or belonging to
aseptic	surgically clean
ashen	deadly pale
asperity	roughness; harshness; ill temper; irritability

aspersion	slander
assiduous	diligent; hard-working; sedulous
assuage	to make something painful or burdensome less severe
astringent	something that draws together; penetrating or severe; substance that shrinks
astute	clever, quick at seeing to get an advantage
atelier	artist's workroom
atonement	repayment
attenuate	to make thin; weaken; enervate
attune	to bring into harmony
audacious	daring; foolishly bold; impudent
augury	omen; sign
august	majestic; venerable
auspicious	favorable; successful; prosperous
austere	severely moral and strict; simple and plain
auxiliary	helping; supporting
aver	to affirm; to assert; to prove
aversion	strong dislike
avid	eager; greedy
avow	admit; declare openly
bacchanalian	riotous, boisterous, or drunken festivity
bait	to persecute
baleful	harmful; ominous; causing evil
balk	obstacle; purposely to get in the way of
baneful	causing harm or ruin; pernicious; destructive
barrage	artificial; obstacle built across a river
barren	not good enough; devoid of value
bask	to enjoy warmth and light
beatify	to bless; to make happy or ascribe a virtue to

bedizen	to adorn, especially in a cheap showy manner
belabor	to beat hard; to assail verbally
bellicose	belligerent; pugnacious; given to fighting
belligerent	(person, nation) waging war
benediction	something that promotes goodness or well-being
benefactor	person who has given help
benevolence	wish or activity in doing good
benign	kind and gentle; mild (climate), not harmful
bequest	act of giving, leaving by will, or passing on to another
berate	to scold sharply
bereft	to leave desolate or alone, especially by death
bewilder	to puzzle; confuse
bigot	stubborn; narrow-minded person
bilge	bulge in the protuberance of a cask
bilk	to cheat
blandishment	flattery; coaxing
blandness	polite manner; comforting; uninteresting
blatant	noisy and rough
blithe	cheerful; casual; carefree
bluster	to talk or act with noisy swaggering threats
bogus	sham; counterfeit; not genuine
boisterous	loud; noisy; rough; lacking restraint
bolster	to give greatly needed support
boorish	crude; offensive; rude
brash	hasty; rush; cheeky; saucy
brass	yellow alloy made by mixing copper and zinc
brazen	made of brass; bold
breach	opening; broken place; breaking

22

brittle	easily broken	chaff	to tease good-naturedly
broach	to bring up; to announce; to begin to talk about	charlatan	quack or fraud
brook	to tolerate, endure	chary	cautious; wary
buoyant	able to float; light-hearted	chastisement	punishment
burgeon	to grow forth; to send out buds	chauvinist	a blindly devoted patriot
burnish	to polish, rub to a shine	chicanery	legal trickery; false argument
cabal	a scheme or plot; a group of plotters	chimera	illusion or fabrication of the mind
cacophony	harsh sound	chisel	steel tool for shaping materials
cadence	rhythmic modulation of sound	chivy	to tease or annoy with persistent petty attacks
cadge	to beg; to get by begging	choleric	irritable; bad-tempered
cajole	to use flattery or deceit; to persuade	chromatic	of color
calumny	slander; aspersion	churl	bad-tempered person
candid	frank; straight-forward	chutzpah	nerve; gall
cant	insincere talk	circumscribe	to draw a line around; to limit
cantankerous	bad-tempered; quarrelsome	clamor	to shout; to complain with a lot of noise
canvass	to discuss thoroughly; sort of touting	clerical	of the clergy or clerk
captious	critical	clientele	customers
carouse	to drink alcohol freely	clinch	to come to grips; to settle conclusively
carp	to find fault or complain querulously	cling	to resist separation
carte blanche	full discretionary power	clot	half-solid lump formed from liquid
castigation	severe punishment	cloture	to force an end to a debate by voting
catalyst	substance that causes speeding up	coagulation	change to a thick and solid state
catatonic	immobile	coalescing	coming together and uniting into one substance
catholic	comprehensive; universal	coax	to persuade or try to persuade by pleading or flattery
caustic	biting; sarcastic	coda	passage that completes a piece of music
cavil	to raise trivial and frivolous objection	coddle	to treat with care and tenderness
cede/cession	to surrender possession of, especially by treaty	coerce	to compel; to force; to make obedient
celerity	rapidity of motion or action	coeval	of the same period; coexisting
censure	expression of blame or disapproval; a rebuke	cogent	strong; convincing
centurion	leader of a unit of 100 soldiers		

25

cogitate	to think deeply; to mediate
cognizant	being fully aware of
collusion	secret agreement for a deceitful purpose
combustion	process of burning
comely	attractive
commemorate	to keep the memory of
commodious	having plenty of space for what is needed
commuter	person who travels regularly
complaisance	tending to comply; obliging willingness to please
compunction	feeling of regret for one's action
conceal	to hide; to keep secret
conceited	having an excessively high opinion of oneself
conciliatory	reconciling; soothing; comforting; mollifying
concomitant	accompanying
concord	agreement or harmony
concur	to agree in opinion; to happen together
condense	to increase in density, strength; to make laconic
condone	to forgive
congeal	to make or become stiff and solid
congenital	existing from birth; inherent
conjoin	to join together
connoisseur	a person with good judgment (e.g., art collector)
connotation	suggestion in addition to
console	to give comfort or sympathy to
conspicuous	easily seen; remarkable
consternation	surprise and fear; dismay
constrain	to compel
constrict	to make tight or smaller
consume	to get to the end of
consummate	perfect; to make perfect, complete

contemn	to scorn or despise
contentious	argumentative; pugnacious; combative; quarrelsome
contiguous	touching; neighboring
contrite	filled with deep sorrow for wrongdoing
contumacious	insubordinate; rebellious
conundrum	a riddle; dilemma; enigma
convalesce	to recover health gradually after sickness
conviction	firm belief
convivial	fond of feasting, drinking, and good company
convoke	to call together; to summon
convoluted	complicated; coiled; twisted
cordial	warm and sincere
cordon	line (of police acting as a guard)
cornucopia	abundant supply
corporeal	physical; of or for the body
corpulent	having a large bulky body
correlate	to have a mutual relation
corroboration	additional strengthening evidence
countenance	to favor or approve of
counterfeit	forgery
countervail	to counterbalance
covert	disguised
covetous	eagerly desirous
cower	to crouch; to shrink back
coy	shy, modest
cozen	to cheat
crass	very great (esp. stupidity)
cravat	piece of linen worn as a necktie
craven	cowardly
crease	a line or mark created by the act of folding
credulous	ready to believe things
cringe	to behave in an excessively servile way

detraction + diatribe
— verbal attack

crotchet	highly individual and usually eccentric opinion
cryptic	secret; with a hidden meaning
cumbersome	burdensome; heavy and awkward to carry
cupidity	greed; lust
curmudgeon	bad-tempered person
curriculum	course of study
cursory	quick; hurried
curtail	to make shorter then was planned
dainty	pretty, delicate (food); difficult to please
dastard	coward
daunt	to intimidate; to make fearful
dawdler	person who is slow; waste of time
dearth	shortage
debacle	a breakup; overthrow; sudden disaster
deciduous	ephemeral, *falling leaves / bark*
declaim/ declamation	to speak pompously or bombastically
declivity	downward inclination
decorum	propriety; properness
decree	order given by authority
decry	to disapprove of
deferential	showing respect
defiance	open disobedience or resistance
deign	to condescend; to give
deleterious	harmful
delineate	to portray, depict, sketch out
deluge	great flood; heavy rush of water
demagogue	person appealing not to reasons
demur	to hesitate; to raise objections
denigrate	to blacken; to belittle; to defame
denouement	an outcome or solution; the unraveling of a plot
deplete	to use until none remains
deposition	dethronement; depositing
deprave	to make morally bad, corrupt

deprecate	to protest against; to express disapproval of
dereliction	deserting and leaving; to fall into ruins
derision	ridicule; mockery; deriding
derivative	unoriginal; obtained from another source
derogatory	insulting; tending to damage
descry	to catch sight of
	In the distance we could barely descry
desiccant	substance used to absorb moisture / *dry*
	how primative desiccated food to preserve it.
desuetude	cessation of use; disuse
desultory	aimless; haphazard; digressing at random
deter	to discourage; to hinder
detraction	slandering; verbal attack; aspersion
detumescence	diminishing or lessening of swelling
deviance	being different in moral standards (from normal)
dexterity	skill (esp. in handling)
diaphanous	transparent; gauzy
	the diaphanous curtain people could see in
diatribe	bitter and violent attack in words
didactic	intended to teach; preachy
diffidence	shyness
	a salesperson needs to overcome his diff.
dilate	to speak comprehensively; to become wider, large
dilatory	intended to delay
	dilatory in paying bills
disabuse	to free from error
	disabuse you of my clients guilt
disallow	to refuse to allow or accept as correct
discern	to see with an effort but clearly
discomfit	to confuse; to embarrass
discompose	to destroy the composure of
disconcert	to upset the self-possession of
disconsolate	cheerless; dejected
discountenance	to refuse to approve of
discourse	speech; lecture

disparage - belittle

25

discredit	to refuse to believe
discreet	careful; prudent
discrete	individually distinct
disdain	to look on with contempt
disencumber	to free from encumbrance
disheveled	untidy
disingenuous	sophisticated; artful; trying to deceive; cunning *insincere*
disinter	to dig up from the earth
dislodge	to move by force from the place occupied
dismal	sad; gloomy; miserable
disparate	essentially different
dispatch	to complete; to put to death; rejection of something regarded as unimportant; a written message
disproof	proof to the contrary
disquiet	to take away the peace or tranquility
dissemble	to conceal the true nature of something / *disguise*
disseminate	to distribute (esp. ideas)
dissent	to have a different opinion; to refuse to assent / *disagree*
dissipate	to be dissolute *squander, scatter*
dissolute	marked by indulgence in vices
dissolution	disintegration; looseness in morals
dissonance	harsh, disagreeable combination of sounds; discord
distraught	distracted violently; upset in mind
divergence	getting farther apart from a point
divestiture	taking off; getting rid of; giving up *deprive*
divulge	to make a secret known
doggerel	trivial, poorly constructed verse
dogmatic	positive; certain; arbitrary without room for discussion
dolorous	marked by misery or grief
dolt	stupid fellow

distend - expand

dormant	in a state of inactivity but awaiting development
dote	to show much fondness; to center one's attention
drawl	slow way of speaking
droll	odd, comical
drone	male bee; idle person
drowsiness	feeling sleepy
drudge	to do hard, menial or monotonous work
dubious	doubtful
dud	failure
dulcet	melodious; harmonious
dupe	to cheat; to make a fool of
duplicity	deliberate deception
duress	coercion
dwarf	much below the usual size
dynamo	a generator; something that produces electric current
earthenware	dishes made of baked clay
ebullience	exuberance; outburst of feeling
ebullient	overflowing with enthusiasm; showing excitement
ecumenical	representing the whole Christian world
edacious	voracious; devouring
eddy	circular or spiral movement (e.g., of water or wind)
edible	fit to be eaten; not poisonous
efface	to make indistinct
effete	infertile; worn out; weak
efficacy	production of a desired result
effluvia	outflow in a stream of particles; a noxious odor or vapor
effrontery	boldness; impudence; arrogance
egregious	flagrant *notorious*
egress	way out; exit
elaborate	worked out with much care, in great detail

36

elegy	a lament; a melancholy composition	epigram	terse or witty and often paradoxical saying
elicit	to draw out	epistle	letter
eloquence	fluent speaking; skillful use of language	epithet	adjective
emaciate	to make thin and weak	epitome	brief summary; representative example; typical model
embellish	to make beautiful	equable	steady; regular
embezzle	to use in a wrong way for one's own benefit	equanimity	calmness of temperament
emollient	soothing to the skin; mollifying	equilibrium	state of being balanced
emote	to stir up; to excite	equipoise	equal distribution of weight; equilibrium
empirical	relying on experiment	equivocal	having a double or doubtful meaning; suspicious
encapsulate	to enclose in a capsule	equivocate	to try to deceive by equivocal language
encomium	warm or glowing praise; eulogy; panegyric	eradicate	to get rid of; to pull up by the roots
encumbrance	burden; things that get in the way of	erratic	irregular in behavior or opinion
endearing	making dear or liked	erudite	learned; scholarly
endorse	to write one's name on the back of	eschew	to avoid
enduring	lasting	esoteric	abstruse; intended only for a small circle of
enervate	to weaken; to deprive of strength; to attenuate	espouse	to marry; to give one's support to
engrave	to impress deeply	eulogy	formal praise; panegyric
engrossing	taking up all the time or attention; writing in large or formal style	euphoria	elation; state of pleasant excitement
engulf	to swallow up	euthanasia	easy and painless death
enigma	puzzle	evasive	tending to evade
enmity	hatred; being an enemy	evince	to show clearly; to indicate
ennui	boredom	evoke	to call up; to bring out
ensign	flag; badge	exacerbate	to make more violent, bitter, or severe
entangle	to put into difficulties	excoriation	severe criticism
enthrall	to captivate	exculpate	to clear from a charge of guilt
entice	to tempt or persuade	execrate	to denounce; to detest utterly
entreat	to ask earnestly	exhaustive	complete; thorough
enunciate	to pronounce (words); to express a theory	exigency	emergency; an urgent situation
enzyme	catalyst	exoneration	to set free from blame
epicurean	devoted to pleasure	exorbitant	much too high or great

attenuate, extenuate

4 7

expatiate	to roam; to wander freely
expedient	likely to be useful for a purpose
expiation	ending; expiring
exploit	brilliant achievement; to develop, to use selfishly
expostulate	to argue earnestly; to dissuade, correct, or protest
expurgate	to remove obscenity; purify; censor
exscind	to cut out; to cut away
extant	still in existence
extempore	without previous thought or preparation
extenuate	to reduce the strength; to lessen seriousness; to partially excuse
extinct	no longer active
extinguish	to end the existence of; to wipe or put out
extirpate	to destroy; to exterminate
extol	to praise highly
extort	to obtain by threats, violence
extralegal	outside the law
extraneous	extrinsic; not forming an essential part
extricable	able to be freed
extrovert	outgoing person
exuberance	state of growing vigorously; being full of life
facetious	humorous; funny; jocular
facile	easily done
fallacious	based on error
falter	to waver; to move in an uncertain manner
fanciful	imaginary
fatuous	without sense; foolish self-satisfaction
fawn	to attempt to please someone
feckless	lacking purpose or vitality; ineffective

fecund	fertile
feint	to pretend
felicitous	apt; suitably expressed; well chosen
felon	person guilty of murder
ferment	substance; to become excited
ferocity	savage cruelty
ferret	to discover by searching; to search
fervid	showing earnest feeling
fervor	warmth of feelings; earnestness
fetid	stinking
fetter	to shackle; to put in chains
feud	bitter quarrel over a long period of time
fidelity	loyalty; accuracy
fidget	to move restlessly; to make nervous
figurehead	carved image on the prow of a ship
finesse	delicate way of dealing with a situation
finical/finicky	difficult to please
fission	splitting or division
fixate	to stare at; to be obsessed with
flak	criticism; antiaircraft guns
flamboyant	brightly colored; florid
flaunting	to show off complacently
flax	pale; a plant
flay	to skin; to excoriate
fledged	able to fly; trained, experienced
fleet	number of ships; quick-moving
flinch	to draw; to move back; to wince
flop	to fail; to move; to fall clumsily
florid	very much ornamented; flushed with rosy color
flounder	to struggle to move; to proceed clumsily
flout	to reject or mock; to go against (as in going against tradition)

fluke	stroke of luck	frugal	careful; economical
fluster	to make nervous or confused	fulmination	bitter protest
foible	defect of character (a person is wrongly proud)	fulsome	disgusting; offensive due to excessiveness
foil	to prevent from carrying out; contrast	fusty	musty; rigidly old-fashioned or reactionary
foment	to promote or incite	gainsay	to deny; to oppose
foolproof	incapable of failure or error	garble	to make unfair selection from facts
foppish	someone who dresses like a fop (pays too much attention to his clothes)	garment	article of clothing
		garner	to gather and save; to store up
forage	food for horses and cattle	garrulity	talkativeness
forbear	to refrain from; to be patient; ancestor	garrulous	too talkative
		gaucherie	socially awkward, tactless behavior
forbearance	patience; willingness to wait	germane	relevant; pertinent to
ford	shallow place in a river (to cross)	gist	the point; general sense
forebode	to foretell or predict	glean	to gather facts in small quantities
forensic	belonging to courts of judicature	glib	ready and smooth but not sincere
forestall	to prevent by taking action in advance; to preempt	glimmer	weak, unsteady light
		gloat	to look at with selfish delight
foretoken	premonitory sign	glut	to supply too much; to fill to excess
forfeit	something surrendered	gnaw	to waste away; to bite steadily
forge	workshop for the shaping of metal; to shape metal, lead	gnomic	characterized by aphorism
		goad	urging a person to action
forgery	counterfeit	gorge	to eat greedily; narrow opening with a stream
forswear	to renounce; to disallow; to repudiate	gossamer	soft light; delicate material
foster	to nurture; to care for	gouge	tool for cutting grooves in wood
fracas	noisy quarrel	grandiloquent	using pompous words
fractious	quarrelsome; irritable	grave	serious; requiring consideration
fragile	easily injured, broken, or destroyed	graze	to touch or scrape lightly in passing
fragrant	sweet-smelling	gregarious	living in societies; liking the company
frantic	wildly excited with joy; anxiety		
frenetic	frantic; frenzied	grievous	causing grief or pain; serious
fret	worry; irritation; to wear away	grovel	to crawl; to humble oneself
fringe	edge; ornamental border; part of hair over the forehead	guile	deceit; cunning
		gullible	easily gulled
froward	intractable; not willing to yield or comply; stubborn	gush	to burst out suddenly; to talk ardently

gust	outburst of feeling; sudden rain, wind, fire, etc.	hyperbole	extravagant exaggeration
hack	to cut roughly; hired horse	hypocrisy	falsely making oneself appear to be what one is not
halcyon	calm and peaceful	iconoclast	person who attacks popular beliefs
hallow	to make holy; to consecrate		
hapless	luckless; unfortunate	idiosyncrasy	personal mannerism
harangue	a long passionate speech	idolatry	excessive admiration of
harbinger	something that indicates or fore-shadows	idyll	a carefree episode or experience
		ignoble	dishonorable; common; undignified
hardihood	resolute; courage and fortitude		
harrow	to distress; to create stress or torment	ignominious	shameful; dishonorable; undignified; disgraceful
haughty	arrogant; conceited	illicit	unlawful; forbidden
heckle	to harass with questions, challenges, or gibes	imbroglio	complicated and embarrassing situation
hector	to bully	immaculate	pure; faultless
heed	attention; to give notice to	imminent	likely to come or happen soon
heinous	odious, awful	immutable	that cannot be changed
heresy	belief contrary to what is generally accepted	impair	to worsen; to diminish in value
		impassioned	filled with passion or zeal
hermetic	sealed by fusion	impassive	unmoved feeling; no sign of passion
heterogeneous	made up of different kinds		
hew	to make by hard work; to cut by striking	impeach	to accuse; to charge with a crime
		impecunious	having little or no money
highbrow	high degree of culture; intellectual	impede	to hinder; to get in the way of
		impending	imminent; being about to happen; expected
hirsute	hairy; shaggy		
hoax	mischievous trick	imperative	urgent; essential
holster	leather case for a pistol	imperious	commanding; haughty; arrogant
homiletics	act of preaching	impermeable	that cannot be permeated
hone	stone used for sharpening tools	impertinent	given to insolent rudeness
honorific	conferring or conveying honor	imperturbable	calm; not capable of being excited
hoodwink	to trick; to mislead	impervious	not allowing to pass through
hospitable	liking; to give hospitality	imperviousness	haughty; arrogant; commanding
hubbub	noise; confusion	impetuous	having sudden energy; impulsive
hubris	arrogant pride	impiety	lack of reverence or dutifulness
hush	make or become silent	implacable	incapable of being placated
husk	worthless outside part of any-thing	implicate	to involve, connect, or incriminate

implicit	implied though not plainly expressed
implosion	collapse; bursting inward
importune	to beg urgently
imprecation	an invocation of evil; a curse
impromptu	without preparation
impudent	rash; indiscreet
impugned	challenged; to be doubted
impunity	exemption from punishment, harm, or loss
impute	to attribute to a cause or source; to ascribe
inadvertent	not paying proper attention
inane	silly senseless
inasmuch	because
incandescent	white, glowing, or luminous with intense heat
incarcerate	to put in prison; to confine
incense	to make angry
incessant	often repeated; continual
inchoate	not yet fully formed; rudimentary; elementary
incipient	beginning
incise	to engrave; to make a cut in
incite	to stir up; to rouse
incongruous	out of place; not in harmony or agreement
incorrigibility	cannot be cured or corrected
incredulous	skeptical; unwilling to believe
inculcate	to fix firmly by repetition
incumbents	official duties
incursion	a raid; a sudden attack
indefatigability	not easily exhaustible; tirelessness
indelible	impossible to remove, erase, or wash away; permanent
indigence	poverty
indigenous	native
indistinct	not easily heard, seen

indolence	laziness
indomitable	not easily discouraged or subdued
indubitable	too evident to be doubted
indulge	to gratify; to give way to; to satisfy; to allow oneself
indulgent	inclined to indulge
ineffable	too great to be described in words
ineluctable	certain; inevitable
inept	unskillful; said or done at the wrong time
ineptitude	quality of being unskillful
inferno	hell
infuriate	fill with fury or rage
infuse	to put; to pour; to fill
ingenuous	naïve; young; artless; frank
ingest	to take in by swallowing
ingress	the act of entering; entrance
inimical	harmful or friendly
inimitable	defying imitation; unmatchable
innocuous	causing no harm
inordinate	exceeding reasonable limits
inscrutable	incapable of being discovered or understood
insensible	unconscious; unresponsive; unaffected
insinuate	suggest or introduce by subtle means
insipid	without taste or flavor
insolvent	unable to pay debts; impoverished
insouciant	unconcerned; carefree
insularity	narrow-mindedness; isolated
insuperable	incapable of being surmounted or solved
insurrection	rising of people to open resistance
inter	to entomb or bury

interdict	to prohibit; to forbid
interim	as an installment
interloper	to encroach; to intrude
interpose	to come between
interregnum	lapse in a continuous series
intersperse	to place here and there
intimate	to announce; to suggest or hint
intractable	not easily managed or controlled; unruly
intransigence	unwillingness to compromise; stubbornness; intractability
intransigent	uncompromising
intrepid	fearless; brave; undaunted
introspection	examining one's own thoughts and feelings
inundate	to flood; to cover by overflowing
inured	accustomed to; adapted
invective	abusive language; curses
inveigh	to attack verbally; to denounce; to deprecate
inveterate	deep-rooted; long-established
invidious	of an unpleasant or objectionable nature
invincible	too strong to be defeated
involute	complex
irascible	irritable; easily angered
irate	angry
ire	to anger
irksome	tiresome
irresolute	hesitating; undecided
irrevocable	final and unalterable
itinerate	to travel from place to place; to peregrinate
jabber	to talk excitedly; to utter rapidly
jejune	lacking nutritive value; dull; juvenile
jettison	to get rid of as superfluous or encumbering
jibe	to make fun of
jocular	meant as a joke
judicious	sound in judgment; wise
knit	to draw together; to unite firmly
labyrinthine	to entangle; the state of affairs
lachrymose	causing tears; tearful
lackluster	(of eyes) dull
lament	to show, feel great sorrow
lassitude	weariness; tiredness
latent	present but not yet active, developed, or visible
laudatory	expressing or giving praise
lavish	giving or producing freely, liberally or generously
legacy	something handed down from an ancestor
levee	formal reception; embankment
levity	lack of seriousness
libel	statement that damages reputation
liberality	free giving; generosity
libertine	immoral person
licentious	lacking legal or moral restraints
lien	legal claim until a debt on it is repaid
limn	to paint; to portray
limp	lacking strength; walking unevenly
limpid	transparent; absolutely serene and untroubled
lionize	to treat as a famous person
listless	characterized by lack of interest, energy, or spirit
lithe	bendable; twistable
loll	to rest; to sit or stand in a lazy way
lope	to move along with long strides
loquacious	talkative; garrulous
lucubrate	to write in scholarly fashion
luculent	easily understood; lucid; clear
lugubrious	mournful; excessively sad
lull	to become quiet or less active

9

lumber	to move in a clumsy, noisy way
luminary	star; light-giving body
lurk	to be out of view, ready to attack
lustrous	being bright, polished
macabre	gruesome; suggesting death
macerate	to make or become soft by soaking in water
machination	plot; scheme
maelstrom	powerful, violent whirlpool
maladroit	tactless; clumsy
malapropism	misuse of a word
malediction	curse; execration
malefaction	evil deed; crime
maleficent	baleful
malevolence	wishing to do evil
malign	to make harmful or untrue statements
malinger	to fake illness or injury in order to shirk a duty
malleable	yielding easily; moldable; adapting
manacle	chains for the hands or feet
massacre	cruel killing of a large number of people
matriculation	be admitted; enter a university as a student
maudlin	sentimental in a silly or tearful way
maul	hurt by rough handling
maverick	rebel; nonconformist
mawkish	sickly sentimental
mellifluous	sweetly flowing
mendacity	dishonesty
mendicant	a beggar
mercurial	quick, changeable in character; fleeting
meretricious	attractive on the surface but of little value

mesmerize	to hypnotize
metamorphose	to change into a different form or appearance; to transform
meticulous	giving great attention to details
mettle	quality of endurance or courage
mettlesome	courageous; high-spirited
miasma	vaporous exhalation causing disease
middling	fairly good but not very good
minatory	menacing; threatening
mince	to pronounce or speak affectedly; to euphemize
misanthrope	person who hates mankind
mischievous	harmful; causing mischief
miscreant	heretical; villainous
miser	person who loves wealth and spends little
misogynist	one who hates women, females
missive	letter
moderation	quality of being limited; not extreme
mollify	to make calmer or quieter
molt	to lose hair, feathers before new growing
monomania	excessive concentration on a single object or idea
morbid	diseased; unhealthy
mordant	biting and caustic; incisive
morose	ill-tempered; unsocial
mottle	surface having colored spots or blotches
muffler	cloth worn round the neck; silencer
mulish	unreasonably and inflexibly obstinate
multifarious	varied; motley; greatly diversified
mundane	worldly as opposed to spiritual; commonplace; everyday

munificent	characterized by great liberality or generosity
myriad	very great number
nadir	lowest, weakest point
nascent	coming into existence; emerging
nebulous	cloud-like; hazy; vague
negligent	taking too little care
neophyte	person who has been converted to a belief
nervy	bold or brash; nervous
nexus	a connection, tie, or link
nibble	to wear away; to eat in small morsels
noisome	offensive; disgusting (smell)
nonchalant	not having interest
nonplused	greatly surprised
nostrum	a quack remedy; an untested cure
novitiate	period of being a novice; house where novices are trained
noxious	harmful
nugatory	trifling; worthless
obdurate	hardened and unrepentant; stubborn; inflexible
obfuscate	to darken; to make obscure; to muddle
oblivious	unaware; having no memory
obloquy	abusively detractive language; sharp criticism
obnoxious	odiously or disgustingly objectionable
obsequious	too eager to obey or serve
obstreperous	noisy; loud
obtain	to be established; accepted or customary
obtrusive	projecting; prominent; undesirably noticeable
obtuse	blunt; stupid
obviate	to make unnecessary; to get rid of
occluded	blocked up

odious	repulsive; hateful
odium	contempt; dislike; aversion
odor	smell; favor; reputation
offal	waste or by-product of a process; rubbish
offhand	without preparation or forethought; extemporaneously
officious	too eager or ready to help; offer advice
ominous	threatening
onerous	needing effort; burdensome
opaqueness	dullness; not allowing light to pass through
opprobrious	showing scorn or reproach
orotund	sonorous; bombastic
ossify	to turn to bone; to settle rigidly into an idea
ostensible	seeming; appearing as such; professed
ostentation	display to obtain admiration or envy
ostracism	shut out from society; refuse to meet, talk
overhaul	examine thoroughly; to learn about the condition
overweening	presumptuously arrogant; being a jerk
paean	song of praise or triumph
palate	roof of the mouth; sense of taste
palatial	magnificent
palliate	lessen the severity of
palpability	can be felt, touched, understood
palpitate	tremble; beat rapidly and irregularly
panegyric	formal praise; eulogy
panoply	a protective covering; impressive array
paradigm	a model; example or pattern

3

parasol	umbrella used as a sunshade, especially by women
pariah	an outcast; a rejected and despised person
parsimonious	too economical; miserly
partisan	one-sided; committed to a party; biased or prejudiced
pathos	emotion of sympathetic pity
patron	regular customer; person who gives support
paucity	scarcity; a lacking of
peccadillo	small sin; small weakness in one's character
pedantic	bookish; showing off learning
pedestrian	commonplace; trite; unremarkable
peevish	bad-tempered; irritable
pellucid	transparent; easy to understand
penchant	strong inclination; a liking
penitent	feeling or showing regret
penurious	poor; stingy
penury	extreme poverty
perambulate	to travel over or through (usually on foot)
percipient	capable of perception; discerning
peregrination	traveling about; wandering
peremptory	urgent; imperative
perfidious	treacherous; faithless
perfunctory	done as a duty; without care
perilous	dangerous
peripatetic	wandering
perish	to be destroyed; to decay
permeate	to spread into every part of
pernicious	harmful; injurious
perpetrate	to be guilty; to commit (usually a crime)
perquisite	gratuity or tip
persevere	to persist in the face of obstacles or discouragement

personable	pleasing in appearance; attractive
perspicacity	quick judging and understanding
pertain	to belong as a part; to have reference
pertinacious	stubbornly unyielding or tenacious
pest	destructive thing or a person who is a nuisance
petrified	taken away power (to think, feel, act)
petrify	to make hard, rocklike
petrous	like a rock, hard, stony
petulant	unreasonably impatient
philistine	a smug, ignorant person; one who lacks knowledge
phlegmatic	calm sluggish temperament; unemotional
picaresque	involving clever rogues or adventurers
pied	of mixed colors
pinch	to be too tight; to take between the thumb and finger
pine	to waste away through sorrow or illness
pious	dutiful to parents; devoted to religion
piquant	agreeably pungent; stimulating
pique	hurt the pride or self-respect; arouse
pitfall	covered hole as a trap; unsuspected danger
pith	essential part; soft liquid substance
pivotal	of great importance (often something others depend on)
placate	to soothe; to pacify; to calm
placid	serenely free of interruption or disturbance
plaintive	mournful melancholy; sorrowful
plaque	flat metal on a wall as a memorial

4

platitude	a trite or banal statement; unoriginality
plea	request
plead	address a court of law as an advocate
plethora	glut
pliant	pliable; easily bent, shaped, or twisted
plod	to continue without rest; to persevere
pluck	to pull the feathers off; to pick
plumb	to get to the root of
plummet	to fall; to plunge steeply
plunge	to move quickly, suddenly, and with force
poignant	deeply moving; keen
polemic	aggressive attack on opinions of another; disputant
poncho	large piece of cloth
ponderous	heavy; bulky; dull
portent	omen; marvelous; threatening
posit	to postulate; to suggest
postulate	to claim; to assume as true, existent, or necessary
potentate	ruler; one who wields great power or sway
prate	to talk long and idly
prattle	to prate; to utter or make meaningless sounds
precarious	uncertain; risky; dangerous
precepts	rules establishing standards of conduct
precipitous	steep
précis	concise summary
preclude	to prevent; to make impossible
precursory	preliminary; anticipating
predilection	special liking; mental preference
predominate	to have more power than others
preen	tidy; show self-satisfaction

premature	occurring before the right time
preponderance	greatness in number, strength, weight
presage	warning sign
presumption	arrogance
preternatural	not normal or usual
prevalent	common
prevaricate	to equivocate; to stray from the truth
prim	neat; formal
primp	to dress or arrange in a very careful or finicky manner
pristine	primitive; unspoiled; pure as in earlier times
probity	uprightness; incorruptibility
proclivity	inclination
procrastination	keeping on putting off
prodigal	wasteful; reckless with money
prodigious	enormous; wonderful
prodigy	portentous event; omen
profane	worldly; having contempt for God
profligacy	shameless immorality
profligate	wasteful; prodigal; extravagant
profundity	depth
profuse	abundant; lavish
prognosticate	to foretell from signs or symptoms; presage
proliferate	to grow; reproduce by rapid multiplication
prolix	tiring because of length
prone	prostrate; inclined to
propagation	increasing the number; spreading; extending
propinquity	nearness in time or place; affinity of nature
propitiatory	conciliatory; appeasing; mitigating

propitious	auspicious; presenting favorable circumstances
prosaic	everyday; mundane; commonplace
proscribe	to denounce as dangerous
protean	displaying great diversity or variety; versatile
protracted	prolonged
provident	frugal; looking to the future
provisional	of the present time only
provoke	to make angry
prudence	careful; forethought
prudish	easily shocked; excessively modest
prune	dried plum; silly person
pry	to inquire too curiously
pucker	to wrinkle
pugnacious	fond of; in the habit of fighting
puissance	strength
pulchritude	physical beauty
pummel	to pound or beat
punctilious	precise; paying attention to trivialities
pundit	pedant; authority on a subject
pungency	sharpness; stinging quality
pungent	marked by a sharp incisive quality; caustic
punitive	inflicting, involving, or aiming at punishment
purvey	to provide; to supply
pusillanimous	cowardly; craven
putative	commonly accepted or supposed
putrefaction	becoming rotten
pyre	large pile of wood for burning
quack	person dishonestly claiming authority
quaff	to drink deeply
quail	to lose courage; to turn frightened
qualm	feeling of doubt; temporary feeling of sickness
quandary	state of doubt or perplexity
quell	to suppress; to subdue
querulous	habitually complaining
quibble	to try to avoid by sophistication
quiescence	state of being passive; motionless
quiescent	at rest; dormant; torpid
quirk	peculiar behavior
quixotic	absurdly idealistic
quotidian	banal; everyday
rabble	mob; crowd; the lower classes of populace
raconteur	person who tells anecdotes
racy	full of zest or vigor; piquant
raffish	low; vulgar
ragamuffin	ragged; often disreputable person
rake	dissolute person; libertine
ramble	to move aimlessly from place to place
ramify	to be divided or subdivided; to branch out
rancorous	feeling bitterness; spitefulness
rant	to use extravagant language
rapacious	greedy (esp. for money)
rarefy	to make thin, less dense; to purify or refine
ratify	to approve and sanction formally
rave	act with excessive enthusiasm
reactionary	opposing progress
rebuff	to snub
recalcitrant	disobedient
recant	to take back as being false; to give up
recast	to cast or fashion anew
recidivism	relapse into antisocial or criminal behavior
reciprocity	granting of privileges in return for similar privileges
recitals	performances of music

6

recluse	person who lives alone and avoids people
recompense	to make payment; to reward; to punish
reconcile	to settle a quarrel; to restore peace
recondite	little known; abstruse
recourse	turning to someone or something for help
recreancy	cowardice; unfaithfulness
recreant	coward; apostate or deserter
rectitude	the quality of being straight; righteousness
recuperate	to become strong after illness, loss, exhaustion
redeem	to get back by payment; to compensate
redoubtable	formidable; causing fear
refine	to make or become pure or cultural
refractory	stubborn; unmanageable; intractable
refulgent	shining; brilliant
regale	to delight or entertain; to feast
regicide	crime of killing a king
reiterate	to say or do again several times
rejuvenation	becoming young in nature or appearance
relapse	to fall back again
remonstrate	to protest or object
renaissance	rebirth or revival
renascent	rising again into being or vigor
render	to deliver; to provide; to represent
renegade	deserter; unconventional or unlawful person
renege	to deny; to renounce; to go back on a promise
renovate	to restore to earlier or better condition

renowned	celebrated; famous
repast	meal
repel	to refuse to accept; to cause dislike
reprisal	recurrence, renewal, or resumption of an action
reproach	to scold; to upbraid
reprobate	person hardened in sin; one devoid of decency
repudiate	to disown; to refuse to accept or pay
repulsive	causing a feeling of disgust
requiem	mass for the dead; solemn chant for the dead
requite	to repay; to give in return
rescind	to repeal; to annul; to cancel
resigned	unresisting; submissive
resilience	quality of quickly recovering the original shape
resort	to frequently visit
restive	refusing to move; reluctant to be controlled
resuscitation	coming back to consciousness
retard	to check; to hinder
reticent	reserved; not talkative
retrograde	tending toward a worse or previous state
revere	to have deep respect for
reverent	feeling or showing deep respect
ribald	crude; characterized by coarse indecent humor
riddle	puzzling person or thing
rift	split; crack; dissension
rivet	to fix; to take up; secure metal pin
roll	call; calling of names
rotund	rich and deep; plump and round
ruffian	tough person, thug
rumple	to wrinkle
sacrosanct	most sacred or holy; immune from criticism or violation

sagacious	having sound judgment; perceptive; wise; like a sage
salacious	obscene
sallow	of a grayish greenish yellow color
salubrious	healthful
salutary	remedial; causing improvement
sanctimony	self-righteousness; hypocritical
sanction	approval (by authority); penalty
sanguinary	bloody
sanguine	cheerful; confident; optimistic
sanity	health of mind; soundness of judgment
sardonic	disdainfully or skeptically humorous; sarcastic
sash	long strip worn around the waist
satiate	satisfy fully
saturnine	gloomy; dark; morose
savant	person of great learning
savor	to taste or smell something
sawdust	tiny bits of wood
scabbard	sheath for a blade
scent	smell (usually pleasant)
scorch	to become discolored; to dry up; to go at high speed
scribble	to write hastily
scruple	minute part or quantity; qualm
scrupulous	having moral integrity; punctiliously exact
scurrilous	given to coarse language
scurvy	mean; contemptible
secede/secession	to withdraw from an organization
secular	material, not spiritual
sedulous	persevering
seminal	like a seed; constituting a source; originative
sententious	short and pithy; full of maxims, proverbs

sequence	succession; connected line of
sere	to make hard and without feeling
serendipity	phenomenon of finding valuable things not sought for
sermon	reproving a person for his faults
serrated	having a toothed edge
servile	like a slave; lacking independence
sever	to break off
severance	severing
shallow	little depth; not earnest
shard	piece of broken earthenware
sheath	cover for the blade of a weapon or a tool
shiftless	lacking in resourcefulness; lacking in ambition
shrew	ill-tempered, scolding woman
shrewd	astute; showing sound judgment
shrill	sharp; piercing
shun	keep away from; avoid
shunt	send from one track to another; lay aside
sidestep	step to one side
simper	to smile in a silly, self-conscious manner
sinew	power; chief supporting force
sinuous	winding; undulating; serpentine
skiff	small boat
skit	short piece of humorous writing
slack	sluggish, dull, not tight
slake	to assuage
slate	kind of blue-grey stone; propose; criticize
sluggard	lazy slow-moving person
slur	to join sounds, words so that they are indistinct
smolder	to burn slowly without flame
snare	to trap
snub	to treat with contempt

soar	to rise; to fly high
sober	self-controlled
sobriety	quality or condition of being sober
sodden	soaked; saturated
soggy	heavy with water
solvent	of the power of forming a solution
somatic	of the body
somnolent	likely to induce sleep; inclined to sleep
soot	black powder in smoke
sophisticated	complex; subtle; refined
sophistry	fallacious reasoning; faulty logic
sophomoric	self-assured though immature
soporific	producing sleep
sordid	wretched; comfortless
specious	illogical; of questionable truth or merit
sphinx	enigmatic or mysterious person
spleen	feelings of anger or ill will; often suppressed
splenetic	bad-tempered; irritable
splice	to join (two ends)
sponge	porous rubber for washing; live at another's expense
spurious	counterfeit
spurn	to have nothing to do with; to reject or refuse
squalid	foul; filthy
squander	to spend wastefully
squat	to crouch; to settle without permission
stanch	to stop the flow of a fluid
steeply	rising or falling sharply
stentorian	extremely loud and powerful
stickler	person who insists on something unyieldingly
stigma	mark of shame or disgrace
stigmatize	to describe as disgraceful
sting	sharp, painful prick
stingy	unwilling to spend or use
stint	to be thrifty; to set limits
stipple	to paint with dots
stipulate	to state or put forward as a necessary condition
stolid	showing no emotion; impassive
stray	to wander; to lose one's way
streak	long; thin; move very fast
striated	striped; grooved or banded
stricture	something that limits; adverse criticism
stride	to walk with long steps
strident	characterized by harsh and discordant sound
strut	a supporting bar
stultify	to cause to appear or be foolish
stygian	dark; gloomy
stymie	to hinder, obstruct, or block
subdue	to overcome; to bring under control
subjugate	to conquer; to subdue
sublime	lofty; astounding worth
submerge	put under water or liquid; sink out of sight
suborn	to induce by bribery; to commit perjury
subpoena	written order requiring a person to appear in a court of law
substantiation	giving facts to support (statement)
subsume	to include under a rule
subterfuge	deception
succor	assistance or relief in time of distress
suffice	to be enough
suffocate	to cause or have difficulty in breathing
suffrage	short prayer usually in a series; right of voting

9

sullied	to be stained or discredited
summarily	briefly; without delay
summary	done without delay or formality
sumptuous	lavish; magnificent
sundry	various; miscellaneous; separate
superannuate	to become retired; to become obsolete
supercilious	disdainful; characterized by haughty scorn
superfluous	more than is needed or wanted
superimpose	to place on the top
supersede	to take the place of
supine	lying on the back; slow to act; passive
suppliant	asking humbly; beseeching
supplicate	to make a humble petition to
suppress	to prevent from being known; put an end to
surcharge	additional load; charge
surfeit	to satiate; to feed to fullness or to excess
susceptibility	sensitiveness
swerve	to change direction suddenly
sybarite	voluptuary
sycophant	person who flatters the rich and powerful
syncopated	abbreviated; stressing the weak beat
synopsis	summary or outline
taciturn	not talkative; silent
tactile	perceptible by touch
tadpole	form of a frog when it leaves the egg
talon	claw of a bird of prey
tamp	to tap or drive down by repeated light blows
tamper	to interfere with
tangential	divergent; incidental
tarnished	lost brightness

tassel	bunch of threads
taunt	contemptuous reproach; hurtful remark
taut	tightly stretched
tautology	a repetition; redundancy
tawdry	cheap; gaudy; showy; tacky
teetotal	opposition to alcohol
temerity	boldness; brashness; intrepidness
temperance	abstinence from alcohol; self-control; moderation
temperate	showing self-control
tenacity	firmness; persistency
tendentious	biased
tenuous	insubstantial; flimsy; weak
tepid	lukewarm
termagant	shrew
terse	brief and to the point
testiness	witness; evidence
threadbare	exhausted of interest or freshness; trite
thrift	care; economy; thriving; prosperous
thwart	obstruct; frustrate
timid	shy; easily frightened
timorous	fearful; timid
toady	obsequious flatterer
tonic	something that gives strength or energy
topple	to be unsteady and overturn
torment	severe pain or suffering
torpid	sleeping; sluggish; lethargic; dormant
torque	twisting force causing rotation
tortuous	devious; not straightforward
tout	to solicit customers; to promote
tractable	easily controlled or managed
traduce	to malign; to violate
transgress	to break; to go beyond a boundary

10

transient	temporary; fleeting
transitory	brief
travesty	parody; imitation
tremulous	characterized by trembling; affected with timidity
trenchant	forceful; effective; vigorous
trepidation	alarm; excited state of mind
trickle	to flow in drops
trifling	unimportant
trite	not new
truce	agreement to cease hostilities
truckle	to act in a subservient manner
truculence	aggressiveness; ferocity
trudge	to walk heavily
turbid	muddy; having the sediment stirred up
turbulence	being uncontrolled; violent
turgid	excessively ornate; swollen or bloated
turmoil	trouble; disturbance; state of extreme confusion, agitation, or commotion
turpitude	wickedness; shamefulness
turquoise	greenish-blue precious stone
tyro	beginner
ubiquitous	present everywhere
ulterior	situated beyond
umbrage	offense; resentment
uncouth	rough; awkward
underbid	to make a lower bid than a competitor
undermine	to weaken gradually at the base
undulate	to move in wavelike fashion; to fluctuate
unearth	to discover and bring to light
unencumbered	easygoing; trifle
unexceptionable	not open to objection or criticism
unfeigned	not pretended; sincere

unscathed	unharmed; unhurt
unseemly	inappropriate; indecorous
untoward	unfortunate; inconvenient
upbraid	to scold; to reproach
urbane	elegant; refined in manners
vacillation	being uncertain; hesitating
vagary	strange act or idea
vain	without use, result; conceited
valedictory	of an act of bidding farewell
valiant	brave
valorous	brave
vanquish	to conquer
vaunt	to boast
veer	to change direction
venal	corruptible
veneer	surface appearance covering the true nature
veneration	regard with deep respect
venial	excusable
veracity	truth
verdant	fresh and green
verisimilitude	appearing true or real
veritable	real; rightly named
verve	spirit; vigor; enthusiasm
vestige	trace or sign
vex	to annoy; to distress; to trouble
vigilance	watchfulness; self-appointed group who maintain order
vigilant	member of a vigilance committee
vigorous	strong; energetic
vilify	to slander; to say evil things
vindicate	to free from allegation or blame; to justify
vindictive	having a desire to revenge
viraginous	of a virago
virago	a loud domineering woman; a scold or nag

visceral	of the internal organs of the body
viscous	sticky; semifluid
vitiate	to lower the quality; to weaken the strength
vituperate	to curse; to abuse in words
vivacious	lively; high-spirited
volatile	changeable; inconstant
volition	power of choosing or determining
volubility	fluency; verbosity; easy use of spoken language
voluble	fluent
voluptuous	full of pleasure to the senses
vouchsafe	to grant
waffle	to talk vaguely and without much result
waft	scent; waving movement; carry lightly through
wag	humorous person
warmonger	person who seeks war
warrant	authority; written order; guarantee
wean	to detach from a habit
welter	turmoil; a bewildering jumble
wend	to go, proceed
wheedle	to influence or entice by words or flattery
whimsical	full of odd ideas, unpredictable
wince	to shrink or flinch with bodily or mental pain
woo	to try to win, to seek the affection of
wrangle	to dispute angrily, to win by argument
writ	written order (usually issued by a court)
yarn	long entertaining story

The CIG to Acing the GRE Roots and Prefixes List

Root or Prefix	Meaning	Examples
a, an	not, without	amoral, atheist, anarchy, anonymous, apathy
ab	away from	absent, abduction, aberrant, abstemious
ambul	to walk	ambulatory, amble, ambulance, somnambulist
ante	before	anteroom, antebellum, antedate, antecedent, antediluvian
anti, ant	against, opposite	antisocial, antiseptic, antithesis, antibody, antichrist, antifreeze, antipathy, antibiotic
audi	to hear	audience, auditory, audible, auditorium, audiovisual, audition
auto	self	automobile, automatic, autograph, autonomous, autoimmune
bene	good, well	benefactor, beneficial, benevolent, benediction, beneficiary, benefit
cede, ceed, cess	to go, to yield	succeed, proceed, precede, recede, secession, exceed, succession

Root or Prefix	Meaning	Examples
chron	time	chronology, chronic, chronicle, chronometer, anachronism
cide, cis	to kill, to cut	fratricide, suicide, incision, excision, circumcision
circum	around	circumnavigate, circumstance, circumcision, circumference, circumlocution, circumvent, circumscribe, circulatory
clud, clus, claus	to close or to close off	include, exclude, clause, claustrophobia, enclose, exclusive, reclusive
con, com	with, together	convene, compress, contemporary, converge, compact, confluence, conjoin, combine
contra, counter	against, opposite	contradict, counteract, contravene, contrary, contrapuntal
cred	to believe	credo, credible, credence, credit, credential, credulity, incredulous
cycl	circle, wheel	bicycle, cyclical, cycle
de	from, down, away	detach, deploy, derange, deodorize, devoid, deflate, degenerate
dei, div	pertaining to God	divinity, divine, deity, divination, deify

Root or Prefix	Meaning	Examples
demo	pertaining to people	democracy, demagogue, epidemic
dict	speak	predict, verdict, malediction, dictate, diction, indict
dis, dys, dif	away, not, negative	dismiss, differ, disallow, disperse, dissuade, disconnect, dysfunction, disproportion, disrespect, distemper, distaste, disarray
duc, duct	to lead, pull	produce, abduct, product, viaduct, aqueduct, induct, deduct, reduce, induce
dyn, dyna	power	dynamic, dynamometer, heterodyne, dynamite, dynamo, dynasty
equi	equal	equidistant, equilateral, equilibrium, equinox, equitable, equation, equator
e, ex	out, away, from	emit, expulsion, exhale, exit, express, exclusive, exceed, explosion
exter, extra	outside of	external, extrinsic, exterior, extraordinary, extracurricular, extrapolate, extraneous
flect, flex	to bend	flexible, reflection, deflect, circumflex

Root or Prefix	Meaning	Examples
flu, flux	flow	effluence, influence, fluctuate, confluence, reflux, influx
graph, gram	to write	polygraph, grammar, biography, graphite, telegram, autograph, lithograph
hetero	other	heterodox, heterogeneous, heterosexual, heterodyne
homo	same	homogenized, homosexual, homonym
hyper	over, above	hyperactive, hypertensive, hyperbolic, hypersensitive, hyperventilate
hypo	below, less than	hypotension, hypodermic, hypoglycemia, hypoallergenic
in, im	not	inviolate, innocuous, intractable, innocent, impregnable, impossible
infra	beneath	infrared, infrastructure
inter, intro	between	international, intercept, interoffice, internal, intermittent
intra	within, into	intranet, intravenous

Root or Prefix	Meaning	Examples
jac, ject	to throw	reject, eject, project, trajectory, interject, dejected, inject
mal	bad, badly	malformation, maladjusted, dismal, malady, malcontent, malfeasance, maleficent
mega	great, million	megaphone, megalomaniac, megabyte, megalopolis
meta	beyond, change	metaphor, metamorphosis, metabolism, metaphysical
meter	measure	perimeter, diameter
micro	small	microscope, microprocessor, microfiche, micrometer, micrograph
mis	bad, badly	misinform, misinterpret, mispronounce, misnomer, mistake
mit, miss	to send	transmit, permit, missile, missionary, remit, admit, missive, mission
morph	shape	polymorphic, amorphous
multi	many	multitude, multiply, multipurpose
neo	new	neologism, neoclassic, neophyte

Root or Prefix	Meaning	Examples
non	not	nonferrous, nonabrasive, nondescript
omni	all	omnipotent, omnivorous, omniscient
para	beside	paraprofessional, paramedic, paraphrase, parachute
per	through, intensive	permit, perspire, perforate, persuade
peri	around	periscope, perimeter, perigee, periodontal
phon	sound	telephone, phonics, phonograph, phonetic, microphone
phot	light	photograph, photon, photosynthesis
poly	many	polytheist, polygon, polygamy, polymorphous
port	to carry	porter, portable, report, transportation, deport, import, export
re	back, again	report, realign, retract, revise, regain, revisit
retro	backwards	retrorocket, retrospect, retrogression, retroactive
sanct	holy	sanctify, sanctuary, sanctimonious, sacrosanct

Root or Prefix	Meaning	Examples
scrib, script	to write	inscription, prescribe, proscribe, manuscript, conscript, scribble, scribe
sect, sec	cut	intersect, dissect, section
semi	half	semiannual, semimonthly, semicircle
spect	to look	inspect, spectator, circumspect, retrospect, prospect, spectacle
sub	under, below	submerge, submarine, substandard, subnormal, subvert
super, supra	above	superior, superscript, supernatural, supersede
syn	together	synthesis, synchronous, syndicate
tele	distance, from afar	television, telephone, telegraph, telemetry
theo, the	pertaining to God	theology, theist, polytheist
therm, thermo	heat	thermal, thermometer, thermocouple, thermodynamic, thermoelectric
tract	to drag, draw	attract, tractor, traction, extract, retract, protract, detract, subtract, contract, intractable

Root or Prefix	Meaning	Examples
trans	across	transoceanic, transmit, transport, transducer
un	not	unharmed, unintended
veh, vect	to carry	vector, vehicle, convection, vehement
vert, vers	to turn	convert, revert, advertise, versatile, vertigo, invert, reversion, extravert, introvert
vita	life	vital, vitality, vitamins, revitalize

The CIG to Acing the GRE Big List of Number Prefixes

Prefix	Meaning	Examples
mono, uni	one	monopoly, monotype, monologue, mononucleosis, monorail, monotheist, unilateral, universal, unity, unanimous, uniform
bi, di	two	divide, diverge, bifurcate, biweekly, bivalve, biannual
tri	three	triangle, trinity, trilateral, triumvirate, tribune, trilogy
quat, quad	four	quadrangle, quadruplets

Prefix	Meaning	Examples
quint, penta	five	quintet, quintuplets, pentagon, pentameter
hex, ses, sex	six	hexagon, hexameter, sextuplets
sept	seven	septet, septennial
oct	eight	octopus, octagon, octogenarian, octave
non	nine	nonagon, nonagenarian
dec	ten	decimal, decade, decalogue, decimate
cent	hundred	centennial, century, centipede
milo, mill, kilo	thousand	millennium, kilobyte, kiloton
mega	million	megabyte, megaton
giga	billion	gigabyte
tera	trillion	terabyte
milli	thousandth	millisecond, milligram
micro	millionth	microgram, microvolt
nano	billionth	nanosecond
pico	trillionth	picofarad, picogram
femto	quadrillionth	femtosecond

Progress Quizzes

Take about ten minutes and write down as many definitions as you can. Then check your definitions against the definitions included in the CIG list or in a dictionary. Don't give yourself half-credit for "sort-of" close answers.

Quiz 1

abscond _____

addle _____

apartheid _____

bellicose _____

bereft _____

brook _____

chivy _____

coeval _____

condense _____

dawdler _____

emollient _____

epitome _____

excoriation _____

exscind _____

fatuous _____

feud _____

fleet _____

forbearance _____

fulmination _____

germane _____

multifarious _____

obdurate _____

officious _____

panegyric _____

peregrination _____

phlegmatic _____

placate _____

pluck _____

portent _____

prattle _____

soporific _____

stigma _____

stultify _____

sumptuous _____

sycophant _____

taunt _____

tenuous _____

thwart _____

tonic _____

wean _____

Quiz 2

abeyance _____

accretion _____

adorn _____

anthropomorphic _____

benefactor _____

bilk _____

calumny _____

carte blanche _____

complaisance _____

congeal _____

contemn _____

convoluted _____

countenance _____

luculent _____

malign _____

mince _____

multifarious _____

novitiate _____

offhand _____

pariah _____

penurious _____

prolix _____

putrefaction _____

rant _____

recompense _____

regale _____

renovate _____

resigned _____

rivet _____

sanity _____

sequence _____

shrewd _____

sobriety _____

spleen _____

stingy _____

subdue _____

suffice _____

sundry _____

valedictory _____

veritable _____

The Least You Need to Know

◆ Vocabulary is tested on the reading and essay sections of the GRE.

◆ Improving your vocabulary increases your accuracy and speed.

◆ Look up any unknown word in a dictionary and write it down.

◆ Start learning *The CIG to Acing the GRE Master Vocabulary List* now!

Part 5

GRE Vocabulary

The real fun begins here. The vocabulary used on the GRE is insane. Take a few minutes to look through our list and you'll discover that working on your vocabulary is probably a good idea. Start soon! It takes a while to improve one's vocabulary. Part 5 also includes quizzes, roots, and prefixes.

A Review of Grammar

This chapter reviews basic grammar and a very specific range of grammar mistakes that may affect your GRE essays. Grammar is not directly tested anywhere on the GRE, but if your writing skills are lacking, you may want to brush up on the rules of basic grammar.

First, we'll be covering some very fundamental concepts (definitions of nouns, verbs, subjects). Then, we'll go over subject agreement with verbs, including compound subjects, singular subjects, and pronoun subjects. Next, we'll cover pronoun and antecedent agreement, and ambiguous pronoun usage. Then, we'll cover a couple more basic concepts (prepositions, objects, and case) and use them to identify incorrect pronoun case usage. These will include the mistake "preposition + I" and when to use "who" or "whom." We'll also review verbs and a few specific tense errors made with the words "since" and "for." Last, we'll cover issues of style and logic, including pronoun shift, faulty comparisons, introductory clauses, and parallelisms.

Exciting List O' Grammatical Definitions

Before we dive in, we should define a few words that will be used throughout the chapter.

Subject: the thing that does something.

> The **monkey** ate the cheese.

Object: the thing receiving the action.

> The monkey ate the **cheese.**

Number: are we talking about one or more? Singular means one. Plural means more than one.

Pronouns: a word used in place of a noun.

> **He** ate the cheese.

Prepositions: "locating" words.

> The monkey ate the cheese **in the atrium**.

Nouns, Pronouns, and Verbs

Nouns are people, places, things, or ideas. For example, the following words are all nouns: Mr. Smith, North Dakota, apple, love. In a sentence, nouns have various roles. If a noun performs some action in a sentence, it is called a *subject*. For example, what are the subjects in these sentences?

> The monkey ate the cheese
> There are three cats in the yard.
> The boy gave his sister a present.

Answers:

In each sentence, the subject is the word that is "doing" something. In the first sentence, the *monkey* is the "doer." What did he do? He *ate*. In the second sentence, the *cats* are the "doers." What are they doing? They *are*. In the last sentence, the *boy* is the "doer." What did he do? He *gave*.

Verbs are action words. For example, the following words are all verbs or verb phrases (in different tenses): run, be, are, to be, swimming, ate, will think, had considered, plan to go, are hitting, would have stopped, will have cheated.

Subjects and *verbs* are always connected in a sentence. One subject can have many verbs. For example:

> The boy hit the ball through the window, ran down the hall, and hid in the closet.

Or one verb can have several subjects:

> The boy, the girls, and the dog are playing on the beach.

The *number* of a noun or verb refers to whether it is singular or plural. When we ask, "What is the number of this noun?" we just mean: is it talking about one thing or more than one thing? *Singular* means one. *Plural* means more than one. For example, "the cat" is singular. "The cats" is plural.

Likewise, when we ask whether a verb is singular or plural, we are asking, are there more than one people/things doing the action, or is one person/thing doing the action? Verbs change their form depending on whether they are singular or plural. For example, *is* is a singular form of the verb "to be," and *are* is the plural form of the verb "to be."

Finally, subjects can be plural. For example, when multiple nouns, joined by the word *and*, are connected to the same action or actions, we call this a *plural subject*. For example, *the chair* is a singular noun, and *the table* is a singular noun, but together, they form a plural subject, because they are both attached to the verb *are*:

> The chair and the table are old.

Try this one:

> The boy hit the ball through the window, ran down the hall, and hid in the closet.

Is the subject singular or plural? Are the verbs singular or plural?

Answer: both the subject, *boy*, and the verbs, *hit, ran, hid*, are singular.

Try this one:

> The boy, the girls, and the dog are
> playing on the beach.

Is the subject singular or plural? Are the verbs singular or plural?

Answer: Both the subject, *boy, girls, and the dog* and the verb, *are playing*, are plural.

This leads us to an important rule about number agreement with verbs: The number of the verb must match the number of the subject. If the subject is singular, the verb takes a singular form. If the subject is plural, the verb takes a plural form. This should be simple, right?

> The cat are happy

just sounds wrong.

So when does this get tricky? It gets tricky when we have to go hunting for the subject and the verb in a sentence. For example, what's the subject and what's the verb in this sentence?

> There are three cats outside on the lawn.

If you rearrange *Cats are there* you should see that *cats* is the "doer," and "being" is what they're doing: *cats are*. But maybe you didn't realize this immediately because the verb came before the subject. When the verb comes before the subject, watch out!

Try this one:

> Expensively outfitted and luxuriously
> maintained in the garden state of New
> Jersey is ETS's golf course and boat
> house.

What's wrong? The phrase "golf course and boat house" is a plural subject. The sentence should be:

> Expensively outfitted and luxuriously
> maintained in the garden state of New
> Jersey **are** ETS's golf course and boat
> house.

What if a lot of words come between the subject and the verb?

> France, a country of 60 million people,
> are located in Western Europe.

Words that come between a subject and its verb don't matter. Delete all the words between the subject and the verb, and you'll see what should agree:

> France … **is** located in Western Europe.

Try this one:

> The wine in these bottles are at least 100
> years old.

What's wrong? *Bottles are* is wrong, because the subject is *wine*. The wine is old, not the bottles!

> The wine in these bottles **is** at least 100
> years old.

X FAIR WARNING

> Moral of the story: watch out if there's a plural word just before the verb — it may not be the subject of the sentence!

Try this one:

> The president's cabinet members are
> convinced that the announcement of the
> investigations, coming just days before

the election, were calculated to derail the president's already struggling campaign.

What's wrong? The *announcement* is the subject: the announcement was calculated to derail the president's campaign, not the investigations. The sentence should read:

> The president's cabinet members are convinced that the announcement of the investigations, coming just days before the election, **was** calculated to derail the president's already struggling campaign.

Compound Subjects

Compound subjects are just a list of "doers" joined by "and." If there's more than one "doer," then the subject is plural. So the verb should be plural, too. Seems simple enough:

> Woody and Bob goes to the store

just sounds wrong.

But sometimes it's less obvious. "The confusion and the hostility in the workplace was overwhelming" is wrong! But it sounds okay, doesn't it? So you can't always trust your ear. (It should be "The confusion and the hostility in the workplace were overwhelming.")

But what if the "doers" are joined by one of these words?

> with
> as well as
> in addition to
> together with
> no less than
> except

Examples:

> Dan along with John …
> Dan in addition to John …
> Dan together with John …
> Dan, no less than John …
> The group, except for Dan …

Are these still plural subjects?

Try this one:

> Woody as well as Bob go to the store.

What's wrong? Phrases like "as well as" link a subject (Woody) to other nouns (Bob) but they don't make the subject plural, they just add information. Woody is still the singular subject. "as well as Bob" is just a little bit of extra information. You can put parentheses around this extra information to make this easy to see, and then delete it:

> Woody (as well as Bob) **goes** to the store.
> Woody (…) **goes** to the store.

! INFO TO GO

Certain compound subjects are considered a unit and take a singular verb. These are idioms—for example, *The long and the short of it is.* You just have to know these; you can't figure them out from grammar rules.

Singular Subjects

Some singular subjects are tricky; for example, is *one of* a singular or plural subject?

Try this one:

> One of the cruelest arch villains who has ever written a test is Dr. Evil.

What's wrong? *One of* is always a singular subject. Think about it:

> One of the cruelest arch villains … is Dr. Evil.

That sounds okay. After all, it would sound wrong if you put in a plural verb, right?

> One of the cruelest arch villains … **are** Dr. Evil.

So far so good. The thing to realize is that the word *who* is talking about *arch villains*, not about Dr. Evil. Since *arch villains* is plural, *who* is plural, too. It must be

> … arch villains who **have** ever written a test …

When you see *one of*, put parentheses after the phrase that follows. Then look at that phrase separately from the rest of sentence, and make sure the subject and verb agree:

> One of (the evilest arch villains who have ever written a test) is Dr. Evil.

Pronoun Subjects

A pronoun is a word that replaces a noun. Usually, pronouns are used to avoid repeating a word in a sentence. For example, *she* is a pronoun, and *it* is a pronoun. See how they can be used to avoid repetition:

> Sara is wearing a new dress. Sara bought the dress yesterday.

Now, with pronouns:

> Sara is wearing a new dress. She bought it yesterday.

Here are some pronouns:

Pronouns

Personal Pronouns (Personal Pronouns for People)	Pronouns to Replace Things, Places, or Ideas
she	it
he	they
they	them
her	which
him	that
them	
who	
that	

Notice that pronouns can be the subjects of sentences. In this sentence,

> She cried yesterday,

"*She*" is the subject of the sentence.

Mostly, singular subjects are obvious: "the monkey," "the book," "she," "he," etc. But some pronoun subjects can be tricky; in spoken English, we often make the mistake of thinking that the following pronoun subjects are plural. In reality, the following pronouns are singular, so they take singular verbs:

> each
> either
> neither
> everyone, everybody
> nobody
> anybody
> someone

In everyday speech, people say things like:

> Everyone in our school hates their teachers.

When people say things like that, they're substituting *all the people* in their mind for "everyone." If you write, *all the people* **hate** *their teachers*, that's fine. But notice that you had to change *everyone* **hate**s to *all the people* **hate**.

Everyone in our school **hate** ... just sounds wrong. *Everyone* takes the singular verb *hates*. That means *everyone* is singular! So we can't use *their*.

> **INFO TO GO**
>
> How do you "hear" grammar mistakes while taking a standardized test? Mutter like a crazy person!
>
> I'm serious: move your lips without making a sound while you read a sentence. You'll catch many errors that way.

Solution:

> Everyone in our schools hates **his** teachers.
> Everyone in our school hates **her** teachers.

The PC-answer is: *Everyone in our school hates his or her teachers.*

It sounds weird, but it's grammatically correct.

Try this one:

> The Empire State Building, the Sears Tower, the Canadian National Tower— each of these buildings were the tallest in the world at the time it was built.

What's wrong? *Each* is a singular subject, so the plural verb *were* is wrong. It should be:

> The Empire State Building, the Sears Tower, the Canadian National Tower— each of these buildings **was** the tallest in the world at the time it was built.

Here are some more examples from that list of singular subjects:

> **Neither** the SAT nor the GRE **is** more fun than a barrel of monkeys.
> **Nobody** remembered his car keys except Sara, so none of us could open our car doors except her.

And what if "each" or "every" comes before the list of doers?

Try this one:

> Every man, woman, and child in the crowd were waiting with fear and a sense of foreboding.

What's wrong? *Each* and *every* are singular subjects. It should be:

> Every man, woman, and child in the crowd **was** waiting with fear and a sense of foreboding.

If *each* or *every* comes before a list of "doers," cross out the list and substitute *one*. Then see what form of the verb sounds correct.

> Every [ONE] ... **was** waiting in anxiety.

There's one big exception to the rule:

Either ... or and *neither ... nor* will agree with the number of the subject closest to the verb:

> **Neither** Dr. Evil nor his **minions are** especially nice.

But:

> **Neither** his minions nor **Dr. Evil is** especially nice.

Pronoun Agreement with Antecedent

When we ask, "What is this pronoun's *antecedent?*" we mean, what noun is it replacing?

For example:

> Sara is wearing a new dress. She bought it yesterday.

The antecedent of *she* is *Sara*. The antecedent of *it* is the *dress*.

It's obvious that a pronoun should agree in number with whatever noun it's describing. We don't say:

> The **cats** are so mean that **he** scratched Susan.

Cats is a plural subject, so we should replace it with *they*, so you'd get:

> The **cats** are so mean that **they** scratched Susan.

So when does this get hard? When you stick a bunch of words between the pronoun and its antecedent! All those extra words can make you lose track of where the original antecedent was.

Try this one:

> The cost of maintaining the home security and surveillance systems is approximately five times what the homeowners paid to purchase it.

What's wrong? What does *it* refer to? In other words, what is the antecedent of *it*? *It* refers to the *systems*.

If you're confused by what word a pronoun is replacing, try rewriting the sentence, and substitute the word you think is correct for the pronoun. For example, in the previous sentence, substitute *systems* for *it* and you'd get:

> The cost of maintaining the … *systems* is approximately five times what the homeowners paid to purchase *the systems*.

If the sentence makes logical sense, then you know you've got it right. In this case, *systems* is a plural subject.

The sentence should read:

> The cost of maintaining the home security and surveillance systems is approximately five times what the homeowners paid to purchase **them**.

Try this one:

> Felix Renggli, a baroque flutist and advocate of stylistic authenticity, has questioned the view that requiring students to copy models prevents them from becoming a creative artist later in life.

What's wrong? *A creative artist* is singular, but the sentence is talking about *students*, which is a plural subject. The sentence should be:

> Felix Renggli, a baroque flutist and advocate of stylistic authenticity, has questioned the view that requiring students to copy models prevents them from becoming **creative artists** later in life.

Note that in this case, we have an agreement between two nouns (*students* and *creative artists*) rather than between a noun and a pronoun. The rule is the same; they must be the same number. Because *creative artists* is connected to *students*, both must be plural.

Ambiguous Pronouns

Sometimes, if we mention more than one noun, it becomes unclear which noun we're talking about when we substitute a pronoun:

> Mary is hardworking and so is her sister Sue. She is going to go to Dartmouth.

Who's going to Dartmouth? Mary or her sister?

Things get even less clear when we substitute a pronoun for a phrase. For example:

> Mike cheated on the SAT, but he got into Harvard and has already started cheating there, too. Ryan thinks **this** is totally unfair, but Jane thinks she'll do **this,** too.

This refers to the various things Mike did (got into Harvard, cheated). In Mike's case, *this* could refer to the fact that Mike got into Harvard, but in Jane's case, *this* could be referring to cheating on her SAT. Generally, using *this, that, it* and so forth to refer to anything more complicated than a noun is bad style. Don't do it. (What is *it* referring to in the phrase *don't do* **it***?*) Repeating a word or phrase is much clearer:

> Mike cheated on his SAT, but he got into Harvard and has already started cheating there, too. Ryan thinks it's totally unfair that Mike got into Harvard, but Jane thinks she'll cheat on her SAT, too.

Case

What is the *case* of a noun? Recall how we ask whether a noun or pronoun is singular or plural? We ask, "What is its *number?*" Similarly, if we want to ask, "Is this noun a subject or something else?" we ask, "What is its *case?*" So the *number* of a noun

refers to whether it consists of one object or more than one object, and the *case* of a noun refers to its role in a sentence: whether the noun is a "doer" (a subject) or whether it's playing some other role.

What other roles can nouns and pronouns play, besides being subjects? They can also be *objects*.

Objects are nouns that receive an action or actions, or are somehow connected to the subject's "performance" of an action. In the sentence,

> Bob gave the box to Barry

Bob is the subject. There are two objects in this sentence. *Box* is the *direct object*, because it most directly receives the action (*gave*). *Barry* is the *indirect object*, because it is slightly "removed from the action," but it's still connected to the action. We wouldn't have the full story about the verb *gave* without the information provided by the indirect object.

A third type of object is the *prepositional object*. *Prepositional objects* are preceded by *prepositions*. A *preposition* is a "locating" word. In other words, a *preposition* gives you information about how the *prepositional object* is located in time, space, or in relationship to other nouns in the sentence. Prepositions answer these questions: when, where, where to?

Examples of prepositions (with example prepositional objects in parentheses):

When?	Where?	Where to?
on (Friday)	in (the house)	up/down (the stairs)
in (spring)	on (the table)	into/out of (the hall)
at (night)	at (the concert)	past (the gas station)
for (three weeks)	behind/in front of (the couch)	through (the alley)

When?	Where?	Where to?
before (two o'clock)	between (the chair and sofa)	
until (yesterday)	among (the flowers)	
since (last year)	by/near/close to (the train station)	

Pronouns change form, depending on whether they're subjects or objects. Prepositional objects, direct and indirect objects, all have the same forms in English (which is not true for many other languages).

You probably automatically change the forms of pronouns when you speak without thinking about it; obviously, no one says:

> I called **he** last night.

Here's the list of pronoun forms.

"Subject" pronouns

Singular	Plural
I	we
you	you
he/she/it	they
who	who

"Object" pronouns

Singular	Plural
me	us
you	you
him/her/it	them
whom	whom

Usually you can depend on your ear to tell you what form a pronoun should have. But things get tricky when you've got more than one subject or object.

Try this one:

> He informed Sandy and I of the circumstances surrounding his decision about them.

What's wrong? *He informed I* sounds wrong, doesn't it? That's because *I* is not the subject, it's an object. The sentence should be:

> He informed Sandy and **me** of the circumstances surrounding his decision.

Try repeating the verb for both objects to "hear" what the correct case of the pronoun should be:

> He informed Sandy and he informed me of the circumstances surrounding his decision.

Identify the problem with each of these sentences:

> To Ira and I, it seemed as if the GREs would never end.
> Except for Irving and I, everyone hates that movie *Snakes on a Plane*.
> These are the golden years for Barb and I, now that we have retired.

All of the above sentences are incorrect! Try repeating the preposition, and you'll see why:

> To Ira and **(to) me**, it seemed as if the GREs would never end. (The preposition "to" is connected to both "Ira" and "me." Both are therefore prepositional objects. "To I" should sound wrong.)

Except for Irving and **(except for) me,** everyone hates that movie *Snakes on a Plane.*

These are the golden years for Barb and **(for) me**, now that we have retired.

Note that we usually skip repeating the preposition, which saves space. However, the preposition still applies to both of its objects even if we don't repeat it.

Bottom line: "preposition + I" is always wrong.

Identify the error in this sentence:

Because the other students and she differed over the correct answer, they all asked for help.

Watch out! Is this wrong? It sounds weird, but it's right, because *students* and *she* are both subjects, and their verb is *differed.*

Identify the error in this sentence:

The theologians of the Middles Ages were greatly troubled that the black plague was an indiscriminate killer; indeed, one priest wrote at the time, "the disease makes no distinction between you and me, rich men and paupers, laity or the clergy."

What's wrong with this sentence? Nothing! *Between you and me* is correct because *between* is a preposition, creating a propositional phase, and prepositional phrases always take objective case pronouns.

Who, Whom

Here's a way to decide whether you need to use "who" or "whom."

Give me an example of a person other than Woody (who, whom) you think is dumber than dirt.

The three-step approach:

1. First, focus on the words that come right after (who/whom):

   you think is dumber than dirt

2. Now, insert a pronoun (he or him) into this phrase right after *think* to make a complete sentence.

   you think _____ is dumber than dirt.

3. Now fill it with either *he* or *him*:

   you think **him** is dumber than dirt, or

   you think **he** is dumber than dirt

Which is correct?

   you think he is dumber than dirt

Sounds right. Now, in the original sentence, use *who* if you chose *he* and use *whom* if you chose *him*. This works every time.

Give me an example of a person other than Woody **who** you think is dumber than dirt.

Try this one:

It is not for me to decide (who, whom) should be punished for breaking the window.

Where do we need to insert a blank in the phrase *should be punished for breaking the window?*

Here:

_____ should be punished for breaking the window.

Fill it with *he* or *him*

> **He** should be punished for breaking the window.

So, *who* is correct.

Why does this work? Because he and him are easy to understand and your ear is usually correct, while who/whom are difficult. Another trick is this: whom almost always appears in a preposition phrase (because whom is objective, and a preposition would require an objective case pronoun). So you would say *to whom, about whom, over whom, in whom, on whom,* and so forth.

Verb Tense

When we ask, "What is this verb's *tense?*" what do we mean? We mean, "When did this action take place?" When we say that the verb is in the *past tense*, we mean the action happened in the past; when we say a verb is in the *future tense*, we mean the action will take place in the future.

One mistake people often make is with the word *since.*

Which of the following sentences is wrong?

> Since 1910 her family **invested** heavily in industrial stocks.
> Since 1910 her family **has invested** heavily in industrial stocks.

The first sentence is wrong. *Since* is a tip-off that you should be using the form has/have plus the past tense of the verb. That's because the form "I have" (worked, played, etc.) is used to describe an action that started at a specific time, and continued up until the present time.

Note: she **has**, he **has,** but I, we, they **have.**

"In the last (months, few days)" also requires the construction "has/have+past tense." For example:

> In the last few days, she has done nothing but study.

Try this one:

> In the last ten months, she increased her GRE scores by 200 points, much to her delight.

What's wrong? The sentence should be:

> In the last ten months, she **has** increased her GRE scores by 200 points, much to her delight.

FAIR WARNING

> *When + had been* is always wrong. Example: "When they had been young, they played in the street."

For is more flexible than *since.* Which of these two sentences is correct?

> For ten years, she **worked** at a law firm.
> For ten years she **has worked** at a law firm.

They're both correct! They just convey different meanings:

> For ten years, she **worked** at a law firm. (We don't know when exactly those 10 years were.)
> For ten years she **has worked** at a law firm. (We know she's worked there up until the present.)

! INFO TO GO

If is often a tip-off that you should use the form *had + past tense:*
If I had studied more
If he had only seen that car coming

Style and Logic

There are a few common style and logic errors. We'll review these errors here. Do keep in mind that such errors are secondary to more basic noun and verb errors, so make sure the basic grammar of a sentence is correct, then concern yourself with the style and logic of the sentence.

Pronoun Shift

Pronoun shift is a type of mistake in written style. *Pronoun shift* means using more than one type of pronoun to talk about a general situation.

Here's an example:

> If you write a sentence that gives advice, one should stick with *you, one,* or *we;* otherwise, we will run into confusion.

What's wrong with the sentence? *If you ... one should ... we get.* Nope! Just stick with one of those choices:

> If **you** write a sentence that gives advice, **you** should stick with *you, one,* or *we;* otherwise, **you** will run into confusion.

Or,

> If **one** writes a sentence that gives advice, **one** should stick with *you, one,* or *we;* otherwise, **one** will run into confusion.

Or,

> If **we** write a sentence that gives advice, **we** should stick with *you, one,* or *we;* otherwise, **we** will run into confusion.

The pronouns *one, you,* and *we* should be warning signals: watch out for pronoun shift when you see these words!

Try this one:

> As one conducts more and more financial transactions through e-mail and the Internet, your need for privacy protection and designs to safeguard information has increased.

What's wrong? *Your* should be replaced with *one:*

> As one conducts more and more financial transactions through e-mail and on the Internet, **one's** need for privacy protection and designs to safeguard information has increased.

Faulty Comparisons

Faulty comparisons are easy to overlook and obvious once you notice them. Faulty comparisons are problems of logic, not of grammar. They compare two things that shouldn't be compared (like "apples and oranges"):

Try this one:

> The Portland zoo, home to such excellent exhibits as the naked mole rat compound and the exotic snake house, is unrivaled by any other city.

What's wrong? Well, who has the excellent exhibits? A zoo. Who else has exhibits, according to the sentence? *Other cities.* So you're comparing a zoo to a city. What, you mean New York has a display on snakes? Where? On the sidewalk?

The sentence should be:

> The Portland zoo, home to such excellent exhibits as the naked mole rat compound and the exotic snake house, is unrivaled by any other zoo.

But we can make it even trickier:

> The Portland zoo has a display on the mating habits of snakes which is unrivaled by any other zoo.

What's wrong now? Well, **what** exactly is unrivaled? Are we comparing zoos, or are we comparing zoo displays? The sentence should be:

> The Portland zoo has a display on the mating habits of snakes which is unrivaled by any other **zoo's display**.

Or,

> The Portland zoo has a display on the mating habits of snakes which is unrivaled by **that of any other zoo**.

Faulty comparisons turn up, not surprisingly, in sentences that compare things. Here's a list of words that should put you on the lookout for faulty comparisons:

> than
> like, similar to
> differing from, in contrast to
> better/worse
> more/less
> adjective + er (smarter, faster, etc.)

Try this one:

> Jean-Baptiste Lamarck's theory that evolution occurred through the inheritance of characteristics acquired during an organism's lifespan in response to external pressures rather than through random genetic mutation differed dramatically from most evolutionary biologists.

What's wrong? The sentence compares a theory with what? Not with another theory, but with evolutionary biologists. The sentence should read:

> Jean-Baptiste Lamarck's theory that evolution occurred through the inheritance of characteristics acquired during an organism's lifespan in response to external pressures rather than through random genetic mutation differed dramatically from most evolutionary **theories**.

All About *Than*

Than is a danger word!

Take a look at this:

> Sentence error identification is more difficult for non-native English speakers than native English speakers.

What's wrong with this sentence? We're essentially saying that sentence error identification is more difficult than native English speakers! This sentence compares sentence error identification to people, and you can't do that.

> Sentence error identification is more difficult … than native English speakers.

That makes no sense. But we can correct this sentence by using one picky little detail:

> Sentence error identification is more difficult *for* non-native English speakers than *for* native English speakers.

Just by repeating the preposition, we can correct the sentence!

So whenever you see *preposition + than* such as:

> for … than
> by … than
> of … than

You need to repeat the preposition!

A few examples:

> **In golf**, running is required much less **than in soccer.**
> **For Jane**, the GRE vocabulary was much harder **than for Sara.**

Introductory Clauses

An *introductory clause* introduces a person or thing. They're just really long, complicated descriptions that end with commas. They can contain information about time, place, the state of something, the cause of something, a comparison to something, and so forth.

Sentences that start like these examples are starting with introductory phrases:

> Walking down the street, …
> While unsure of her feelings for Ricardo, …
> Like his other books, …
> Differing from previous legislation on many accounts, …
> When presented with the new proposal, …

All of these phrases are describing something, but you don't yet know what they describe. You need to keep reading the sentence, because the first part was only an introduction. In order to avoid confusion about what is being described, we have a rule about where the word that is being described should appear in the sentence: the thing that is being described must come immediately after the introductory clause! So after an introductory clause, a noun or a pronoun must come next!

Let's revisit those example introductory clauses, and now we'll insert what they're describing after the commas.

> Walking down the street, **Bob** noticed a new store …
> While unsure of her feelings for Ricardo, **she** knew at least that …
> Like his other books, **Professor Hoppenstadt's new book** …
> Differing from previous legislation on many accounts, **the new law** …
> When presented with the new proposal, **the stubborn president** reacted with indignation …

Notice that an adjective or **other describer** can come before the subject:

> Professor Hoppenstadt's new book …
> the stubborn president …

But any other type of word, or any noun that's *not* described by the introductory clause, is wrong if it comes immediately after the comma!

> Walking down the street, the new store caught Bob's eye.

The new store isn't walking, so this is wrong.

> While unsure of her feelings for Ricardo, he on the other hand was sure that he loved her.

We know that a female name should follow the comma because the word "her" means the introductory clause is describing someone female.

> Like his other books, in his new book Professor Hoppenstadt ...

His other *books* can't be compared to *in his new book*. *Prepositions cannot come between the comma and the thing being described.*

> Differing from previous legislation on many accounts, the arguments over the new law were ...

Previous legislation is being compared to *a new law*, not to *arguments*. This is actually a faulty comparison.

> When presented with the new proposal, **the stubborn attitude of the president** proved difficult.

The *proposal* was presented to the *president*, not to his *attitude*.

Try this one:

> Loaded down with three duffle bags and a snowboard, John's search for a baggage cart was increasingly desperate.

What's wrong? The *search* isn't loaded down with bags; John is! In this case, *John's* is just like an adjective describing the search, it's not a subject. The sentence should be:

> Loaded down with three duffle bags and a snowboard, John desperately searched for a baggage cart.

Parallel Construction

If a sentence has some sort of repetition, the repeated parts of it are all "treated the same." In other words, if you've got a list, you want all the things in the list to be the same part of speech (either verbs or nouns or clauses). You don't want to mix nouns and verbs in a list!

Doesn't make sense? Let's get down to examples.

A noun and an infinitive are not parallel (an infinitive is *to* + *verb*):

> His duties were the coordination of the project and to write the grant proposal.

What's wrong? Look at the sentence structure. *His duties were X and Y.* Okay, we've got a list. So the items in the list, X and Y, should both be nouns, or they should both be verbs, or they should both be infinitives.

Either of these solutions would work:

> His duties were the coordination of the project and the composition of the grant proposal.
> His duties were to coordinate the project and to write the grant proposal.

A gerund and an infinitive are not parallel (a gerund = *verb* + *ing*):

> Gerald's favorite pastimes were playing basketball and to swim.

What's wrong? Again, it's a list:

> Gerald's favorite pastimes were X and Y.

X and Y need to both be infinitives or both gerunds:

> Gerald's favorite pastimes were playing basketball and swimming.
>
> Gerald's favorite pastimes were to play basketball and swim.

Both of these examples are correct. Often, defaulting to the infinitive is preferred, but, in every case, the words in the list must be the same parts of speech.

A noun and a clause are not parallel:

> To criticize a problem superficially and the true evaluation of an argument are not one and the same thing.

Try this one:

> In order for the audience to believe in and be engaged by an actor in a movie, they have to convincingly portray the emotions of a character.

What's wrong? *To believe … be engaged* is actually parallel! They are both infinitives, it's just that there's an implied *to* which has been left out. That's okay. If you stuck the *to* back in, it would just be unnecessary: *to believe in and (**to**) be engaged by.*

So there's a different problem going on. To whom does *they* refer? It refers to *an actor*. Because *an actor* is singular, the problem is with *they have*. The sentence should read:

> In order for the audience to believe in and be engaged by an actor in a movie, **he (or she)** has to convincingly portray the emotions of the character.

Sometimes you may think a sentence has multiple problems. Always fix the biggest mistake, which usually means the mistake in fundamental grammar. For example, parallelisms are a matter of style; so if you have the choice between fixing a perceived parallelism problem, and fixing a mistake in number or tense, which do you choose? You choose the mistake in number or tense! Number and tense are basic to good grammar and you can never let those mistakes slip through.

What would you fix with this example?

> Storing pastries in a breadbox delays drying and the growth of mold but increase the rate at which baked goods lose flavor.

Solution: The big problem is *increase*. It should be *increases*, so you'd get

> Storing pastries delays drying … **but increases** the rate at which ….

This is an error in subject/verb agreement, so it is a more egregious error than the fact that *drying* and *the growth of mold* are not parallel.

Sounds Right but Is Wrong

Sometimes, constructions that sound correct when we say them are actually wrong when written down. For example, in spoken English, it's fine to say:

> I plan on jogging today.

However, when we write about a future event, we must use the following construction:

> I plan **to jog** today.

Wrong Word

Occasionally writers use a word that sounds a lot like the right word but isn't. For example, what's the difference between the following words?

> implicated vs. implies
> defensible vs. defensive

If you're not sure, look them up. Just make sure that you are always using the right word. Often these words that look similar are very different. To be implicated means to be involved or accused of being involved, but to imply means to suggest. They aren't related.

Repetition/Redundancy

Double negatives and repeating words are common mistakes.

For example:

> I'm so tired I cannot hardly keep my eyes open.

The corrected sentence should be either:

> I'm so tired I can hardly keep my eyes open.

Or,

> I'm so tired I cannot keep my eyes open.

Here's another example:

> The amount of revision was not sufficient enough to ensure that all errors had been corrected.

The correct sentence should be either:

> The amount of revision was not sufficient to ensure that all errors had been corrected.

Or,

> The amount of revision was not enough to ensure that all errors had been corrected.

Factually Wrong

Occasionally, writers produce sentences that are grammatically correct but, given the logic of the sentence, factually wrong. For example:

> It is predicted that Western Europe will experience the most significant phase of the Industrial Revolution in the nineteenth century.

There is nothing grammatically wrong with this sentence. It's just that historically, the nineteenth century has already occurred, so you can't talk about it as if it were in the future. (Had this sentence been written in the eighteenth century, then it would be right.)

Graduate School Admissions Details

In This Chapter

- When to start
- The players
- Application components

In many ways, graduate school seems like college: the same football team, the same library, the same professors. Most likely, the graduate school you attend will be integrated into the college. And so many graduate school hopefuls think about grad school in the context of college. But in almost every way, grad school will be different from college.

Admissions Nuts and Bolts

The level of competition for many graduate schools is fierce. Many grad programs are very small, some with fewer than 10 students enrolled. Such a program may only receive 200 applications, which is tiny compared to the 5,000–30,000 applications most colleges receive, but that grad school will often admit only 5 applicants with the assumption that 1 or 2 will attend. Most graduate programs admit fewer than 20 percent of applicants. Many grad-school applicants have above-average GPAs for their colleges, but their GPAs will be average in the grad school pool. College students applying to grad school are typically the most academically gifted and motivated students, so, on average, their GPAs will be above average.

The Application Process: When to Start

When should you start the graduate school application process? As soon as possible!

First, you'll need the necessary coursework. Grad schools want to see not only an impressive academic record, but also a record of participation. You should get involved in clubs, journals, and conferences that relate to your area of concentration. It's difficult to wake up midway through your senior year, decide that you want to attend grad school, and put together an impressive application. You should subscribe to the journals that cover your area, attend the conferences, and become a member of the appropriate associations.

And just as getting employed out of grad school will depend on recommendations from your grad school advisor, getting admitted to grad school will depend somewhat on your undergraduate advisor's recommendation. It's important that one of your professors, usually your advisor, thinks that you've got what it takes to succeed in grad school.

Keep in mind that grad schools are not only interested in your ability to complete the work, but they're also interested in your ability to graduate and become employed. Many grad schools are filled with Ph.D. candidates in their sixth or seventh year, who just can't seem to complete everything. So punctuality, organization, and motivation are often as important as pure intellectual ability.

You will need to take one or more standardized tests. Most graduate schools require the GRE, and some require GRE Subject Tests and perhaps the TOEFL (Test of English as a Foreign Language) or GMAT (Graduate Management Admissions Test). GRE scores are good for five years. No graduate school requires a GRE score that's less than two years old. If you're going to apply for grad school in your senior year in college, you should take the GRE at the end of your junior year or during the summer between junior and senior year. Studies show that test-takers score higher on standardized tests such as the GRE if they take the test while still in school. So if you have a choice, take the GRE while you're still in school. In any case, you should take the GRE one to two years before you apply, and choose a time when you can devote yourself to preparing for the GRE. Expect to spend 20–40 hours preparing for the GRE.

Beginnings

The grad-school application process begins when you start to make relationships with college professors. They are informally evaluating your ability to succeed in grad school. The process continues as you prepare for the GRE: your GRE score will partially determine that outcome of the process. So while many think the process begins when you request an application, it actually begins many months—perhaps even years—earlier.

Most graduate schools will have a single, general application that asks for your basic information such as name, test scores, transcripts, and recommendations. So the Graduate School of Arts and Sciences will have a general application and a set of general requirements that apply to anyone interested in any school within the Graduate School of Arts and Sciences. In many cases, individual departments will also have additional requirements and application forms—don't forget about these! A history department may require an additional essay or writing sample. An English-literature department may require a GRE Subject Test in Literature. Be sure to check the specific department's website for information about unique application requirements. In some cases, individual departments use their own applications and no general application exists.

Once you've requested or downloaded all the applications, you should make a list of the requirements of each school. Some will require GRE subject tests, which are typically only offered in November, December, and April. Some will require writing samples or multiple recommendations. After you've made a list of all the requirements, make a list of deadlines.

The process usually involves a general application form, a personal statement (or statement of intent), obtaining recommendations, requesting transcripts, and sending test scores. Some programs will require writing samples, a portfolio, or an interview.

Regardless of the office to which you mail your application, it will always be evaluated on the departmental level. Even though universities may have university-wide admissions requirements, admissions decisions are almost always made by department committees. These committees review your application and make an initial determination: yes, no, or maybe. The "yes" pile will be very small—perhaps 2 percent of the applicants. The "no" pile is often quite large, sometimes as high as 50 percent of the applicants. The rest will be in the "maybe" pile, and their application will await further review. Usually, the few applicants who are admitted will receive an offer of admission fairly quickly.

The admissions committee will then await more applications, sometimes receiving 10 per day, and other times receiving a few each week. It's common for an admissions committee to review applications every four to six weeks during the admissions season. At the end, they will review the number of applicants they've admitted and compare that to the number they wanted to admit. They know that not everyone admitted will accept. A yield of 50 percent would be very high. So a department that has budgeted for 10 new students may admit 20 applicants. If the department admitted fewer applicants than they

want or if their yield is low (fewer students accepting than expected), the committee will review again the applications in the "maybe" pile. Obviously, it's important to get your application in early and get all supporting material in early. Committees don't review (and often won't even receive) applications that aren't complete.

Unlike with colleges, waitlists aren't that common for graduate programs. Larger or lesser competitive programs will sometimes have waitlists. But small or very competitive programs usually don't have waitlists.

Pieces and Players

This may surprise you, but the one person with whom you'll have the most contact is the department secretary (who may be the Graduate Admissions Secretary or the Admissions Coordinator or Administrator). Often, this person has been in the department for years, will be there when you're there, and will be there after you leave. The secretary has far more influence than most think. It's up to the secretary to assemble your application and present it to the committee. The secretary knows better than most how the application process works, where everything is, and how to make things happen. The secretary will also know about department research, grants, and the other students. Assuming everything goes well, you'll probably speak to the secretary several times. In fact, you should speak to the secretary several times. You'll request information from him or her, ask questions about professors and the program, and confirm that the office has received your materials. You should do your best to make a friend with the secretary.

The secretary forwards your completed application to the Admissions Committee. The committee is usually composed of professors within the department. Sometimes professors volunteer, while other times they are assigned. Some professors like being on committees; many do not. Some programs will have an administrator or a graduate student on the committee. Keep in mind that admissions committees are often very small, sometimes just two or three professors.

Deadlines

After you've received all the information from the schools, confirm their deadlines. Committees have meeting dates set far in advance, so if you miss a deadline, it's likely that no one will be available to consider your application. Be sure to investigate each department's deadlines. Sometimes such deadlines are earlier than the general deadlines for the school. Finally, deadlines for students seeking financial aid are often much earlier than the general deadlines, and financial aid is often granted on a first-come, first-served basis. In all cases, you should apply early.

Transcripts

Your transcript will be sent directly from the registrar. It will be stamped, sealed, and signed. If you get a sealed official transcript from your registrar, don't open it. You may include the sealed transcript directly with your application. Open, unsealed transcripts aren't acceptable. You will need to request transcripts from all colleges and universities you've attended. Registrars usually take two to three weeks to process such requests, so do it early. And if any college you've attended uses an obscure grading system, the registrar will need to include an explanation of the grading system.

Application Fee

Your main application should always be submitted with the application fee or fee waiver. Your

application won't be considered without the fee. Application fees range from $30 to $100. Fee waivers are usually offered by schools; ask the secretary if you're interested. Usually, if you qualified for the fee waiver for the GRE, you'll get one for the application, too.

GRE Scores

You need to send official test scores from ETS. Most graduate schools will require GRE General Test scores. Some will require Subject Tests or TOEFL scores if you're an international student.

Recommendations

Letters of recommendation are an extremely important part of the admissions process. Department committee members will thoroughly review these letters and attempt to get a good idea of your personality and potential. Your recommender should know you well and be able to set you apart from the competition. A good recommender won't be one who will simply recount your grades, but rather one who can attest that you are a hard worker and are well-organized, motivated, competent, and excited about the field. A good recommender will have some insight into whether you can handle the grueling load of grad school work, whether you would be able to teach and conduct research, and whether you have the maturity to succeed in a professional environment.

Some applications have forms that ask your recommenders to rate specific attributes, and some simply have open-ended questions about your potential. And still other schools simply ask your recommenders to write a letter. In many cases, recommenders will write and attach a letter regardless of the school's instructions.

Schools will ask for one to three recommendation letters. The number may vary by the program and degree for which you're applying; often, Ph.D. programs will ask for more recommendations than a Master's program. Or you may be required to submit more recommendations if you're applying for funding. If you have questions, call the department secretary. In all cases, your recommenders should be professors in your area of concentration and have taught you in your junior or senior year.

Usually, you should try to get one more recommendation than you need in case one is lost or something else happens. Keep in mind that professors are not usually the most organized people, so ask for the recommendation early, and ask for more than one to insure against accidents.

Unwritten Recommendations

As previously noted, your application begins long before you actually mail in an application. The people with whom you speak, the meetings and conferences you attend, the interactions you have with all people involved will all affect your application. The people you know and what they think of you can significantly affect your application.

Make a point of networking, and bolstering your image and people's impression of you. Too many applicants think that the entire application is simply a form they complete and mail back. On the contrary, a successful application will be composed of written and unwritten components, each one weighing on the admissions committee's decision. Because most graduate programs only receive 50–300 applications, these unwritten components can make a big difference. Unlike colleges, graduate programs receive so few applications that admissions committee members can make phone calls, meet applicants, and talk to professors. So impressions and reputations can make a difference.

You should be sure that your professors and recommenders know what your interests and strengths are, make some phone calls to professors and the schools in which you're interested, send e-mails and attend conferences. Your chances of being admitted are greatly increased if everyone involved knows who you are, what you're doing, why you're doing it, and why you should be admitted to graduate programs. There's no official incorporation of the human factor in the admissions process, but it's difficult for an admissions committee member to reject an application when that member has personally met the applicant, knows the recommenders, has exchanged phone calls and e-mails with all of them, and has attended conferences with them.

Statement of Purpose

Graduate programs usually require a statement of purpose, letter of intent, or personal essay. The graduate school essentially wants you to confirm that you're motivated to take on graduate study.

The statement prompt may be open-ended or ask specifically what you wish to study and why. You should discuss your preparation for grad school, your interest and ability to pursue graduate study, and the area you wish to pursue. In most cases, you should address, very specifically, what you wish to study in graduate school. If you're applying to a history department, stating that you wish to study history is obvious and helpful. You should have a very specific issue or problem in which you're interested (for example, U.S. Colonial history focusing on the issue of property rights in Boston in the 1760s). Finally, your statement should connect your interests and strengths to the program's interests and strengths. You may cite professors, conferences, and publications associated with the program to strengthen your argument that you would thrive in and contribute to the school.

Members of the admissions committee will evaluate your ability to construct and support your argument. Start with the statement of purpose early and plan to rewrite it several times. Have your friends and professors review it. Have your recommenders read it (if they aren't too busy). Plan for your statement to take two to three months to perfect.

Interviews

Many schools don't offer formal interviews, but if the school suggests or offers interviews, even if informal, you must go unless it's financially unfeasible. A visit to the school will provide you with valuable information and demonstrate interest to the admissions committee. Make sure you've alerted the department that you will be on campus. Ask to meet with a professor whose work you're interested in. Make sure you've done your research before any meetings. Ask smart questions about the students in the program, the publications of the professors, and the research interests of all involved. Don't ask obvious questions such as the books the professors have published; that sort of information is readily available online.

Residency Forms

If you're applying as an in-state student to a public school, you will need to prove your residency. Often, you'll need to prove that you've lived in the state for at least 12 months prior to starting the program. Some schools will have lengthier requirements, often 18 or 20 months. Proof usually entails having a dated document or identification that shows you've lived in the state for the required period of time. In-state students usually are charged much lower tuition, so it's worth your time.

International Student Forms

If you're applying to a U.S. grad school as an international student, you will have a few more forms. Usually, you'll need to take the TOEFL. A high verbal score on the GRE may preclude you from needing to take the TOEFL. In most cases, schools will have minimum GRE Verbal or TOEFL scores. Ask the department secretary if such minimums exist. You will also need to provide translations of any documents you submit, including transcripts and recommendations. These transcripts need to be certified as accurate. You will also need to provide health forms showing that you've been immunized.

Perhaps more importantly, you will need to prove that you are capable of paying for graduate school. Usually, you will need to certify that you have funds to cover at least nine months of living in the United States; this means having nine months' worth of cash in the bank and having the bank send an official letter stating that these funds are available.

Once admitted, you will need to supply the U.S. government with information regarding your plans. The school will mail the forms to you, including Form I-20 or IAP-66, which is a Certificate of Eligibility for Non-Immigrant Status. You will typically submit the certificate together with an application, your acceptance documents, your passport, and your evidence of financial support.

All these documents will be submitted to the local U.S. embassy or consulate. With these forms, you should be able to secure an international student visa. If you submit Form I-20, you will get an F-1 visa. If you submit Form IAP-66, you will get a J-1 visa.

Help! The 24-Hour Guide

In This Chapter

◆ Intro chapters

◆ Verbal

◆ Math

◆ Writing

If you're reading this chapter, you probably only have a few hours until the GRE. Perhaps you've got two hours, or perhaps you have a day. Maybe you just don't want to read this entire book but want quick points. You're in the right place.

The purpose of this appendix is to guide you to the parts of this book that will most quickly maximize your score. Part of this process will require you to assess your strengths and weaknesses.

Intro Chapters

Skip Chapter 1. It's a great chapter, but if you only have a few hours, this isn't a necessary chapter. You do need to spend 30 minutes on Chapter 2. This chapter outlines a few very important ideas, including pinpointing your strengths, pacing, process of elimination, and the new GRE. Chapter 3 should be read after you take the test.

Verbal

If you have two hours

Spend 30 minutes on the sentence completion chapters (6 and 7). You need to master sentence completions—they are easy, fast points and you should fully understand how sentence completions work.

Next, spend 30 minutes on the analogies chapter. You probably won't see too many analogies, but there are techniques that will allow you to get them correct without really knowing the definitions of the words. So focusing a little on analogy guessing techniques can be a quick way to pick up some points!

Then spend an hour reading the reading passages and short reading passages chapters (8 and 9). While sentence completions are short and fast, your verbal score will be largely determined by your ability to perform well on short and long reading passages. Get good at them! If you have any time remaining, try putting it all together with some practice reading passages from Chapters 11 and 12.

If you have four hours

Read Chapters 6 and 7, and spend 90 minutes on chapters 8 and 9, as described previously.

Now spend 30 minutes on Chapter 10. There aren't too many of these on the GRE, but you should be able to get most of them correct with a little practice.

After you've reviewed sentence completions, short and long reading passages, and logic passages, put it all together by spending some time on Chapters 11 and 12.

If you still have time remaining, read the analogies chapter. Focus on the techniques for guessing when you don't know the definition of the words.

Math

If you have two hours … and poor math skills

Start with Chapter 13. This chapter alone may take two hours, but it will be worth it. Quite simply, everything in this chapter is essential. The concepts in this chapter are guaranteed to be on the GRE—learn and understand them!

If you have time, go to Chapter 17. There will be chart/data questions on every GRE, so you should prepare for them if you can. They usually aren't that difficult, so a little review can really help.

If you have two hours … and good math skills

In Chapter 13, skip to the middle and do the "Averages," "Simultaneous Equations," and "D = RT" sections to warm up.

Now review Chapter 17. These can be a bit odd, so practice on a few.

Now skip to Chapter 19 and complete the practice sets.

If you have four hours … and poor math skills

Start with Chapter 13. This chapter alone may take two hours, but it will be worth it. Quite simply, everything in this chapter is essential. The concepts in this chapter are guaranteed to be on the GRE—learn and understand them!

Now move on to Chapter 14, on algebra. You should spend about 30 minutes and try to complete the entire chapter.

Skip Chapters 15 and 16. There's not a lot of geometry on the new GRE and not enough time to work on quant comps.

Skip Chapter 18 and try a practice set. If you're consistently missing a particular problem type, go back to the section that covers that problem type and review it.

Now spend a good hour, if you need it, on Chapter 17. There will be chart/data questions on every GRE, so you should prepare for them.

If you have four hours … and good math skills

In Chapter 13, skip to the middle and do the "Averages," "Simultaneous Equations," and "D = RT" sections to warm up.

Now review Chapter 17.

Spend an hour completing Chapter 18. You probably know how to do all of this, but you probably haven't tried problems like these in years.

Finally, complete the math practice sets in Chapter 19.

Analytical Writing

Read Chapter 20 and skip the other essay chapters. Chapter 20 will tell you the most important concepts for writing good essays. If you have time, you should practice writing one timed essay; practicing writing a timed essay can be very helpful to understanding the time constraints you'll be under.

Anything Else?

Studying vocabulary would be great, but you need three to four months, not three to four hours, to really improve your vocabulary.

And the appendixes are important, but not critically so. If you have time or are taking the GRE again, you should reread this entire book and start studying vocabulary now.

The CIG Practice GRE

This CIG sample test is designed to help you gauge your knowledge and pacing. No two GREs are the same, so the frequency and distribution of question types will vary. You should obtain real practice GREs from ETS in order to get a better sense of your abilities and potential score.

It's important to strictly time yourself on this. You should take this test as if it were a computer-based GRE, which means you should …

♦ Pretend as if this paper were a computer screen; don't write on the paper.

♦ Record your answers on another piece of paper.

♦ Simulate the computer environment for essay answers by writing the essays on a computer; don't use spell-check.

♦ Answer each question in order to go on to the next question.

♦ Remember that you can't go back or skip ahead.

Section 1

Analytical Writing
Perspective on an Issue

45 minutes.

Present your perspective on one of the issues below using relevant examples.

> Topic No. 321: "Technology and the application thereof increase loneliness."

> Topic No. 322: "Environmental politics will divide the world into factions and will be more divisive than communism."

Section 2

Analytical Writing
Analyze an Argument

30 minutes.

Present your opinion on the reasoning of this argument.

> Topic No. 323: "Eight months ago, Grenville raised its speed limit on its single major highway by 20 miles per hour. A recent study concluded that Grenville's accident rate declined by 2 percent during that period. Wonkasville, 2 miles from Grenville, witnessed a 1 percent decrease in accidents during the same period. If Wonkasville wishes to further decrease its accident rate, it should increase the speed limit on their major highways."

Section 3

28 questions. 45 minutes.

The following question consists of a word printed in capital letters followed by five words or phrases. Choose the word or phrase that most nearly means the opposite of the word in capital letters.

1. ADVENTITIOUS:
   a. shy
   b. solicitous
   c. reticent
   d. innate
   e. garrulous

Each of the following questions includes a sentence with a blank indicating that something has been omitted. Select the answer choice that best completes the sentence.

2. It is pointless to disagree over facts; if a phenomenon is subject to quantification, observation, and analysis, than neither opinion nor intuition can take the place of _____ verification.
   a. empirical
   b. independent
   c. subjective
   d. personal
   e. a priori

3. A quintessential _____, Mrs. Streng abstained from alcohol, tobacco, and refined sugar, ate only twice a day, and took every opportunity to deny herself those pleasures she perceived as "indulgences."
   a. aesthetic
   b. ascetic
   c. moderate
   d. intellectual
   e. hedonist

4. Michael Thompson Michelson was _____ by nature; he never seemed to have much of an opinion about anything, and was unmoved by either serendipity or misfortune.

    a. facetious

    b. sprightly

    c. tedious

    d. phlegmatic

    e. sanguine

Each of the following questions includes a sentence with a blank indicating that something has been omitted. Select the two answer choices that best complete the sentence.

5. Although the rigors of a musical education at a music conservatory are in large part emotional and psychological, practicing an instrument six hours daily is also physically _____ _____.

    a. strenuous

    b. indulgent

    c. dubious

    d. taxing

    e. illusory

6. In *Invisible Man*, the protagonist _____ _____ aspects of American society, critically examining the assumptions and values, not only of Caucasian-American, but also African-American culture.

    a. scrutinizes

    b. excludes

    c. beautifies

    d. idealizes

    e. questions

Questions 7–9 are based on the following reading passage:

From the book Robert Louis Stevenson *by Walter Raleigh*

When a popular writer dies, it has become the fashion with a nervous generation to ask the question, "Will he live?" There is no idler question, none more hopelessly impossible and unprofitable to answer. It is one of the many vanities of criticism to promise immortality to the authors that it praises, to patronize a writer with the assurance that our great-grandchildren, whose time and tastes are thus <u>frivolously mortgaged</u>, will read his works with delight. Let us make sure that our sons will care for Homer before we pledge a more distant generation to a newer cult.

Nevertheless, without handling the prickly question of literary immortality, it is easy to recognize that the literary reputation of Robert Louis Stevenson is made of good stuff. His fame has spread, as lasting fame is wont to do, from the few to the many. Fifteen years ago his essays and fanciful books of travel were treasured by a small and discerning company of admirers; long before he chanced to fell the British public with *Treasure Island* and *Dr. Jekyll and Mr. Hyde* he had shown himself a delicate marksman. And although large editions are nothing, standard editions, richly furnished and complete, are worthy of remark. Stevenson is one of the very few authors in our literary history who have been honored during their lifetime by the appearance of such an edition; the best of his public, it would seem, do not only wish to read his works, but to possess them, and all of them, at the cost of many pounds, in library form. It would be easy to mention more voluminous and more popular authors than Stevenson whose publishers could not find five subscribers for an adventure like this. He has made a brave beginning in that race against Time which all must lose.

7. The passage that begins with: "and although large editions are nothing, standard editions, richly furnished and complete, are worthy of remark" implies which of the following?

   a. Stevenson's publishers did not find his works of sufficient quality to warrant a hardcover edition.

   b. The format in which an author's works are published is possibly predicative of his posthumous fame, at least among those readers he acquired during his lifetime.

   c. Large editions are superior to standard editions.

   d. Standard editions of an author's work published posthumously are unusual.

   e. If an author's work is published in several editions during his lifetime, his works will likely become classics.

8. In context, the phrase <u>frivolously mortgaged</u> most nearly means:

   a. carelessly bantered

   b. presumptuously sold

   c. lightheartedly loaned

   d. unthinkingly committed

   e. blindly predicted

9. Which of the following statements would the author most likely agree with?

   a. Robert Louis Stevenson's fame will most likely be immortal.

   b. Robert Louis Stevenson will most likely be forgotten within three generations.

   c. Robert Louis Stevenson's literary reputation will not likely survive his death.

   d. All authors must inevitably be forgotten.

   e. The celebration of an author during his lifetime has nothing to do with his posthumous reputation.

Questions 10–11 are based on the following reading passage:

Excerpted from "Historical and Political Essays" by William Edward Hartpole Lecky

Ancient* art was essentially the glorification of the body, a representation of the full strength and beauty of developed manhood. The saint of the medieval mosaic represents the body in its extreme maceration and humiliation. The rhetorician, Dio Chrysostom, in a somewhat whimsical passage, which was suggested by a remark of Plato, found a special moral significance in the fact that Homer, though he places his heroes on the banks of what he calls "the fishy Hellespont," never makes them eat fish, but always flesh and the flesh of oxen, for this, as he says, is "strength-producing food" and is therefore suited for the formation of heroes and the proper diet for men of virtue. Compare this judgment with the protracted, and indeed incredible, fasts which the monkish writers delighted in attributing to the saints of the desert, and we have a vivid picture of the change that had passed over the ideal.

*meaning Hellenic, or ancient Greek

10. With which of the following statements would the author most likely agree?

   a. The morality or ideals of a culture may be deduced from its artwork and literature.

   b. The ancient Greeks were more concerned with physical prowess than spiritual well being.

   c. Medieval artists and writers were more interested in detailing the physical feats of endurance of saints rather than in dealing with their spiritual fortitude.

   d. Both medieval and ancient writers associated certain moral virtues to certain types of foods.

   e. Neither medieval nor ancient writers were as concerned with the health aspects of diet as contemporary society is.

11. The author implies that the rhetorician Dio Chrysostom's analysis of Homer's verse:

    a. is closely analogous with medieval writers' analysis of the hardships endured by saints.

    b. is a completely accurate reflection of Homeric society.

    c. is a reflection, not of Homeric society, but of Dio Chrysostom's society.

    d. is frivolous and without relevance.

    e. was perhaps written in a less than serious spirit, but reflects a conviction, shared by medieval monks, that the physical aspects of life may influence the spiritual aspects.

Each of the following questions includes a sentence with a blank indicating that something has been omitted. Select the answer choice that best completes the sentence.

12. According to legend, the maze constructed by the ancient Minoans to house the Minator was so _____ that only the most _____ hero, Theseus, managed to escape its complicated paths unscathed.

    a. nefarious … unharmed

    b. reticular … lackadaisical

    c. devious … obtuse

    d. convoluted … resourceful

    e. treacherous … timorous

13. Following legislation banning _____ speech, suspected _____ could be seized and jailed without access to a lawyer.

    a. controversial … artists

    b. belligerent … pacifists

    c. nugatory … debunkers

    d. illegal … conformists

    e. seditious … insurrectionists

14. The eyespots of a butterfly's wings are extremely responsive to evolutionary pressures such as _____; rather than being merely _____, they are integral to these insects' ability to elude birds and other predators.

    a. deforestation … aesthetic

    b. fecundity … reproductive

    c. predation … decorative

    d. ostracism … communicative

    e. levees … adaptive

15. The medicinal properties of ginger are well known; the herb may be used to treat coughs or to _____ the pain of an upset stomach.

    a. exacerbate

    b. abjure

    c. bolster

    d. mitigate

    e. enervate

16. An understanding of any national literature depends in large part on _____; without a thorough knowledge of a nation's language, history, and culture, how can a literary work be anything but _____ to the reader?

    a. endorsement … unrelated

    b. encumbrance … engrossing

    c. contextualization … impenetrable

    d. canon … extraneous

    e. forbearance … relevant

17. As a medium of cultural transmission, television has never been _____ respect, but in spite of contemporary criticism, it often serves as a vehicle for important, informative, and high-quality content.

    a. invoked with

    b. lavished with

    c. bilked of

    d. cowed with

    e. chastised without

Questions 18–20 are based on the following reading passage:

Excerpted from the introduction to Life of Johnson *by James Boswell*

In reading biography three men meet one another in close intimacy—the subject of the biography, the author, and the reader. Of the three the most interesting is, of course, the man about whom the book is written. The most privileged is the reader, who is thus allowed to live familiarly with an eminent man. Least regarded of the three is the author. It is his part to introduce the others, and to develop between them an acquaintance, perhaps a friendship, while he, though ever busy and solicitous, withdraws into the background … Biography is the literature of realized personality, of life as it has been lived, of actual achievements or shortcomings, of success or failure; it is not imaginary and embellished, not what might be or might have been, not reduced to prescribed or artificial forms, but it is the unvarnished story of that which was delightful, disappointing, possible, or impossible, in a life spent in this world.

Some think that Boswell, in his *Life of Johnson*, did not sufficiently realize his duty of self-effacement. He is too much in evidence, too bustling, too anxious that his own opinion, though comparatively unimportant, should get a hearing. In general, Boswell's faults are easily noticed, and have been too much talked about. He was morbid, restless, self-conscious, vain, insinuating; and, poor fellow, he died a drunkard. But the essential Boswell, the skilful and devoted artist, is almost unrecognized. As the creator of the *Life of Johnson* he is almost as much effaced as is Homer in the *Odyssey*. Boswell's performance looks easy enough—merely the more or less coherent stringing together of a mass of memoranda. He is indeed so closely concealed that the reader suspects no art at all. Nevertheless it was rare

and difficult, as is the highest achievement in art. Boswell is primarily the artist, and he has created one of the great masterpieces of the world. He created nothing else, though his head was continually filling itself with literary schemes that came to naught. But into his *Life of Johnson* he poured all his artistic energies, as Milton poured his into *Paradise Lost*, and Virgil his into the *Aeneid*.

18. The author states that all of the following authors poured all of their artistic energies into one endeavor, EXCEPT:

    a. Boswell

    b. Milton

    c. Virgil

    d. Homer

19. The proper role of the biographer, according to the author, could most closely be compared to:

    a. a puppeteer who, by remaining invisible himself, creates a drama onstage.

    b. a painter who creates a portrait of a literary figure.

    c. a curator who organizes letters and memorabilia into a well-designed museum display.

    d. a researcher who interprets the results of his experiments in order to draw new conclusions.

    e. a writer who creates a novel out of the prosaic details of his neighbors' lives.

20. Consider EACH of the following three answer choices and select ALL that apply:

    The author suggests which of the following:

    a. the work *Life of Johnson* receives less critical recognition than it deserves because of the poor reputation of its author.

b. the faults of Boswell's *Life of Johnson* are superficial ones.

c. boswell was the perfect biographer, in that he did not impose his subjective opinions upon the reader, but rather presented Johnson's life through skillfully organized details.

Question 21 is based on the following reading passage:

Under a 1990 law known as the Clery Act, American universities must report statistics on burglaries that occur on campus to the Education Department and to students and staff. Schools report larceny statistics, which do not involve unlawful entry, separately to the FBI, which then releases an annual report. Last year, Hinterlands University reported just fifty burglaries, a decrease of 200% from the previous year, leading a campus police officer to call the university an "oasis compared to crime in the rest of the city of Hinterlands." In fact, campus officials believe that these statistics may have been the main reason Hinterlands University experienced an increase in applications this year of 50%.

21. Which of the following would most directly undermine campus officials' assumptions about the increase in applications?

    a. Crime statistics represent a sensitive issue for colleges, many of whom resisted passage of the Clery Act when it was first introduced.

    b. Had statistics on larcenies been reported by Hinterlands University, potential applicants would have learned that nine hundred larcenies took place last year on campus.

    c. The Clery Act requires that statistics be released to current students as well as potential applicants.

    d. The majority of applicants did not learn of crime statistics through the FBI's annual report.

    e. The majority of applicants last year learned through the FBI's annual report that nine hundred larcenies took place last year on campus, which represented an increase of 200% from the previous year.

Select the answer choice that best completes the sentence:

22. Erasmus was respected by his peers because he was both a _____ negotiator and a _____ diplomat; he often succeeded in winning concessions from his opponents through his determination, but his subtle handling of sensitive situations ensured that he never offended them.

    a. pugnacious … sensitive
    b. bellicose … belligerent
    c. tenacious … tactful
    d. auxiliary … immaculate
    e. astringent … disingenuous

23. The Romans may have argued that they brought civilization (in the form of roads, government, and a settled agrarian lifestyle) to those they conquered. However, the purportedly humanitarian aspects of conquest are regarded as _____ at best by contemporary scholars, who are aware that such actions are, on the contrary, _____.

    a. dubious … self-serving
    b. hallowed … hypocritical
    c. effete … insincere
    d. villainous … generous
    e. agnostic … dogmatic

24. Quantum physicists must often rely on a
_____ style in presenting their findings to
the general public, because the _____ mathematics underlying quantum mechanics are
incomprehensible without extensive education.

    a. concrete ... prosaic
    b. abstruse ... basic
    c. philosophical ... agile
    d. colloquial ... esoteric
    e. elegant ... unsophisticated

Question 25 is based on the following reading passage:

The architectural firm BauerInc has
made it a policy for the last three years to
assign their top clients to available senior
architects within the firm if a suitably
qualified subordinate can be found to
support the efforts of that senior architect.
Strict adherence to this rule has been
observed in the last three years, yet during
that time, some top clients have been
assigned to freelance architects outside
the firm, although numerous BauerInc
employees have received education
qualifying them for such assignments.

Select the best answer choice:

25. If the information provided is true, which of
the following **must** also be true about BauerInc
during the past two years?

    a. Freelance architects assigned to
    the jobs must have had higher
    qualifications than BauerInc
    employees.

    b. Some assignments to top clients
    were available, but were not
    advertised to BauerInc employees.

    c. At the time some assignments were
    offered to senior architects, no
    qualified BauerInc employees were
    available as assistants.

    d. BauerInc hired certain people
    for jobs for which they had no
    qualifications.

    e. BauerInc employees who received
    an education qualifying them for
    assignments were unable to complete
    their education in time.

Questions 26–28 are based on the following reading passage:

Excerpted from Language: An Introduction to the Study of Speech *by Edward Sapir*

Languages are more to us than systems of thought-transference. They are invisible garments that drape themselves about our spirit and give a predetermined form to all its symbolic expression. When the expression is of unusual significance, we call it literature. Art is so personal an expression that we do not like to feel that it is bound to predetermined form of any sort. The possibilities of individual expression are infinite, language in particular is the most fluid of mediums. Yet some limitation there must be to this freedom, some resistance of the medium. In great art there is the illusion of absolute freedom. The formal restraints imposed by the material—paint, black and white, marble, piano tones, or whatever it may be—are not perceived; it is as though there were a limitless margin of elbow-room between the artist's fullest utilization of form and the most that the material is innately capable of. The artist has intuitively surrendered to the inescapable tyranny of the material, made its brute nature fuse easily with his conception. The material "disappears" precisely because there is nothing in the artist's conception to indicate that any other material exists. For the time being, he, and we with him, move in the artistic medium as a fish moves in the water, oblivious of the existence of an alien atmosphere. No sooner, however, does the artist transgress the law of his medium than we realize with a start that there is a medium to obey.

Language is the medium of literature as marble or bronze or clay are the materials of the sculptor. Since every language has its distinctive peculiarities, the innate formal limitations—and possibilities—of one literature are never quite the same as those of another. The literature fashioned out of the form and substance of a language has the color and the texture of its matrix. The literary artist may never be conscious of just how he is hindered or helped or otherwise guided by the matrix, but when it is a question of translating his work into another language, the nature of the original matrix manifests itself at once. All his effects have been calculated, or intuitively felt, with reference to the formal "<u>genius</u>" of his own language; they cannot be carried over without loss or modification. Croce is therefore perfectly right in saying that a work of literary art can never be translated. Nevertheless literature does get itself translated, sometimes with astonishing adequacy. This brings up the question whether in the art of literature there are not intertwined two distinct kinds or levels of art—a generalized, non-linguistic art, which can be transferred without loss into an alien linguistic medium, and a specifically linguistic art that is not transferable. I believe the distinction is entirely valid, though we never get the two levels pure in practice. Literature moves in language as a medium, but that medium comprises two layers, the latent content of language—our intuitive record of experience—and the particular conformation of a given language—the specific how of our record of experience. Literature that draws its sustenance mainly—never entirely—from the lower level, say a play of Shakespeare's, is translatable without too great a loss of character. If it moves in the upper rather than in the lower level—a fair example is a lyric of Swinburne's—it is as good as untranslatable. Both types of literary expression may be great or mediocre.

26. With which of the following would the author agree?

    a. The great author is never conscious of the limitations of his medium.

    b. The great author is more bound by the limitations of his material than a great sculptor is bound by the limitations of clay or bronze.

    c. The great author creates the impression of unusual freedom precisely through his recognition—conscious or unconscious—of restrictions imposed by language.

    d. The great author is always conscious of the limitations of his medium.

    e. Language is a limitless medium of communication and expression.

27. The author mentions Croce's opinion of translated literary works in order to:

    a. introduce a refutation of Croce's opinion.

    b. offer an explanation for why translated literature is inferior to the original.

    c. acknowledge that, in any literary work, certain elements of expression specific to a particular language will be lost or modified in translation.

    d. introduce a discussion of the formal components of literary style and substance.

    e. introduce further support for Croce's opinion.

28. "Genius" most nearly means which of the following?

    a. protégé

    b. prose

    c. opportunity

    d. capacity

    e. intelligence

For questions 29–30, a related pair of words or phrases is followed by five pairs of words of phrases. Choose the answer choice that best expresses the same relationship as that expressed in the original pair of words or phrases.

29. Amorphous : structure ::

    a. gnarled : exposure

    b. ghastly : trepidation

    c. flaccid : firmness

    d. torpid : stillness

    e. cavernous : area

30. Flushed : ruddiness

    a. alluring : repulsion

    b. gaudy : dowdiness

    c. opalescent : iridescence

    d. effervescent : stasis

    e. fluorescent : obscurity

Section 4

28 questions. 45 minutes.

Numbers: All numbers in this section are real numbers.

Figures: Position of points, etc., are in the order shown unless otherwise noted. Lines are straight unless otherwise noted. Figures lie on a plane unless otherwise noted. Figures are intended to be helpful but it should not be assumed that they are drawn to scale or are visually accurate unless otherwise noted.

For questions 1–11, choose the answer choice that best answers the question.

1. If x is a positive integer, what is 40 percent of $20x$?

    a. $10x$
    b. $2x$
    c. 10
    d. 8
    e. $8x$

2. In a fish store, a tank has 10 fish in it. If 6 of the fish are female, what is the probability that a fish selected at random will be female?

    a. $\frac{3}{5}$
    b. $\frac{1}{6}$
    c. $\frac{2}{3}$
    d. $\frac{2}{5}$
    e. $\frac{4}{10}$

3. When k is divided by 4, the remainder is 1. What happens to the remainder when $k + 2$ is divided by 4?

    a. Nothing.
    b. It increases by 1.
    c. It is multiplied by 3.
    d. The remainder is 0.
    e. It cannot be determined by the information given.

4. A store bought an item for $200. The store increased the item's price by 30 percent to sell it. Two months later, the store has a sale. They discount the item by 30 percent. What is the price of the item during the sale?

    a. $182
    b. $198
    c. $200
    d. $230
    e. $260

5. Mr. Wallace averages 60 miles per hour for the first t hours on an 800 mile trip. If $t < 13$, in terms of t, how many miles does Mr. Wallace have left?

    a. $60t - 800$
    b. $48,000 - 60t$
    c. $800 - 60t$
    d. $\frac{800}{t} - 60$
    e. $\frac{3}{40} - t$

6. If x is a positive integer and $\frac{2\sqrt{x}}{\sqrt{2}} = 0.5 \cdot \frac{\sqrt{2}}{\sqrt{x}}$, then $x =$

    a. 2
    b. 2.5
    c. $\sqrt{2}$
    d. 4
    e. 0.5

7. If $0 < a < b < c$ and the average (arithmetic mean) of a, b, and c is equal to the median of the three numbers, then which of the following is equal to b?

   a. $\dfrac{a+c}{3}$

   b. $\sqrt{ac}$

   c. $\dfrac{a+c}{2}$

   d. $\dfrac{c-a}{3}$

   e. $a + c$

8. If a circle with a radius of 8 inches is cut in half along the diameter, what is the perimeter of the resulting semicircle?

   a. 16π

   b. 8π

   c. $16\pi + 8$

   d. $8\pi + 8$

   e. $8\pi + 16$

9. If $8x + y = 3$ and $2z - 16x = 2$, what is $y + z$?

   a. 4

   b. 5

   c. 6

   d. 7

   e. 8

10. If $2^{x+1} = y$, which of the following is equal to y?

   a. 2^x

   b. 2^y

   c. y^2

   d. $y - 1$

   e. $y - 2$

11. If $3xy = 4$ and $x - 2y = 7$, what is $3x^2y - 6xy^2$?

   a. 3

   b. 12

   c. 28

   d. 42

   e. 60

For questions 12–18, there are no answer choices. Answer the question and type your answer into the computer.

12. What is $(x + y)^2$ if $x = 3y$ and $y = 2$?

13. On an hour-long drive, 40 minutes were spent in traffic. What fraction of the drive was <u>not</u> in traffic?

14. The first term of a sequence is 3. Each term after the first is 5 less than three times the term right before it. What is the 4th term of the sequence?

15. If the quotient when 0.56 is divided by an integer is $\frac{7}{25}$ (0.28), what is the integer?

16. In any triangle ABC, if the lengths of the sides are a, b, and c, what could be a value of $\dfrac{b}{a+c}$?

17. A total of 3,500 people were surveyed on the street. On a specific question, the possible answers were yes, no, or undecided. Only 90 percent of the people who were asked answered that particular question. If 30 percent of the people who answered said "yes," and 37 people said "undecided," how many people said no?

18. If $50x(x^2 + \frac{1}{2}x + \frac{1}{5} + \frac{1}{x}) = ax^3 + bx^2 + cx + d$,

    what is the value of $\dfrac{a+d}{2b+5c}$?

The CIG Practice GRE   **339**

For questions 19–25 determine whether:

a. Quantity A is greater

b. Quantity B is greater

c. The two quantities are equal

d. The relationship cannot be determined from the given information

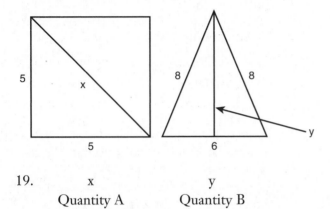

19.   x   y

    Quantity A   Quantity B

20. $(x + a)(x + b) = x^2 - 4x + 4$

         a   b

    Quantity A   Quantity B

21. Dietrich and Günther live in a city whose streets are laid out as a grid of equally spaced blocks, as shown below. Each city block is a distance of .1 miles:

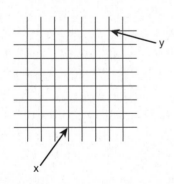

Dietrich travels from x to y by car, and so is forced to stay on the streets. His car travels at a constant rate of 10 mph.

Günther travels from x to y by a direct underground tunnel, and runs through this tunnel at a constant rate of 7 mph.

If Dietrich takes the fastest possible route open to him, and Günther takes the underground tunnel, which lies on a straight line connecting x and y, consider the quantities:

A = The time it takes Dietrich to get from *x* to *y*

B = The time it takes Günther to get from *x* to *y*

22. Paisley sells lemonade out of a stand. If *n* represents the number of glasses he sells in a day, his profit (represented by P) for that day in dollars is given by the formula:

P = (*m*/100) × *n* - *x* where *m* and *x* are constants.

If Paisley sells 10 glasses on Monday and makes a profit of $4, and then sells 15 glasses on Tuesday for a profit of $7.50, then compare:

A = *nx*

B = 2

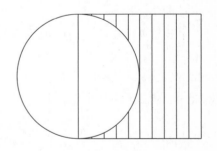

23. If the side of the square in the above diagram forms a diagonal of the inscribed circle, then consider:

A = the area of the lined region

B = the area of the circle

24. Scott and Jeremy are driving a distance of 50 miles. They both drive at a constant rate, and Jeremy drives 10 miles per hour faster than Scott.

   > A = 10 minutes
   >
   > B = the difference in the amount of time it takes Scott and Jeremy to drive the 50 miles

25. Let $y = 2x + 1$, with $x, y < 0$

   > A = $10/y$
   >
   > B = $5/x$

For questions 26–28, choose the answer choice that best answers the question.

26. Which is the diameter of a circle with area of 9π?

   > a. 3
   > b. 4
   > c. 5
   > d. 6
   > e. 9

27. The percent decrease from 20 to 13 is equal to the percent decrease from 34 to what number?

   > a. 13
   > b. 15.2
   > c. 18
   > d. 22.1
   > e. 34

28. How much did Michelle weigh last year if she now weighs p pounds, but immediately gained 10 over the last year's weight q?

   > a. $p + q + 10$
   > b. $p - q - 10$
   > c. $p - q + 10$
   > d. $q - p - 10$
   > e. $p + q - 10$

Answers

Section 3: Verbal Answers

1. d. innate

   "Adventitious" means "added onto," so its opposite is "innate." It's on our GRE vocab list!

2. a. empirical

   "Empirical" means concerning facts or observable phenomena.

3. b. ascetic

   An ascetic is one who denies himself or herself pleasures and who abstains from indulgences.

4. d. phlegmatic

   "Phlegmatic" means undemonstrative or indifferent.

5. a. strenuous; d. taxing

   The clue is that conservatory is both emotional and psychologically demanding ("rigors" means difficulties) but *also* physically demanding: "strenuous" or "taxing."

6. a. scrutinizes; e. questions

   The clue is that the protagonist "critically examines" values. "Scrutinizes" meaning examine, and "questions," meaning criticize, are both encompassed by this phrase.

7. b. The format in which an author's works are published is possibly predicative of his posthumous fame, at least among those readers he acquired during his lifetime.

   The implication is that large edition books are built to last; those readers who purchase such books presumably plan to keep the author's works for the long-term, and probably already have a high opinion of the author.

8. d. unthinkingly committed

   In this sense, "mortgaged" means "pledged," i.e., promised or committed, while "frivolously" implies, not so much silliness, as "unworthy of serious attention."

9. d. All authors must inevitably be forgotten.

   The clue is the quote, "there is no antidote against the opium of time"; although the author acknowledges that literary fame may last for generations, or indeed for thousands of years, he also implies that, because human memory is finite, all authors will eventually be forgotten: "He has made a brave beginning in that race against Time which all must lose."

10. a. The morality or ideals of a culture may be deduced from its artwork and literature.

    The clue lies in the last sentence: according to the author, the comparisons of ancient art with medieval mosaics, and of the remarks of Plato with the writing of monks, creates "a vivid picture of the change" that has passed over a cultural ideal.

11. d. was perhaps written in a less than serious spirit, but reflects a conviction, shared by medieval monks, that the physical aspects of life may influence the spiritual aspects.

    The author mentions Plato in order to make a connection to the authors of the medieval period who described the diets of saints. Though Plato and the monks drew opposite conclusions about the effects of diet, they both shared the belief that diet could influence morality and personality, i.e., "spirituality."

12. d. convoluted … resourceful

    The maze is "complicated"; therefore it is "convoluted." Logically, the only person who could escape a complicated maze is someone who is resourceful, or who is capable of dealing with difficult situations.

13. e. seditious … insurrectionists

    "Seditious" means "rebellious" and "insurrectionists" means "rebels."

14. c. predation … decorative

    The clue is that the eyespots enable the butterflies to escape "predators," i.e., other animals that want to eat them. Therefore the eyespots, rather than being merely "pretty" or "decorative," help the butterflies avoid being eaten—i.e., preyed upon ("predation").

15. d. mitigate

    "Mitigate" means to lesson or relieve.

16. c. contextualization … impenetrable

    The clue is that a knowledge of history, language, and culture provide a "context" in which the reader can understand, or "penetrate," a literary work ("impenetrable" here means "incomprehensible").

17. b. lavished with

    The clue is "in spite of" criticism. This implies that TV has received more criticism than praise. "Lavished with respect" means to be given a great deal of respect or praise.

18. d. Homer

    The author never states that Homer's sole masterpiece was the *Odyssey*.

19. c. a curator who organizes letters and memorabilia into a well-designed museum display.

    The author states that biography is a presentation of "actual achievements or shortcomings, of success or failure; it is not imaginary and embellished. It is the unvarnished story."

20. b. the faults of Boswell's *Life of Johnson* are superficial ones.

    The author states that the faults of Boswell's work are "easily noticed," i.e., "on the surface," but also states that "the essential Boswell, the skilful and devoted artist, is almost unrecognized."

21. e. The majority of applicants last year did learn through the FBI's annual report that 900 larcenies took place last year on campus, which represented an increase of 200% from the previous year.

If the majority of applicants learned that overall crime statistics actually went up, a decrease in crime statistics could not be responsible for the rise in applications.

22. c. tenacious ... tactful

The clue is that Erasmus was both determined and never caused offense; "tenacious" means "determined" and "tactful" means diplomatic or careful not to give offense.

23. a. dubious ... self-serving

The clue is that contemporary scholars *doubt* the "humanitarian" or generous aspects of the Romans' conquests (dubious means doubtful); instead, they consider the Romans selfish, or self-serving.

24. d. colloquial ... esoteric

The clue is that the mathematics underlying quantum mechanics are known only to a few people; they are "esoteric." Therefore, the physicists must rely on "everyday" or "colloquial" speech in order to make their ideas understandable to the public.

25. c. At the time some assignments were offered to senior architects, no qualified BauerInc employees were available as assistants.

The company policy states that BauerInc will "assign their top clients to available senior architects within the firm if a suitably qualified subordinate can be found to support the efforts of that senior architect." Therefore,

the only circumstance in which an assignment would be assigned to someone outside the company would be when no assistant was available.

26. c. The great author creates the impression of unusual freedom precisely through his recognition—conscious or unconscious—of restrictions imposed by language.

The passage states that any artist who "surrenders" to the "formal restraints imposed by the material" is then free to exploit that material, creating the "illusion of absolute freedom."

27. c. acknowledge that, in any literary work, certain elements of expression specific to a particular language will be lost or modified in translation.

The passage states that Croce's opinion highlights the fact that certain elements in any literary work are untranslatable.

28. d. capacity

"Capacity" is a synonym for "genius." The "formal capacity" of a language would mean the special environment created by its rules for the writer.

29. c. flacid : firmness

Both are "means without" relationships.

30. c. opalescent : iridescence

Flushed is to exhibit ruddiness as opalescent is to exhibit iridescence.

Section 4: Math Answers

Multiple choice questions:

1. e.
2. a.
3. c.

4. a.

5. c.

6. a.

7. c.

8. e.

9. a.

10. a.

11. c.

Produce your own response questions:

12. 64

13. ⅓

14. 16

15. 2

16. $0 < x < 1$

17. 2,168

18. 1

Quantitative comparison questions:

19. b.

20. c.

21. b.

22. a.

23. b.

24. d.

25. b.

Multiple choice questions:

26. d.

27. d.

28. e.

Index

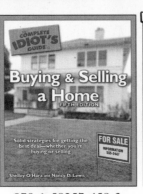
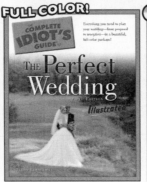
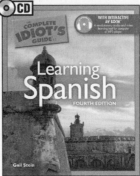